SPC SIMPLIFIED WORKBOOK

Practical Steps to Quality

SECOND EDITION

DAVIDA M. AMSDEN

HOWARD E. BUTLER

ROBERT T. AMSDEN

PRODUCTIVITY

Productivity Press
P.O. Box 13390
Portland, Oregon 97213-0390
United States of America
Telephone: 503-235-0600
Telefax: 503-235-0909
E-mail: info@productivityinc.com

Printed in the United States of America

ISBN 0-527-76341-1

The paper used in this publication meets the minimum requirements of American National Standard for Information Sciences—Permanence of Paper for Printed Library Materials. ANSI Z39.48-1984.

The Variable Control Chart ($\bar{X}$ and R) and ASQ logo are copyright © American Soceity for Quality. Reprinted by permission.

05 04 03 02 01 00   7 6 5 4 3 2

Contents

MODULE 4: ATTRIBUTE CONTROL CHARTS

p-Control Charts

np-Control Charts

c-Control Charts

MODULE 5: MACHINE AND PROCESS CAPABILITY

MODULE 6: QUALITY PROBLEM-SOLVING TOOLS

Brainstorming

Cause and Effect Diagrams

Pareto Analysis and Pareto Diagram

Flow Charts

MODULE 7: ELEMENTS OF A TOTAL QUALITY MANAGEMENT SYSTEM

BLANK CHARTS AND WORKSHEETS

ACKNOWLEDGMENTS

Like the textbook *SPC Simplified*, this workbook has grown out of our experiences with the people who are "making it happen" on the shop floor. They, together with teachers in community colleges, vocational schools, and companies, have asked for more practice problems and case studies. We developed this workbook to meet that need, and we are grateful for the encouragement and suggestions.

There are some special people we want to thank. The spring 1990 DSC-430 class at the University of Dayton and other seminar participants tested the case studies in Module 6. Our reviewers, Vivian Amsden and Jim Pressnell, made invaluable contributions to the clarity and shape of the manuscript. Karen Feinberg, the editor, has done her usual thorough job, as well as Steve Gstalder and the team at Quality Resources. Doug Relyea, who gave us initial encouragement for the project. To all of these people, our deepest gratitude.

D.M.A.
R.T.A.
H.E.B.

INTRODUCTION

As you use the textbook *SPC Simplified*, this workbook will provide you with an easy way to review and practice statistical process control techniques and to increase your ability to use these techniques in the workplace.

The arrangement of the workbook provides a self-learning method for better understanding of material in the textbook. Each module includes review questions that lead you through the corresponding module of *SPC Simplified*. These review questions follow the text closely, but in some cases you may need to turn back a page or two to find the answer. You can and should compare your answers with the text and with the solutions key. Such a comparison will help you determine whether you need to go back to the textbook to study the module further.

Modules 2 through 6 in the workbook include two series of exercises for each major subject are in each module. They allow you to practice the calculations required for each of the statistical techniques. These exercises are simple and are designed to help you build your confidence in doing these calculations. In the back of this workbook you'll find blank masters of the worksheets you'll need to copy.

Modules 2 though 6 of *SPC Simplified* deal with the statistical and problem-solving techniques used most often in the analysis and control of repetitive operations. The corresponding modules in the workbook contain case studies of manufacturing situations. The case studies present data and ask questions related to the operation, just as you would find in an actual manufacturing situation. We strongly recommend that you complete the necessary calculations and charts and answer the questions before you turn to the case study analysis in the solutions key. Then you can compare your charts and answers with those provided.

REVIEW QUESTIONS

To use statistical tools effectively, you need to understand the six principles of statistical process control.

1. Since no two things are exactly alike, what do we need to do to make parts interchangeable?

_____

_____

2. (a) What can we do with the variation in a product or process?

_____

(b) Why is it important to monitor normal variation?

_____

_____

_____

3. (a) How do things vary?

_____

_____

(b) How can you see this pattern take shape?

_____

_____

(c) What is another name for this pattern?

_____

(d) What does the frequency curve show about the measurements in the middle?

_____

_____

(e) What is this curve shaped like?

_____

4. (a) Whenever things of the same kind are measured, where will a large group of the measurements tend to cluster?

_____

(b) If you measure 100 pieces from a process, how many of the 100 pieces are likely to fall within the two middle sections of the graph in Figure 1-3 in the textbook?

_____

_____

(c) How many of the 100 pieces are likely to fall in the two outside sections of the graph?

_____

(d) What is the name of the curve in Figure 1-3?

_____

_____

5. It's possible to determine the shape of the distribution curve for parts produced by any process.

   (a) What are the five sources of variation?

      (1) _____

      (2) _____

      (3) _____

      (4) _____

      (5) _____

   (b) Variation in the measurements from a process result from what two types of causes?

      (1) _____

      (2) _____

   (c) Which type of cause can we normally do nothing about?

      _____

   (d) What is another name for this type of cause?

      _____

   (e) Which type of cause can we do something about?

      _____

   (f) What is another name for this type of cause?

      _____

   (g) If variations are due to the first type of cause alone, what can we say about this product?

      _____

      _____

   (h) What can we say about the process?

      _____

6. (a) What kind of variations tend to distort the normal distribution curve?

      _____

   (b) What does the frequency distribution or tally show?

      _____

      _____

   (c) What does the frequency distribution help us do?

      _____

      _____

      _____

      _____

7. When properly used, what three things will control charts tell you?

   (a) _____

      _____

   (b) _____

      _____

   (c) _____

      _____

TOOLS OF QUALITY

1. To improve or to maintain the quality of your products and sevices, you need to know the answers to these three questions:

   (a) _____

      _____

   (b) _____

      _____

   (c) _____

      _____

2. (a) Why is it important to demonstrate that your job is operating in a stable manner?

   _____

   _____

   _____

   _____

   _____

   (b) What can you say about the quality and productivity of a stable operation?

   _____

THE HISTOGRAM OR FREQUENCY DISTRIBUTION

1. Why is the histogram more like a "snapshot" of a process than like a "motion picture"?

   _____

   _____

   _____

2. A quick look at the pattern of the histogram helps answer the following questions.

   (a) To what curve should the process be producing parts?

   _____

   (b) When can we say that a process is well centered?

   _____

   _____

   _____

   (c) Under what conditions can we say that the process is capable of meeting the engineering specifications?

   _____

   _____

3. (a) How can we tell whether the process is making parts outside the specifications?

   _____

   _____

   _____

   (b) What does *sigma* describe?

   _____

   _____

   _____

4. We can use the frequency distribution and the histogram to

   (a) _____

   _____

   (b) _____

   _____

   (c) _____

   _____

   (d) _____

   _____

   (e) _____

   _____

   (f) _____

   _____

THE CONTROL CHART

1. What is the difference between the frequency distribution and the control chart?

   _____

   _____

   _____

   _____

2. (a) What does a control chart tell us about a job?

_____

_____

_____

   (b) What are control limits?

_____

_____

_____

   (c) On what are they based?

_____

   (d) What do they show?

_____

_____

_____

3. What two things do control limits warn us about?

   (a) _____

   (b) _____

4. What are the two general types of control chart?

   (a) _____

   (b) _____

Variables Charts: Average and Range Chart

1. What variables chart is the most commonly used?

_____

2. The measurements in Figure 1-10 in the textbook have been coded. Why is this method helpful?

_____

_____

3. (a) How do we find the average of the measurements in a sample?

_____

_____

   (b) What is another name for the average?

_____

4. How do we find the range of the readings in a sample?

_____

_____

_____

5. The average and range chart is really two charts.

   (a) For what purpose do we use the average chart?

_____

_____

   (b) For what purpose do we use the range chart?

_____

_____

6. (a) Where do we want the plotted points to stay?

_____

_____

   (b) What do we say about a job if a point falls outside one of these limits?

_____

Attribute Charts

1. What kind of inspection results calls for attribute charts?

_____

_____

2. (a) What do points inside the control limits indicate?

   _____

   (b) What does a point outside the control limits indicate?

   _____

SUMMARY

1. What is the greatest use of control charts?

   _____

   _____

   _____

2. (a) If a process is in statistical control, what is the source of the only variation we see in the process?

   _____

   (b) How can this type of problem be solved effectively?

   _____

   _____

   (c) Who could solve this type of problem?

   _____

3. (a) If a process is out of statistical control, what kind of cause is present?

   _____

   (b) What is this type of problem called?

   _____

2 Frequency Histograms and Checksheets

FREQUENCY HISTOGRAMS: REVIEW QUESTIONS

VARIATION

1. Since no two items are exactly the same, why is single measurement not enough?

_____

_____

2. What do we need instead of a single example or measurement?

_____

FREQUENCY HISTOGRAMS

1. (a) What does the frequency histogram do for us?

   _____

   _____

   (b) The histogram is like a snapshot of a process. What two things does it show us about the process?

   (1) _____

   _____

   (2) _____

   _____

2. Refer to Figure 2-1 in the textbook.

   (a) What is the lower edge of this chart called?

   _____

(b) What does it do?

_____

_____

(c) What does the vertical scale along the left-hand edge record?

_____

_____

3. What three things does the frequency histogram in Figure 2-1 show quickly and easily without the use of tables?

   (a) _____

   (b) _____

   (c) _____

4. What two things does the frequency histogram not tell you about variation?

   (a) _____

   _____

   (b) _____

   _____

CONSTRUCTING A FREQUENCY HISTOGRAM

Step 1. Collect the measurements.

You may be able to find data that have already been collected by a production associate.

How should you arrange the measurements?

_____

Step 2. Find and mark the largest and the smallest number in each group.

What is an easy way to mark the largest and the smallest number in each group?

_____

_____

Step 3. Find the largest and the smallest number in the whole set.

How do you mark the largest and the smallest number in the whole set? (You may wish to refer to Table 2-3 in the textbook.)

_____

_____

Step 4. Calculate the range of the measurements.

How do you calculate the range?

_____

_____

Step 5. Determine the intervals.

Measurements for the histogram cover a large interval.

(a) To construct the histogram, how should you handle this large interval?

_____

_____

(b) What is one rule of thumb to use?

_____

It is important to choose the right number of intervals for the number of readings. Table 2-4 in the textbook gives further guidelines.

(c) What is one problem with using too few intervals?

_____

_____

(d) What is the problem with using too many?

_____

_____

(e) What is the advantage of choosing the right number of intervals?

_____

_____

Step 6. Determine intervals, boundaries, and midpoints.

(a) How do you find the width of the interval?

_____

For example, suppose the range of a set of 50 observations is 45.

(b) When you divide this range by 8 intervals (Table 2-4), what is the width of the interval?

_____

(c) Rounded off, what is the width of the interval?

_____

(d) Into how many intervals can you group the data?

_____

(e) How many units wide will the intervals be?

_____

(f) What is the next step?

_____

_____

(g) Where must every reading fall?

_____

Suppose that the smallest reading in the set of measurements is 32. The intervals are 6 units wide.

(h) If the lower endpoint of the first interval is 32, what is the upper endpoint?

_____

(i) What is the lower endpoint of the second interval?

_____

(j) What is the upper endpoint of the second interval?

_____

Suppose you have a series of intervals, each 6 units wide, going from 50 to 56, 56 to 62, 62 to 68, and so on.

(k) What is the problem with a measurement of exactly 56?

_____

_____

(l) What can you do to solve this problem?

_____

(m) What is an easy way to do this?

_____

_____

For the intervals and measurements we are looking at, the numbers have no decimal places. Subtract 0.5 from the endpoint of each interval.

(n) The endpoint of 50 becomes

_____

(o) The endpoint of 56 becomes

_____

(p) Into what interval will the reading of 56 fall?

_____

(q) Where do you set the midpoint?

_____

(r) For the interval between 61.5 and 67.5, what is the width?

_____

(s) What is the midpoint?

_____

Step 7. Determine the frequencies.

(a) What are the steps you should use for determining the frequencies for each class interval?

_____

_____

_____

_____

_____

_____

(b) What are the two ways to check your work? (See Table 2-6 in the textbook.)

(1) _____

_____

(2) _____

_____

Step 8. Prepare the frequency histogram.

(a) There are two main principles to follow in preparing the frequency histogram. Write them below.

(1) _____

_____

(2) _____

_____

(b) In drawing the frequency histogram, what four things must you do?

(1) _____

(2) _____

(3) _____

(4) _____

(c) How do you identify the intervals?

_____

(d) How can you make the histogram easy to read?

(1) _____

_____

(2) _____

_____

(3) _____

_____

(4) _____

_____

SOME CAUTIONS

To make the histogram tell the story of the data it represents, keep these questions in mind.

1. Why should you use equal width intervals?

_____

_____

2. (a) Is it OK to use open intervals?

_____

(b) Why or why not?

_____

_____

_____

_____

3. Why shouldn't you make breaks in the vertical or horizontal scales?

_____

_____

4. Why shouldn't you have too few or too many intervals?

_____

_____

_____

_____

5. What is the problem with putting too much information on one histogram?

_____

_____

6. What is the problem with not giving enough information?

_____

_____

WHAT FREQUENCY HISTOGRAMS TELL YOU ABOUT UNDERLYING FREQUENCY DISTRIBUTIONS

1. Why will histograms coming from the same process not look the same?

_____

_____

2. (a) What do we call the pattern created by taking all the items in a group of the same kind of items and arranging them in a frequency histogram?

_____

_____

(b) Why does it always create the same pattern?

_____

_____

3. (a) What is the problem with taking very small samples?

_____

_____

   (b) Why will histograms based on very small samples usually be different from each other?

_____

_____

_____

4. (a) Why should you take samples of at least 50 pieces?

_____

_____

   (b) What is a better sample size?

_____

FREQUENCY HISTOGRAMS IN PRODUCTION SITUATIONS

1. The frequency histogram can show whether production situations are good or not so good.

   (a) What is a good situation?

_____

_____

_____

   (b) What is one caution?

_____

_____

_____

2. Why is a histogram like a "snapshot" of the process rather than a "motion picture?"

_____

_____

3. Figure 2-15 in the textbook shows a process in trouble.

   (a) What would happen in this case if the center of the process is moved?

_____

_____

   (b) Who could probably solve this problem?

_____

   (c) What are three possible solutions?

   (1) _____

   (2) _____

   (3) _____

4. (a) If your histogram shows that the process is off center, what might you do to improve the situation?

_____

_____

   (b) What is necessary before you take this step?

_____

_____

   (c) Even if the process is centered perfectly, what problem is still possible?

_____

_____

5. See Figure 2-17 in the textbook. It is really two histograms.

   (a) What does this pattern suggest?

_____

_____

(b) What are four possible reasons for this?

(1) _____

_____

(2) _____

_____

(3) _____

_____

(4) _____

_____

(c) To correct the situation, you need to understand what is going on. What could you do to bring the two histograms into focus? Give an example.

_____

_____

_____

_____

_____

FREQUENCY HISTOGRAMS: EXERCISES, SERIES 1

For each of the following sets of data, you will construct a separate frequency histogram. First, answer Questions 1 through 7 on the top part of the frequency histogram worksheet. In Question 8, draw the histogram on the graph portion of the worksheet. You will find the specifications with each data set. Keep them in mind as you prepare the histograms.

SET 1.

Specifications: Lower = 67, Upper = 109

a) 69, 68, 76, 68, 75

b) 79, 82, 81, 67, 62

c) 77, 76, 77, 83, 84

d) 76, 79, 83, 83, 77

e) 75, 77, 73, 72, 74

f) 72, 66, 80, 77, 81

g) 70, 75, 70, 70, 71

h) 80, 77, 75, 77, 75

i) 75, 73, 78, 77, 76

j) 80, 76, 75, 68, 70

k) 71, 77, 73, 80, 77

l) 80, 78, 72, 78, 77

m) 80, 78, 77, 75, 71

n) 61, 70, 76, 77, 78

o) 82, 74, 77, 82, 74

p) 75, 83, 80, 77, 75

q) 83, 77, 74, 78, 74

r) 77, 72, 77, 77, 78

s) 70, 77, 75, 74, 78

t) 71, 71, 72, 61, 80

SET 2.

Specifications: Lower = .77, Upper = 1.07

a) .983, .888, .986, .976, .986

b) .897, .972, .979, .889, .884

c) .972, .983, .908, .984, .887

d) .886, .899, .885, .884, .889

e) .986, .883, .982, .972, .889

f) .957, .933, .921, .977, .893

g) .923, .930, .894, .949, .893

h) .919, .934, .901, .977, .957

i) .942, .949, .935, .886, .893

j) .871, .954, .934, .941, .969

k) .884, .933, .948, .892, .821

l) .885, .933, .953, .968, .934

m) .885, .932, .948, .900, .933

n) .890, .884, .949, .933, .955

o) .905, .920, .898, .927, .935

p) .968, .930, .950, .925, .940

q) .872, .931, .886, .956, .984

r) .926, .928, .885, .891, .858

s) .970, .928, .898, .872, .888

t) .938, .883, .892, .928, .931

SET 3.

Specifications: Lower = 30, Upper = 42

a) 26, 41, 30, 38, 28

b) 37, 32, 31, 29, 43

c) 39, 40, 29, 29, 43

d) 42, 37, 38, 42, 34

e) 37, 29, 32, 34, 32

f) 40, 38, 37, 35, 31

g) 31, 31, 32, 21, 40

h) 34, 42, 37, 34, 42

i) 40, 38, 32, 38, 37

j) 37, 40, 33, 37, 31

k) 38, 37, 37, 32, 37

l) 32, 26, 40, 37, 41

m) 34, 38, 34, 37, 43

n) 30, 37, 35, 34, 38

o) 30, 35, 30, 30, 31

p) 40, 37, 35, 37, 35

q) 38, 37, 36, 30, 21

r) 35, 43, 40, 37, 35

s) 30, 28, 35, 36, 40

t) 35, 33, 38, 37, 36

SET 4.

Specifications: Lower = 5, Upper = 55

a) 40, 43, 38, 30, 50

b) 32, 23, 35, 30, 37

c) 30, 19, 22, 22, 52

d) 24, 38, 29, 33, 31

e) 10, 31, 13, 44, 35

f) 21, 30, 29, 21, 25

g) 11, 23, 27, 22, 25

h) 24, 30, 20, 29, 16

i) 33, 33, 16, 45, 36

j) 21, 24, 31, 29, 29

k) 27, 15, 44, 26, 43

l) 25, 29, 34, 29, 13

m) 36, 9, 30, 42, 50

n) 16, 27, 27, 37, 32

o) 34, 24, 49, 11, 30

p) 35, 41, 29, 32, 26

q) 29, 21, 33, 30, 33

r) 21, 10, 28, 32, 35

s) 32, 32, 38, 36, 24

t) 40, 34, 44, 32, 16

1. Find the largest and the smallest reading for each group of readings in each data set. Circle the largest and draw a box around the smallest.

2. Next, find the very largest and the very smallest reading for each set. Double circle the very largest and draw a double box around the very smallest. When you have done this, write those numbers on a frequency histogram worksheet for each data set.

3. Now you are ready to find the range for each set. Write your answer in the space provided on each worksheet.

4. Determine the intervals. Remember that the readings for each set cover large intervals.

   (a) To construct the histogram, what do you do with the large interval? (Refer to Table 2-4 in the textbook.)

   _____

   _____

   (b) If there are 50 observations, how many intervals might you want to use?

   _____

   (c) When may you round off?

   _____

   (d) Determine the width of each interval. Write your answer in the "Interval width" space provided on each worksheet.

   (e) List the intervals in the "Interval" column.

5. Next, set up boundaries for the intervals.

   (a) Why must every reading fall between two boundaries?

   _____

   _____

   (b) How can you make this happen?

   _____

   _____

   Write in the boundaries for each data set on the frequency histogram worksheets.

6. Set midpoints at the center of each interval. How do you do this?

   _____

   _____

   _____

   Write in the midpoints for each set on the frequency histogram worksheets.

7. Determine the frequencies.

   (a) What are the steps you should use in determining the frequencies?

   _____

   _____

   _____

   (b) How can you check your work?

   _____

   _____

Follow these steps for each set on the frequency histogram worksheets.

8. Prepare a frequency histogram for each set of data. Use the graph area of the histogram worksheet.

9. Once you have constructed the histogram, draw in the specifications for each histogram. Then answer the following questions for each histogram.

   (a) In relation to the width of the specifications, is the variation for this process small or large?

   Set 1. _____

   Set 2. _____

   Set 3. _____

   Set 4. _____

(b) Have all the units shown in the histogram been produced inside the specifications?

Set 1. _____

Set 2. _____

Set 3. _____

Set 4. _____

(c) If not, what is the histogram telling you?

Set 1. _____

_____

Set 2. _____

_____

Set 3. _____

_____

Set 4. _____

_____

(d) Who could probably solve this problem?

Set 1. _____

Set 2. _____

Set 3. _____

Set 4. _____

(e) Where does the process appear to be centered?

Set 1. _____

Set 2. _____

Set 3. _____

Set 4. _____

(f) If the process were to be centered at the midpoint between the specifications, could you be sure that all the units would be produced within the specifications?

Set 1. (yes/no) _____

Set 2. (yes/no) _____

Set 3. (yes/no) _____

Set 4. (yes/no) _____

(g) If the process is properly centered and there is still product outside the specifications, who could solve this problem?

Set 1. _____

_____

Set 2. _____

_____

Set 3. _____

_____

Set 4. _____

_____

FREQUENCY HISTOGRAMS: EXERCISES, SERIES 2

For each of the following sets of data, you will construct a separate frequency histogram. First, answer Questions 1 through 7 on the top part of the frequency histogram worksheet. In Question 8, draw the histogram on the graph portion of the worksheet. You will find the specifications with each data set. Keep them in mind as you prepare the histograms.

SET 1.

Specifications: Lower = 50.5, Upper = 58.5

a) 53, 53, 55, 61, 57

b) 55, 50, 53, 55, 57

c) 56, 58, 58, 53, 52

d) 53, 48, 55, 58, 55

e) 62, 57, 54, 56, 60

f) 51, 57, 59, 52, 50

g) 52, 51, 53, 57, 54

h) 54, 48, 52, 55, 54

i) 51, 50, 53, 57, 55

j) 57, 54, 52, 56, 53

k) 56, 55, 59, 55, 57

l) 58, 53, 59, 54, 52

m) 56, 54, 52, 55, 53

n) 53, 57, 59, 56, 60

o) 61, 60, 57, 57, 55

p) 54, 52, 57, 53, 54

q) 56, 51, 59, 57, 57

r) 56, 55, 58, 52, 53

s) 51, 49, 53, 52, 55

t) 55, 56, 60, 59, 57

SET 2.

Specifications: Lower = .115, Upper = .245

a) .149, .107, .139, .143, .142

b) .130, .122, .133, .140, .148

c) .120, .122, .137, .136, .107

d) .136, .177, .140, .121, .136

e) .122, .110, .133, .119, .132

f) .135, .145, .120, .129, .151

g) .107, .130, .128, .127, .108

h) .123, .131, .119, .126, .144

i) .140, .136, .129, .127, .112

j) .130, .133, .145, .143, .114

k) .133, .135, .123, .129, .132

l) .118, .129, .133, .131, .117

m) .146, .154, .145, .151, .130

n) .117, .132, .140, .127, .132

o) .121, .143, .111, .122, .140

p) .137, .127, .140, .125, .122

q) .133, .141, .136, .134, .133

r) .132, .126, .135, .146, .133

s) .133, .126, .148, .126, .130

t) .133, .120, .124, .121, .150

SET 3.

Specifications: Lower = 64.5, Upper = 84.5

a) 73, 73, 81, 75, 77

b) 73, 68, 75, 78, 75

c) 75, 70, 73, 77, 83

d) 77, 75, 75, 77, 70

e) 70, 75, 77, 75, 73

f) 67, 72, 70, 73, 73

g) 72, 75, 68, 72, 75

h) 75, 70, 70, 68, 72

i) 79, 82, 70, 71, 70

j) 80, 73, 74, 70, 78

k) 72, 68, 83, 77, 77

l) 75, 67, 70, 75, 68

m) 69, 78, 74, 70, 66

n) 73, 76, 76, 70, 72

o) 80, 76, 72, 74, 75

p) 74, 69, 77, 69, 81

q) 72, 73, 69, 75, 77

r) 77, 75, 82, 72, 70

s) 73, 70, 70, 72, 73

t) 78, 78, 77, 77, 74

SET 4.

Specifications: Lower = −46, Upper = 44

a)	7,	−3,	10,	−5
b)	3,	11,	6,	4
c)	2,	−4,	5,	16
d)	3,	−4,	18,	−4
e)	3,	−10,	−6,	−9
f)	−9,	−13,	16,	−12
g)	13,	2,	24,	−1
h)	−19,	10,	13,	3
i)	−8,	−3,	21,	1
j)	10,	2,	0,	−13
k)	21,	−1,	−10,	15
l)	−22,	−3,	−2,	0
m)	14,	−4,	−11,	1
n)	−18,	−3,	−1,	6
o)	−16,	13,	15,	3
p)	2,	−11,	3,	−20
q)	−23,	−9,	10,	−13
r)	6,	6,	7,	−8
s)	18,	10,	3,	−8
t)	12,	13,	9,	−23

1. Find the largest and the smallest reading for each group of readings in each data set. Circle the largest and draw a box around the smallest.

2. Next, find the very largest and the very smallest reading for each set. Double circle the very largest and draw a double box around the very smallest. When you have done this, write those numbers on a frequency histogram worksheet for each data set.

3. Now you are ready to find the range for each set. Write your answer in the space provided on each worksheet.

4. Determine the intervals. Remember that the readings for each set cover large intervals.

    (a) To construct the histogram, what do you do with the large interval? (Refer to Table 2-4 in the textbook.)

    _____

    _____

    (b) If there are 50 observations, how many intervals might you want to use?

    _____

    (c) When may you round off?

    _____

    (d) Determine the width of each interval. Write your answer in the "Interval width" space provided on each worksheet.

    (e) List the intervals in the "Interval" column.

5. Next, set up boundaries for the intervals.

    (a) Why must every reading fall between two boundaries?

    _____

    _____

    (b) How can you make this happen?

    _____

Write in the boundaries for each data set on the frequency histogram worksheets.

6. Set midpoints at the center of each interval. How do you do this?

   _____

   _____

   _____

   Write in the midpoints for each set on the frequency histogram worksheets.

7. Determine the frequencies.

   (a) What are the steps you should use in determining the frequencies?

      _____

      _____

      _____

   (b) How can you check your work?

      _____

      _____

   Follow these steps for each set on the frequency histogram worksheets.

8. Prepare a frequency histogram for each set of data. Use the graph area of the histogram worksheet.

9. Once you have constructed the histogram, draw in the specifications for each histogram. Then answer the following questions for each historgram.

   (a) In relation to the width of the specifications, is the variation for this process small or large?

      Set 1. _____

      Set 2. _____

      Set 3. _____

      Set 4. _____

(b) Have all the units shown in the histogram been produced inside the specifications?

   Set 1. _____

   Set 2. _____

   Set 3. _____

   Set 4. _____

(c) If not, what is the histogram telling you?

   Set 1. _____

      _____

   Set 2. _____

      _____

   Set 3. _____

      _____

   Set 4. _____

      _____

(d) Who could probably solve this problem?

   Set 1. _____

   Set 2. _____

   Set 3. _____

   Set 4. _____

(e) Where does the process appear to be centered?

   Set 1. _____

   Set 2. _____

   Set 3. _____

   Set 4. _____

(f) If the process were to be centered at the midpoint between the specifications, could you be sure that all the units would be produced within the specifications?

Set 1. (yes/no) _____

Set 2. (yes/no) _____

Set 3. (yes/no) _____

Set 4. (yes/no) _____

(g) If the process is properly centered and there is still product outside the specifications, who could solve this problem?

Set 1. _____

_____

Set 2. _____

_____

Set 3. _____

_____

Set 4. _____

_____

CHECKSHEETS: REVIEW QUESTIONS

1. What are variable data?

2. Why is the checksheet a useful tool when we need to work with non-variable data?

3. List the five common types of checksheets.

(a) _____

(b) _____

(c) _____

(d) _____

(e) _____

THE FREQUENCY HISTOGRAM CHECKSHEET

1. What type of information does the frequency histogram checksheet provide?

_____

_____

2. What are some advantages to using a frequency histogram checksheet?

_____

_____

_____

_____

3. When might you use the frequency histogram checksheet?

_____

_____

4. When should you not use the frequency histogram checksheet? Why not?

_____

_____

_____

_____

THE CHECKLIST CHECKSHEET

1. How do you use a checklist checksheet?

   _____

   _____

2. There are many uses for this type of checksheet. The textbook mentions several. Give three examples from your own work experience.

   (a) _____

   (b) _____

   (c) _____

THE ITEM CHECKSHEET

1. What is an item checksheet?

   _____

   _____

2. (a) How is this type of checksheet helpful?

   _____

   _____

   (b) What is one important use of this checksheet?

   _____

   _____

3. Give three examples from your own work experience.

   (a) _____

   (b) _____

   (c) _____

THE LOCATION CHECKSHEET

1. What is the main use of the location checksheet?

   _____

2. Give three examples from your own work experience.

   (a) _____

   (b) _____

   (c) _____

THE MATRIX CHECKSHEET

1. What does a matrix checksheet allow you to record?

   _____

2. Give three examples of a matrix checksheet from your own work experience.

   (a) _____

   (b) _____

   (c) _____

CHECKSHEETS: EXERCISES, SERIES 1

FREQUENCY HISTOGRAM CHECKSHEET

In real life, you collect and record the data directly onto a frequency histogram checksheet. The following instructions are given as if you were collecting the data live. However, to practice constructing and using this type of checksheet, you will have to use data that have already been collected. Refer to the data sets given for the Frequency Histogram Exercises, Series 1 on pages 11-12. For each of these data sets, construct a separate frequency histogram checksheet.

First, photocopy the frequency histogram checksheet form provided at the back of this workbook and follow the directions in numbers 1 through 6 to prepare the checksheet. The specifications are included with the data sets for frequency histograms—keep them in mind as you set up the checksheets. Then answer the questions in number 7.

1. (a) What are the anticipated largest and smallest readings for each set? Record your answers in the spaces provided on the frequency histogram checksheet form.

   (b) Find the anticipated range of the data and record your answer as "Range" on the checksheet.

2. Write the anticipated number of observations under "No. of observations" on the checksheet.

3. Follow the directions for determining the number of intervals and interval widths that are given on page 18 in the textbook. Indicate the number of intervals and the widths in the spaces provided on the checksheet.

4. Set up the intervals. For the frequency histogram checksheet, you don't have to determine boundaries or find the midpoints of the intervals as you did for histograms. However, you do need to make sure that an observation will fall in only one interval. Do this by making the lower end of the interval greater than the upper end of the previous interval. Write out the first two intervals in the spaces provided at the top of the checksheet as a way of double-checking.

5. Next, prepare the frequency histogram checksheet on the graph portion of the worksheet. Write in the intervals at the bottom of the graph, starting with the two intervals you have already determined. Set the vertical scale and label this "Frequency."

6. Now fill in the graph. Write a small "x" for each observation in the appropriate interval, one above the other. See Figure 2-18 in the textbook.

7. Once you have prepared the frequency histogram checksheet, draw in the specifications. Then answer the next three questions for each checksheet.

   (a) In relation to the width of the specifications, is the variation for each process large or small?

   Set 1. _____

   Set 2. _____

   Set 3. _____

   Set 4. _____

   (b) Have all the units shown on the checksheet been produced within the specifications?

   Set 1. _____

   Set 2. _____

   Set 3. _____

   Set 4. _____

   (c) Where does the process appear to be centered?

   Set 1. _____

   Set 2. _____

   Set 3. _____

   Set 4. _____

CHECKLIST CHECKSHEET

1. Create a checklist checksheet for an example from your workplace. You might set up a checklist checksheet for starting up a process or shutting a process down.

2. Create a checklist checksheet for changing an automobile tire.

ITEM CHECKSHEET

1. Your company makes small plastic parts. In an effort to improve the quality of these parts, your work group decides to collect information about the kinds of defects and other quality problems. You and the group know from your own experience and from talking with customers what kinds of defects are occurring: parts have excess flashing; parts are torn, cracked, or discolored; there are holes and breaks; parts are too soft, too hard. Create an item checksheet for your team to use for collecting data.

2. A labeling operation is having problems. The labels are misprinted or they are unclear because they are smudged. Sometimes the labeling machine is not working properly or there is a problem with the glue. The labels are torn or they are the wrong ones. Many times there are not enough labels or there are none at all. A problem-solving team creates an item checksheet so that they can gather data for an improvement project. How would you make this kind of checksheet?

LOCATION CHECKSHEET

1. Develop a location checksheet for your workplace. You might set this up for a machine to see where oil leaks are occurring around the machine or where maintenance work should be performed on the machine itself.

2. Develop a location checksheet for your workplace. You might set this up for a parking lot to show where the paint lines need to be repainted or accidents occur.

MATRIX CHECKSHEET

1. A problem-solving team at Tasty Pastry Bakery wants to improve product quality. The team decides to compare the performance of three bread-mixing machines, so members collect data on problems for each machine. They found the following types of problems: the mixer sticks; oil leak; speed is too fast; speed is too slow; motor overheats; mixing machine is not clean. How would you set up a matrix checksheet for collecting these data?

2. You are working with an improvement team to find the causes of cracks in springs your company makes for compact cars. You and the group think part of the cause has something to do with the heat treatments and variation in the length of the treatments. You plan an experiment to test your ideas. Build a matrix checksheet on which you can collect data for the number of cracks that occur for two heat treat processes, H1 and H2, and four times, T1, T2, T3, and T4.

CHECKSHEETS: EXERCISES, SERIES 2

FREQUENCY HISTOGRAM CHECKSHEET

In real life, you should collect and record the data directly onto a frequency histogram checksheet. The following instructions are given as if you were collecting the data live. However, to practice constructing and using this type of checksheet, you will have to use data that have already been collected. Refer to the data sets given for the Frequency

Histogram Exercises, Series 2 on pages 15-16. For each of these data sets, construct a separate frequency histogram checksheet.

First, photocopy the frequency histogram checksheet form provided at the back of this workbook and follow the directions in numbers 1 through 6 to prepare the checksheet. The specifications are included with the data sets for frequency histograms—keep them in mind as you set up the checksheets. Then answer the questions in number 7.

1. (a) What are the anticipated largest and smallest readings for each set? Record your answers in the spaces provided on the frequency histogram checksheet form.

   (b) Find the anticipated range of the data and record your answer as "Range" on the checksheet.

2. Write the anticipated number of observations under "No. of observations" on the checksheet.

3. Follow the directions for determining the number of intervals and interval widths that are given on page 18 in the textbook. Indicate the number of intervals and the widths in the spaces provided on the checksheet.

4. Set up the intervals. For the frequency histogram checksheet, you don't have to determine boundaries or find the midpoints of the intervals as you did for histograms. However, you do need to make sure that an observation will fall in only one interval. Do this by making the lower end of the interval greater than the upper end of the previous interval. Write out the first two intervals in the spaces provided at the top of the checksheet, as a way of double-checking.

5. Next, prepare the frequency histogram checksheet on the graph portion of the worksheet. Write in the intervals at the bottom of the graph, starting with the two inter-

vals you have already determined. Set the vertical scale and label this "Frequency."

6. Now fill in the graph. Write a small "x" for each observation in the appropriate interval, one above the other. See Figure 2-18 in the textbook.

7. Once you have prepared the frequency histogram checksheet, draw in the specifications. Then answer the next three questions for each checksheet.

   (a) In relation to the width of the specifications, is the variation for each process large or small?

       Set 1. _____

       Set 2. _____

       Set 3. _____

       Set 4. _____

   (b) Have all the units shown on the checksheet been produced within the specifications?

       Set 1. _____

       Set 2. _____

       Set 3. _____

       Set 4. _____

   (c) Where does the process appear to be centered?

       Set 1. _____

       Set 2. _____

       Set 3. _____

       Set 4. _____

CHECKLIST CHECKSHEET

1. Create a checklist checksheet for a home emergency kit.

2. Create a checklist checksheet for an example from your workplace. You might make a checklist checksheet for a new associate who is learning the simultaneous operational steps of two injection mold machines.

ITEM CHECKSHEET

1. Develop an item checksheet for collecting data on defects in a soldering process. Defects include problems with: commutator; wire breaks; short circuits; soldering; resistance; and dirt.

2. Construct an item checksheet for defects in a filter unit for an aquarium. Defects from recent warranty claims have included: scratches on filter tank; filter motor is noisy; motor won't function or sticks; component missing; electrical short; return tube is defective.

LOCATION CHECKSHEET

1. Build a location checksheet for your workplace. You might do this for locations of baskets of parts in the plant or for locations of tools.

2. Build a location checksheet for your workplace. You might do this for locations of PCs throughout the workplace or of slippery places in the floor.

MATRIX CHECKSHEET

1. You are part of a training unit in your company. There will be a series of eight skill-building classes; class size has to be limited to 12 participants. Develop a matrix checksheet for training sessions for the associates in the Merrimac Plant.

2. E.M. Company produces envelopes, both personal and business sizes. From time to time the quality coordinator has some of the team leaders do audits on each of seven envelope machines, one team leader for each of three shifts. To do the audits, the team leader carefully examines a sample of 100 envelopes. If there are eight or more defective envelopes in the sample, the team leader writes it down as a "Reject;" otherwise as "OK." Prepare a matrix checksheet to be used for a one-week period.

FREQUENCY HISTOGRAMS: CASE STUDIES

The following case studies are taken from actual use in manufacturing organizations.

CASE 2-1

The first step in a process that manufactures rubber products is to prepare the raw or unvulcanized rubber for molding by extruding it and cutting it into blocks The blocks are loaded into a mold and vulcanized into a final shape. The blocks of unvulcanized rubber must be large enough to fill all of the cavities in the mold completely but not so large that the amount of material used is excessive.

The weights of 125 consecutive pieces were recorded at the stock preparation operation. The results are recorded in the table "Weights of Unvulcanized Rubber Blocks." Construct a frequency histogram using the recorded weights and draw the specification limits of 730/790 grams on the graph.

Is the operation set up such that we could expect all the cavities in the molding operation to be filled completely?

Is the output of the stock preparation operation set at the optimum weight to assure that all cavities will be filled and the material used will be minimized?

Weights of Unvulcanized Rubber Blocks (g) (Case 2-1)

Part Number: 3140242
Operation: Extrude stock preparation
Specification: 730/790 grams
Equipment: Precision scales to nearest gram
Note: Pieces were weighed individually in groups of five. The individual weights were recorded as listed.

No.	Weight	No.	Weight	No.	Weight	No.	Weight	No.	Weight
1	765	26	788	51	776	76	788	101	784
2	760	27	758	52	798	77	782	102	776
3	748	28	755	53	778	78	783	103	794
4	749	29	767	54	781	79	800	104	780
5	756	30	787	55	776	80	798	105	780
6	775	31	779	56	772	81	791	106	792
7	766	32	786	57	783	82	790	107	779
8	767	33	774	58	776	83	785	108	804
9	765	34	766	59	770	84	786	109	781
10	758	35	785	60	778	85	789	110	772
11	777	36	748	61	765	86	776	111	773
12	756	37	783	62	785	87	773	112	772
13	758	38	784	63	795	88	769	113	763
14	749	39	784	64	797	89	766	114	793
15	762	40	741	65	794	90	793	115	796
16	756	41	791	66	752	91	785	116	764
17	781	42	790	67	779	92	789	117	763
18	780	43	780	68	777	93	780	118	779
19	789	44	786	69	762	94	794	119	773
20	760	45	771	70	789	95	753	120	788
21	786	46	780	71	780	96	777	121	778
22	785	47	756	72	787	97	798	122	778
23	784	48	756	73	782	98	800	123	768
24	797	49	757	74	784	99	787	124	799
25	786	50	782	75	779	100	773	125	801

CASE 2-2

A company that forges metal parts has two sets of tooling for producing the same part. The orders from the customer are such that only one set of tooling is needed to produce the number of parts required at this time.

The forging being produced contains two cylindrical sections that must be concentric with each other within .040 inch. This measurement is made by rotating the forging on one of the sections and using a dial indicator gage to measure the maximum variation in the other section. The total variation observed on the indicator gage is recorded. This is referred to as the total indicator reading, or TIR.

One hundred forgings were made in each of the two forging hammer and die setups in the shop. The total indicator reading (TIR) was recorded for each setup. As a member of a quality improvement team you are asked to recommend which production setup should be run to fill the current orders.

Construct a frequency histogram for each setup, using the measurements listed in the tables for Hammer #2—Die #1 and Hammer #3—Die #2. On the basis of the frequency histograms, which setup would you recommend?

Hammer #2—Die #1 (Case 2-2)

TOTAL INDICATOR READING (TIR) (in)

Subgroup	Sample #1	Sample #2	Sample #3	Sample #4	Sample #5
1	.015	.020	.012	.015	.004
2	.008	.010	.015	.003	.018
3	.005	.011	.016	.016	.000
4	.011	.016	.024	.010	.009
5	.002	.010	.014	.020	.008
6	.016	.007	.012	.020	.019
7	.020	.017	.005	.012	.015
8	.014	.021	.013	.016	.022
9	.024	.002	.006	.005	.022
10	.015	.022	.006	.019	.007
11	.015	.010	.020	.012	.021
12	.015	.012	.017	.010	.010
13	.017	.007	.019	.015	.014
14	.014	.018	.003	.003	.004
15	.024	.004	.015	.001	.012
16	.007	.010	.022	.008	.020
17	.010	.014	.020	.015	.022
18	.010	.015	.015	.007	.030
19	.021	.010	.005	.011	.020
20	.026	.010	.025	.012	.012

Hammer #3—Die #2 (Case 2-2)

Subgroup	Sample #1	Sample #2	Sample #3	Sample #4	Sample #5
	TOTAL INDICATOR READING (TIR) (in)				
1	.028	.010	.010	.022	.010
2	.010	.022	.017	.007	.023
3	.008	.016	.010	.039	.003
4	.011	.009	.020	.015	.012
5	.030	.022	.018	.025	.020
6	.011	.018	.023	.015	.007
7	.003	.021	.013	.017	.011
8	.066	.022	.025	.015	.012
9	.015	.014	.004	.015	.015
10	.014	.022	.021	.014	.028
11	.017	.005	.018	.025	.017
12	.001	.022	.015	.015	.010
13	.017	.015	.019	.009	.007
14	.028	.010	.033	.021	.015
15	.050	.027	.035	.015	.050
16	.015	.017	.021	.010	.015
17	.033	.025	.015	.030	.010
18	.050	.010	.025	.015	.010
19	.006	.023	.047	.017	.020
20	.041	.020	.015	.002	.031

CASE 2-3

An assembly operation requires the production associate to assemble a left-hand stationary snap to an adjustable retainer. The dimension from the stationary snap to the adjustable retainer after assembly is 323.0 ± 3.2 millimeters (mm). This dimension is measured using a metric scale.

Develop a frequency histogram based on the measurements in the table "Dimension from

Left-Hand Stationary Snap to Adjustable Retainer." Using the histogram, determine whether the process is centered on the specified dimension. Is the process stable or are assignable causes present?

The measurements were taken in groups of five and are recorded to the nearest whole millimeter.

Dimension from Left-Hand Stationary Snap to Adjustable Retainer (mm) (Case 2-3)

Subgroup	Sample #1	Sample #2	Sample #3	Sample #4	Sample #5
1	324.0	323.0	324.0	322.0	321.0
2	323.0	322.0	324.0	324.0	321.0
3	323.0	321.0	323.0	324.0	324.0
4	324.0	323.0	322.0	324.0	325.0
5	323.0	323.0	324.0	323.0	322.0
6	323.0	324.0	324.0	322.0	325.0
7	322.0	324.0	325.0	323.0	321.0
8	324.0	324.0	324.0	323.0	321.0
9	323.0	322.0	324.0	323.0	322.0
10	324.0	323.0	325.0	324.0	321.0
11	324.0	323.0	325.0	324.0	323.0
12	324.0	324.0	325.0	323.0	323.0
13	323.0	324.0	325.0	323.0	323.0
14	323.0	321.0	324.0	325.0	322.0
15	323.0	323.0	324.0	323.0	323.0
16	324.0	321.0	324.0	323.0	321.0
17	324.0	322.0	324.0	324.0	324.0
18	322.0	323.0	324.0	324.0	323.0
19	322.0	323.0	323.0	323.0	324.0
20	321.0	323.0	324.0	323.0	323.0

CASE 2-4

This case is very similar to Case 2-3. The measurements were taken at a companion operation, namely the assembly of the right-hand stationary snap to the adjustable retainer. The dimension and the tolerance are 323.0 ± 3.2 mm, the same as in the previous case. The samples were taken and the measurements were recorded as in Case 2-3, in the table showing dimensions to the nearest 1 mm.

Construct a frequency histogram and use this histogram to answer the following questions:

1. Is the process centered on the specification?
2. Is the process stable—that is, free from assignable causes?

The measurements were recorded in groups of five.

The data, in fact, were created to be similar to the data in Case 2-3 for comparison pur-

Dimension from Right-Hand Stationary Snap to Adjustable Retainer (to the nearest mm) (Case 2-4)

Subgroup	Sample #1	Sample #2	Sample #3	Sample #4	Sample #5
1	323.0	322.0	322.0	323.0	322.0
2	324.0	321.0	322.0	325.0	322.0
3	321.0	323.0	324.0	324.0	322.0
4	321.0	325.0	323.0	324.0	322.0
5	321.0	321.0	324.0	323.0	324.0
6	321.0	322.0	325.0	322.0	321.0
7	322.0	322.0	320.0	324.0	320.0
8	322.0	322.0	324.0	325.0	324.0
9	324.0	321.0	325.0	324.0	324.0
10	322.0	324.0	324.0	322.0	320.0
11	323.0	320.0	324.0	324.0	323.0
12	322.0	321.0	324.0	323.0	325.0
13	322.0	322.0	323.0	325.0	322.0
14	324.0	324.0	320.0	322.0	325.0
15	323.0	322.0	325.0	320.0	321.0
16	322.0	325.0	322.0	325.0	321.0
17	322.0	322.0	324.0	320.0	321.0
18	322.0	322.0	322.0	323.0	324.0
19	322.0	322.0	323.0	324.0	321.0
20	324.0	321.0	324.0	322.0	323.0

poses. When these measurements were made, the associate realized that the measurements should be taken with at least the same precision as expressed in the specification, so the dimensions were measured and recorded to the nearest tenth of a millimeter. The measurements had been adjusted by merely replacing all numbers after the decimal point with a zero. Use the measurements listed in the table showing dimensions to the nearest 0.1 mm to construct a frequency histogram. Examine this histogram and determine whether you can answer more readily the two questions asked before.

Dimension from Right-Hand Stationary Snap to Adjustable Retainer (to the nearest 0.1 mm) (Case 2-4)

Subgroup	Sample #1	Sample #2	Sample #3	Sample #4	Sample #5
1	323.2	322.2	322.3	323.7	322.9
2	324.2	321.6	322.4	325.4	322.6
3	321.2	323.3	324.6	324.5	322.7
4	321.0	325.0	323.3	324.7	322.6
5	321.4	321.6	324.0	323.8	324.4
6	321.3	322.5	325.6	322.6	321.7
7	322.3	322.7	320.1	324.8	320.2
8	322.4	322.6	324.2	325.3	324.4
9	324.1	321.2	325.7	324.7	324.6
10	322.5	324.3	324.9	322.4	320.1
11	323.7	320.7	324.2	324.1	323.6
12	322.6	321.5	324.7	323.3	325.1
13	322.2	322.8	323.0	325.6	322.5
14	324.0	324.6	320.6	322.3	325.2
15	323.5	322.2	325.3	320.8	321.3
16	322.6	325.2	322.8	325.7	321.5
17	322.0	322.6	324.2	320.6	321.6
18	322.9	322.1	322.4	323.9	324.5
19	322.0	322.6	323.2	324.6	321.8
20	324.0	321.7	324.2	322.5	323.2

CASE 2-5

A certain rubber material is produced by a batch-type process. A quantity, or batch, is made by mixing powdered chemicals with various oils in an established sequence.

The completed batch is the raw material used to make vulcanized rubber products. Each batch is sampled, and various tests are conducted to determine the degree of conformance to specified properties. The tests result in variable measurements. The values were accumulated over a fairly long period, but the manufacturing conditions were basically the same throughout the period. The ingredients used in the material, the equipment used in weighing and mixing, the methods used, and the environmental conditions in the mixing area should produce successive batches with a tensile strength that varies around an average in a normal or bell-shaped manner.

The figures recorded on the data record sheet for tensile strength are values obtained from samples taken from 100 consecutive batches of the same formulation produced on the same mixer. The tensile strength specification is 1840 to 1900 pounds per square inch (psi). Using these values, construct a frequency histogram and estimate the average tensile strength of the batches. Can we expect the batches that follow this to be within the specification limits?

Data Record Sheet—Tensile Strength (psi) (Case 2-5)

Rubber Compound 9765-3
Tensile Strength Specification 1840/1900 psi

Sample	Value	Sample	Value	Sample	Value	Sample	Value
1	1862	26	1858	51	1852	76	1858
2	1860	27	1864	52	1863	77	1853
3	1853	28	1853	53	1869	78	1868
4	1861	29	1844	54	1858	79	1862
5	1851	30	1845	55	1855	80	1865
6	1859	31	1859	56	1850	81	1860
7	1860	32	1858	57	1850	82	1860
8	1860	33	1855	58	1845	83	1865
9	1860	34	1855	59	1858	84	1855
10	1866	35	1860	60	1855	85	1860
11	1850	36	1856	61	1862	86	1865
12	1862	37	1850	62	1865	87	1854
13	1855	38	1860	63	1861	88	1860
14	1861	39	1838	64	1861	89	1860
15	1850	40	1864	65	1868	90	1860
16	1860	41	1851	66	1860	91	1862
17	1869	42	1853	67	1858	92	1870
18	1861	43	1862	68	1858	93	1860
19	1860	44	1861	69	1845	94	1860
20	1860	45	1864	70	1860	95	1860
21	1845	46	1852	71	1865	96	1855
22	1851	47	1857	72	1855	97	1863
23	1860	48	1860	73	1862	98	1855
24	1855	49	1863	74	1860	99	1853
25	1860	50	1862	75	1851	100	1854

CHECKSHEETS: CASE STUDIES

CASE 2-6

A company has been experiencing excessive scrap rates on several of their products. Cross-functional continuous improvement (CI) teams have been formed and are attacking some potential problems. One of the products being studied by a CI team is a seal that has been found to contain defects in many of the dimensions or characteristics critical to the function of the product. The CI team has listed the characteristics and is considering how they can best analyze the performance of this product to prepare a plan of action to improve the quality performance of the product in question.

As a member of the team, you have agreed to present the results of your inspection of the production of the seal over five days at the next meeting of the team. The parts were produced on three shifts each day for five days. They are produced using a 15-cavity mold. Each cavity is numbered. An individual part can be identified by the cavity in which it was molded.

The dimensions or characteristics are inspected using various gages and measuring instruments. Following is a list of the dimensions checked:

- Diameter.
- Ovality.
- Squareness.
- Shelf height.
- Parallelism.
- Outside diameter.
- TIR (Total Indicator Reading).
- Bent insert.
- Overall height.

You have taken the time to record the cavity number of each of the rejected parts and have organized the rejects by cause, being careful to note the total number of rejects for each cause. Here is the list you have made:

24 parts rejected for ovality

1 from cavity 4	4 from cavity 9
2 from cavity 5	2 from cavity 10
3 from cavity 6	1 from cavity 11
11 from cavity 7	

3 parts rejected for parallelism

1 from cavity 8
1 from cavity 10
1 from cavity 11

131 parts rejected for TIR

6 from cavity 2	28 from cavity 7
1 from cavity 3	15 from cavity 8
1 from cavity 4	23 from cavity 9
2 from cavity 5	12 from cavity 10
3 from cavity 6	40 from cavity 11

105 parts rejected for shelf height

2 from cavity 5	14 from cavity 10
14 from cavity 6	18 from cavity 11
48 from cavity 7	1 from cavity 12
8 from cavity 9	

14 parts rejected for bent insert

6 from cavity 5	1 from cavity 7
4 from cavity 6	3 from cavity 9

The total number of parts rejected for the five days is 277 and the total number of parts produced and inspected is 5,577.

Before the CI team meets, you must prepare this inspection data in a presentable form for the team members. From this information the team should be able to make decisions that will result in identifying the source, or sources, of the high rejection rate.

Using the data provided prepare a checksheet for the CI team to use to analyze this problem.

CASE 2-7

A company has been having trouble meeting the shipping schedule for a certain product. You are a member of a continuous improvement team with the task of finding the cause of the problem and developing corrective action.

One of the sources of delays in the production of the product involves an operation performed on a machine that receives raw stock from another department. The production associates operating this machine have said that they often experience broken tools, which cause delays in the production of the product and headaches for them.

A preliminary examination of the situation on the production floor leads you to identify the following major causes of downtime and delays on this operation:

• No stock on hand.
• Broken tool.
• Overage stock.
• Machine maintenance.
• Miscellaneous.

Using these five categories, design a checksheet that the production associates on all three shifts can use to record each instance when their machine is down and not producing parts. The checksheet should cover five days of production. Instruct the associates to make a tally by cause and by day for each five-minute period that the operation is down. That is, if the machine is down for 10 minutes on Monday due to overage stock, the associates will place two tally marks in the appro-

priate block on the checksheet. These tally marks will be in the row called "Overage Stock" and the column headed "Monday".

At the end of the five days, you pick up the checksheet and complete it by totalling the times tallied in each of the blocks of the checksheet along with the total times for each cause and each day for all causes. You found the following information.

No stock on hand
Monday — 18 tallies
Tuesday — 6 tallies
Wednesday — 0 tallies
Thursday — 30 tallies
Friday — 1 tally

Overage stock
Monday — 2 tallies
Tuesday — 6 tallies
Wednesday — 8 tallies
Thursday — 0 tallies
Friday — 10 tallies

Machine maintenance
Monday — 0 tallies
Tuesday — 1 tally
Wednesday — 0 tallies
Thursday — 0 tallies
Friday — 1 tally

Broken tool
Monday — 1 tally
Tuesday — 4 tallies
Wednesday — 7 tallies
Thursday — 0 tallies
Friday — 8 tallies

Miscellaneous
Monday — 2 tallies
Tuesday — 0 tallies
Wednesday — 3 tallies
Thursday — 1 tally
Friday — 0 tallies

Using the information supplied by the production associates, construct a checksheet for the CI team to use in your next meeting.

3 Variable Control Charts

AVERAGE AND RANGE CHARTS: REVIEW QUESTIONS

1. One of the best-known and most widely used control charts is the average and range control chart. What is another name for this control chart?

_____

2. (a) What are two other names we sometimes use for the average?

    (1) _____

    (2) _____

    (b) How do you find the average?

    _____

    _____

    _____

3. (a) To figure the range of your sample data, what do you need to do first?

    _____

    _____

    _____

    _____

    (b) Write the directions for finding the range:

    _____

    _____

4. The average and range control chart has control limits.

    (a) What does UCL on the chart mean?

    _____

    (b) What does LCL on the chart mean?

    _____

5. (a) When the averages and the ranges are inside the control limits, how do we describe the process?

    _____

    _____

    (b) What should the production associate do by way of adjusting the process?

    _____

    _____

    (c) If a point on the average chart is outside the control limits, what should the associate do?

    _____

    _____

6. (a) Why do the points move up and down inside the limits?

    _____

    _____

    (b) What is another name for this?

    _____

(c) Generally speaking, can the associate get rid of these causes?

_____

(d) Why or why not?

_____

_____

_____

_____

7. (a) When an average is outside the control limits, what does the chart tell you to do?

_____

_____

_____

_____

(b) What does this situation tell you about the process?

_____

(c) What additional factor is now operating along with the inherent variation?

_____

_____

(d) What is this factor doing to the overall average of the process?

_____

_____

(e) Is this natural to the process?

_____

8. What are the main categories of sources of assignable causes?

(a) _____

(b) _____

(c) _____

(d) _____

(e) _____

9. (a) If the range goes outside the limits, what should we ask first?

_____

_____

(b) Does the operator usually have control over the inherent variation in the process?

_____

(c) What does a range outside the control limits usually mean?

_____

_____

10. What are the five purposes of control charts that are given in the textbook?

(a) _____

(b) _____

(c) _____

(d) _____

(e) _____

SETTING UP AVERAGE AND RANGE CHARTS

Step 1. Choose what to measure.

There are many different things in a process that can be measured. In choosing what to measure, what two points should you keep in mind?

(a) _____

_____

_____

(b) _____

_____

_____

_____

Step 2. Take the samples.

To set up an average and range chart, you will need a series of samples.

(a) What does a sample consist of?

_____

_____

(b) What kind of variation should be seen within the sample?

_____

(c) How should you choose your samples?

_____

_____

(d) Should you take your sample over a long or a short period of time?

_____

(e) What kind of data source should you look for when taking samples for the initial control chart?

_____

_____

_____

Step 3. Set up forms or data and graphs.

Step 4. Collect the samples and record the measurements.

When you write down the measurements on the form, in what order do you record them?

_____

_____

Step 5. Calculate the averages.

(a) How do you find the average?

_____

_____

_____

(b) Where do you write this answer on the chart?

_____

_____

Step 6. Calculate the overall average.

(a) What is another name for the overall average?

(b) Write the symbol for overall average:

_____

(c) How do you find the overall average?

_____

_____

_____

Step 7. Determine the ranges for the samples.

(a) To determine the range for each sample, which two measurements must you find?

_____

_____

(b) How do you find the range?

_____

_____

Step 8. Calculate the average range.

(a) How do you find the average range?

_____

_____

(b) Write the symbol for average range:

_____

Step 9. Determine scales for the graphs and plot the data.

(a) How should you set the scales for the graphs?

_____

_____

_____

(b) Where do we usually set the lower scale for ranges?

_____

(c) What must you be sure to leave room for on the graphs?

_____

_____

_____

Step 10. Determine control limits for ranges.

(a) Why do we calculate control limits for ranges before we calculate limits for averages?

_____

_____

_____

(b) Figure 3-14 in the textbook is a table of average and range chart factors. Which factor do you use to determine control limits for ranges?

_____

(c) Must you use the factor that corresponds to your sample size?

_____

(d) The usual sample size is 5. What is the correct value of the factor for this size sample?

_____

(e) Another commonly used sample size is 4. What is the correct value of the factor to use in this case?

_____

(f) Write the formula for finding the upper control limit for ranges:

_____

(g) Under what conditions is the lower control limit for ranges always zero?

_____

_____

Step 11. Are the ranges in statistical control?

What are the three possible answers to this question?

(a) _____

_____

(b) _____

_____

(c) _____

_____

Figure 3-16 in the textbook is a decision chart that shows all the possibilities in picture form.

(d) When can we say that the ranges are in statistical control?

_____

_____

(e) What does this mean about the inherent variation?

_____

(f) What does this mean about special causes?

_____

(g) When you are first setting up the range chart, what should you do if one or two ranges fall outside the control limits?

_____

_____

_____

(h) What recalculations should you make?

_____

_____

_____

(i) Should you use the out-of-control ranges?

_____

(j) What would be true if one or more of the remaining ranges still fall outside the new control limits?

_____

_____

(k) What should you do?

_____

_____

_____

(l) What may you do if all the ranges are inside the new control limits?

_____

_____

(m) What is the situation when three or more ranges are outside the original limits?

_____

_____

(n) What does this mean about the inherent variation?

_____

(o) What is happening to the ranges?

_____

_____

(p) What should you do?

_____

_____

_____

_____

Step 12. Determine control limits for averages.

(a) Only under what condition can you work on control limits for averages?

_____

_____

(b) Figure 3-17 in the textbook is a table of average and range chart factors. Which factor do you use to determine control limits for averages?

_____

(c) The usual sample size is 5. What is the correct value of the factor for this sample size?

_____

(d) Another commonly used sample size is 4. What is the correct value of the factor to use in this case?

_____

(e) Write the formula for the upper control limit for averages:

_____

(f) Write the formula for the lower control limit for averages:

_____

Step 13. Are the averages in statistical control?

(a) Just as for ranges, what are the three possible answers to this question?

(1) _____

_____

(2) _____

_____

(3) _____

_____

The decision chart in Figure 3-19 in the textbook shows the possible situations.

(b) Under what conditions can we say that the averages are in statistical control?

_____

_____

(c) What does this mean about the inherent variation?

_____

(d) What does this mean about special causes?

_____

(e) What must be true in order for you to use this chart to control production?

_____

_____

_____

(f) When first setting up a control chart, what should you do if one or two averages fall outside the control limits?

_____

_____

_____

(g) Do you use the out-of-control averages?

_____

(h) If one or more of the remaining averages still fall outside the new control limits, what would then be true?

_____

_____

(i) What should you do?

_____

_____

_____

(j) What can you do if all the averages are new inside the new control limits?

_____

_____

(k) What is the situation when three or more averages are outside the original limits?

_____

_____

(l) What does this mean about the inherent variation?

_____

_____

_____

(m) What should you do?

_____

_____

_____

_____

HOW TO USE CONTROL CHARTS IN CONTINUED PRODUCTION

1. (a) Under what conditions can we say that a process is in statistical control?

_____

_____

_____

(b) What kind of variation is probably at work?

_____

(c) Why is this type of variation present?

_____

(d) What do we know about the variation if the range chart is in control?

_____

_____

2. (a) What does being in control show about the process?

_____

(b) What kind of products are being produced?

_____

(c) What can happen if there is a large amount of variation?

_____

3. (a) What is the difference between specifications and control limits?

_____

_____

_____

_____

(b) Are they the same?

_____

4. What does adjusting the overall mean do to the control limits for averages?

_____

_____

_____

_____

_____

_____

AVERAGE AND RANGE CHARTS: EXERCISES, SERIES 1

For each of the following sets of data, you will prepare a separate average and range chart. Write your answers for Question 1 in the appropriate space on the average and range chart form. Write the calculations for Questions 2 through 9 and the answers to all questions in the space provided in the workbook. Draw in the lines for the overall average, the average range, and the upper and lower control limits for ranges and averages as directed in Questions 2, 3, 5, 8, and 9.

SET 1.

a) 26, 41, 30, 38, 28

b) 37, 32, 31, 29, 43

c) 39, 40, 29, 29, 43

d) 42, 37, 38, 42, 34

e) 37, 29, 27, 34, 32

f) 40, 38, 37, 35, 31

g) 31, 31, 32, 21, 40

h) 34, 42, 37, 34, 42

i) 40, 38, 32, 38, 37

j) 37, 40, 33, 37, 31

k) 38, 37, 37, 32, 37

l) 32, 26, 40, 37, 41

m) 34, 38, 34, 37, 43

n) 30, 37, 35, 34, 38

o) 30, 35, 30, 30, 31

p) 40, 37, 35, 37, 35

q) 38, 37, 36, 30, 21

r) 35, 43, 40, 37, 35

s) 30, 28, 35, 36, 40

t) 35, 33, 38, 37, 36

SET 2.

a) 69, 68, 76, 68, 75

b) 79, 82, 81, 67, 62

c) 77, 76, 77, 83, 84

d) 76, 79, 83, 83, 77

e) 75, 77, 73, 72, 74

f) 72, 66, 80, 77, 81

g) 70, 75, 70, 70, 71

h) 80, 77, 75, 77, 75

i) 75, 73, 78, 77, 76

j) 80, 76, 75, 68, 70

k) 71, 77, 73, 80, 77

l) 80, 78, 72, 78, 77

m) 80, 78, 77, 75, 71

n) 61, 70, 76, 77, 78

o) 82, 74, 77, 82, 74

p) 75, 83, 80, 77, 75

q) 83, 77, 74, 78, 74

r) 77, 72, 77, 77, 78

s) 70, 77, 75, 74, 78

t) 71, 71, 72, 61, 80

SET 3.

a) .983, .888, .986, .976, .986

b) .897, .972, .979, .889, .884

c) .972, .983, .908, .984, .887

d) .886, .899, .885, .884, .889

e) .986, .883, .982, .972, .889

f) .957, .933, .921, .977, .893

g) .923, .930, .894, .949, .893

h) .919, .934, .901, .977, .957

i) .942, .949, .935, .886, .893

j) .871, .954, .934, .941, .969

k) .884, .933, .948, .892, .821

l) .885, .933, .953, .968, .934

m) .885, .932, .948, .900, .933

n) .890, .884, .949, .933, .955

o) .905, .920, .898, .927, .935

p) .968, .930, .950, .925, .940

q) .872, .931, .886, .956, .984

r) .926, .928, .885, .891, .858

s) .970, .928, .898, .872, .888

t) .938, .883, .892, .928, .931

SET 4.

a)	8,	3,	−6,	6,	4
b)	−8,	4,	6,	−5,	4
c)	−2,	3,	4,	6,	1
d)	1,	0,	9,	6,	−1
e)	8,	6,	−3,	9,	5
f)	3,	−2,	5,	2,	−5
g)	−5,	5,	2,	−5,	−5
h)	−1,	−4,	−5,	5,	8
i)	7,	3,	−5,	2,	1
j)	−1,	−9,	−1,	8,	−5
k)	3,	0,	−3,	4,	1
l)	0,	3,	−14,	−2,	3
m)	7,	7,	0,	3,	5
n)	4,	−1,	7,	3,	−1
o)	0,	−9,	−7,	0,	5
p)	8,	−2,	−2,	−3,	0
q)	−4,	−4,	3,	4,	0
r)	−2,	5,	3,	6,	5
s)	7,	0,	0,	2,	−3
t)	2,	2,	0,	0,	2

1. Calculate the averages and ranges for each set and plot them on the charts.

2. Calculate the overall average for each set.

   Set 1. _____

   Set 2. _____

   Set 3. _____

   Set 4. _____

Draw a line for each overall average on its own chart and label it.

3. Calculate the average range for each set.

   Set 1. _____

   Set 2. _____

   Set 3. _____

   Set 4. _____

Draw a line for each average range on the range chart and label it.

4. Refer to the table of average and range chart factors in Figure 3-14 in the textbook.

   (a) To calculate the upper control limits for ranges, which factor do you use?

   _____

   (b) What is the sample size in these exercises?

   _____

   (c) What value of the factor should you use to calculate the upper control limit for ranges?

   _____

   (d) Write the formula you use to calculate the upper control limit for ranges:

   _____

   (e) Under what conditions is the lower control limit for ranges always zero?

   _____

   _____

5. Using the average ranges you calculated in Question 3, determine the upper control limit for the range in each data set. Draw it in on its own chart and label it.

   Set 1. _____

   Set 2. _____

Set 3. _____

Set 4. _____

6. (a) Do any of the ranges fall outside the upper control limit for ranges?

Set 1. (yes/no) _____

If so, how many? _____

Set 2. (yes/no) _____

If so, how many? _____

Set 3. (yes/no) _____

If so, how many? _____

Set 4. (yes/no) _____

If so, how many? _____

(b) What, if anything, should you do in each case?

Set 1. _____

_____

Set 2. _____

_____

Set 3. _____

_____

Set 4. _____

_____

7. Refer to the table of average and range chart factors in Figure 3-17 in the textbook.

(a) To calculate the control limits for averages, which factor do you use?

_____

(b) What is the sample size in these exercises?

_____

(c) What value of the factor should you use to calculate the control limits for averages?

_____

(d) Write the formula for the upper control limit for averages:

_____

(e) Write the formula for the lower control limit for averages:

_____

8. Using the overall averages you calculated in Question 2, determine the upper control limit for the averages in each data set. Then draw it in on its own chart. Be sure to label it.

Set 1. _____

_____

Set 2. _____

_____

Set 3. _____

_____

Set 4. _____

_____

9. Using the overall averages you calculated in Question 2, determine the lower control limit for the averages in each data set. Draw it in on its own chart. Be sure to label it.

Set 1. _____

_____

Set 2. _____

_____

Set 3. _____

_____

Set 4. _____

_____

10. (a) Do any averages fall outside either the upper or the lower control limits?

Set 1. (yes/no) _____

If so, how many? _____

Set 2. (yes/no) _____

If so, how many? _____

Set 3. (yes/no) _____

If so, how many? _____

Set 4. (yes/no) _____

If so, how many? _____

(b) What, if anything, should you do in each case?

Set 1. _____

_____

Set 2. _____

_____

Set 3. _____

_____

Set 4. _____

_____

AVERAGE AND RANGE CHARTS: EXERCISES, SERIES 2

For each of the following sets of data, you will prepare a separate average and range chart. Write your answers for Question 1 in the appropriate space on the average and range chart form. Write the calculations for Questions 2 through 9 and the answers to all questions in the space provided in the workbook. Draw in the lines for the overall average, the average range, and the upper and lower control limits for ranges and averages as directed in Questions 2, 3, 5, 8, and 9.

SET 1.

a) 40, 43, 38, 30, 50

b) 32, 23, 35, 30, 37

c) 30, 19, 22, 22, 52

d) 24, 38, 29, 33, 31

e) 10, 31, 13, 44, 35

f) 21, 30, 29, 21, 25

g) 11, 23, 27, 22, 25

h) 24, 30, 20, 29, 16

i) 33, 33, 16, 45, 36

j) 21, 24, 31, 29, 29

k) 27, 15, 44, 26, 43

l) 25, 29, 34, 29, 13

m) 36, 9, 30, 42, 50

n) 16, 27, 27, 37, 32

o) 34, 24, 49, 11, 30

p) 35, 41, 29, 32, 26

q) 29, 21, 33, 30, 33

r) 21, 10, 28, 32, 35

s) 32, 32, 38, 36, 24

t) 40, 34, 44, 32, 16

SET 2.

a) 42, 54, 26, 44

b) 46, 48, 34, 42

c) 42, 38, 20, 45

d) 43, 40, 31, 43

e) 39, 42, 51, 36

f) 59, 21, 37, 47

g) 40, 52, 44, 39

h) 54, 36, 40, 42

i) 60, 23, 53, 34

j) 37, 19, 39, 25

k) 39, 41, 34, 39

l) 26, 43, 46, 55

m) 40, 26, 39, 30

n) 56, 32, 37, 33

o) 31, 29, 40, 35

p) 41, 23, 54, 45

q) 39, 43, 42, 48

r) 32, 62, 29, 32

s) 47, 33, 45, 40

t) 60, 40, 46, 53

SET 3.

a) .149, .107, .139, .143, .142

b) .130, .122, .133, .140, .148

c) .120, .122, .137, .136, .107

d) .136, .117, .140, .121, .136

e) .122, .110, .133, .119, .132

f) .135, .145, .120, .129, .151

g) .107, .130, .128, .127, .108

h) .123, .131, .119, .126, .144

i) .140, .136, .129, .127, .112

j) .130, .133, .145, .143, .114

k) .133, .135, .123, .129, .132

l) .118, .129, .133, .131, .117

m) .146, .154, .145, .151, .130

n) .117, .132, .140, .127, .132

o) .121, .143, .111, .122, .140

p) .137, .127, .140, .125, .122

q) .133, .141, .136, .134, .133

r) .132, .126, .135, .146, .133

s) .133, .126, .148, .126, .130

t) .133, .120, .124, .121, .150

SET 4.

a) 7, −3, 10, −5

b) 3, 11, 6, 4

c) 2, −4, 5, 16

d) 3, −4, 18, −4

e) 3, −10, −6, −9

f) −9, −13, 16, −12

g) 13, 2, 24, −1

h) −19, 10, 13, 3

i) −8, −3, 21, 1

j) 10, 2, 0, −13

k) 21, −1, −10, 15

l) −22, −3, −2, 0

m) 14, −4, −11, 1

n) −18, −3, −1, 6

o) −16, 13, 15, 3

p) 2, −11, 3, −20

q) −23, −9, 10, −13

r) 6, 6, 7, −8

s) 18, 10, 3, −8

t) 12, 13, 9, −23

1. Calculate the averages and ranges for each set and plot them on the charts.

2. Calculate the overall average for each set.

   Set 1. _____

   Set 2. _____

   Set 3. _____

   Set 4. _____

   Draw a line for each overall average on its own chart and label it.

3. Calculate the average range for each set.

   Set 1. _____

   Set 2. _____

   Set 3. _____

   Set 4. _____

   Draw a line for each average range on the range chart and label it.

4. Refer to the table of average and range chart factors in Figure 3-14 in the textbook.

   (a) To calculate the upper control limits for ranges, which factor do you use?

   _____

   (b) For a sample size of 5, what value of the factor should you use to calculate the upper control limit for ranges?

   _____

   (c) For a sample size of 4, what value of the factor should you use to calculate the upper control limit for ranges?

   _____

   (d) Write the formula you use to calculate the upper control limit for ranges:

   _____

   (e) Under what conditions is the lower control limit for ranges always zero?

   _____

   _____

5. Using the average ranges you calculated in Question 3, determine the upper control limit for the range in each data set. Draw it in on its own chart and label it.

   Set 1. _____

   Set 2. _____

   Set 3. _____

   Set 4. _____

6. (a) Do any of the ranges fall outside the upper control limit for ranges?

   Set 1. (yes/no) _____

   If so, how many? _____

   Set 2. (yes/no) _____

   If so, how many? _____

   Set 3. (yes/no) _____

   If so, how many? _____

   Set 4. (yes/no) _____

   If so, how many? _____

   (b) What, if anything, should you do in each case?

   Set 1. _____

   _____

   Set 2. _____

   _____

   Set 3. _____

   _____

   Set 4. _____

   _____

7. Refer to the table of average and range chart factors in Figure 3-17 in the textbook.

   (a) To calculate the control limits for averages, which factor do you use?

   _____

(b) For a sample size of 5, what value of the factor should you use to calculate the control limits for averages?

_____

(c) For a sample size of 4, what value of the factor should you use to calculate the control limits for averages?

_____

(d) Write the formula for the upper control limit for averages:

_____

(e) Write the formula for the lower control limit for averages:

_____

8. Using the overall averages you calculated in Question 2, determine the upper control limit for the averages in each data set. Then draw it in on its own chart. Be sure to label it.

Set 1. _____

_____

Set 2. _____

_____

Set 3. _____

_____

Set 4. _____

_____

9. Using the overall averages you calculated in Question 2, determine the lower control limit for the averages in each data set. Draw it on its own chart. Be sure to label it.

Set 1. _____

_____

Set 2. _____

_____

Set 3. _____

_____

Set 4. _____

_____

10. (a) Do any averages fall outside either the upper or the lower control limits?

Set 1. (yes/no) _____

If so, how many? _____

Set 2. (yes/no) _____

If so, how many? _____

Set 3. (yes/no) _____

If so, how many? _____

Set 4. (yes/no) _____

If so, how many? _____

(b) What, if anything, should you do in each case?

Set 1. _____

_____

Set 2. _____

_____

Set 3. _____

_____

Set 4. _____

_____

MEDIAN AND RANGE CHARTS: REVIEW QUESTIONS

1. (a) Under what circumstances is the median and range control chart a good chart to use?

   _____

   _____

   _____

   _____

   (b) If your operation does not fit these requirements, what kind of chart should you use?

   _____

2. (a) When using the median and range chart, what sample sizes can you work with?

   _____

   (b) What sample sizes are easiest to work with?

   _____

DEVELOPING THE MEDIAN AND RANGE CHARTS

If you relabel the average and range chart form, you can use it for the median and range chart.

Step 1. Collect samples.

What time frame do you use when taking your samples?

_____

Step 2. Measure the dimension you want to chart.

Where do you record the results of your measurements on the median and range chart?

_____

_____

Step 3. Determine the median measurement.

(a) What is a median?

_____

(b) How do you find the median?

_____

_____

_____

(c) In a three-piece sample, what is the median?

_____

_____

(d) In a five-piece sample, where does the median fall?

_____

_____

_____

(e) How do you figure the median for an even-numbered sample?

_____

_____

(f) Where do you record the median measurement of a sample?

_____

(g) What is the difference between the median and the mean of a group of measurements?

_____

_____

_____

(h) In this set of five measurements—46, 41, 47, 49, 40—what is the average?

_____

(i) How would you find the median of this set measurements?

_____

_____

(j) What is the median for this set?

_____

Step 4. Determine the ranges for the samples.

(a) How do you calculate the range for the median and range chart?

_____

(b) Where do you record the range on the chart?

_____

A three-piece sample has the measurements 17, 12, 15.

(c) Rank them and write your answer here:

_____

(d) Which is the largest?

_____

(e) Which is the smallest?

_____

(f) What is the median?

_____

(g) What is the range for this sample?

_____

Step 5. Determine the median of medians ($\widetilde{\widetilde{X}}$) and the median of ranges ($\widetilde{R}$).

Suppose you measure and record 15 samples on a median and range chart. There are three readings in each of your samples, and you have found the median and range for each sample. Now you are ready to figure the median of the medians and the median of the ranges.

(a) How do you figure the median of the medians in a group of 15 medians?

_____

_____

(b) Write the symbol for median of the medians:

_____

(c) How do you find the median range in a group of 15 measurements?

_____

_____

(d) Write the symbol for median range:

_____

Step 6. Set the scale for the median ($\widetilde{X}$) chart.

How much of the available chart space should you allow for the spread of the measurements?

_____

Step 7. Set the scale for the range.

How should you set the scale for ranges in the median chart?

_____

_____

Step 8. Plot the measurements on the control chart.

(a) Should you plot the individual measurements in the sample on the median and range chart?

_____

(b) How do we plot the medians on the median and range chart?

_____

(c) Why might you want to connect the medians with straight lines?

_____

(d) How do you plot the ranges on the median and range chart?

_____

_____

Step 9. Determine the control limits for medians and ranges.

Figure 3-23 in the textbook is the table of factors for the median and range chart.

(a) Are the factors for the median and range chart the same as the factors for the average and range chart?

_____

(b) To calculate the upper control limit for ranges, which factor do you use?

_____

(c) What is the correct value for a sample size of 3?

_____

(d) What is the correct value for a sample size of 5?

_____

(e) What is the formula for finding the upper control limit for ranges?

_____

(f) What is the lower control limit for ranges?

_____

As you did for the average and range chart, check to see whether all the ranges are inside the control limits.

(g) What should you do if one or two ranges are outside the upper control limit?

_____

_____

_____

(h) What should you do if three or more ranges are outside the control limits?

_____

_____

_____

_____

(i) Only under what condition can you work on control limits for medians?

_____

_____

(j) To calculate control limits for medians, which factor should you use?

_____

(k) For a sample size of 3, what is the correct value of the factor to use?

_____

(l) For a sample size of 5, what is the correct value?

_____

(m) Write the formula for the upper control limit for medians:

_____

(n) Write the formula for the lower control limit for medians:

_____

(o) What should you do if one or two of the medians fall outside the control limits?

_____

_____

(p) What recalculations should you make, if any?

_____

_____

(q) If one or more of the remaining medians still fall outside the new control limit, what would then be true?

_____

_____

(r) What should you do?

_____

_____

_____

(s) What is the situation if three or more medians fall outside the control limits when you are first setting up the chart?

_____

_____

(t) What should you do?

_____

_____

_____

HOW TO USE MEDIAN AND RANGE CHARTS IN CONTINUED PRODUCTION

(a) What kind of measurements do you plot on the median and range chart?

_____

_____

_____

(b) Can you compare the plotted points to the specifications?

_____

(c) Under what circumstances is corrective action necessary?

_____

_____

_____

_____

_____

_____

(d) Can individual points appear outside control limits even when the job is running normally?

_____

(e) Does an individual point falling outside the specification mean that an assignable cause is operating?

_____

(f) Under what circumstances may you say that the process is out of control?

_____

_____

_____

MEDIAN AND RANGE CHARTS: EXERCISES, SERIES 1

1. Determine the medians in the following set of data. Write each answer in the space provided.

PRACTICE SETS

a) 44, 41, 39, 47, 48 _____

b) 13, 27, 17, 20, 22 _____

c) 63, 59, 68, 67, 63 _____

d) 73, 81, 75, 77, 80 _____

e) 34, 38, 36, 31, 30 _____

f) 29, 31, 30 _____

g) 77, 73, 76 _____

h) 8, 11, 12 _____

i) 63, 66, 60 _____

j) 21, 24, 25 _____

k) 17, 13, 18, 16 _____

l) 56, 54, 59, 55 _____

m) 97, 103, 98, 96 _____

n) 30, 28, 34, 33 _____

o) 61, 60, 65, 64 _____

p) 56, 68, 46, 59, 51 _____

q) 8, 6, −3, 9, 5 _____

r) 43, 46, 40, 53 _____

s) 88, 85, 78, 91, 82 _____

t) 1.56, 1.68, 1.59 _____

2. For each of the following sets of data, you will prepare a separate median and range

chart. Write your answers for Question 3 in the appropriate spaces on the median and range chart forms. Write the calculations for Questions 4, 5, 7, 10, and 11 and the answers to all questions in the space provided in the workbook. Draw in the lines for the median of the medians, the median of the ranges, and the upper and lower control limits for medians and ranges as directed in Questions 4, 5, 7, 10, and 11.

SET 1.

a) 73, 73, 81, 75, 77

b) 73, 68, 75, 78, 75

c) 75, 70, 73, 77, 83

d) 77, 75, 75, 77, 70

e) 70, 75, 77, 75, 73

f) 67, 72, 70, 73, 73

g) 72, 75, 68, 72, 75

h) 75, 70, 70, 68, 72

i) 79, 82, 70, 71, 70

j) 80, 73, 74, 70, 78

k) 72, 68, 83, 77, 77

l) 75, 67, 70, 75, 68

m) 69, 78, 74, 70, 66

n) 73, 76, 76, 70, 72

o) 80, 76, 72, 74, 75

p) 74, 69, 77, 69, 81

q) 72, 73, 69, 75, 77

r) 77, 75, 82, 72, 70

s) 73, 70, 70, 72, 73

t) 78, 78, 77, 77, 74

SET 2.

a) 38, 35, 33, 37

b) 32, 34, 31, 31

c) 29, 33, 39, 38

d) 31, 30, 29, 34

e) 34, 35, 39, 36

f) 31, 35, 32, 32

g) 37, 29, 30, 37

h) 32, 38, 30, 37

i) 30, 35, 32, 41

j) 35, 32, 33, 38

k) 30, 38, 27, 36

l) 37, 32, 35, 32

m) 39, 37, 30, 31

n) 40, 31, 38, 30

o) 37, 37, 32, 30

p) 32, 32, 33, 31

q) 38, 36, 30, 33

r) 32, 35, 36, 40

s) 35, 34, 37, 36

t) 37, 29, 32, 31

SET 3.

a) 11, 15, 14

b) 14, 13, 18

c) 18, 14, 12

d) 19, 13, 16

e) 17, 17, 14

f) 16, 18, 12

g) 17, 13, 13

h) 17, 11, 15

i) 14, 14, 17

j) 12, 15, 16

k) 13, 15, 16

l) 17, 12, 18

m) 19, 17, 15

n) 15, 16, 13

o) 12, 12, 17

p) 13, 17, 18

q) 14, 15, 16

r) 18, 13, 15

s) 19, 14, 14

t) 17, 12, 17

3. Find the medians and ranges for the three data sets. Write your answers in the appropriate places on the median and range chart forms. Then plot the individual points, medians, and ranges, each on their own chart.

4. Find the median of the medians for each set in Question 2.

   Set 1. _____

   Set 2. _____

   Set 3. _____

   Draw a line to represent the median of the medians for each set on its own median and range chart. Label it.

5. Find the median range for each set.

   Set 1. _____

   Set 2. _____

   Set 3. _____

   Draw a line for each median of ranges on its own median and range chart. Label it.

6. Refer to the table of factors for the median and range chart in Figure 3-23 in the textbook.

(a) To calculate the upper control limits for ranges, which factor do you use?

_____

(b) What is the sample size in Set 1?

_____

(c) Which value of the factor should you use when calculating the control limit for ranges with this sample size?

_____

(d) What is the sample size in Set 2?

_____

(e) Which value of the factor should you use?

_____

(f) What is the sample size in Set 3?

_____

(g) Which value of the factor should you use?

_____

(h) Write the formula for calculating the upper control limit for ranges:

_____

(i) What is the lower control limit for ranges?

_____

7. Using the median ranges you found in Question 5, determine the upper control limit for the range in each data set.

Set 1. _____

Set 2. _____

Set 3. _____

Draw in the upper control limit for each set on its median and range control chart.

8. (a) Do any of the ranges fall outside the upper control limit for ranges?

Set 1. (yes/no) _____

If so, how many? _____

Set 2. (yes/no) _____

If so, how many? _____

Set 3. (yes/no) _____

If so, how many? _____

(b) What, if anything, should you do in each case?

Set 1. _____

_____

Set 2. _____

_____

Set 3. _____

_____

9. Refer to Figure 3-23 in the textbook for the median and range chart factors.

(a) To calculate the control limits for medians, which factor do you use?

_____

The sample size for each data set in Question 2 is different.

(b) What is the sample size in Set 1?

_____

(c) Which value of the factor do you use?

_____

(d) What is the sample size for Set 2?

_____

(e) Which value of the factor do you use?

_____

(f) What is the sample size for Set 3?

_____

(g) Which value of the factor do you use?

_____

(h) Write the formula you use to calculate the upper control limit for medians:

_____

(i) Write the formula you use to calculate the lower control limit for medians:

_____

10. Using the median of the medians you found in Question 4, first determine the upper control limit for the medians for each data set. Then draw in the upper control limit for each set on its own median and range control chart.

   Set 1. _____

   _____

   Set 2. _____

   _____

   Set 3. _____

   _____

11. Using the median of the medians you found in Question 4, first determine the lower control limit for the medians for each data set. Then draw in the lower control limit for each set on its own median and range control chart.

   Set 1. _____

   _____

   Set 2. _____

   _____

   Set 3. _____

   _____

12. (a) Do any medians fall outside either the upper or the lower control limits?

Set 1. (yes/no) _____

If so, how many? _____

Set 2. (yes/no) _____

If so, how many? _____

Set 3. (yes/no) _____

If so, how many? _____

(b) What, if anything, should you do in each case?

   Set 1. _____

   _____

   Set 2. _____

   _____

   Set 3. _____

   _____

(c) Do any individuals points fall outside the control limits?

   Set 1. (yes/no) _____

   Set 2. (yes/no) _____

   Set 3. (yes/no) _____

(d) What, if anything, should you do in each case?

   Set 1. _____

   _____

   Set 2. _____

   _____

   Set 3. _____

   _____

MEDIAN AND RANGE CHARTS: EXERCISES, SERIES 2

1. Determine the medians in the following set of data. Write each answer in the space provided.

PRACTICE SETS

a) 40, 37, 35, 44, 43 _____

b) 25, 39, 29, 32, 34 _____

c) 162, 159, 165, 164, 158 _____

d) 11, 13, 20, 17, 15 _____

e) 74, 76, 70, 78, 77 _____

f) 52, 49, 48 _____

g) 93, 86, 87 _____

h) 5, 8, 7 _____

i) 71, 76, 70 _____

j) 25, 34, 27 _____

k) 11, 14, 18, 19 _____

l) 65, 64, 69, 72 _____

m) 197, 183, 198, 189 _____

n) 50, 47, 54, 53 _____

o) 19, 21, 20, 25 _____

p) 35, 37, 40, 32 _____

q) .72, .77, .73, .68, .67 _____

r) 10, 6, 5, 18, 12 _____

s) −13, 9, −23 _____

t) 129, 145, 123, 133 _____

2. For each of the following sets of data, you will prepare a separate median and range chart. Write your answers for Question 3 in the appropriate spaces on the median and range chart forms. Write the calculations for Questions 4, 5, 7, 10, and 11 and the answers to all questions in the space provided in the workbook. Draw in the lines for the median of the medians, the median of the ranges, and the upper and lower control limits for medians and ranges as directed in Questions 4, 5, 7, 10, and 11.

SET 1.

a) 103, 98, 95, 102

b) 97, 95, 104, 98

c) 93, 97, 94, 98

d) 97, 95, 102, 96

e) 101, 103, 95, 97

f) 99, 93, 96, 97

g) 96, 95, 98, 101

h) 101, 95, 94, 97

i) 94, 93, 98, 96

j) 99, 101, 97, 98

k) 96, 92, 101, 93

l) 95, 101, 102, 97

m) 104, 96, 99, 98

n) 104, 99, 101, 99

o) 97, 95, 98, 96

p) 99, 95, 94, 97

q) 98, 101, 97, 98

r) 103, 98, 94, 97

s) 99, 96, 98, 97

t) 99, 101, 103, 98

SET 2.

a) 40, 42, 39

b) 37, 39, 38

c) 46, 43, 41

d) 42, 42, 47

e) 38, 41, 47

f) 40, 42, 39

g) 37, 42, 39

h) 48, 45, 44

i) 43, 42, 45

j) 47, 44, 46

k) 45, 39, 41

l) 40, 38, 45

m) 46, 47, 43

n) 45, 46, 44

o) 42, 41, 40

p) 43, 41, 39

q) 42, 45, 41

r) 43, 44, 41

s) 38, 41, 40

t) 42, 45, 42

SET 3.

a) 53, 53, 55, 61, 57

b) 55, 50, 53, 55, 57

c) 56, 58, 58, 53, 52

d) 53, 48, 55, 58, 55

e) 62, 57, 54, 56, 60

f) 51, 57, 59, 52, 50

g) 52, 51, 53, 57, 54

h) 54, 48, 52, 55, 54

i) 51, 50, 53, 57, 55

j) 57, 54, 52, 56, 53

k) 56, 55, 59, 55, 57

l) 58, 53, 59, 54, 52

m) 56, 54, 52, 55, 53

n) 53, 57, 59, 56, 60

o) 61, 60, 57, 57, 55

p) 54, 52, 57, 53, 54

q) 56, 51, 59, 57, 57

r) 56, 55, 58, 52, 53

s) 51, 49, 53, 52, 55

t) 55, 56, 60, 59, 57

3. Find the medians and ranges for the three data sets. Write your answers in the appropriate places on the median and range chart forms. Then plot the individual points, medians, and ranges, each on their own chart.

4. Find the median of the medians for each set in Question 2.

   Set 1. _____

   Set 2. _____

   Set 3. _____

   Draw a line to represent the median of the medians for each set on its own median and range chart. Label it.

5. Find the median range for each set.

   Set 1. _____

   Set 2. _____

   Set 3. _____

   Draw a line for each median of ranges on its own median and range chart. Label it.

6. Refer to the table of factors for the median and range chart in Figure 3-23 in the textbook.

(a) To calculate the upper control limits for ranges, which factor do you use?

_____

(b) What is the sample size in Set 1?

_____

(c) Which value of the factor should you use when calculating the control limit for ranges with this sample size?

_____

(d) What is the sample size in Set 2?

_____

(e) Which value of the factor should you use?

_____

(f) What is the sample size in Set 3?

_____

(g) Which value of the factor should you use?

_____

(h) Write the formula for calculating the upper control limit for ranges:

_____

(i) What is the lower control limit for ranges?

_____

7. Using the median ranges you found in Question 5, determine the upper control limit for the range in each data set.

Set 1. _____

Set 2. _____

Set 3. _____

Draw in the upper control limit for each set on its median and range control chart.

8. (a) Do any of the ranges fall outside the upper control limit for ranges?

Set 1. (yes/no) _____

If so, how many? _____

Set 2. (yes/no) _____

If so, how many? _____

Set 3. (yes/no) _____

If so, how many? _____

(b) What, if anything, should you do in each case?

Set 1. _____

_____

Set 2. _____

_____

Set 3. _____

_____

9. Refer to Figure 3-23 in the textbook for the median and range chart factors.

(a) To calculate the control limits for medians, which factors do you use?

_____

The sample size for each data set in Question 2 is different.

(b) What is the sample size in Set 1?

_____

(c) Which value of the factor do you use?

_____

(d) What is the sample size for Set 2?

_____

(e) Which value of the factor do you use?

_____

(f) What is the sample size for Set 3?

_____

(g) Which value of the factor do you use?

_____

(h) Write the formula you use to calculate the upper control limit for medians:

_____

(i) Write the formula for calculating the lower control limit for medians:

_____

10. Using the median of the medians you found in Question 4, first determine the upper control limit for the medians for each data set. Then draw in the upper control limit for each set on its own median and range control chart.

    Set 1. _____

    _____

    Set 2. _____

    _____

    Set 3. _____

    _____

11. Using the median of the medians you found in Question 4, first determine the lower control limit for the medians for each data set. Then draw in the lower control limit for each set on its own median and range control chart.

    Set 1. _____

    _____

    Set 2. _____

    _____

    Set 3. _____

    _____

12. (a) Do any medians fall outside either the upper or the lower control limits?

    Set 1. (yes/no) _____

    If so, how many? _____

Set 2. (yes/no) _____

If so, how many? _____

Set 3. (yes/no) _____

If so, how many? _____

(b) What, if anything, should you do in each case?

Set 1. _____

_____

_____

Set 2. _____

_____

_____

Set 3. _____

_____

(c) Do any individual points fall outside the control limits?

Set 1. (yes/no) _____

Set 2. (yes/no) _____

Set 3. (yes/no) _____

(d) What, if anything, should you do in each case?

Set 1. _____

_____

Set 2. _____

_____

Set 3. _____

_____

INDIVIDUAL AND RANGE CHARTS: REVIEW QUESTIONS

1. (a) When is it best to use the individual and range chart?

   _____
   _____
   _____

   (b) What is a drawback to the individual and range chart in comparison to the average and range chart?

   _____
   _____

2. (a) What are two situations given in the textbook in which it is a good idea to use the individual and range chart?

   (1) _____
   _____

   (2) _____
   _____

   (b) What are some examples of this type of process?

   _____
   _____

   (c) In these situations, what can you say about the measurements?

   _____
   _____
   _____

DEVELOPING AN INDIVIDUAL AND RANGE CHART

1. How do you adapt the standard average and range chart form for use as an individual and range chart?

   _____
   _____
   _____
   _____
   _____
   _____

2. (a) To develop an individual and range chart, how many measurements will you need?

   _____

   (b) Where do you record the values on the control chart?

   _____
   _____

   (c) Because this is an individual chart, how many measurements do you have for each batch?

   _____

   (d) Where should you record the batch number?

   _____

   (e) What is a useful way to show the order of the samples?

   _____

3. (a) How do you figure the range values for the individual and range chart?

   _____

   _____

   _____

   (b) Where do you record the range value?

   _____

   (c) Is there a range value for the first batch measurement?

   _____

   (d) Is the number of range values the same as the number of measurements?

   _____

4. (a) How much of the available "individuals" chart space do you allow for the difference between the largest and the smallest measurements?

   _____

   (b) Where does the scale for the "ranges" chart start?

   _____

   (c) How should the divisions on the scale for ranges compare with the divisions on the "individuals" chart?

   _____

CONTROL LIMITS

1. Refer to Figure 3-14 in the textbook, the table for average and range chart factors. How do you calculate control limits for individual and range charts?

   _____

   _____

2. (a) When determining the upper control limit for ranges for the individual and range chart, which factor do you use?

   _____

(b) What is the size of the sample?

   _____

(c) What is the correct value of the factor?

   _____

(d) Write the formula for the upper control limit for ranges:

   _____

3. (a) How do you calculate the average range?

   _____

   _____

   (b) In the individual and range chart, is the number of ranges the same as the number of individual readings?

   _____

4. Where is the lower control limit for ranges on the individual and range chart always set?

   _____

5. After calculating the upper control limit for the ranges, check whether any ranges fall outside the control limit.

   (a) What is the situation if three or more ranges are greater than the upper control limit?

   _____

   _____

   (b) What should you do?

   _____

   _____

   _____

   (c) What should you do if one or two ranges are outside the control limit?

   _____

   (d) Should you throw out the corresponding individual measurements?

   _____

(e) Should you calculate a new upper control limit for ranges?

_____

6. (a) If one or more of the remaining ranges are still greater than the new control limits, what condition is true?

_____
_____

(b) What should you do?

_____
_____
_____

(c) If none of the remaining ranges is greater than the new control limits, what should you do?

_____
_____

7. What must be true of the ranges before you can work on control limits for individuals?

_____
_____

8. To determine the upper and the lower control limits for individuals, you need to calculate the average of the individuals.

(a) How do you do this?

_____
_____
_____

(b) What is the sample size for the individuals?

_____

(c) What is the value of the factor that corresponds to this sample size? (To find the value of the factor you need,

see the appendix at the end of the textbook.)

_____

(d) Write the formula for the upper control limit for individuals:

_____

(e) Write the formula for the lower control limit for individuals:

_____

9. Once you have determined the control limits for individuals, you apply the same tests to the individual measurements as you applied to the range values.

(a) What is the situation if three or more measurements are outside the control limits?

_____
_____

(b) What should you do?

_____
_____
_____

(c) What should you do if one or two individuals are outside the control limits?

_____
_____
_____

(d) What does it mean if you recalculate the control limits and there are still measurements outside the new control limits?

_____
_____

(e) What should you do?

_____

_____

_____

10. (a) Under what circumstances can you use the individual and range chart to monitor and control your operation?

_____

_____

_____

   (b) Is this chart used in the same way as other variable control control charts?

_____

   (c) What kind of measurements does the individual and range chart control?

_____

11. (a) Can you compare measurements plotted on the individual chart to specification limits as well as to control limits?

_____

   (b) What type of problem do you have when an individual measurements falls outside the control limits?

_____

   (c) Who should take action?

_____

(d) What should they do?

_____

_____

(e) When points on the control chart fall outside the specifications but not outside the control limits, what type of problem is it?

_____

_____

(f) Who should correct this situation?

_____

(g) What should they do?

_____

_____

(h) If either the upper or the lower control limit for individual measurements falls outside the specifications, what does that tell you about the operation or the process?

_____

_____

_____

(i) To gain confidence in the accuracy of the control limits, what should you do?

_____

_____

_____

INDIVIDUAL AND RANGE CHARTS: EXERCISES, SERIES 1

1. Calculate ranges between the individual measurements for the following data sets.

PRACTICE SET 1.

a) 73 _____

b) 68 _____

c) 70 _____

d) 75 _____

e) 75 _____

f) 72 _____

g) 75 _____

h) 70 _____

i) 82 _____

j) 73 _____

k) 68 _____

l) 67 _____

m) 78 _____

n) 76 _____

o) 76 _____

p) 69 _____

q) 73 _____

r) 75 _____

s) 70 _____

t) 78 _____

PRACTICE SET 2.

a) .137 _____

b) .122 _____

c) .122 _____

d) .142 _____

e) .133 _____

f) .145 _____

g) .130 _____

h) .131 _____

i) .136 _____

j) .133 _____

k) .135 _____

l) .129 _____

m) .154 _____

n) .132 _____

o) .143 _____

p) .127 _____

q) .141 _____

r) .126 _____

s) .126 _____

t) .120 _____

2. For each of the following sets of data, you will prepare a separate individual and range chart. Write your answers for Question 3 in the appropriate spaces on the individual and range chart forms. Write the calculations for Questions 4, 5, 7, 10, and 11 and the answers to all questions in the space provided in the workbook. Draw in the line for each average of the individuals, average range, and upper and lower control limits for individuals and ranges as directed in Questions 4, 5, 7, 10, and 11.

SET 1.

a) 103 _____

b) 98 _____

c) 102 _____

d) 95 _____

e) 99 _____

f) 104 _____

g) 101 _____

h) 99 _____

i) 95 _____

j) 101 _____

k) 102 _____

l) 97 _____

m) 97 _____

n) 95 _____

o) 103 _____

p) 101 _____

q) 102 _____

r) 97 _____

s) 95 _____

t) 104 _____

SET 2.

a) 43 _____

b) 40 _____

c) 36 _____

d) 21 _____

e) 19 _____

f) 29 _____

g) 27 _____

h) 26 _____

i) 27 _____

j) 43 _____

k) 29 _____

l) 31 _____

m) 51 _____

n) 27 _____

o) 22 _____

p) 25 _____

q) 34 _____

r) 46 _____

s) 26 _____

t) 21 _____

SET 3.

a) 53 _____

b) 50 _____

c) 58 _____

d) 48 _____

e) 57 _____

f) 57 _____

g) 51 _____

h) 48 _____

i) 50 _____

j) 54 _____

k) 55 _____

l) 53 _____

m) 54 _____

n) 55 _____

o) 60 _____

p) 52 _____

q) 51 _____

r) 55 _____

s) 49 _____

t) 56 _____

SET 4.

a) 13.6 _____

b) 11.2 _____

c) 11.7 _____

d) 14.2 _____

e) 15.0 _____

f) 14.8 _____

g) 10.8 _____

h) 12.2 _____

i) 13.2 _____

j) 13.3 _____

k) 10.7 _____

l) 11.4 _____

m) 15.1 _____

n) 14.4 _____

o) 13.2 _____

p) 13.2 _____

q) 13.3 _____

r) 12.6 _____

s) 14.0 _____

t) 13.0 _____

3. For each of the data sets from Question 2, plot the individual measurements on their own chart. Then determine the ranges and plot them on the charts.

4. Calculate the average of the individuals for each set in Question 2. Draw a line for each average of individuals on its own chart. Label it.

Set 1. _____

Set 2. _____

Set 3. _____

Set 4. _____

5. Calculate the average range for each data set in Question 2. Draw in a line for each average range on its range chart and label it.

Set 1. _____

Set 2. _____

Set 3. _____

Set 4. _____

6. Refer to the table of average and range chart factors in Figure 3-14 in the textbook.

(a) To calculate the upper control limit for ranges, which factor do you use?

_____

(b) What is the sample size you use when determining the range for the individual and range chart?

_____

(c) For this sample size, what value of the factor should you use to calculate the upper control limit for ranges?

_____

(d) Write the formula you use to calculate the upper control limit for ranges:

_____

(e) Where must you always set the lower control limit for ranges on the individual and range chart?

_____

7. Using the average ranges you calculated in Question 5, determine the upper control limit for the ranges in each data set. Draw it in on its own range chart and label it.

Set 1. _____

Set 2. _____

Set 3. _____

Set 4. _____

8. (a) Do any of the ranges fall outside the upper control limit for ranges?

Set 1. (yes/no) _____

If so, how many? _____

Set 2. (yes/no) _____

If so, how many? _____

Set 3. (yes/no) _____

If so, how many? _____

Set 4. (yes/no) _____

If so, how many? _____

(b) What, if anything, should you do in each case?

Set 1. _____

_____

Set 2. _____

_____

Set 3. _____

_____

Set 4. _____

_____

9. Refer to the table of individual and range chart factors in the appendix at the end of the textbook.

(a) To calculate upper and lower control limits for the individuals chart, what sample size do you use?

_____

(b) What is the value of the factor that corresponds to this sample size?

_____

(c) Write the formula for the upper control limit for individuals:

_____

(d) Write the formula for the lower control limit for individuals:

_____

10. Using the average of the individuals you calculated in Question 4, determine the upper control limit for the individuals in each data set. Draw it in on its own chart and label it.

Set 1. _____

_____

Set 2. _____

_____

Set 3. _____

_____

Set 4. _____

_____

11. Using the average of the individuals you calculated in Question 4, determine the lower control limit for the individuals in each data set.

Set 1. _____

_____

Set 2. _____

_____

Set 3. _____

_____

Set 4. _____

_____

Draw in the lower control limit for each set on its chart. Label it.

12. (a) Do any individual measurements fall outside either the upper or the lower control limits?

Set 1. (yes/no) _____

If so, how many? _____

Set 2. (yes/no) _____

If so, how many? _____

Set 3. (yes/no) _____

If so, how many? _____

Set 4. (yes/no) _____

If so, how many? _____

(b) What, if anything, should you do in each case?

Set 1. _____

_____

Set 2. _____

_____

Set 3. _____

_____

Set 4. _____

_____

INDIVIDUAL AND RANGE CHARTS: EXERCISES, SERIES 2

1. Calculate ranges between the individual measurements for the follow data sets.

s) 97.0 _____

t) 93.8 _____

PRACTICE SET 1.

a) 98.3 _____

b) 98.7 _____

c) 97.2 _____

d) 88.6 _____

e) 98.6 _____

f) 95.7 _____

g) 92.3 _____

h) 91.9 _____

i) 94.2 _____

j) 87.1 _____

k) 88.4 _____

l) 88.5 _____

m) 88.4 _____

n) 89.0 _____

o) 90.5 _____

p) 96.8 _____

q) 87.2 _____

r) 92.6 _____

PRACTICE SET 2.

a) 37 _____

b) 31 _____

c) 38 _____

d) 34 _____

e) 36 _____

f) 32 _____

g) 37 _____

h) 37 _____

i) 41 _____

j) 38 _____

k) 36 _____

l) 32 _____

m) 31 _____

n) 30 _____

o) 30 _____

p) 31 _____

q) 33 _____

r) 40 _____

s) 36 _____

t) 31 _____

2. For each of the following sets of data, you will prepare a separate individual and range chart. Write your answers for Question 3 in the appropriate spaces on the individual and range chart forms. Write the calculations for Questions 4, 5, 7, 10, and 11 and the answers to all questions in the space provided in the workbook. Draw in the line for each average of the individuals, average range, and upper and lower control limits for individuals and ranges as directed in Questions 4, 5, 7, 10, and 11.

SET 1.

a) 16 _____

b) 24 _____

c) 35 _____

d) 33 _____

e) 26 _____

f) 30 _____

g) 32 _____

h) 50 _____

i) 13 _____

j) 43 _____

k) 29 _____

l) 36 _____

m) 16 _____

n) 25 _____

o) 22 _____

p) 35 _____

q) 31 _____

r) 52 _____

s) 37 _____

t) 50 _____

SET 2.

a) −3 _____

b) 11 _____

c) −4 _____

d) −10 _____

e) −13 _____

f) −4 _____

g) 2 _____

h) 10 _____

i) −3 _____

j) 2 _____

k) −1 _____

l) −3 _____

m) −4 _____

n) −3 _____

o) 13 _____

p) −11 _____

q) −9 _____

r) 6 _____

s) 10 _____

t) 13 _____

SET 3.

a) 43 _____

b) 23 _____

c) 19 _____

d) 38 _____

e) 31 _____

f) 30 _____

g) 23 _____

h) 30 _____

i) 33 _____

j) 24 _____

k) 15 _____

l) 29 _____

m) 9 _____

n) 27 _____

o) 24 _____

p) 41 _____

q) 21 _____

r) 10 _____

s) 32 _____

t) 34 _____

SET 4.

a) .119 _____

b) .126 _____

c) .131 _____

d) .144 _____

e) .123 _____

f) .132 _____

g) .127 _____

h) .140 _____

i) .136 _____

j) .141 _____

k) .132 _____

l) .135 _____

m) .126 _____

n) .133 _____

o) .146 _____

p) .150 _____

q) .121 _____

r) .114 _____

s) .120 _____

t) .133 _____

3. For each of the data sets from Question 2, plot the individual measurements on their own chart. Then determine the ranges and plot them on the charts.

4. Calculate the average of the individuals for each set in Question 2. Draw a line for each average of individuals on its own chart. Label it.

Set 1. _____

Set 2. _____

Set 3. _____

Set 4. _____

5. Calculate the average range for each data set in Question 2. Draw in a line for each average range on its range chart and label it.

Set 1. _____

Set 2. _____

Set 3. _____

Set 4. _____

6. Refer to the table of average and range chart factors in Figure 3-14 in the textbook.

(a) To calculate the upper control limit for ranges, which factor do you use?

_____

(b) What is the sample size you use when determining the range for the individual and range chart?

_____

(c) For this sample size, what value of the factor should you use to calculate the upper control limit for ranges?

_____

(d) Write the formula you use to calculate the upper control limit for ranges:

_____

(e) Where must you always set the lower control limit for ranges on the individual and range chart?

_____

7. Using the average ranges you calculated in Question 5, determine the upper control limit for the ranges in each data set. Draw it on its own range chart and label it.

Set 1. _____

Set 2. _____

Set 3. _____

Set 4. _____

8. (a) Do any of the ranges fall outside the upper control limit for ranges?

Set 1. (yes/no) _____

If so, how many? _____

Set 2. (yes/no) _____

If so, how many? _____

Set 3. (yes/no) _____

If so, how many? _____

Set 4. (yes/no) _____

If so, how many? _____

(b) What, if anything, should you do in each case?

Set 1. _____

_____

Set 2. _____

_____

Set 3. _____

_____

Set 4. _____

_____

9. Refer to the table of individual and range chart factors in the appendix at the end of the textbook.

(a) To calculate upper and lower control limits for the individuals chart, what sample size do you use?

_____

(b) What is the value of the factor that corresponds to this sample size?

_____

(c) Write the formula for the upper control limit for individuals:

_____

(d) Write the formula for the lower control limit for individuals:

_____

10. Using the average of the individuals you calculated in Question 4, determine the upper control limit for the individuals in each data set. Draw it in on its own chart and label it.

Set 1. _____

_____

Set 2. _____

_____

Set 3. _____

_____

Set 4. _____

_____

11. Using the average of the individuals you calculated in Question 4, determine the lower control limit for the individuals in each data set.

Set 1. _____

_____

Set 2. _____

_____

Set 3. _____

_____

Set 4. _____

_____

Draw in the lower control limit for each set on its chart. Label it.

12. (a) Do any individual measurements fall outside either the upper or the lower control limits?

Set 1. (yes/no) _____

If so, how many? _____

Set 2. (yes/no) _____

If so, how many? _____

Set 3. (yes/no) _____

If so, how many? _____

Set 4. (yes/no) _____

If so, how many? _____

(b) What, if anything, should you do in each case?

Set 1. _____

_____

Set 2. _____

_____

Set 3. _____

_____

Set 4. _____

_____

VARIABLE CONTROL CHARTS: CASE STUDIES

The following case studies are taken from actual use in manufacturing organizations.

CASE 3-1

A rubber products manufacturing company starts the process of molding rubber by extruding the unvulcanized rubber into blocks of a certain weight. It is necessary to control the weight of these blocks to be assured that the products will be filled out completely when removed from the press that vulcanizes the rubber into the desired shape. It is also desirable that the prepared blocks of rubber be no larger than necessary to make a good product, thereby keeping material costs down.

At the point where the rubber coming from the extruder is cut automatically to a set length,

the stock preparation operator has a precision scale for weighing individual pieces of the rubber as they pass along on a moving belt. The weight of each piece of rubber is a dimension that varies within limits determined by the process. When the weight of the blocks of rubber is found to vary outside those limits, we know that the variation is caused by something not normal to the process (an assignable cause).

Using the information and the weights listed in the table "Weights of Unvulcanized Rubber Blocks," prepare a variable control chart and decide whether the stock preparation operation was free of assignable causes when the measurements were obtained. Also decide whether the control chart you make could be used on a continuing basis to detect the presence of assignable causes in this operation.

Weights of Unvulcanized Rubber Blocks (g) (Case 2-1)

Part Number: 3140242
Operation: Extrude stock preparation
Specification: 730/790 grams
Equipment: Precision scales to nearest gram
Note: Pieces were weighed individually in groups of five. The individual weights were recorded as listed.

No.	Weight	No.	Weight	No.	Weight	No.	Weight	No.	Weight
1	765	26	788	51	776	76	788	101	784
2	760	27	758	52	798	77	782	102	776
3	748	28	755	53	778	78	783	103	794
4	749	29	767	54	781	79	800	104	780
5	756	30	787	55	776	80	798	105	780
6	775	31	779	56	772	81	791	106	792
7	766	32	786	57	783	82	790	107	779
8	767	33	774	58	776	83	785	108	804
9	765	34	766	59	770	84	786	109	781
10	758	35	785	60	778	85	789	110	772
11	777	36	748	61	765	86	776	111	773
12	756	37	783	62	785	87	773	112	772
13	758	38	784	63	795	88	769	113	763
14	749	39	784	64	797	89	766	114	793
15	762	40	741	65	794	90	793	115	796
16	756	41	791	66	752	91	785	116	764
17	781	42	790	67	779	92	789	117	763
18	780	43	780	68	777	93	780	118	779
19	789	44	786	69	762	94	794	119	773
20	760	45	771	70	789	95	753	120	788
21	786	46	780	71	780	96	777	121	778
22	785	47	756	72	787	97	798	122	778
23	784	48	756	73	782	98	800	123	768
24	797	49	757	74	784	99	787	124	799
25	786	50	782	75	779	100	773	125	801

CASE 3-2

A company that forges metal parts has two sets of tooling for producing the same part. The orders from the customer are such that only one set of tooling needs to be used to make the number of parts required at this time.

An important requirement of the forging includes two cylindrical sections that must be concentric with each other within .040 inch. This measurement is made by rotating the forging on one of the sections and using a dial indicator gage to measure the maximum variation in the other section. The total varia-tion observed on the indicator gage is recorded. This is referred to as the total indi-cator reading, or TIR.

One hundred forgings were made in each of the two forging hammer and die setups in the shop. The total indicator reading (TIR) was recorded in groups of five. As a member of a quality improvement team you are asked to recommend which production setup should be run to fill the current orders.

Using the measurements recorded in the tables for Hammer #2—Die #1 and Hammer #3—Die #2, construct average and range charts to make your decision.

Hammer #2—Die #1 (Case 3-2)

| Subgroup | TOTAL INDICATOR READING (TIR) (in) | | | | |
	Sample #1	Sample #2	Sample #3	Sample #4	Sample #5
1	.015	.020	.012	.015	.004
2	.008	.010	.015	.003	.018
3	.005	.011	.016	.016	.000
4	.011	.016	.024	.010	.009
5	.002	.010	.014	.020	.008
6	.016	.007	.012	.020	.019
7	.020	.017	.005	.012	.015
8	.014	.021	.013	.016	.022
9	.024	.002	.006	.005	.022
10	.015	.022	.006	.019	.007
11	.015	.010	.020	.012	.021
12	.015	.012	.017	.010	.010
13	.017	.007	.019	.015	.014
14	.014	.018	.003	.003	.004
15	.024	.004	.015	.001	.012
16	.007	.010	.022	.008	.020
17	.010	.014	.020	.015	.022

(table continues on next page)

Hammer #2—Die #1 (Case 3-2) **(continued)**

	TOTAL INDICATOR READING (TIR) (in)				
Subgroup	Sample #1	Sample #2	Sample #3	Sample #4	Sample #5
18	.010	.015	.015	.007	.030
19	.021	.010	.005	.011	.020
20	.026	.010	.025	.012	.012

Hammer #3—Die #2 (Case 3-2)

	TOTAL INDICATOR READING (TIR) (in)				
Subgroup	Sample #1	Sample #2	Sample #3	Sample #4	Sample #5
1	.028	.010	.010	.022	.010
2	.010	.022	.017	.007	.023
3	.008	.016	.010	.039	.003
4	.011	.009	.020	.015	.012
5	.030	.022	.018	.025	.020
6	.011	.018	.023	.015	.007
7	.003	.021	.013	.017	.011
8	.066	.022	.025	.015	.012
9	.015	.014	.004	.015	.015
10	0.14	.022	.021	.014	.028
11	.017	.005	.018	.025	.017
12	.001	.022	.015	.015	.010
13	.017	.015	.019	.009	.007
14	.028	.010	.033	.021	.015
15	.050	.027	.035	.015	.050
16	.015	.017	.021	.010	.015
17	.033	.025	.015	.030	.010
18	.050	.010	.025	.015	.010
19	.006	.023	.047	.017	.020
20	.041	.020	.015	.002	.031

CASE 3-3

An assembly operation requires the associate to assemble a left-hand stationary snap to an adjustable retainer. The dimension from the stationary snap to the adjustable retainer after assembly is 323.0 ± 3.2 millimeters. This dimension is measured using a metric scale.

Develop an average and range chart based on the data listed in the table "Dimension from Left-Hand Stationary Snap to Adjustable Retainer." Using the chart, determine whether the process is centered on the specified dimension. Is the process stable or are assignable causes present?

The measurements were taken in groups of five and are recorded to the nearest whole millimeter.

Dimension from Left-Hand Stationary Snap to Adjustable Retainer (mm) (Case 3-3)

Subgroup	Sample #1	Sample #2	Sample #3	Sample #4	Sample #5
1	324.0	323.0	324.0	322.0	321.0
2	323.0	322.0	324.0	324.0	321.0
3	323.0	321.0	323.0	324.0	324.0
4	324.0	323.0	322.0	324.0	325.0
5	323.0	323.0	324.0	323.0	322.0
6	323.0	324.0	324.0	322.0	325.0
7	322.0	324.0	325.0	323.0	321.0
8	324.0	324.0	324.0	323.0	321.0
9	323.0	322.0	324.0	323.0	322.0
10	324.0	323.0	325.0	324.0	321.0
11	324.0	323.0	325.0	324.0	323.0
12	324.0	324.0	325.0	323.0	323.0
13	323.0	324.0	325.0	323.0	323.0
14	323.0	321.0	324.0	325.0	322.0
15	323.0	323.0	324.0	323.0	323.0
16	324.0	321.0	324.0	323.0	321.0
17	324.0	322.0	324.0	324.0	324.0
18	322.0	323.0	324.0	324.0	323.0
19	322.0	323.0	323.0	323.0	324.0
20	321.0	323.0	324.0	323.0	323.0

CASE 3-4

This case is very similar to Case 3-3. The measurements were taken at a companion operation, namely the assembly of the right-hand stationary snap to the adjustable retainer. The dimension and the tolerance are 323.0 ± 3.2 mm, the same as in the previous case. The samples were taken and the measurements were recorded in groups of five, as in Case 3-3, except that the measurements were recorded to the nearest tenth of a millimeter. Using these measurements, construct an average and range chart.

Is the process centered on the specification? Are any assignable causes present? When you use measurements that are recorded to tenths of a millimeter, do you produce a chart that shows more variation than if the decimals were ignored?

Dimension from Right-Hand Stationary Snap to Adjustable Retainer (to the nearest 0.1 mm) (Case 3-4)

Subgroup	Sample #1	Sample #2	Sample #3	Sample #4	Sample #5
1	323.2	322.2	322.3	323.7	322.9
2	324.2	321.6	322.4	325.4	322.6
3	321.2	323.3	324.6	324.5	322.7
4	321.0	325.0	323.3	324.7	322.6
5	321.4	321.6	324.0	323.8	324.4
6	321.3	322.5	325.6	322.6	321.7
7	322.3	322.7	320.1	324.8	320.2
8	322.4	322.6	324.2	325.3	324.4
9	324.1	321.2	325.7	324.7	324.6
10	322.5	324.3	324.9	322.4	320.1
11	323.7	320.7	324.2	324.1	323.6
12	322.6	321.5	324.7	323.3	325.1
13	322.2	322.8	323.0	325.6	322.5
14	324.0	324.6	320.6	322.3	325.2
15	323.5	322.2	325.3	320.8	321.3
16	322.6	325.2	322.8	325.7	321.5
17	322.0	322.6	324.2	320.6	321.6
18	322.9	322.1	322.4	323.9	324.5
19	322.0	322.6	323.2	324.6	321.8
20	324.0	321.7	324.2	322.5	323.2

CASE 3-5

A company purchases metal tubing that is approximately 2 inches in diameter and several feet long. This tubing is fed into an automatic cutoff machine, which cuts the tubing into shorter lengths for use in subsequent operations.

One of these shorter lengths is 615.0 ± 3.2 mm, or approximately 24 inches ± 1/8 of an inch. The cutoff operation is very fast, and the production associate is responsible for keeping material supplied to several machines as well as measuring the output of each machine on a continuing basis. When the measure-ments show that corrective action is required, the associate notifies a setup person, who takes the necessary corrective action. A control chart is used to tell the associate when everything is running satisfactorily or when an assignable cause is present and corrective action is required.

At about 15-minute intervals, the associate takes five consecutive pieces from the machine and measures the length of each. Using the measurements taken, develop a control chart that can be used to detect the presence of assignable causes requiring corrective action.

Lengths of Metal Tubing (mm) (Case 3-5)

Subgroup	Sample #1	Sample #2	Sample #3	Sample #4	Sample #5
1	616.0	612.0	614.0	615.0	615.0
2	616.0	614.0	615.0	618.0	615.0
3	613.0	617.0	614.0	612.0	614.0
4	613.0	616.0	614.0	615.0	614.0
5	616.0	618.0	614.0	615.0	614.0
6	614.0	616.0	614.0	615.0	612.0
7	615.0	612.0	614.0	615.0	612.0
8	614.0	612.0	615.0	614.0	613.0
9	612.0	613.0	615.0	615.0	615.0
10	612.0	615.0	615.0	613.0	615.0
11	616.0	614.0	612.0	616.0	612.0
12	613.0	612.0	616.0	615.0	615.0
13	614.0	615.0	612.0	613.0	613.0
14	615.0	615.0	615.0	615.0	615.0
15	614.0	612.0	615.0	614.0	613.0
16	614.0	613.0	615.0	614.0	612.0
17	615.0	612.0	615.0	615.0	615.0
18	613.0	615.0	614.0	615.0	615.0
19	612.0	614.0	612.0	615.0	613.0
20	612.0	615.0	615.0	616.0	615.0

CASE 3-6

The production associate in Case 3-5 has several machines to tend, and the output of the machines is very fast. In this operation it is possible to use a control chart that is different from the average and range chart and still is almost as effective for control as the average and range chart. This is the median and range chart.

Using only the first three measurements of each sample of five in Case 3-5, create a median and range chart. Does this chart show a pattern of control similar to the pattern in the average and range chart developed in Case 3-5? Are the average of the averages ($\overline{\overline{X}}$) and the average range ($\overline{R}$) the same for both charts? Are the control limits the same?

CASE 3-7

A company manufactures a product called a crank arm. During the manufacturing process a dimension is created that is .800 inch ± .020 inch. A production associate was concerned about the ability of the machine to make all pieces within the specification, so at random times over a two-month period he measured and recorded the .800 dimension as the parts came from the machine. Fortunately, he measured three pieces each time he came to the machine to check on the operation.

After doing this 20 times, the associate decided that he would not have any problems with the .800 dimension and stopped his random checks. Would you agree with his decision? Can the operation be expected always to produce the .800 dimension within tolerance? Is the operation stable? That is, are no assignable causes present and will it be safe to ignore the .800 dimension from now on?

Construct an average and range chart and attempt to answer the previous questions using the measurements that the supervisor collected.

Crank Arm Dimensions (in) (Case 3-7)

Date	Sample #1	Sample #2	Sample #3
5/9	.800	.802	.796
5/10	.803	.800	.793
5/11	.797	.793	.797
5/12	.793	.796	.798
5/14	.792	.799	.801
5/15	.795	.797	.797
5/16	.793	.796	.791
5/24	.796	.794	.790
5/25	.794	.795	.796
5/29	.793	.791	.793
6/1	.805	.802	.803
6/4	.805	.806	.803
6/5	.800	.800	.803
6/13	.801	.796	.800
6/14	.801	.804	.804
6/19	.805	.790	.790
6/22	.805	.807	.803
6/25	.798	.799	.800
6/27	.800	.798	.800
6/28	.804	.803	.803

CASE 3-8

The median and range chart is similar to the average and range chart, but it is quicker to use because it requires less arithmetic and usually makes use of a smaller sample size.

Average and range charts most often use five-piece samples; median and range charts often use smaller samples. Median and range charts are easier to use when the sample size is an uneven number, such as three, because in that case it is easy to determine the median value to plot. The measurements in Case 3-7 are well suited to a median and range chart. There are three measurements in each sample.

Using the data from Case 3-7, construct a median and range chart and compare it to the average and range chart constructed in that problem. How do the average range and the overall average values compare to the median range and the median of the medians measurement values? How do the control limits compare? Do the two control charts tell the same story?

CASE 3-9

A certain rubber material is produced by a batch-type process. A quantity, or batch, of material is made by mixing powdered chemicals with various oils in an established sequence.

The completed batch is the raw material used to make vulcanized rubber products. Each batch is sampled, and various tests are conducted to determine the degree of conformance to specified properties. Although the tests result in variable measurements, the time between batches is so long that an average and range chart is not satisfactory for monitoring such a process.

Using the values listed on the data record sheet, develop individual and range charts. The values recorded are tensile strength values obtained from samples taken from 100 consecutive batches of the same formulation produced on the same mixer.

Does the process require adjustment to meet the specification? Were any assignable causes present during the production of the 100 batches? Should adjustments be made to the process or to the control charts?

Data Record Sheet—Tensile Strength (psi) (Case 3-9)

Rubber Compound 9765-3
Tensile Strength Specification 1840/1900 psi

Sample	Value	Sample	Value	Sample	Value	Sample	Value
1	1862	26	1858	51	1852	76	1858
2	1860	27	1864	52	1863	77	1853
3	1853	28	1853	53	1869	78	1868
4	1861	29	1844	54	1858	79	1862
5	1851	30	1845	55	1855	80	1865
6	1859	31	1859	56	1850	81	1860
7	1860	32	1858	57	1850	82	1860
8	1860	33	1855	58	1845	83	1865
9	1860	34	1855	59	1858	84	1855
10	1866	35	1860	60	1855	85	1860
11	1850	36	1856	61	1862	86	1865
12	1862	37	1850	62	1865	87	1854
13	1855	38	1860	63	1861	88	1860
14	1861	39	1838	64	1861	89	1860
15	1850	40	1864	65	1868	90	1860
16	1860	41	1851	66	1860	91	1862
17	1869	42	1853	67	1858	92	1870
18	1861	43	1862	68	1858	93	1860
19	1860	44	1861	69	1845	94	1860
20	1860	45	1864	70	1860	95	1860
21	1845	46	1852	71	1865	96	1855
22	1851	47	1857	72	1855	97	1863
23	1860	48	1860	73	1862	98	1855
24	1855	49	1863	74	1860	99	1853
25	1860	50	1862	75	1851	100	1854

4 Attribute Control Charts

p-CONTROL CHARTS: REVIEW QUESTIONS

1. When you are doing quality improvement work, you base your chart on one of two kinds of information.

   (a) Which type of information do you need to construct an average and range chart?

   _____

   (b) Where do these data come from?

   _____

   _____

   _____

2. Sometimes you have a different situation in manufacturing. The product has an important characteristic that you want to control, but the characteristic cannot be measured or is difficult to measure.

   (a) What do we call nonmeasurable characteristics?

   (b) What kind of data do they provide?

   _____

   _____

3. To monitor a nonmeasurable characteristic in your product, what three kinds of charts can you use?

   (a) _____

   (b) _____

   (c) _____

What does each type of chart help to monitor or control?

   (d) _____

   _____

   (e) _____

   _____

   (f) _____

   _____

   (g) What does "p" stand for?

   _____

   (h) What does "np" stand for?

   _____

   (i) What does "c" stand for?

   _____

4. (a) What does the word "defective" describe?

   _____

   (b) What is the difference between a defect and a defective piece?

   _____

   _____

   _____

   _____

PERCENT DEFECTIVE p-CHARTS

1. (a) What does the term "percentage" mean?

_____

_____

(b) What do we call the p-chart that uses percentages?

_____

2. (a) Write the formula to find the percentage:

_____

_____

(b) In a sample of 100 units where six pieces are defective, what does p equal?

_____

(c) In a sample of 50 units where four pieces are defective, what does p equal?

_____

3. (a) Do p-charts have control limits like those on the average and range chart?

_____

(b) What does UCL on the chart mean?

_____

(c) What does LCL on the chart mean?

_____

4. (a) What can you say about a process when the point you plot falls between the upper and the lower control limits on the p-chart?

_____

_____

(b) How should you keep running the process?

_____

_____

(c) If a point on the p-chart is very close to one of the control limits, what should the operator do?

_____

_____

_____

_____

_____

_____

5. (a) When points move up and down inside the limits, what are you probably seeing?

_____

(b) What is another name for this?

_____

(c) What causes it?

_____

_____

_____

(d) Generally speaking, can the production associate do anything about it?

_____

6. (a) If a point falls outside the control limits, what does it show about the process?

_____

_____

(b) What kind of cause is present?

_____

(c) What should you do?

_____

_____

7. What are possible sources of assignable causes?

(a) _____

(b) _____

(c) _____

(d) _____

(e) _____

SETTING UP PERCENT DEFECTIVE p-CHARTS

1. What are three reasons why you might want to use p-charts?

(a) _____

(b) _____

(c) _____

2. Where can control charts help to focus attention?

_____

_____

Step 1. Take the sample.

(a) Keep these questions in mind when determining the size of your sample:

(1) How many units should your sample include?

_____

(2) On the average, how many defectives should there be per sample?

_____

(3) What kind of samples should you avoid?

_____

_____

(4) How can you do this?

_____

_____

(5) What should you do if sample sizes are more than 20% greater or 20% less than the average sample size?

_____

_____

_____

(b) What kind of variation should the sample show?

_____

(c) What does this kind of variation tell you about the defects?

_____

_____

(d) To show only this kind of variation, how should you take your samples?

_____

_____

_____

_____

(e) If a process has been running at 10% defective, about how many defectives should a sample of 50 include?

_____

(f) Would a sample of this size meet the guideline?

_____

Step 2. Fill in background information.

Refer to the form for p-charts, Figure 4-9 in the textbook.

Step 3. Collect samples and record the data.

What three pieces of information do you need to record?

(a) _____

_____

(b) _____

_____

(c) _____

_____

Step 4. Calculate p, percent defective.

Write the formula for calculating p in words:

_____

_____

_____

Step 5. Calculate p̄, the average percent defective for the process.

(a) How do you calculate p̄, the average percent defective for the process?

_____

_____

_____

_____

_____

(b) If you look at 50 pieces 20 times, how many parts in all have you inspected?

_____

Step 6. Determine scales for the graph and plot the data.

(a) How should you set the scale for the graph?

_____

_____

_____

(b) For what do you need to leave enough space above the largest p?

_____

(c) What do you do next?

_____

_____

(d) What does the solid line you draw on the chart represent?

_____

_____

Step 7. Calculate control limits.

First, answer the following questions.

(a) What is $\sqrt{}$ the symbol for?

_____

(b) What is the symbol for multiplication?

_____

(c) What is n?

_____

(d) What is p̄?

_____

(e) Write the formula for calculating the upper control limit for p:

_____

When you determine the upper control limit for p, always follow the order of calculations outlined in *SPC Simplified.* Suppose you have a sample size of 50 and the p̄ is 21.3%. Answer the following questions as you calculate the upper control limit for p. In the order of calculations, begin inside the $\sqrt{}$.

(f) What is the first calculation?

_____

(g) What is the result?

_____

(h) After you multiply this result by $\bar{p}$, what do you do next?

_____

_____

(i) What is the result for this calculation?

_____

(j) Once you have done all these calculations, what do you do next?

_____

_____

(k) What answer did you get?

_____

(l) By what number do you multiply the answer?

_____

(m) What is the result for this calculation?

_____

(n) What do you do next?

_____

_____

(o) What is the upper control limit for p in this example?

_____

Your answer should be 38.67%. If you did not produce the correct answer, check to see whether you followed the order of calculations laid out in the textbook.

Work the following problem for more practice. Suppose you have to calculate the upper control limit for p for a process that has been running at 11.6% defective. The sample size is 50.

(p) In this case, what is n?

_____

(q) What is $\bar{p}$?

_____

(r) Determine the upper control limit for p for this example. Follow the directions and the example that are given in *SPC Simplified*. Work in the space provided.

What is the upper control limit for p in this example?

_____

Check your answer with the answer key. If you did not produce the correct answer, check to see whether you followed the order of calculations laid out in the textbook.

(s) Write the formula for calculating the lower control limit for p:

_____

(t) What is the difference between the calculations for the lower control limit and for the upper control limit?

_____

_____

_____

_____

(u) If your answer is a negative number when you figure the lower control limit, where should you set the lower limit?

_____

FRACTION DEFECTIVE p-CHARTS

(a) What is another kind of p-chart?

_____

(b) What does it show?

_____
_____
_____

The fraction defective chart looks just about the same as the percent defective chart, but there are three differences. The first difference is in the formula for determining p.

(c) What does the formula for determining p, the fraction defective, calculate instead of a percentage?

_____

(d) Write the formula for p in words:

_____
_____
_____

(e) When you calculate p, the fraction defective, are you multiplying by 100%?

_____

(f) What kind of number is your answer?

_____

(g) Where is the decimal point?

_____
_____

(h) How do you calculate $\bar{p}$?

_____
_____

The second difference is in how you determine the upper and lower control limits.

(i) Write the formula for the upper control limit for p, the fraction defective:

_____

(j) Write the formula for the lower control limit for p, the fraction defective:

_____

(k) When we calculate control limits for the fraction defective, the numbers inside the square root symbol are different from the numbers we use to calculate the percent defective. In what two ways are these numbers different.

(1) _____
_____
_____

(2) _____
_____
_____

(l) Are the calculations the same as those for the percent defective chart?

_____
_____

The third difference is the scale for the fraction defective p-chart.

(m) How is this scale shown?

_____
_____

Step 8. Interpret the p-chart you have just set up.

Whether you use a percent defective or a fraction defective p-chart, there are three possible situations you could face when you interpret the chart. (For easy reference see the decision chart for working with p's, Figure 4-15 in the textbook.)

1. (a) In the first case, if all the p's lie inside the control limits, what can you say about the process?

_____

_____

   (b) As far as you can tell, what kind of variation is at work?

_____

2. (a) In the second case, if one or two p's are outside the limits, what is the usual practice?

_____

_____

   (b) What recalculations, if any, should you make?

_____

_____

_____

If you have recalculated the control limits, there are two situations to check.

   (c) First, if there are any p's still outside the new control limits, what is true of the process?

_____

_____

   (d) What should you do?

_____

_____

_____

   (e) If there are no p's outside the recalculated control limits, what can you do?

_____

   (f) What should you watch for?

_____

_____

3. (a) In the third case, if you find three or more p's outside the original control limits, what is true of the process?

_____

_____

   (b) What should you do?

_____

_____

_____

_____

Step 9. Fill in the kinds of defects.

Once the p's are in control, you can start collecting information about the different kinds of defects.

   (a) Can the total count of defects be larger than the number of defective pieces?

_____

   (b) Can a defective piece have more than one defect?

_____

_____

HOW TO USE THE P-CHART IN CONTINUED PRODUCTION

1. (a) Under what conditions can you say that the process is in statistical control?

_____

_____

   (b) Only one kind of variation is at work. What kind?

_____

2. (a) Why should you review your p-chart from time to time?

_____

_____

_____

_____

(b) How do you calculate the check?

_____

_____

_____

(c) What does this step allow you to do?

_____

_____

p-CONTROL CHARTS: EXERCISES, SERIES 1, A

1. For the following 20 samples, find the percent defective, p, for each sample. Write each percentage in the space provided. The sample size is 50 pieces.

PRACTICE SET

%

a) 10 _____

b) 3 _____

c) 6 _____

d) 3 _____

e) 8 _____

f) 3 _____

g) 9 _____

h) 8 _____

i) 7 _____

j) 6 _____

k) 11 _____

l) 6 _____

m) 4 _____

n) 3 _____

o) 5 _____

p) 8 _____

q) 7 _____

r) 9 _____

s) 8 _____

t) 10 _____

2. For each of the following sets of inspection data, prepare a separate percent defective p-chart. First calculate the p's (percents defective) and write your answer in the space provided. Then plot the p's on the charts.

SET 1.

Sample size 50 pieces

%

a) 6 _____

b) 3 _____

c) 3 _____

d) 5 _____

e) 6 _____

f) 9 _____

g) 6 _____

h) 7 _____

i) 3 _____

j) 5 _____

k) 7 _____

l) 6 _____

m) 7 _____

n) 5 _____

o) 7 _____

p) 6 _____

q) 7 _____

r) 5 _____

s) 8 _____

t) 2 _____

SET 2.

Sample size 50 pieces

%

a) 11 _____

b) 15 _____

c) 15 _____

d) 7 _____

e) 15 _____

f) 16 _____

g) 21 _____

h) 13 _____

i) 16 _____

j) 13 _____

k) 11 _____

l) 14 _____

m) 18 _____

n) 16 _____

o) 21 _____

p) 13 _____

q) 13 _____

r) 20 _____

s) 13 _____

t) 16 _____

SET 3.

Sample size 50 pieces

%

a) 9 _____

b) 6 _____

c) 3 _____

d) 8 _____

e) 8 _____

f) 11 _____

g) 8 _____

h) 8 _____

i) 6 _____

j) 6 _____

k) 8 _____

l) 6 _____

m) 8 _____

n) 6 _____

o) 8 _____

p) 8 _____

q) 9 _____

r) 6 _____

s) 9 _____

t) 2 _____

SET 4.

Sample size 48 pieces

%

a) 4 _____

b) 4 _____

c) 12 _____

d) 6 _____

e) 5 _____

f) 8 _____

g) 13 _____

h) 14 _____

i) 8 _____

j) 8 _____

k) 8 _____

l) 9 _____

m) 8 _____

n) 7 _____

o) 7 _____

p) 7 _____

q) 10 _____

r) 9 _____

s) 6 _____

t) 12 _____

3. Calculate the average percent defective for the process, $\bar{p}$, for each set in Question 2. Draw a line for each $\bar{p}$ on its own chart and label it.

   Set 1. _____

   Set 2. _____

   Set 3. _____

   Set 4. _____

4. Now you are ready to calculate the control limits for p. Write the formula for determining the upper control limit for p:

   _____

5. In the space provided, determine the upper control limit for p for each set. Use the $\bar{p}$'s, average percents defective, that you calculated in Question 3. Draw in the control limit for p on its own chart. Be sure to label it.

   Set 1.

   Set 2.

Set 3.

(c) When you calculate the lower control limit, what do you do if your answer is a negative number?

_____

_____

7. Determine the lower control limit for p using the $\bar{p}$, average percents defective, that you calculated in Question 3. Use the space provided. Draw in the control limit for p on the p-chart and label it.

Set 1.

Set 4.

Set 2.

6. (a) Write the formula for calculating the lower control limit for p:

_____

(b) What is the difference between the calculations for the lower control limit and for the upper control limit?

_____

_____

_____

_____

Set 3.

Set 4.

8. (a) Do any of the p's, percents defective, fall outside either the upper or the lower control limit for p's?

Set 1. (yes/no) _____

If so, how many? _____

Set 2. (yes/no) _____

If so, how many? _____

Set 3. (yes/no) _____

If so, how many? _____

Set 4. (yes/no) _____

If so, how many? _____

(b) What, if anything, should you do in each case?

Set 1. _____

_____

Set 2. _____

_____

Set 3. _____

_____

Set 4. _____

_____

p-CONTROL CHARTS: EXERCISES, SERIES 1, B

1. For the following 20 samples, find the fraction defective, p, for each sample. Write each answer in the space provided. The sample size is 50 pieces.

PRACTICE SET

a) 16 _____

b) 5 _____

c) 7 _____

d) 6 _____

e) 12 _____

f) 9 _____

g) 13 _____

h) 12 _____

i) 9 _____

j) 10 _____

k) 14 _____

l) 9 _____

m) 5 _____

n) 5 _____

o) 8 _____

p) 12 _____

q) 11 _____

r) 12 _____

s) 14 _____

t) 11 _____

g) 12 _____

h) 7 _____

i) 13 _____

j) 9 _____

k) 8 _____

l) 6 _____

m) 12 _____

n) 12 _____

o) 15 _____

p) 10 _____

q) 9 _____

r) 16 _____

s) 6 _____

t) 12 _____

2. For each of the following sets of inspection data, prepare a separate fraction defective p-chart. In this exercise you are to calculate the p's (fractions defective) and plot them on the charts.

(a) Write the formula for p, fraction defective, in words:

_____

_____

_____

(b) Do you multiply by 100% when you calculate p, the fraction defective?

_____

(c) What kind of number is your answer?

_____

SET 1.

Sample size 50 pieces

a) 7 _____

b) 7 _____

c) 10 _____

d) 3 _____

e) 10 _____

f) 11 _____

SET 2.

Sample size 48 pieces

a) 14 _____

b) 9 _____

c) 9 _____

d) 8 _____

e) 10 _____

f) 8 _____

g) 16 _____

h) 15 _____

i) 14 _____

j) 10 _____

k) 11 _____

l) 14 _____

m) 15 _____

n) 11 _____

o) 13 _____

p) 14 _____

q) 9 _____

r) 18 _____

s) 13 _____

t) 16 _____

3. Calculate the average fraction defective for the process, $\bar{p}$, for each set in Question 2. Draw a line for each $\bar{p}$ on its own chart and label it.

   Set 1. _____

   Set 2. _____

4. Now you are ready to calculate the control limits for p. Write the formula for determining the upper control limit for p, fraction defective:

   _____

5. Using the $\bar{p}$'s, average fractions defective, that you calculated in Question 3, determine the upper control limit for p for each set. Work in the space provided. Draw in each control limit for p on its chart. Be sure to label it.

   Set 1.

Set 2.

6. (a) Write the formula for calculating the lower control limit for p, fraction defective:

   _____

   (b) What is the difference between the calculations for the lower control limit and for the upper control limit?

   _____

   _____

   _____

   _____

   (c) When you calculate the lower control limit, what do you do if your answer is a negative number?

   _____

   _____

7. Using the $\bar{p}$'s, average fractions defective, that you calculated in Question 3, determine the lower control limit for p for each set. Work in the space provided. Draw in each control limit for p on its chart. Be sure to label it.

Set 1.

8. (a) Do any of the p's, fractions defective, fall outside either the upper or the lower control limit for p's?

Set 1. (yes/no) _____

If so, how many? _____

Set 2. (yes/no) _____

If so, how many? _____

(b) What, if anything, should you do in each case?

Set 1. _____

_____

Set 2.

Set 2. _____

_____

---

p-CONTROL CHARTS: EXERCISES, SERIES 2, A

1. For the following 20 samples, find the percent defective, p, for each sample, Write each percentage in the space provided. The sample size is 50 pieces.

PRACTICE SET

%

a) 7 _____

b) 8 _____

c) 4 _____

d) 5 _____

e) 6 _____

f) 9 _____

g) 8 _____

h) 7 _____

i) 7 _____

j) 4 _____

k) 4 _____

l) 4 _____

m) 7 _____

n) 7 _____

o) 5 _____

p) 3 _____

q) 4 _____

r) 6 _____

s) 9 _____

t) 6 _____

2. For each of the following sets of inspection data, prepare a separate percent defective p-chart. First calculate the p's (percents defective) and write your answer in the space provided. Then plot the p's on the charts.

SET 1.

Sample size 50 pieces

%

a) 19 _____

b) 9 _____

c) 9 _____

d) 11 _____

e) 16 _____

f) 14 _____

g) 17 _____

h) 16 _____

i) 13 _____

j) 12 _____

k) 19 _____

l) 12 _____

m) 12 _____

n) 9 _____

o) 13 _____

p) 16 _____

q) 16 _____

r) 15 _____

s) 17 _____

t) 12 _____

SET 2.

Sample size 50 pieces

%

a) 4 _____

b) 6 _____

c) 10 _____

d) 1 _____

e) 8 _____

f) 7 _____

g) 11 _____

h) 4 _____

i) 8 _____

j) 8 _____

k) 5 _____

l) 5 _____

m) 10 _____

n) 8 _____

o) 13 _____

p) 9 _____

q) 8 _____

r) 13 _____

s) 4 _____

t) 9 _____

SET 3.

Sample size 100 pieces

%

a) 14 _____

b) 9 _____

c) 16 _____

d) 4 _____

e) 16 _____

f) 10 _____

g) 20 _____

h) 12 _____

i) 15 _____

j) 14 _____

k) 16 _____

l) 11 _____

m) 14 _____

n) 11 _____

o) 18 _____

p) 14 _____

q) 15 _____

r) 22 _____

s) 12 _____

t) 19 _____

SET 4.

Sample size 48 pieces

%

a) 6 _____

b) 8 _____

c) 15 _____

d) 10 _____

e) 11 _____

f) 18 _____

g) 19 _____

h) 19 _____

i) 17 _____

j) 11 _____

k) 10 _____

l) 13 _____

m) 11 _____

n) 11 _____

o) 10 _____

p) 10 _____

q) 16 _____

r) 15 _____

s) 11 _____

t) 13 _____

3. Calculate the average percent defective for the process, $\overline{p}$, for each set in Question 2. Draw a line for each $\overline{p}$ on its own chart and label it.

Set 1. _____

Set 2. _____

Set 3. _____

Set 4. _____

4. Now you are ready to calculate the control limits for p. Write the formula for determining the upper control limit for p:

_____

5. In the space provided, determine the upper control limit for p for each set. Use the $\overline{p}$'s, average percents defective, that you calculated in Question 3. Draw in the control limit for p on its own chart. Be sure to label it.

Set 1.

Set 2.

Set 3.

Set 4.

6. (a) Write the formula for calculating the lower control limit for p:

_____

(b) What is the difference between the calculations for the lower control limit and for the upper control limit?

_____
_____
_____
_____

(c) When you calculate the lower control limit, what do you do if your answer is a negative number?

_____
_____

7. Determine the lower control limit for p using the p̄'s, average percents defective, that you calculated in Question 3. Use the space provided. Draw in the control limit for p on the p-chart and label it.

Set 1.

Set 4.

Set 2.

8. (a) Do any of the p's, percents defective, fall outside either the upper or the lower control limit for p's?

Set 1. (yes/no) _____

If so, how many? _____

Set 2. (yes/no) _____

If so, how many? _____

Set 3. (yes/no) _____

If so, how many? _____

Set 4. (yes/no) _____

If so, how many? _____

(b) What, if anything, should you do in each case?

Set 1. _____

_____

Set 2. _____

_____

Set 3. _____

_____

Set 4. _____

_____

Set 3.

P-CONTROL CHARTS: EXERCISES, SERIES 2, B

1. For the following 20 samples, find the fraction defective, p, for each sample. Write each answer in the space provided. The sample size is 50 pieces.

PRACTICE SET.

a) 7 _____

b) 9 _____

c) 5 _____

d) 6 _____

e) 7 _____

f) 9 _____

g) 10 _____

h) 8 _____

i) 8 _____

j) 5 _____

k) 6 _____

l) 8 _____

m) 8 _____

n) 8 _____

o) 7 _____

p) 3 _____

q) 5 _____

r) 6 _____

s) 9 _____

t) 6 _____

2. For each of the following sets of inspection data, prepare a separate fraction defective p-chart. In this exercise you are to calcu-

late the p's (fraction defective) and plot them on the charts.

(a) Write the formula for p, fraction defective, in words:

_____

_____

_____

(b) Do you multiply by 100% when you calculate p, the fraction defective?

_____

(c) What kind of number is your answer?

_____

SET 1.

Sample size 50 pieces

a) 10 _____

b) 4 _____

c) 8 _____

d) 5 _____

e) 10 _____

f) 6 _____

g) 11 _____

h) 11 _____

i) 8 _____

j) 7 _____

k) 15 _____

l) 9 _____

m) 10 _____

n) 6 _____

o) 9 _____

p) 10 _____

q) 10 _____

r) 11 _____

s) 10 _____

t) 11 _____

SET 2.

Sample size 48 pieces

a) 3 _____

b) 4 _____

c) 9 _____

d) 5 _____

e) 5 _____

f) 6 _____

g) 10 _____

h) 11 _____

i) 7 _____

j) 6 _____

k) 8 _____

l) 9 _____

m) 5 _____

n) 4 _____

o) 5 _____

p) 6 _____

q) 9 _____

r) 8 _____

s) 6 _____

t) 10 _____

3. Calculate the average fraction defective for the process $\bar{p}$, for each set in Question 2.

Draw a line for each $\bar{p}$ on its own chart and label it.

Set 1. _____

Set 2. _____

4. Now you are ready to calculate the control limits for p. Write the formula for determining the upper control limit for p, fraction defective:

_____

5. Use the $\bar{p}$'s, average fractions defective, that you calculated in Question 3, determine the upper control limit for p for each set. Work in the space provided. Draw in each control limit for p on its own chart. Be sure to label it.

Set 1.

Set 2.

6. (a) Write the formula for calculating the lower control limit for p, fraction defective:

_____

(b) What is the difference between the calculations for the lower control limit and for the upper control limit?

_____

_____

_____

_____

(c) When you calculate the lower control limit, what do you do if your answer is a negative number?

_____

_____

7. Using the $\overline{p}$'s, average fractions defective, that you calculated in Question 3, determine the lower control limit for p for each set. Work in the space provided. Draw in the control limit for p on its chart. Be sure to label it.

Set 1.

Set 2.

8. (a) Do any of the p's, fractions defective, fall outside either the upper or the lower control limit for p's?

Set 1. (yes/no) _____

If so, how many? _____

Set 2. (yes/no) _____

If so, how many? _____

(b) What, if anything, should you do in each case?

Set 1. _____

_____

Set 2. _____

_____

np-CONTROL CHARTS: REVIEW QUESTIONS

1. What is the difference between what the np-chart plots and what the p-chart plots?

   _____

   _____

   _____

2. When you use the np-chart, must the size of every sample be the same?

   _____

SETTING UP THE np-CHARTS

1. Setting up the np-chart is similar to setting up a p-chart. What is the only difference?

   _____

   _____

   _____

Step 1. Take the sample.

(a) How large should the sample be?

   _____

   _____

(b) How do you take the samples?

   _____

   _____

(c) How frequently do you take the samples?

   _____

   _____

Step 2. Fill in the form for the data and the graph.

(a) Can you use the same chart form as you do for the p-chart?

   _____

(b) To identify the chart as an np-chart, what do you write in place of "PERCENT DEFECTIVE"?

   _____

Step 3. Collect samples and record the data.

(a) Is this step identical to the p-chart procedure?

   _____

(b) Will "NO. INSP." always show the same number for each sample?

   _____

(c) What are you plotting in each sample?

   _____

   _____

Step 4. Calculate the $n\bar{p}$.

(a) What is $n\bar{p}$?

   _____

(b) How do you calculate it?

   _____

   _____

   _____

(c) In the np-chart, if you inspect 50 pieces at a time, do those 50 pieces make up a single sample?

_____

(d) Is "total number of samples" the same as "total number of times you looked at pieces"?

_____

Suppose you inspect 20 samples and find a total of 176 defective parts.

(e) How would you calculate the average number defective for the process?

_____

(f) What is the n$\bar{p}$ for this sample?

_____

Step 5. Determine the scale for the graph and plot the np's.

(a) How do you set the scale?

_____
_____
_____
_____

(b) What will the lower control limit often be?

_____

Step 6. Calculate the control limits.

(a) The formula for determining control limits for np is similar to which other formula?

_____
_____

(b) Write the formula for the upper control limit for np:

_____
_____

(c) What is $\sqrt{}$ the symbol for?

_____

(d) What is the symbol for multiplication?

_____

(e) What is n?

_____

(f) What is n$\bar{p}$?

_____
_____

When you determine the upper control limit for np, always follow the order of calculations outlined in Step 6 for np-charts in *SPC Simplified.* Suppose you inspect 20 samples of 50 pieces in each sample. The n$\bar{p}$ is 5.9. Answer the following questions as you calculate the upper control limit for np. In the order of calculations, begin inside the $\sqrt{}$.

(g) What is the first calculation?

_____

(h) What is the result?

_____

(i) After you subtract this result from 1, what do you do next?

_____

(j) What is the result for this calculation?

_____

(k) Once you have done all these calculations, what do you do next?

_____

(l) What answer did you get?

_____

(m) By what number do you multiply the answer?

_____

(n) What is the result for this calculation?

_____

(o) What do you do next?

_____

(p) What is the upper control limit for np in this example?

_____

Your answer should be 12.74. If you did not produce the correct answer, check to see whether you followed the order of calculations laid out in the textbook.

Work the following problem for more practice. Suppose you have to calculate the upper control limit for np for a process that has been running with an average number defective of 7.2. The sample size is 50.

(q) In this case, what is n?

_____

(r) What is $\overline{np}$?

_____

(s) Determine the upper control limit for np for this example. Follow the directions and the example in *SPC Simplified*. Work in the space provided.

What is the upper control limit for np in this example?

_____

Check your answer with the answer key. If you did not produce the correct answer, check

to see whether you followed the order of calculations laid out in the textbook.

(t) Write the formula for the lower control limit for the number defective, np:

_____

(u) When you calculate the lower control limit, what do you do if your answer is a negative number?

_____

_____

Step 7. Interpret the np-chart.

Once you have set up the np-chart, there are three possible situations you could face in interpreting the chart.

1. (a) In the first case, if all the np's lie inside the control limits, what can you say about the process?

_____

_____

   (b) As far as you can tell, what kind of variation is at work?

_____

2. (a) In the second case, if one or two np's are outside the limits, what is the usual practice?

_____

_____

_____

   (b) What recalculations, if any, should you make?

_____

_____

If you have recalculated the control limits, there are two situations to check.

(c) In the first situation, if there are any np's still outside the new control limits, what is true of the process?

_____

_____

(d) What should you do?

_____

_____

_____

(e) If there are no np's outside the recalculated control limits, what can you do?

_____

_____

(f) What should you watch for?

_____

(g) Why?

_____

_____

3. (a) In the third case, if you find three or more np's outside the original control limits, what is definitely true of the process?

_____

_____

(b) What should you do?

_____

_____

_____

_____

np-CONTROL CHARTS: EXERCISES, SERIES 1

1. The following is an inspection report of 20 samples taken from a process. The sample size consists of 50 pieces.

(a) In calculating $n\overline{p}$, do you use the sample size of 50?

_____

(b) Why or why not?

_____

_____

Sample:

a) 8	f) 7	k) 9	p) 5
b) 10	g) 8	l) 8	q) 3
c) 6	h) 4	m) 7	r) 10
d) 6	i) 8	n) 7	s) 5
e) 9	j) 6	o) 10	t) 6

(c) Find the average number defective, $n\overline{p}$:

_____

2. For each of the following sets of inspection data, prepare a separate np, number defective, chart. Plot the np's for each process on their own charts.

SET 1.

Twenty samples of 50 pieces

a) 11	f) 7	k) 10	p) 6
b) 13	g) 9	l) 11	q) 5
c) 6	h) 7	m) 11	r) 11
d) 6	i) 9	n) 8	s) 5
e) 9	j) 9	o) 11	t) 8

SET 2.

Twenty samples of 50 pieces

a) 8	f) 7	k) 11	p) 6
b) 13	g) 8	l) 9	q) 3
c) 8	h) 5	m) 8	r) 11
d) 7	i) 10	n) 8	s) 5
e) 11	j) 6	o) 10	t) 6

SET 3.

Twenty-five samples of 50 pieces

a) 8	f) 11	k) 5	p) 5	u) 8
b) 7	g) 11	l) 5	q) 11	v) 6
c) 15	h) 2	m) 8	r) 7	w) 8
d) 9	i) 5	n) 8	s) 2	x) 15
e) 5	j) 8	o) 5	t) 6	y) 3

SET 4.

Twenty-five samples of 40 pieces

a) 7	f) 6	k) 5	p) 5	u) 5
b) 5	g) 5	l) 7	q) 3	v) 5
c) 4	h) 5	m) 3	r) 7	w) 4
d) 7	i) 4	n) 3	s) 4	x) 7
e) 4	j) 5	o) 2	t) 11	y) 4

3. Calculate the average number defective for the process, $\bar{np}$, for each set in Question 2. Write your answer in the space provided. Then draw a line for each $\bar{np}$ on its own chart and label it.

Set 1. _____

Set 2. _____

Set 3. _____

Set 4. _____

4. Now you are ready to calculate the control limits for np.

(a) Write the formula for determining the upper control limit for np:

_____

(b) Write the formula for the lower control limit for np:

_____

(c) When you calculate the lower control limit, what do you do if your answer is a negative number?

_____

_____

5. Working in the space provided, determine the upper and the lower control limit for np for each set. Use the $\bar{np}$'s, average numbers defective, that you calculated in Question 3. When you find the control limits, draw them in on their own charts and label them.

Set 1: UCL_{np}

Set 1: LCL_{np}

Set 2: UCL$_{np}$

Set 3: LCL$_{np}$

Set 2: LCL$_{np}$

Set 4: UCL$_{np}$

Set 3: UCL$_{np}$

Set 4: LCL$_{np}$

6. (a) Do any of the np's, numbers defective, fall outside either the upper or the lower control limit for np's?

Set 1. (yes/no) _____

If so, how many? _____

Set 2. (yes/no) _____

If so, how many? _____

Set 3. (yes/no) _____

If so, how many? _____

Set 4. (yes/no) _____

If so, how many? _____

(b) What, if anything, should you do in each case:

Set 1. _____

_____

Set 2. _____

_____

Set 3. _____

_____

Set 4. _____

_____

np-CONTROL CHARTS: EXERCISES, SERIES 2

1. The following is an inspection report of 20 samples taken from a process. The sample size consists of 50 pieces.

    (a) In calculating $n\bar{p}$, do you use the sample size of 50?

    _____

    (b) Why or why not?

    _____

    _____

Sample:

a) 8	f) 6	k) 10	p) 10
b) 6	g) 6	l) 10	q) 7
c) 16	h) 8	m) 11	r) 8
d) 7	i) 3	n) 7	s) 7
e) 9	j) 4	o) 4	t) 3

(c) Find the average number defective, $n\bar{p}$:

_____

2. For each of the following sets of inspection data, prepare a separate np, number defective, chart. Plot the np's for each process on their own charts.

SET 1.

Twenty samples of 50 pieces

a) 8	f) 6	k) 12	p) 11
b) 9	g) 6	l) 11	q) 7
c) 18	h) 9	m) 12	r) 9
d) 8	i) 5	n) 8	s) 7
e) 11	j) 4	o) 4	t) 3

SET 2.

Twenty samples of 50 pieces

a) 11	f) 6	k) 11	p) 11
b) 9	g) 7	l) 13	q) 9
c) 16	h) 11	m) 15	r) 9
d) 7	i) 4	n) 8	s) 7
e) 9	j) 7	o) 5	t) 5

SET 3.

Twenty-five samples of 50 pieces

a) 12	f) 12	k) 12	p) 12	u) 11
b) 10	g) 12	l) 10	q) 14	v) 9
c) 17	h) 6	m) 10	r) 11	w) 11
d) 13	i) 9	n) 10	s) 5	x) 9
e) 8	j) 10	o) 8	t) 9	y) 17

SET 4.

Twenty-five samples of 40 pieces

a) 11	f) 9	k) 6	p) 5	u) 9
b) 8	g) 6	l) 6	q) 6	v) 7
c) 8	h) 7	m) 8	r) 9	w) 7
d) 8	i) 9	n) 6	s) 9	x) 8
e) 6	j) 8	o) 4	t) 15	y) 9

3. Calculate the average number defective for the process, $n\bar{p}$, for each set in Question 2. Write your answer in the space provided. Then draw a line for each $n\bar{p}$ on its own chart and label it.

    Set 1. _____

    Set 2. _____

    Set 3. _____

    Set 4. _____

4. Now you are ready to calculate the control limits for np.

    (a) Write the formula for determining the upper control limit for np:

    _____

    (b) Write the formula for the lower control limit for np:

    _____

    (c) When you calculate the lower control limit, what do you do if your answer is a negative number?

    _____

    _____

5. Working in the space provided, determine the upper and the lower control limit for np for each set. Use the $n\bar{p}$'s, average numbers defective, that you calculated in Question 3. When you find the control limits, draw them in on their own charts and label them.

    Set 1: UCL_{np}

    Set 1: LCL_{np}

Set 2: UCL$_{np}$

Set 3: LCL$_{np}$

Set 2: LCL$_{np}$

Set 4: UCL$_{np}$

Set 3: UCL$_{np}$

Set 4: LCL$_{np}$

6. (a) Do any of the np's, numbers defective, fall outside either the upper or the lower control limit for np's?

Set 1. (yes/no) _____

If so, how many? _____

Set 2. (yes/no) _____

If so, how many? _____

Set 3. (yes/no) _____

If so, how many? _____

Set 4. (yes/no) _____

If so, how many? _____

(b) What, if anything, should you do in each case?

Set 1. _____

_____

Set 2. _____

_____

Set 3. _____

_____

Set 4. _____

_____

c-CONTROL CHARTS: REVIEW QUESTIONS

1. (a) What kind of control chart do you use to control a nonmeasurable characteristic?

_____

_____

(b) What does the p-chart allow you to control?

_____

(c) What does the np-chart allow you to control?

_____

(d) What does the c-chart help you control?

_____

(e) When do you use the c-chart?

_____

_____

2. Don't confuse the c-chart with the np-chart.

(a) What does the np-chart plot?

_____

_____

(b) What does the c-chart plot?

_____

_____

3. (a) What kinds of data do p-, np-, and c-charts use?

_____

_____

(b) What do the p-chart and the np-chart count in the sample?

_____

_____

_____

(c) What does the c-chart count?

_____

_____

_____

(d) What is an inspection unit?

_____

_____

_____

(e) How many defects may an inspection unit have?

_____

_____

(f) How do you calculate c?

_____

_____

4. Under the heading "KINDS OF DEFECTS" on the c-chart, there will be several readings. Why are kinds of defects more important for the c-chart than for the p-chart?

_____

_____

_____

_____

_____

INTERPRETING c-CHARTS

1. Charts for averages, ranges, and percents defective have upper and lower control limits.

(a) Do charts for defect counts or c's also have control limits?

_____

(b) If the c lies within the control limits, what can you say about the process?

_____

_____

(c) Can you continue to run the job without any correction or adjustment?

_____

_____

(d) What three things does the c-chart tell you?

(1) _____

_____

(2) _____

_____

(3) _____

_____

(e) If you see a point or points outside the control limits, what must you do?

_____

_____

_____

_____

(f) What are the sources of assignable causes?

_____

_____

_____

_____

SETTING UP c-CHARTS

1. A c-chart of a process helps you do what three things?

(a) _____

_____

(b) _____

_____

(c) _____

_____

Step 1. Take the sample.

(a) The sample should show only one kind of variation. What kind?

_____

(b) How many sources of data must the sample represent?

_____

(c) Therefore how should you take the sample?

_____

_____

_____

(d) Once you have established the inspection unit, must you stay with it?

_____

Step 2. Fill in background information.

Is the layout of the c-chart similar to the layout of the p-chart?

_____

_____

Step 3. Collect and record the data.

Follow the established plan for how often you sample and for the size of the inspection unit.

(a) How do you find the numbers of kinds of defects in each inspection unit?

_____

_____

(b) Where do you record these numbers?

_____

_____

_____

_____

(c) For how many samples (inspection units) do you need data?

_____

_____

Step 4. Calculate the average number of defects for the process.

How do you calculate the average number of defects for the process, $\bar{c}$?

_____

_____

_____

_____

Step 5. Determine the scale for the graph and plot the data.

(a) How do you set the scales on the graph?

_____

_____

_____

(b) Beside plotting the c's, what do you do with the overall mean, $\bar{c}$?

_____

_____

Step 6. Calculate the upper and the lower control limits.

(a) What is $\sqrt{}$ the symbol for?

_____

(b) What is $\bar{c}$?

(c) Write the formula for the upper control limit for c:

_____

When you determine the upper control limit for c, always follow the order of calculations outlined in Step 6 for c-charts in *SPC Simplified*. For practice, suppose you have a situation where the average count of defects for the process is 2.03. Answer the following questions as you calculate the upper control limit for c.

(d) What is the first calculation?

_____

(e) What is the result?

_____

(f) What do you do next?

_____

(g) What is the result?

_____

(h) After you have made these calculations, what do you do next?

_____

(i) What answer did you get?

_____

(j) What is the upper control limit for c in this example?

_____

Check your answer with the answer key. If you did not produce the correct answer, check to see whether you followed the order of calculations outlined in the textbook.

(k) Write the formula for the lower control limit for c:

_____

(l) When you calculate the lower control limit, what do you do if the answer is a negative number?

_____

_____

Step 7. Interpret the c-chart

Once you have set up the c-chart, there are three possible situations. Either (1) all the c's are inside the control limits; (2) one or two c's are outside the limits; or (3) three or more c's are outside the limits. You may wish to refer to the questions for the p-chart.

1. (a) If all the c's lie inside the control limits, what can you say about the process?

_____

_____

(b) As far as you can tell, there is only one kind of variation at work. What kind?

_____

_____

2. (a) If one or two c's are outside the limits, what is the usual practice?

_____

_____

_____

(b) What recalculations, if any, should you make?

_____

_____

After recalculating the control limits, there are two situations to check.

(c) First, if there are any c's still outside the new control limits, what is true of the process?

_____

_____

(d) What should you do?

_____

_____

_____

(e) If there are no c's outside the recalculated control limits, what can you do?

_____

(f) What should you watch for?

_____

_____

3. (a) If you find three or more c's outside
the control limits, what is definitely true
of the process?

_____

_____

(b) What should you do?

_____

_____

_____

_____

c-CONTROL CHARTS: EXERCISES, SERIES 1

1. For the following two sets of 20 inspection
units, find the count of defects, c. Write
each answer in the space provided.

PRACTICE SET 1.

	defect type	count
	v x y z	
a)	1, 1, 1, 0	_____
b)	0, 1, 3, 0	_____
c)	3, 0, 2, 1	_____
d)	1, 0, 4, 0	_____
e)	3, 1, 5, 0	_____
f)	3, 0, 5, 0	_____
g)	1, 0, 9, 0	_____
h)	2, 1, 2, 0	_____

i)	0, 0, 2, 0	_____
j)	0, 0, 4, 0	_____
k)	3, 0, 3, 0	_____
l)	3, 1, 3, 0	_____
m)	2, 0, 3, 0	_____
n)	1, 1, 2, 0	_____
o)	1, 1, 3, 2	_____
p)	1, 1, 5, 0	_____
q)	0, 1, 4, 0	_____
r)	2, 0, 1, 0	_____
s)	0, 0, 6, 0	_____
t)	2, 2, 8, 0	_____

PRACTICE SET 2.

defect type v x y z	count
a) 0, 1, 5, 0	_____
b) 2, 1, 3, 0	_____
c) 3, 1, 0, 0	_____
d) 1, 0, 4, 1	_____
e) 3, 0, 3, 0	_____
f) 2, 0, 1, 0	_____
g) 2, 1, 5, 1	_____
h) 3, 2, 5, 0	_____
i) 1, 1, 5, 0	_____
j) 2, 1, 4, 0	_____
k) 1, 0, 2, 0	_____
l) 3, 0, 5, 0	_____
m) 3, 2, 4, 0	_____
n) 2, 1, 2, 0	_____
o) 2, 0, 4, 1	_____
p) 2, 1, 2, 0	_____
q) 2, 0, 3, 1	_____
r) 2, 1, 3, 2	_____
s) 2, 0, 2, 0	_____
t) 1, 2, 2, 1	_____

2. What is the total number of defects for each set of inspection units in Question 1? What is the average number of defects, $\bar{c}$, for each set?

	total number of defects	average number of defects
Set 1.	_____	_____
Set 2.	_____	_____

3. The following data sets represent groups of inspection units. Prepare a c-chart for each set. First count the defects in each inspection unit and write your answer in the place provided. Then plot the c's on their own charts.

SET 1.

defect type v x y z	count
a) 0, 2, 3, 0	_____
b) 2, 0, 0, 1	_____
c) 1, 1, 1, 1	_____
d) 2, 2, 2, 1	_____
e) 2, 2, 2, 1	_____
f) 3, 2, 4, 0	_____
g) 3, 1, 3, 1	_____
h) 2, 2, 1, 2	_____
i) 1, 2, 5, 1	_____
j) 1, 1, 1, 1	_____
k) 4, 1, 3, 2	_____
l) 3, 0, 1, 4	_____
m) 6, 1, 2, 1	_____
n) 3, 1, 4, 1	_____
o) 4, 1, 2, 2	_____
p) 2, 0, 1, 0	_____
q) 3, 2, 1, 1	_____
r) 2, 0, 3, 0	_____
s) 2, 0, 1, 1	_____
t) 1, 0, 3, 0	_____

SET 2.

defect type v x y z	count
a) 0, 4, 2, 0	_____
b) 0, 7, 1, 1	_____

c) 0, 4, 0, 2 _____

d) 3, 0, 2, 2 _____

e) 5, 0, 3, 2 _____

f) 2, 4, 2, 0 _____

g) 0, 7, 2, 2 _____

h) 1, 4, 1, 3 _____

i) 1, 2, 2, 0 _____

j) 1, 1, 3, 0 _____

k) 4, 1, 4, 0 _____

l) 3, 0, 3, 1 _____

m) 6, 1, 5, 0 _____

n) 3, 1, 3, 0 _____

o) 4, 1, 3, 1 _____

p) 2, 0, 2, 1 _____

q) 0, 3, 2, 3 _____

r) 2, 0, 3, 1 _____

s) 0, 7, 0, 2 _____

t) 1, 0, 3, 1 _____

SET 3.

defect type v x y z	count
a) 0, 3, 1, 6	_____
b) 1, 1, 2, 2	_____
c) 1, 0, 1, 0	_____
d) 1, 2, 3, 1	_____
e) 1, 2, 0, 4	_____
f) 0, 4, 0, 6	_____
g) 2, 1, 0, 4	_____
h) 1, 3, 0, 4	_____
i) 1, 5, 1, 2	_____
j) 1, 1, 0, 4	_____

k) 2, 3, 0, 3 _____

l) 4, 1, 0, 3 _____

m) 1, 2, 0, 1 _____

n) 1, 4, 0, 2 _____

o) 2, 2, 0, 3 _____

p) 0, 1, 2, 4 _____

q) 1, 1, 0, 4 _____

r) 0, 3, 1, 3 _____

s) 0, 2, 1, 6 _____

t) 0, 3, 0, 1 _____

SET 4.

defect type v x y z	count
a) 1, 2, 1, 0	_____
b) 2, 0, 4, 0	_____
c) 2, 1, 5, 0	_____
d) 2, 0, 3, 2	_____
e) 2, 1, 2, 0	_____
f) 2, 0, 3, 0	_____
g) 2, 1, 3, 0	_____
h) 3, 2, 3, 0	_____
i) 3, 0, 4, 0	_____
j) 1, 0, 2, 0	_____
k) 2, 1, 2, 0	_____
l) 1, 1, 9, 0	_____
m) 3, 2, 5, 0	_____
n) 2, 1, 5, 0	_____
o) 2, 0, 8, 0	_____
p) 3, 0, 6, 0	_____
q) 1, 0, 4, 0	_____
r) 3, 1, 2, 1	_____
s) 2, 1, 3, 0	_____
t) 0, 1, 1, 0	_____

4. Determine the total number of defects for each set of inspection units in Question 3 and write the answer in the space provided. Then calculate the average number of defects for the process, $\bar{c}$. Write that answer in the space provided. On each chart, draw in a line for $\bar{c}$ and label it.

	total number of defects	average number of defects, $\bar{c}$
Set 1.	_____	_____
Set 2.	_____	_____
Set 3.	_____	_____
Set 4.	_____	_____

5. Now you are ready to calculate the control limits for c.

   (a) Write the formula for determining the upper control limit for c:

   _____

   (b) Write the formula for determining the lower control limit for c:

   _____

   (c) When you calculate the lower control limit for c, what do you do if the answer is a negative number?

   _____

   _____

6. In the space provided, determine the upper and the lower control limits for c for each set. Use the $\bar{c}$'s, average numbers of defects for the process, that you calculated in Question 4. On each chart, draw in the control limits for c. Be sure to label them.

Set 1: UCL_c

Set 1: LCL_c

Set 2: UCL_c

Set 2: LCL_c

Set 3: UCL_c

Set 3: LCL$_c$

Set 1. (yes/no) _____

If so, how many? _____

Set 2. (yes/no) _____

If so, how many? _____

Set 3. (yes/no) _____

If so, how many? _____

Set 4: UCL$_c$

Set 4. (yes/no) _____

If so, how many? _____

(b) What, if anything, should you do in each case?

Set 1. _____

_____

Set 4: LCL$_c$

Set 2. _____

_____

Set 3. _____

_____

Set 4. _____

7. (a) Do any of the c's, count of defects, fall outside either the upper or the lower control limit for c's?

_____

---

c-CONTROL CHARTS: EXERCISES, SERIES 2

1. For the following two sets of 20 inspection units, find the count of defects, c. Write each answer in the space provided.

PRACTICE SET 1.

defect type				count
v	x	y	z	
a) 5,	0,	0,	0	_____
b) 3,	0,	0,	4	_____

c) 3, 2, 2, 3 _____

d) 4, 1, 1, 0 _____

e) 8, 0, 3, 5 _____

f) 7, 0, 0, 3 _____

g) 2, 0, 1, 4 _____

h) 7, 0, 0, 1 _____

i) 3, 0, 2, 3 _____

j) 2, 0, 1, 1 _____

k) 3, 0, 1, 4 _____

l) 2, 0, 1, 0 _____

m) 6, 1, 1, 2 _____

n) 3, 1, 2, 3 _____

o) 4, 0, 1, 2 _____

p) 1, 0, 0, 5 _____

q) 5, 0, 2, 1 _____

r) 5, 0, 0, 5 _____

s) 6, 0, 0, 2 _____

t) 4, 0, 0, 6 _____

PRACTICE SET 2.

defect type v x y z	count
a) 3, 4, 5, 0	_____
b) 0, 0, 3, 0	_____
c) 1, 1, 3, 2	_____
d) 1, 2, 4, 1	_____
e) 3, 1, 8, 0	_____
f) 1, 2, 7, 0	_____
g) 3, 2, 2, 0	_____
h) 2, 2, 7, 0	_____
i) 0, 2, 3, 0	_____
j) 3, 4, 2, 0	_____
k) 4, 1, 3, 0	_____
l) 1, 4, 2, 0	_____
m) 0, 4, 6, 1	_____
n) 1, 2, 3, 1	_____
o) 1, 2, 4, 0	_____
p) 0, 3, 1, 0	_____
q) 0, 4, 5, 0	_____
r) 3, 0, 5, 0	_____

s) 1, 2, 6, 0 _____

t) 2, 6, 4, 0 _____

2. What is the total number of defects for each set of inspection units in Question 1? What is the average number of defects, $\bar{c}$, for each set?

	total number of defects	average number of defects
Set 1.	_____	_____
Set 2.	_____	_____

3. The following data sets represent groups of inspection units. Prepare a c-chart for each set. First count the defects in each inspection unit and write your answer in the place provided. Then plot the c's on their own charts.

SET 1.

defect type v x y z	count
a) 3, 0, 3, 4	_____
b) 5, 0, 1, 1	_____
c) 6, 0, 3, 1	_____
d) 2, 1, 3, 2	_____
e) 7, 0, 0, 2	_____
f) 4, 0, 4, 1	_____
g) 6, 0, 0, 4	_____
h) 3, 0, 1, 2	_____
i) 3, 0, 0, 4	_____
j) 7, 1, 1, 2	_____
k) 2, 0, 0, 0	_____
l) 5, 0, 1, 2	_____
m) 2, 0, 1, 2	_____

n) 7, 0, 2, 2 _____

o) 4, 0, 3, 4 _____

p) 2, 0, 1, 4 _____

q) 3, 0, 1, 2 _____

r) 1, 1, 0, 3 _____

s) 2, 0, 2, 0 _____

t) 3, 0, 2, 6 _____

SET 2.

defect type				count
v	x	y	z	
a) 3,	0,	0,	0	_____
b) 2,	0,	0,	4	_____
c) 5,	0,	2,	3	_____
d) 5,	0,	1,	0	_____
e) 6,	0,	3,	5	_____
f) 2,	0,	0,	3	_____
g) 2,	1,	1,	4	_____
h) 7,	0,	0,	1	_____
i) 7,	0,	2,	3	_____
j) 4,	0,	1,	1	_____
k) 4,	0,	1,	4	_____
l) 2,	0,	1,	0	_____
m) 6,	0,	1,	2	_____
n) 3,	0,	2,	3	_____
o) 3,	0,	1,	2	_____
p) 1,	1,	0,	5	_____
q) 3,	0,	2,	1	_____
r) 2,	0,	0,	5	_____
s) 7,	1,	0,	2	_____
t) 3,	0,	0,	6	_____

SET 3.

defect type				count
v	x	y	z	
a) 3,	4,	4,	0	_____
b) 0,	0,	0,	4	_____
c) 1,	1,	2,	3	_____
d) 1,	2,	1,	0	_____
e) 3,	1,	3,	5	_____
f) 1,	2,	0,	3	_____
g) 3,	2,	1,	4	_____
h) 2,	2,	0,	1	_____
i) 0,	2,	2,	3	_____
j) 3,	4,	1,	1	_____
k) 4,	1,	1,	4	_____
l) 1,	4,	1,	0	_____
m) 0,	4,	1,	2	_____
n) 1,	2,	2,	3	_____
o) 2,	6,	2,	6	_____
p) 0,	3,	0,	5	_____
q) 0,	4,	2,	1	_____
r) 3,	0,	0,	5	_____
s) 1,	2,	0,	2	_____
t) 1,	2,	1,	2	_____

SET 4.

defect type				count
v	x	y	z	
a) 3,	0,	5,	0	_____
b) 2,	3,	0,	0	_____
c) 5,	0,	3,	2	_____
d) 5,	0,	4,	1	_____
e) 6,	0,	8,	0	_____

f) 0, 2, 7, 0 _____

g) 2, 1, 2, 0 _____

h) 7, 0, 7, 0 _____

i) 7, 0, 3, 0 _____

j) 0, 4, 0, 2 _____

k) 0, 3, 0, 4 _____

l) 0, 2, 2, 0 _____

m) 1, 6, 0, 6 _____

n) 3, 1, 3, 0 _____

o) 3, 0, 4, 0 _____

p) 0, 1, 1, 1 _____

q) 0, 5, 3, 0 _____

r) 2, 5, 0, 0 _____

s) 0, 6, 1, 7 _____

t) 3, 0, 0, 4 _____

4. Determine the total number of defects for each set of inspection units in Question 3 and write the answer in the space provided. Then calculate the average number of defects for the process, $\bar{c}$. Write that answer in the space provided. On each chart, draw in a line for $\bar{c}$ and label it.

	total number of defects	average number of defects, $\bar{c}$
Set 1.	_____	_____
Set 2.	_____	_____
Set 3.	_____	_____
Set 4.	_____	_____

5. Now you are ready to calculate the control limits for c.

(a) Write the formula for determining the upper control limit for c:

_____

(b) Write the formula for determining the lower control limit for c:

_____

(c) When you calculate the lower control limit, what do you do if the answer is a negative number?

_____

_____

6. In the space provided, determine the upper and the lower control limits for c for each set. Use the $\bar{c}$'s, average numbers of defects for the process, that you calculated in Question 4. On each chart, draw in the control limits for c. Be sure to label them.

Set 1: UCL_c

Set 1: LCL_c

Set 2: UCL_c

Set 2: LCL$_c$

Set 3: UCL$_c$

Set 3: LCL$_c$

Set 4: UCL$_c$

Set 4: LCL$_c$

7. (a) Do any of the c's, count of defects, fall outside either the upper or the lower control limit for c's?

Set 1. (yes/no) _____

If so, how many? _____

Set 2. (yes/no) _____

If so, how many? _____

Set 3. (yes/no) _____

If so, how many? _____

Set 4. (yes/no) _____

If so, how many? _____

(b) What, if anything, should you do in each case?

Set 1. _____

_____

Set 2. _____

_____

Set 3. _____

Set 4. _____

_____

ATTRIBUTE CONTROL CHARTS: CASE STUDIES

The following case studies are taken from actual use in manufacturing organizations.

CASE 4-1

From a box containing 1000 beads, samples were drawn in such a manner as to assure that they were random. Each bead in the box had the same chance of being included in a sample as every other bead. The purpose was to produce data that would simulate the output of stable process. In other words, no assignable causes would be present.

Most of the beads in the box were of a natural color, but some beads were one of five other colors: red, white, brown, blue, and yellow. Samples of 100 beads were drawn. As each sample was drawn, the number of beads of each color was counted and recorded.

Using the data in the table "Bead Samples," prepare a percent defective chart (p-chart) in which any colored bead is considered to be a defective piece.

Construct p-charts for the individual colored beads and compare them with the p-chart you constructed based on all the colors combined.

Bead Samples (Case 4-1)

Sample No.	Red	White	Brown	Blue	Yellow
1	14	10	5	1	0
2	16	7	5	0	1
3	13	10	2	2	0
4	12	6	5	1	0
5	12	10	9	5	0
6	11	6	4	0	2
7	17	6	3	0	0
8	20	12	1	1	0
9	11	6	5	1	1
10	9	10	7	0	0
11	6	7	7	2	0
12	8	6	8	3	0
13	21	6	3	3	0
14	17	7	3	3	0

(table continues on next page)

Bead Samples (Case 4-1)*(continued)*

Sample No.	Red	White	Brown	Blue	Yellow
15	15	11	2	3	0
16	10	10	4	2	0
17	9	9	3	3	0
18	17	5	2	3	1
19	12	11	2	1	0
20	14	7	5	4	0

CASE 4-2

A company that makes an assembled product has been receiving complaints from a customer. The products, when received, are reported to have scratches on the outer surface. The customer considers these scratches detrimental. The manufacturer has been aware of the existence of the scratches, but has not considered them to be cause for rejection. Before the customer's complaints can be answered, the manufacturer must obtain further information.

The assemblies are packed for shipment in containers holding 80 assemblies each. An inspect/pack operation is the final step of the process: a production associate makes a final check of the assemblies and places them in the container. This associate has started to keep a record of the number of assemblies with scratches. Four times each day for five days, he has recorded the number of scratches found on the 80 assemblies packed in each container. Construct a number defective control chart using the results of his inspections, and answer these questions: How many of

Assemblies with Surface Scratches (Case 4-2)

Container No.	Number of Assemblies with Scratches	Container No.	Number of Assemblies with Scratches
1	8	11	17
2	6	12	14
3	9	13	9
4	9	14	7
5	7	15	6
6	5	16	5
7	8	17	4
8	10	18	3
9	8	19	5
10	11	20	7

the assemblies contain scratches? Are the scratches part of the normal system or are they the result of unusual occurrences in the process?

CASE 4-3

A manufacturer receives a tubing assembly from a customer. After a coating of epoxy is sprayed on, it is conveyed through a bake oven. The tubing assembly is inspected, packed, and shipped back to the customer.

The inspection operation is performed visually. The inspector looks for five different types of defects in the coating: thin coating, poor adhesion on tubes, poor adhesion on bosses, blisters, and dirt. The inspection results for 20 assemblies are recorded in the table.

What type of statistical process control chart can be used most effectively to monitor the quality of the coating at this inspection operation? Is the process stable? Can the associates on the production floor do a better job?

Inspection Results for Tubing Assemblies (Case 4-3)

Sample No.	Thin Coating	Adhesion on Tubes	Adhesion on Bosses	Blisters	Dirt
1	0	0	2	3	0
2	0	2	0	0	0
3	0	0	1	0	0
4	0	0	1	0	5
5	0	0	2	0	0
6	2	0	0	1	0
7	0	0	0	3	0
8	1	0	0	0	0
9	1	0	0	1	0
10	0	0	0	0	0
11	1	0	2	1	0
12	0	0	2	0	0
13	1	0	0	2	0
14	1	0	0	1	0
15	0	0	0	1	0
16	0	0	0	0	0
17	1	0	0	3	0
18	2	0	1	0	0
19	2	0	1	1	0
20	1	0	1	1	0

CASE 4-4

A manufacturer of an assembled unit tests each unit before it is packed and sent to the warehouse. The test data show that five defects appear to cause most of the rejections and repairs. For purposes of this problem, the defects have been coded and identified as Defects 1, 2, 3, 4, and 5.

The results from the tests of 20 units are shown. Using this data, develop control charts that can be used to monitor the quality performance of the manufacturing process. They must be available for the plant manager to review and act upon. The production floor associates must be able to use them to detect the need for corrective aciton.

Test Results Showing Five Types of Defects (Case 4-4)

Sample No.	Defect 1	Defect 2	Defect 3	Defect 4	Defect 5
1	7	8	2	6	1
2	12	4	1	1	0
3	13	6	1	0	0
4	13	6	6	3	2
5	13	5	3	0	0
6	7	5	5	3	1
7	11	7	6	1	0
8	12	5	2	0	0
9	13	10	3	3	1
10	12	7	0	1	0
11	7	12	7	0	0
12	12	6	3	2	2
13	14	3	0	2	0
14	10	10	5	2	2
15	10	9	2	2	1
16	22	3	3	1	0
17	12	3	6	2	1
18	14	6	4	2	1
19	18	11	0	1	1
20	12	13	5	5	1

CASE 4-5

A company applies a coating of Teflon to a portion of the outer surface of a small tubular assembly as the last operation before inspecting and packing it for shipment. The inspection records show that in recent months, tubular assemblies have been rejected and repaired because of six different defects: thin coating, thick coating, chipped coating, overspray, poor adhesion, and dirt.

A management team decided to monitor the rejection rate of this part, using a control chart. Over a period of about one month the finished products were sampled and inspected, and the results were recorded. The sample size was 100 parts, and the parts were inspected by the person who inspected them regularly.

Using the inspection results, develop a control chart that can be used to monitor future production of these parts.

Defects in Teflon Coating (Case 4-5)

Sample No.	Thin Coat	Thick Coat	Chipped Coat	Overspray	Poor Adhesion	Dirt
1	1	0	1	1	1	0
2	4	0	0	0	0	0
3	4	0	1	0	0	0
4	0	5	0	0	0	0
5	3	0	0	0	0	3
6	7	0	0	0	0	0
7	4	0	0	0	0	0
8	0	0	1	0	0	2
9	0	0	1	0	0	0
10	2	0	0	0	0	0
11	2	0	0	0	0	0
12	0	0	0	0	0	0
13	0	0	0	0	0	0
14	3	0	0	0	0	0
15	3	0	0	0	0	0
16	6	0	0	0	0	0
17	4	0	3	0	0	0
18	2	0	0	0	0	0
19	5	0	0	0	0	0
20	6	0	0	0	0	0
21	5	0	0	0	0	0

(table continues on next page)

Defects in Teflon Coating (Case 4-5) *(continued)*

Sample No.	Thin Coat	Thick Coat	Chipped Coat	Overspray	Poor Adhesion	Dirt
22	2	0	0	0	0	0
23	2	0	0	0	0	0
24	6	0	3	0	0	0
25	7	0	0	0	0	0
26	20	0	0	0	0	3
27	0	6	0	0	0	0
28	3	0	0	0	0	0
29	0	0	0	0	0	0
30	1	0	0	0	0	0
31	4	0	4	0	0	0
32	0	0	0	0	0	0

CASE 4-6

Rubber parts are molded and trimmed before being fed onto a moving conveyor belt. The parts are inspected for visual defects as they move down the belt and into the shipping carton. Parts with defects are removed as they pass the inspectors. Approximately twice each shift, an inspector collects 100 consecu-tive parts from the belt, inspects them, and records the results on a control chart.

Construct a p-chart using the data from this inspect/pack operation. Each sample is 100 parts.

Is the manufacturing process in control?

Visual Defects in Rubber Parts (Case 4-6)

Sample No.	Non-Fills	Bad Trim	Foreign Material	Blisters
1	7	0	0	0
2	2	5	0	0
3	2	4	0	0
4	4	3	0	0
5	0	4	0	0
6	0	0	0	0
7	2	0	0	0
8	0	0	0	0

(table continues on next page)

Visual Defects in Rubber Parts (Case 4-6) *(cont'd)*

Sample No.	Non-Fills	Bad Trim	Foreign Material	Blisters
9	0	7	0	2
10	1	8	0	3
11	0	11	0	0
12	0	12	0	0
13	0	3	0	0
14	0	10	0	0
15	0	0	0	0
16	0	2	5	5
17	0	0	2	3
18	0	1	0	0
19	0	0	0	6
20	0	3	3	7
21	0	0	7	0
22	0	14	0	2
23	0	4	0	5
24	0	0	0	4
25	0	4	0	5
26	0	3	0	3
27	2	0	3	0
28	0	4	0	3
29	0	0	0	5
30	0	3	1	0
31	0	1	1	1
32	0	0	1	1

CASE 4-7

A team of employees is working to improve the quality of Part 8719, which was discussed in Case 4-6. The inspection results were plotted on a p-chart. Using the data from Case 4-6, determine which type of defect you would recommend that the team attack first to improve the quality of the part.

Can any of the defect types be improved by action on the production floor? Should the team concentrate on developing changes for improvement that they will recommend to management for action? If so, which defect types need this kind of action?

5 Machine and Process Capability

REVIEW QUESTIONS

1. (a) Under what conditions may we say that a process or an operation is stable?

   _____

   _____

   (b) What do most of the "tools of quality" measure?

   _____

2. (a) Once we have made the process or operation stable, what is the next question we should ask?

   _____

   _____

   _____

   _____

   _____

   (b) If a machine or a process is not capable of producing parts within specifications, who has the responsibility to solve this problem?

   _____

3. (a) What are the two ways to measure the capability of a machine or a process?

   (1) _____

   (2) _____

   (b) How can you get the best estimate of capability?

   _____

4. (a) What is the difference between machine capability and process capability?

   _____

   _____

   _____

   _____

   _____

   (b) When would you want to make a machine capability study?

   _____

   _____

   _____

   (c) When would you want to make a process capability study?

   _____

   _____

   _____

MACHINE CAPABILITY

1. What are the sources of variation in a process?

   _____

   _____

   _____

2. (a) Where should you perform a machine capability study?

_____

_____

(b) What kind of variation should the measurements show?

_____

_____

(c) How can you minimize unwanted variation?

_____

_____

_____

AVERAGE AND RANGE CHART METHOD

1. (a) With how many dimension(s) of a product is a machine capability study concerned?

_____

(b) What is one purpose of the machine capability study?

_____

_____

(c) Why is this important?

_____

_____

2. What is another purpose of the machine capability study?

_____

_____

3. (a) To develop the average and range chart, what measurements to you use?

_____

_____

(b) Why?

_____

_____

_____

(c) On what do you base the estimate of capability?

_____

_____

4. (a) What is the best way to determine stability?

_____

(b) Why?

_____

_____

_____

5. (a) What tool can you use to estimate the average of a dimension and its spread?

_____

(b) How can you use a histogram to estimate machine capability?

_____

(c) When can you use it?

_____

_____

(d) What is a more precise tool than the histogram?

_____

6. (a) When can you say that a process is stable?

_____

_____

(b) What condition is necessary for you to proceed with a capability study?

_____

_____

7. Why might you want to "code" measurements?

_____

_____

8. (a) When using the control chart method for machine capability, over what period of time should you take and record the measurements?

_____

_____

   (b) Why is it important to do it in this way?

_____

_____

9. (a) After taking and recording the measurements, what calculations do you make?

_____

_____

   (b) Which should you develop first, the average chart or the range chart?

_____

   (c) Why? (See Module 3.)

_____

_____

_____

_____

10. (a) Why should you try to eliminate all assignable causes before performing a capability study?

_____

_____

_____

_____

_____

LIMITS FOR INDIVIDUALS

1. After you have set up the average and range chart and have determined that no points lie outside the control limits, what is the next step?

_____

_____

2. Refer to Figure 5-2 in the textbook and the text following. Answer these questions:

   (a) What is $\bar{\bar{X}}$?

_____

   (b) What is $\bar{R}$?

_____

   (c) What is "sigma"?

_____

   (d) Write the symbol for "sigma":

_____

   (e) What is d_2?

_____

_____

   (f) What value of the d_2 factor should you use if the sample size is five?

_____

   (g) What is the value of the factor if the sample size is four?

_____

   (h) Write the formula for finding 3 sigma:

_____

   (i) Find 3 sigma in the following examples. The sample size is five.

   (1) $\bar{R}$ is 10.2

_____

   (2) $\bar{R}$ is 9.55

_____

(3) $\bar{R}$ is .0772

_____

(4) $\bar{R}$ is 10.6

_____

(j) What do we mean by UL_x?

_____

_____

_____

(k) Write the formula for UL_x:

_____

(l) Determine the UL_x in the following examples, using the values of $\bar{R}$ given in Question (i) (1) through (4).

(1) $\bar{\bar{X}}$ is 35.12

_____

(2) $\bar{\bar{X}}$ is 75.38

_____

(3) $\bar{\bar{X}}$ is .92464

_____

(4) $\bar{\bar{X}}$ is 1.13

_____

(m) What do we mean by LL_x?

_____

_____

_____

(n) Write the formula for LL_x:

_____

(o) Determine the LL_x. The $\bar{\bar{X}}$'s and $\bar{R}$'s are the same as in Question (l).

(1) _____

(2) _____

(3) _____

(4) _____

(p) What does US mean?

_____

(q) What does LS mean?

_____

(r) Write the formula for determining tolerance here:

_____

(s) What is the tolerance for a machine when the US is 18.43 and the LS is 4.02?

_____

(t) Tolerance describes the designer's wishes and the customer's requirements. What is another name for tolerance?

_____

(u) Process spread tells how the process is actually doing. Write the formula for process spread:

_____

(v) What is the process spread of a machine if the $\bar{R}$ is 7.013? The sample size is 5.

_____

_____

3. (a) Under what circumstances can you say that the operation or machine is capable of meeting the specification?

_____

_____

(b) This is true only under what condition?

_____

_____

4. Refer to Figure 5-3 in the textbook.

   (a) What kind of condition is this?

   _____

   _____

   (b) How do you know?

   _____

   _____

   (c) What will happen in such an operation if anything changes?

   _____

   _____

   _____

5. Refer to Figure 5-4 in the textbook.

   (a) What is the situation here?

   _____

   _____

   (b) Are parts being produced outside the specification?

   _____

6. Refer to Figure 5-5 in the textbook.

   (a) What is the situation here?

   _____

   (b) Are parts being produced outside the specification?

   _____

   (c) What should you do to correct this situation?

   _____

   _____

7. Refer to Figure 5-6 in the textbook.

   (a) Where is this process centered?

   _____

   (b) What is the relation of the process spread to the specifications?

   _____

   _____

   _____

   (c) Is this a good or a bad situation?

   _____

   _____

   _____

8. How could other sources of variation eventually affect the output of the machine?

   _____

   _____

   _____

   _____

9. What is the expected and required situation when you perform a machine capability study?

   _____

   _____

   _____

   _____

   _____

   _____

10. What is an advantage of using the average and range chart to predict process or machine capability?

   _____

   _____

THE PROBABILITY PLOT

1. (a) What is a simple way to test the estimates you made from control chart measurements?

   _____
   _____

   (b) How do you use the measurements from the average and range chart?

   _____
   _____

2. When making the probability plot, you use special graph paper called normal probability paper. This paper will show the following:

   (a) _____

   (b) _____

   (c) _____

   (d) _____

Step 1. Gather information and fill in the heading.

(a) How many measurements do you need?

   _____
   _____

(b) If you estimate normality with fewer measurements, what risk do you take?

   _____
   _____

Step 2. Tally the measurements.

(a) What kind of tally do you use for the normal probability plot?

   _____
   _____

(b) About how many divisions should you use?

   _____
   _____

(c) What kind of values do you use from the average and range chart?

   _____
   _____

(d) Where do you record the number of tallies in each division?

   _____
   _____

Step 3. Find the estimated accumulated frequencies.

(a) What is the first thing you do before placing the plot points on the normal probability chart?

   _____
   _____
   _____
   _____

(b) What does EAF mean?

   _____

(c) Why do you convert the measurements?

   _____
   _____
   _____
   _____

(d) How do you calculate the first EAF?

   _____
   _____
   _____

(e) How do you calculate the second EAF?

   _____
   _____
   _____
   _____
   _____

(f) What is the procedure for finding the remaining EAFs?

_____

_____

(g) What is an easy way to check your addition?

_____

_____

_____

(h) Using the frequencies in the probability worksheet at the bottom of this page, find the EAFs. The sample size is 100.

(i) What is the total of the frequencies in this example?

_____

(j) Is the highest EAF exactly twice the sample size in this example?

_____

_____

Step 4. Place the plot points.

(a) How do you obtain the plot points you put on the graph?

_____

_____

(b) What is the formula for determining the plot points?

_____

(c) Using the EAFs from Step 3, determine the plot points. Write your answer in the appropriate space on the probability worksheet in Step 3. For this example, N = 100.

(d) How is the left-hand edge of the graph marked?

_____

(e) Which numbers do you plot on the graph, EAFs or plot points (%)?

_____

(f) In the example you have been working, what would this first number be?

_____

(g) How do you place the point?

_____

_____

_____

_____

_____

_____

_____

FREQUENCY			2	10	29	23	6	11	15	2	2					
Follow arrows and perform additions as shown (N ≥ 25)																
EST. ACCUM. FREQ. (EAF)																
PLOT POINTS (%) (EAF/2N) X 100																

Step 5. Draw the line of best fit.

(a) If the points you plot fall in a straight line on the graph paper, what do you know about the measurements from your study?

_____

_____

_____

(b) What does a trend away from a straight line tell you?

_____

_____

(c) How can you judge the accuracy of the estimate of the process spread?

_____

_____

_____

_____

_____

Step 6. Estimate the process spread.

(a) What value do you get when you extend the line of best fit to the bottom edge of the graph?

_____

_____

(b) What value do you get when you extend the line of best fit to the top edge of the graph?

_____

_____

(c) What does "6 sigma" represent?

_____

_____

(d) What is machine capability?

_____

_____

_____

_____

ESTIMATING THE PROPORTION OF PARTS OUT OF SPECIFICATION

1. (a) Suppose the line of best fit crosses a specification limit line before it crosses the top edge of the graph. What does this allow you to do?

_____

_____

(b) Suppose the line of best fit crosses a specification limit line before it crosses the bottom edge of the graph. What does this allow you to do?

_____

_____

(c) How do you use these estimates even if the line of best fit is not a straight line?

_____

_____

_____

2. Refer to Figure 5-12 in the textbook. What four things tell you that this process is capable of meeting the specification?

(a) _____

_____

(b) _____

_____

(c) _____

_____

(d) _____

_____

3. Refer to Figure 5-13 in the textbook.

   (a) What is the relationship between the line of best fit and the upper specification limit?

   _____

   _____

   (b) What does this lead you to expect about parts produced by this operation?

   _____

   (c) Would this operation be considered capable?

   _____

   (d) Why or why not?

   _____

   _____

   _____

4. Even if a capability study does not give a clear decision about the capability of the machine under study, what can it tell you?

   _____

   _____

   _____

PROCESS CAPABILITY

1. What is the basic difference between machine or operation capability and process capability?

   _____

   _____

   _____

   _____

   _____

2. (a) What must the measurements include when you do a process capability study?

   _____

   (b) What are some examples?

   _____

   _____

   _____

   _____

   _____

3. What kind of time period do you need to make a process capability study?

   _____

4. (a) What is the first step you take in making a process capability study?

   _____

   (b) How much time do you need?

   _____

5. What are the next three steps in making the process capability study?

   (a) _____

   _____

   (b) _____

   _____

   (c) _____

   _____

6. (a) Why do you use the average and range chart when making a process capability study?

   _____

   _____

(b) What two things does the range chart tell you?

(1) _____

_____

(2) _____

_____

(c) What does the average chart tell you?

_____

_____

_____

7. (a) Over a long period of time, how should you expect the range to behave?

_____

(b) Over the same period of time, how should you expect the average to behave?

_____

_____

_____

8. Why do you use the individual measurements making up the averages when you estimate process capability?

_____

_____

_____

9. When you make a process capability study, what three things does the probability plot help to estimate?

(a) _____

(b) _____

(c) _____

10. Refer to Figure 5-14 in the textbook.

(a) Is this process stable?

_____

(b) How can you tell?

_____

_____

11. Refer to Figure 5-15 in the textbook.

(a) Is this process capable?

_____

(b) On what is the estimate of capability based?

_____

_____

12. Refer to Figure 5-16 in the textbook. Are the measurements distributed normally?

_____

13. How do you find the estimated process average?

_____

_____

_____

14. (a) When you compare the specification limits to the line of best fit in Figure 5-16, is the total process spread (6σ) greater than or less than the specification spread?

_____

(b) How can you tell?

_____

_____

_____

_____

_____

_____

15. In summary, once the process is stable, what four things must be true before you can say that a process is capable?

    (a) _____

    _____

    (b) _____

    _____

    (c) _____

    _____

    (d) _____

    _____

CAPABILITY INDEX

1. (a) What is the capability index?

    _____

    _____

    (b) How do you find it?

    _____

    _____

    _____

    _____

2. (a) What does C_p mean?

    _____

    (b) What does a C_p of 1.0 or greater mean?

    _____

    _____

    (c) What would be the C_p of a machine if the 6σ equals the tolerance?

    _____

    (d) Write the formula for the C_p index:

    _____

    _____

3. (a) Find the C_p for a process that has a total tolerance of 0.93 degrees and a process spread of 0.77 degrees.

    _____

    _____

    (b) Is this process capable of producing parts with a spread less than the tolerance?

    _____

4. (a) Is it possible for a machine or a process to be capable but still produce some or all parts outside the tolerance?

    _____

    (b) What one thing does the C_p index not tell you?

    _____

5. (a) What is another type of capability index?

    _____

    (b) If this index is a negative number, what does it tell you about the process average?

    _____

    _____

    _____

    (c) What does a number less than 1 tell you about the capability of the machine or the process?

    _____

    (d) Write the formulas for calculating this index:

    (1) _____

    (2) _____

    (e) Which of these two calculations do you use?

    _____

6. (a) What is the process spread?

_____

(b) Where does half of the spread fall?

_____

_____

CAPABILITY RATIO

1. (a) What is the capability ratio (CR)?

_____

_____

(b) Write the formula:

_____

2. What does a CR of more than 100% indicate?

_____

_____

3. What does the CR not tell you?

_____

_____

4. What is the one thing that the CR does tell you?

_____

_____

_____

_____

CAPABILITY STUDIES: EXERCISES, SERIES 1

1. You will make machine or process capability studies for each of the following data sets. Questions 1 through 4 relate to the frequency histogram method for determining machine or process capability. First draw a frequency histogram for each data set. For each histogram, draw in the design specifications that are given with each data set. Then answer Questions 2 through 4 in the space provided in this workbook.

SET 1.

Specifications: Lower = −10, Upper = 65

a) 31, 43, 28, 33, 27

b) 19, 32, 47, 7, 46

c) 36, 35, 26, 35, 41

d) 43, 38, 50, 34, 31

e) 17, 37, 23, 27, 28

f) 12, 34, 45, 47, 30

g) 25, 42, 29, 24, 34

h) 29, 39, 11, 27, 45

i) 26, 37, 14, 39, 16

j) 13, 26, 27, 2, 46

k) 18, 29, 37, 29, 43

l) 36, 14, 35, 29, 31

m) 7, 18, 31, 26, 39

n) 6, 37, 12, 31, 34

o) 34, 48, 32, 42, 32

p) 25, 30, 36, 43, 32

q) 24, 47, 24, 33, 11

r) 18, 46, 17, 31, 44

s) 16, 32, 30, 27, 20

t) 25, 43, 33, 34, 30

SET 2.

You may want to code the date for Set 2.
Specifications:
For coded data: Lower = 5, Upper = 50
For original data: Lower = 0.205, Upper = 0.250

a) .221, .222, .234, .240, .216

b) .235, .228, .224, .246, .235

c) .248, .230, .246, .237, .221

d) .242, .232, .232, .228, .226

e) .236, .229, .238, .223, .239

f) .200, .244, .215, .235, .236

g) .234, .233, .239, .232, .244

h) .236, .239, .246, .227, .220

i) .216, .240, .241, .229, .216

j) .233, .226, .243, .233, .218

k) .232, .225, .231, .236, .242

l) .229, .243, .244, .227, .240

m) .229, .233, .247, .213, .232

n) .235, .237, .217, .215, .229

o) .232, .230, .227, .219, .235

p) .243, .225, .228, .236, .242

q) .232, .229, .208, .243, .232

r) .229, .234, .251, .226, .231

s) .227, .213, .223, .231, .231

t) .232, .244, .210, .233, .223

SET 3.

Specifications: Lower = 0.0, Upper = 4.0

a) 1.4, 1.8, 3.3, 1.8, 2.6

b) 2.1, 3.0, 1.3, 3.3, 0.8

c) 2.8, 4.3, 1.9, 2.7, 3.5

d) 2.3, 2.8, 4.1, 3.0, 1.9

e) 2.2, 3.2, 3.2, 3.8, 2.9

f) 2.7, 4.3, 3.6, 3.2, 3.5

g) 3.6, 4.5, 4.3, 3.7, 4.9

h) 2.2, 3.8, 2.9, 2.4, 2.5

i) 4.0, 2.5, 2.5, 3.8, 4.9

j) 4.0, 3.0, 2.7, 4.4, 3.6

k) 2.6, 1.7, 2.8, 1.9, 1.6

l) 2.9, 2.9, 3.5, 3.3, 2.1

m) 1.4, 1.9, 2.6, 2.4, 3.4

n) 2.7, 1.9, 2.4, 4.6, 3.8

o) 4.7, 2.0, 2.7, 1.3, 3.6

p) 2.2, 3.5, 4.1, 3.7, 1.4

q) 2.8, 3.2, 3.5, 3.8, 3.1

r) 3.4, 1.8, 3.4, 3.4, 2.6

s) 1.9, 4.1, 4.3, 1.2, 2.5

t) 3.2, 1.7, 2.2, 4.2, 3.4

SET 4.

Specifications: Lower = 10, Upper = 250

a) 90, 105, 57, 87, 45

b) 45, 138, 69, 66, 72

c) 54, 93, 78, 141, 60

d) 126, 99, 90, 111, 81

e) 117, 72, 84, 87, 96

f) 92, 54, 81, 78, 60

g) 60, 126, 114, 171, 63

h) 108, 111, 66, 99, 57

i) 132, 120, 102, 99, 132

j) 9, 102, 153, 84, 81

k) 117, 102, 87, 96, 120

l) 78, 72, 30, 105, 123

m) 69, 117, 75, 66, 90

n) 57, 72, 39, 72, 114

o) 117, 96, 72, 90, 105

p) 102, 123, 81, 45, 150

q) 123, 105, 24, 90, 111

r) 114, 108, 78, 114, 78

s) 33, 69, 99, 63, 93

t) 99, 93, 87, 87, 75

2. Estimate the average for each operation.

Set 1. _____

Set 2. _____

Set 3. _____

Set 4. _____

3. Is the operation average centered close to the midpoint between the specifications?

Set 1. _____

Set 2. _____

Set 3. _____

Set 4. _____

4. Do you think each operation is capable of producing parts with a spread less than the tolerance?

Set 1. _____

Set 2. _____

Set 3. _____

Set 4. _____

5. Questions 5 through 11 relate to the average and range chart method for determining machine or process capability. Using the data sets from Question 1, construct average and range charts, as you have already learned to do. Then answer Questions 5 through 11 in the space provided in this workbook.

(a) Which chart should you develop first, the average chart or the range chart?

_____

(b) Why?

_____

_____

6. Tell whether or not each operation is stable.

Set 1. _____

_____

Set 2. _____

_____

Set 3. _____

_____

Set 4. _____

_____

7. Refer to Figure 5-2 in *SPC Simplified* and the text following. Explain what we mean by the following terms:

(a) $\bar{\bar{X}}$

_____

(b) $\bar{R}$

_____

(c) "sigma"

_____

(d) Write the symbol for sigma:

_____

(e) d_2

_____

_____

(f) What value of the d_2 factor should you use if the sample size is 5?

_____

(g) What is the value of the factor if the sample size is 4?

_____

(h) Write the formula for finding 3 sigma:

_____

(i) What does UL_x mean?

_____

_____

_____

_____

(j) Write the formula for UL_x:

_____

(k) What does LL_x mean?

_____

_____

_____

(l) Write the formula for LL_x:

_____

8. Using each average and range chart that you have developed, determine the UL_x and the LL_x, the upper and lower limits for individuals. Work in the space provided.

Set 1.

Set 2.

Set 3.

Set 4.

9. Determine the tolerance for each operation and write that answer in the space provided. First answer the following questions.

(a) What does US mean?

_____

(b) What does LS mean?

_____

(c) Write the formula for determining tolerance:

_____

_____

Now do the calculations. (See data sets for specifications.)

Set 1. _____

Set 2. _____

Set 3. _____

Set 4. _____

10. (a) Write the formula for process spread:

_____

(b) Find the process spread for each operation.

_____

Set 1. _____

_____

Set 2. _____

_____

Set 3. _____

_____

Set 4. _____

_____

11. Compare the tolerance for each operation with the process spread. You may want to refer to Figure 5-4 in the textbook. Will the operation be capable of producing parts with a spread less than the tolerance? Write your answer in the space provided.

	tolerance	process spread	capable?
Set 1.	_____	_____	_____
Set 2.	_____	_____	_____

Set 3. _____   _____   _____
Set 4. _____   _____   _____

Questions 12 through 21 relate to the probability plot method for determining machine and process capability. Question 12 gives you practice in calculating estimated accumulated frequencies and determining plot points. Record your answers on the worksheet portion of the probability chart in Question 12.

12. (a) First find the estimated accumulated frequencies.

(b) Now determine the plot points for these examples. The total number of measurements for each set may not be 100. Remember: do not calculate the plot point for the last EAF.

Part No. & Name	12-1 (Series 1)														Char. Measured				
Operation No. & Desc.														Spec.					
VALUE																			
FREQUENCY				3	0	5	12	14	37	18	10	1							
Follow arrows and perform additions as shown (N ≥ 25)																			
EST. ACCUM. FREQ. (EAF)																			
PLOT POINTS (%) (EAF/2N) X 100																			

Part No. & Name	12-2 (Series 1)												Char. Measured					
Operation No. & Desc.													Spec.					

VALUE																								
FREQUENCY				1	1	3	31	5	25	15	11	8												
Follow arrows and perform additions as shown (N ≥ 25)																								
EST. ACCUM. FREQ. (EAF)																								
PLOT POINTS (%) (EAF/2N) X 100																								

Part No. & Name	12-3 (Series 1)												Char. Measured					
Operation No. & Desc.													Spec.					

VALUE																								
FREQUENCY				2	0	5	17	15	31	20	10	0												
Follow arrows and perform additions as shown (N ≥ 25)																								
EST. ACCUM. FREQ. (EAF)																								
PLOT POINTS (%) (EAF/2N) X 100																								

Part No. & Name	12-4 (Series 1)																		Char. Measured			
Operation No. & Desc.																			Spec.			

VALUE																						
FREQUENCY			5	5	9	16	27	16	7	6	4											
Follow arrows and perform additions as shown (N ≥ 25)																						
EST. ACCUM. FREQ. (EAF)																						
PLOT POINTS (%) (EAF/2N) X 100																						

Go back to the data sets from Question 1. For each set, construct a probability plot. Use the entire sheet of the normal probability plot chart. Answer Questions 13 and 14 and record your answers on the worksheet part of the probability chart. You should use the graph portion of the probability chart for Questions 15 and 16. Then follow the directions for answering Questions 17 through 28.

13. Find the frequencies of the measurements for each set. Be sure that the first frequency you write in on the left is the lowest value. You may copy the tallies from the frequency histogram worksheet onto the worksheet part of the probability chart.

14. Determine the estimated accumulated frequencies for each set.

15. Now determine the plot points. The total number of measurements for each set may not be 100. Remember: do not figure a plot point for the very largest EAF.

Record the plot points on the graph portion of the probability chart.

16. (a) Draw the line of best fit. If the line of best fit is straight or nearly straight, are the measurements used in the studies distributed normally?

   _____

   (b) When you look at your plots, are the data distributed normally?

   Set 1. (yes/no) _____

   Set 2. (yes/no) _____

   Set 3. (yes/no) _____

   Set 4. (yes/no) _____

17. Estimate the process spread for each probability plot.

   (a) First determine the lowest value and the highest value you can expect from the operation.

	lowest	highest
Set 1.	_____	_____
Set 2.	_____	_____
Set 3.	_____	_____
Set 4.	_____	_____

(b) How do you find the process spread?

_____

_____

_____

_____

(c) Find the process spread for each operation.

Set 1. _____

Set 2. _____

Set 3. _____

Set 4. _____

18. Draw in the specifications for each operation. The specifications were given with each data set. Now you will be able to compare the process spread with the tolerance and determine whether or not the operation is capable of producing parts with a spread less than the tolerance. Remember: the tolerance is the difference between the upper specification and the lower specification and is a single number.

	tolerance	process spread	capable?
Set 1.	_____	_____	_____
Set 2.	_____	_____	_____
Set 3.	_____	_____	_____
Set 4.	_____	_____	_____

19. Does the line of best fit cross a specification limit before it crosses either the top edge or the bottom edge of the graph?

Set 1. (yes/no) _____

Set 2. (yes/no) _____

Set 3. (yes/no) _____

Set 4. (yes/no) _____

20. If the answer is yes for any of the probability plots, what percentage of the production will be out of specification?

	% above	% below
Set 1.	_____	_____
Set 2.	_____	_____
Set 3.	_____	_____
Set 4.	_____	_____

21. (a) How do we define the estimated process average?

_____

_____

_____

_____

(b) Find the estimated process average for each operation.

Set 1. _____

Set 2. _____

Set 3. _____

Set 4. _____

(c) Is the operation average centered close to the midpoint between the specifications?

Set 1. (yes/no) _____

Set 2. (yes/no) _____

Set 3. (yes/no) _____

Set 4. (yes/no) _____

22. (a) Write the formula for the C_p index:

_____

CAPABILITY STUDIES: EXERCISES, SERIES 2

1. You will make machine or process capability studies for each of the following data sets. Questions 1 through 4 relate to the frequency histogram method for determining machine or process capability. First draw a frequency histogram for each data set. For each histogram, draw in the design specifications that are given with each data set. Then answer Questions 2 through 4 in the space provided in this workbook.

SET 1.

Specifications: Lower = 10, Upper = 90

a) 79, 94, 94, 91, 83

b) 81, 72, 85, 86, 60

c) 79, 76, 86, 76, 86

d) 88, 66, 88, 89, 88

e) 69, 71, 76, 74, 87

f) 68, 92, 62, 79, 82

g) 64, 75, 93, 77, 76

h) 70, 92, 97, 82, 78

i) 90, 73, 89, 60, 77

j) 75, 82, 91, 88, 74

k) 96, 84, 93, 93, 82

l) 97, 99, 98, 65, 97

m) 87, 73, 84, 86, 83

n) 73, 84, 69, 95, 92

o) 85, 97, 83, 83, 90

p) 97, 83, 75, 79, 74

q) 96, 67, 98, 94, 82

r) 87, 106, 85, 63, 88

s) 76, 53, 73, 68, 79

t) 83, 65, 83, 79, 77

SET 2.

Specifications: Lower = .100, Upper = .470

a) .22, .37, .26, .19, .43

b) .47, .44, .32, .29, .29

c) .13, .27, .18, .36, .20

d) .41, .30, .36, .35, .33

e) .46, .25, .34, .14, .42

f) .42, .33, .35, .45, .28

g) .31, .36, .25, .35, .24

h) .14, .33, .32, .27, .26

i) .24, .28, .47, .20, .32

j) .15, .19, .24, .25, .23

k) .25, .26, .26, .27, .34

l) .15, .30, .42, .34, .29

m) .15, .38, .38, .47, .33

n) .22, .30, .30, .32, .44

o) .13, .33, .49, .24, .35

p) .45, .11, .33, .33, .26

q) .30, .25, .25, .26, .15

r) .31, .31, .27, .22, .23

s) .52, .38, .28, .24, .33

t) .42, .19, .42, .37, .42

SET 3.

Specifications: Lower = 400, Upper = 470

a) 424, 423, 418, 424, 423

b) 441, 433, 438, 435, 421

c) 413, 418, 424, 442, 450

d) 422, 415, 422, 426, 424

e) 429, 428, 439, 446, 426

f) 431, 413, 444, 417, 426

g) 433, 447, 448, 425, 455

h) 432, 431, 428, 426, 457

i) 455, 429, 423, 442, 419

j) 425, 441, 425, 429, 430

k) 442, 439, 425, 434, 439

l) 438, 446, 429, 440, 421

m) 425, 433, 427, 424, 431

n) 419, 435, 430, 423, 433

o) 435, 432, 434, 441, 437

p) 430, 423, 420, 431, 415

q) 429, 425, 439, 420, 419

r) 426, 424, 439, 441, 425

s) 424, 435, 421, 415, 435

t) 435, 415, 423, 423, 427

SET 4.

Specifications: Lower = 5, Upper = 55

a) 40, 43, 38, 30, 50

b) 32, 23, 35, 30, 37

c) 30, 19, 22, 22, 52

d) 24, 38, 29, 33, 31

e) 10, 31, 13, 44, 35

f) 21, 30, 29, 21, 25

g) 11, 23, 27, 22, 25

h) 24, 30, 20, 29, 16

i) 33, 33, 16, 45, 36

j) 21, 24, 31, 29, 29

k) 27, 15, 44, 26, 43

l) 25, 29, 34, 29, 13

m) 36, 9, 30, 42, 50

n) 16, 27, 27, 37, 32

o) 34, 24, 49, 11, 30

p) 35, 41, 29, 32, 26

q) 29, 21, 33, 30, 33

r) 21, 10, 28, 32, 35

s) 32, 32, 38, 36, 24

t) 40, 34, 44, 32, 16

2. Estimate the average for each operation.

Set 1. _____

Set 2. _____

Set 3. _____

Set 4. _____

3. Is the operation average centered close to the midpoint between the specifications?

Set 1. _____

Set 2. _____

Set 3. _____

Set 4. _____

4. Do you think each operation is capable of producing parts with a spread less than the tolerance?

Set 1. _____

Set 2. _____

Set 3. _____

Set 4. _____

5. Questions 5 through 11 relate to the average and range chart method for determining machine or process capability. Using the data sets from Question 1, construct average and range charts, as you have already learned to do. Then answer Questions 5 through 11 in the space provided in this workbook.

   (a) Which chart should you develop first, the average chart or the range chart?

   _____

   (b) Why?

   _____

   _____

6. Tell whether or not each operation is stable.

   Set 1. _____

   Set 2. _____

   Set 3. _____

   Set 4. _____

7. Refer to Figure 5-2 in *SPC Simplified* and the text following. Explain what we mean by the following terms:

   (a) $\overline{\overline{X}}$

   _____

   (b) $\overline{R}$

   _____

   (c) "sigma"

   _____

   (d) Write the symbol for sigma:

   _____

   (e) d_2

   _____

   _____

   (f) What value of the d_2 factor should you use if the sample size is 5?

   _____

   (g) What is the value of the factor if the sample size is 4?

   _____

   (h) Write the formula for finding 3 sigma:

   _____

   (i) What does UL_x mean?

   _____

   _____

   _____

   _____

   (j) Write the formula for UL_x:

   _____

   (k) What does LL_x mean?

   _____

   _____

   _____

   _____

   (l) Write the formula for LL_x:

   _____

8. Using each average and range chart that you have developed, determine the UL_x and the LL_x, the upper and lower limits for individuals. Work in the space provided.

   Set 1.

   Set 2.

Set 3.

Set 4.

9. Determine the tolerance for each operation and write that answer in the space provided. First answer the following questions.

(a) What does US mean?

_____

(b) What does LS mean?

_____

(c) Write the formula for determining tolerance:

_____

_____

Now do the calculations. (See data sets for specifications.)

Set 1. _____

Set 2. _____

Set 3. _____

Set 4. _____

10. (a) Write the formula for process spread:

_____

(b) Find the process spread for each operation.

Set 1. _____

_____

Set 2. _____

_____

Set 3. _____

_____

Set 4. _____

_____

11. Compare the tolerance for each operation with the process spread. You may want to refer to Figure 5-4 in the textbook. Will the operation be capable of producing parts with a spread less than the tolerance? Write your answer in the space provided.

	tolerance	process spread	capable?
Set 1.	_____	_____	_____
Set 2.	_____	_____	_____
Set 3.	_____	_____	_____
Set 4.	_____	_____	_____

Questions 12 through 21 relate to the probability plot method for determining machine and process capability. Question 12 gives you practice in calculating estimated accumulated frequencies and determining plot points. Record your answers on the worksheet portion of the probability chart in Question 12.

12. (a) First find the estimated accumulated frequencies.

(b) Now determine the plot points for these examples. The total number of measurements for each set may not be 100. Remember: do not calculate the plot point for the last EAF.

Part No. & Name	12-1 (Series 2)										Char. Measured					
Operation No. & Desc.											Spec.					

VALUE																			
FREQUENCY				1	5	11	10	14	22	27	6	4							
Follow arrows and perform additions as shown (N ≥ 25)																			
EST. ACCUM. FREQ. (EAF)																			
PLOT POINTS (%) (EAF/2N) X 100																			

Part No. & Name	12-2 (Series 2)										Char. Measured					
Operation No. & Desc.											Spec.					

VALUE																			
FREQUENCY				3	0	5	12	16	25	19	13	7							
Follow arrows and perform additions as shown (N ≥ 25)																			
EST. ACCUM. FREQ. (EAF)																			
PLOT POINTS (%) (EAF/2N) X 100																			

Part No. & Name	12–3 (Series 2)												Char. Measured					
Operation No. & Desc.													Spec.					
VALUE																		
FREQUENCY			1	2	5	8	15	21	30	12	3	2	1					
Follow arrows and perform additions as shown (N ≥ 25)																		
EST. ACCUM. FREQ. (EAF)																		
PLOT POINTS (%) (EAF/2N) X 100																		

Part No. & Name	12–4 (Series 2)												Char. Measured					
Operation No. & Desc.													Spec.					
VALUE																		
FREQUENCY			5	12	23	37	15	5	1									
Follow arrows and perform additions as shown (N ≥ 25)																		
EST. ACCUM. FREQ. (EAF)																		
PLOT POINTS (%) (EAF/2N) X 100																		

Go back to the data sets from Question 1. For each set, construct a probability plot. Use the entire sheet of the normal probability plot chart. Answer Questions 13 and 14 and record you answers on the worksheet part of the probability chart. You should use the graph portion of the probability chart for Questions 15 and 16. Then follow the directions for answering Questions 17 through 28.

13. Find the frequencies of the measurements for each set. Be sure that the first frequency you write in on the left is the lowest value. You may copy the tallies from the frequency histogram worksheet onto the worksheet part of the probability chart.

14. Determine the estimated accumulated frequencies for each set.

15. Now determine the plot points. The total number of measurements for each set may not be 100. Remember: do not figure a plot point for the very largest EAF. Record the plot points on the graph portion of the probability chart.

16. (a) Draw the line of best fit. If the line of best fit is straight or nearly straight, are the measurements used in the studies distributed normally?

    _____

    (b) When you look at your plots, are the data distributed normally?

    Set 1. (yes/no) _____

    Set 2. (yes/no) _____

    Set 3. (yes/no) _____

    Set 4. (yes/no) _____

17. Estimate the process spread for each probability plot.

    (a) First determine the lowest value and the highest value you can expect from the operation.

	lowest	highest
Set 1.	_____	_____
Set 2.	_____	_____
Set 3.	_____	_____
Set 4.	_____	_____

(b) How do you find the process spread?

_____

_____

_____

_____

(c) Find the process spread for each operation.

Set 1. _____

Set 2. _____

Set 3. _____

Set 4. _____

18. Draw in the specifications for each operation. The specifications were given with each data set. Now you will be able to compare the process spread with the tolerance and determine whether or not the operation is capable of producing parts with a spread less than the tolerance. Remember: the tolerance is the difference between the upper specification and the lower specification and is a single number.

	tolerance	process spread	capable?
Set 1.	_____	_____	_____
Set 2.	_____	_____	_____
Set 3.	_____	_____	_____
Set 4.	_____	_____	_____

19. Does the line of best fit cross a specification limit before it crosses either the top edge or the bottom edge of the graph?

    Set 1. (yes/no) _____

    Set 2. (yes/no) _____

    Set 3. (yes/no) _____

    Set 4. (yes/no) _____

20. If the answer is yes for any of the probability plots, what percentage of the production will be out of specification?

	% above	% below
Set 1.	_____	_____
Set 2.	_____	_____
Set 3.	_____	_____
Set 4.	_____	_____

21. (a) How do we define the estimated process average?

    _____

    _____

    _____

    _____

    (b) Find the estimated process average for each operation.

    Set 1. _____

    Set 2. _____

    Set 3. _____

    Set 4. _____

    (c) Is the operation average centered close to the midpoint between the specifications?

    Set 1. (yes/no) _____

    Set 2. (yes/no) _____

    Set 3. (yes/no) _____

    Set 4. (yes/no) _____

22. (a) Write the formula for the C_p index:

    _____

    (b) Find the C_p index for each of the operations.

    Set 1. _____

    Set 2. _____

    Set 3. _____

    Set 4. _____

23. On the basis of the C_p index you have found, can you say that each operation is capable?

    Set 1. (yes/no) _____

    Set 2. (yes/no) _____

    Set 3. (yes/no) _____

    Set 4. (yes/no) _____

24. (a) Write the formula for the C_{pk} index:

    _____

    _____

    _____

    (b) Find the C_{pk} index for each of the operations.

    Set 1.

    Set 2.

    Set 3.

    Set 4.

25. On the basis of the C_{pk} index you have found, is the operation average inside or outside the specification tolerance?

    Set 1. (inside/outside) _____

    Set 2. (inside/outside) _____

    Set 3. (inside/outside) _____

    Set 4. (inside/outside) _____

26. On the basis of the C_{pk} index you have found, can you say that each operation is capable?

    Set 1. _____

    Set 2. _____

    Set 3. _____

    Set 4. _____

27. (a) Write the formula for the capability ratio (CR):

    _____

(b) Find the CR for each operation.

    Set 1. _____

    _____

    Set 2. _____

    _____

    Set 3. _____

    _____

    Set 4. _____

    _____

28. On the basis of the CR you have found, would you say that each operation is capable of producing parts with a spread less than the tolerance?

    Set 1. _____

    Set 2. _____

    Set 3. _____

    Set 4. _____

MACHINE AND PROCESS CAPABILITY: CASE STUDIES

The following case studies are taken from actual use in manufacturing organizations.

CASE 5-1

The weights of stock preparation pieces of rubber were used in Cases 2-1 and 3-1. They were collected at the operation as the pieces came from the extruder. The 125 weights recorded were obtained from consecutive pieces. Using these weights, construct the proper charts and estimate the capability of this operation.

Is this a machine capability analysis or a process capability analysis?

What is the capability ratio (CR)?

What is the capability index (C_{pk})?

CASE 5-2

In Cases 2-2 and 3-2 you were asked to make decisions about two forging tool setups. You can make a more complete analysis of the output of these operations with the same measurements. Using the data from Cases 2-2 and 3-2, develop a capability analysis of each of the two forging tool setups. Determine the machine capability index for each setup.

Which production setup would you recommend running to fill current orders?

CASE 5-3

The assembly operation described in Case 2-3 required the production associate to assemble a left-hand stationary snap to an adjustable retainer. The dimension involved is 323.0 ± 3.2 mm.

Using the measurements taken at this operation and employed in Case 2-3 and using the average and range chart developed in Case 3-3, complete the necessary calculations and chart to complete a process capability analysis.

What is the capability ratio of this operation?

Should the operation be classified as capable or not capable?

CASE 5-4

This problem is very similar to Case 5-3. The measurements were taken at the assembly of the right-hand stationary snap to the adjustable retainer.

Using the measurements from Case 2-4 and the average and range chart developed in Case 3-4, complete a process capability analysis of this operation.

What is the capability ratio?

Should the operation be classified as capable or not capable?

CASE 5-5

This problem uses the measurements from Case 2-5 and the average and range chart from Case 3-5. Steel tubing is cut into short lengths for use in subsequent operations.

Using the information for Case 2-5 and the control chart developed in Case 3-5, complete a machine capability analysis of this operation.

What is the capability ratio?

Should the operation be classified as capable or not capable?

Does the analysis of the measurements from this operation indicate a problem other than stability or capability?

CASE 5-6

This problem deals with the crank arm operation and measurements from Cases 2-6 and 3-7.

The production associate in charge of the operation that created the .800 dimension was concerned about the capability of the machine to make all pieces within the specification. Using the measurements recorded by the associate, complete a capability analysis of this operation.

What is the capability ratio?

Is the operation capable?

Was the associate correct in deciding that the operation no longer needed to be checked?

CASE 5-7

This problem uses the measurement information from Case 2-7 and the control charts developed in Case 3-9. The material in this operation is produced in a batch-type process. The batches are a mixture of various materials that make up a rubber compound, which is then vulcanized into rubber products. The dimension measured is the tensile strength of the rubber when it is finally vulcanized. These measurements are obtained by taking a sample from each batch and molding it into a test specimen.

Using the measurements from Case 2-7 and the control chart from Case 3-9, complete the capability analysis of this operation.

Is the mixing operation capable?

6 Quality Problem-Solving Tools

BRAINSTORMING: REVIEW QUESTIONS

1. (a) What do we mean by a chronic production problem?

   _____

   _____

   (b) What do we mean by a sporadic production problem?

   _____

   _____

   (c) For which type of production problem
can we use quality problem-solving
tools?

   _____

2. What are the benefits of finding solutions
to chronic production problems?

   _____

   _____

   _____

   _____

BRAINSTORMING

1. How does brainstorming help in the problem-solving process?

   (a) _____

   _____

   (b) _____

   _____

2. (a) What kind of problem-solving method
is brainstorming?

   _____

   _____

   (b) In what two ways does brainstorming
help build people?

   (1) _____

   _____

   (2) _____

   _____

WHAT IS NEEDED
FOR BRAINSTORMING?

1. (a) To begin a brainstorm, what kind of
group do you need?

   _____

   _____

   (b) Who should be included in the group?

   _____

   _____

   (c) What are two reasons for including
these people?

   (1) _____

   _____

   (2) _____

   _____

(d) What is the benefit of doing this?

_____

_____

2. (a) Who can lead a brainstorm?

   (b) What are three things the leader must do?

      (1) _____

      _____

      (2) _____

      _____

      (3) _____

      _____

The effective leader also puts aside personal goals for the benefit of the group.

3. What kind of meeting place does the group need?

_____

_____

4. What equipment does the group need?

   (a) _____

   (b) _____

   (c) _____

HOW DOES A BRAINSTORM WORK?

Answer the following questions on the general rules for a good brainstorming session.

1. What is the very first thing to do at the start of a brainstorming session?

_____

2. What should everyone understand?

_____

3. (a) How many ideas may a person give per turn?

_____

(b) What should you do if you can't think of anything?

_____

(c) What should you do if you think of an idea when it is not your turn?

_____

_____

4. (a) What is the recorder's job?

_____

   (b) Should the recorder give his or her ideas?

_____

5. Are all ideas written down?

_____

6. Why are wild ideas important?

_____

_____

7. (a) Why is it important to hold criticism until after the brainstorming session?

_____

_____

   (b) What is the aim of the brainstorm?

_____

8. How should laughter be handled?

_____

_____

_____

9. Why is it a good idea to allow time for further thought?

_____

_____

_____

Additional questions:

10. How does the brainstorm start?

_____

_____

11. What time limit should the brainstorm have?

_____

12. When will a brainstorm leader have to do most of the work?

_____

_____

13. When can other members begin to share leadership?

_____

_____

PRODDING TECHNIQUES

1. Why is it important to be careful when using prodding techniques?

_____

_____

Encouraging Ideas

2. (a) What is piggybacking?

_____

_____

(b) When is it helpful to use this technique?

_____

_____

(c) What are two other techniques for "priming the pump"?

(1) _____

(2) _____

3. You can prod the brainstorm by tossing out ideas in certain directions. What are two ways to do this?

(a) _____

_____

(b) _____

_____

The Silent Member

4. (a) What is the best advice for working with a silent member of the team?

_____

(b) What is a simple, effective way to help bring out a silent member?

_____

_____

(c) How does this help?

_____

_____

_____

(d) What is another method for bringing out the silent member?

_____

(e) What are some cautions to keep in mind with this method?

_____

_____

_____

The Second Pass

5. (a) Why is it helpful to have another session after the initial one?

_____

_____

(b) What is one way to handle a second pass?

_____

_____

(c) What is the purpose of this method?

_____

_____

_____

(d) Another method for handling the second pass is to post the brainstorm sheets in the work area. Why is this a good idea?

_____

_____

_____

(e) What is another advantage of this method?

_____

_____

COMPLETING THE BRAINSTORM

1. How can you make sure the brainstorm covers all general areas of possible causes?

_____

_____

_____

2. What are some of these general areas?

_____

_____

DIFFICULTIES WITH BRAINSTORMING AND WHAT TO DO ABOUT THEM

1. (a) How should you handle possible resentment toward ideas from outsiders?

_____

_____

_____

(b) Why is it helpful to have an outsider's perspective?

_____

_____

2. Where should criticism be directed?

_____

_____

3. (a) How should you deal with a difficult member?

_____

(b) What are some ways to do this?

_____

_____

_____

(c) What are two ways to confront a person directly in a brainstorming session?

(1) _____

_____

(2) _____

_____

BRAINSTORMING: EXERCISES, SERIES 1

1. Brainstorming is a group process. If you are not part of a problem-solving group, you can try brainstorming with your family or with a few friends at lunch. Here are some topics for further practice. Develop a brainstorm for each topic, with at least 12 ideas per topic. Be sure to review the rules for brainstorming before you begin.

   • Uses for former gas stations
   • Uses for discarded Christmas trees
   • Reasons why the car won't start
   • Causes for variation in gas mileage
   • Sources of contamination in paint

2. This exercise gives you an opportunity to practice piggybacking. We have listed the main brainstorm topic and one possible cause in the table at the bottom of this page. Piggyback on each cause by offering two more ideas.

3. One way to prod a brainstorm session is by suggesting opposites. For the following ideas, give a pair of opposites. For example, opposite suggestions for "tension on a line" could be "too tight" and "too slack."

(a) Mesh of strainer

_____

_____

(b) Amount of catalyst

_____

_____

(c) Mixing speed

_____

_____

(d) Process specifications

_____

_____

[Series 1] Brainstorm Topic	Possible Cause		Additional Cause
(a) Cookie mix isn't selling	Proportion of flour and eggs	(1)	_____
		(2)	_____
(b) Bad process for plastic seal	Thermometer in oven is not always accurate	(1)	_____
		(2)	_____
(c) Misalignment of steel support beams	Steel beams are too short	(1)	_____
		(2)	_____
(d) Cracked caps in bottling	Speed of capper	(1)	_____
		(2)	_____
(e) Malfunction of pouring machine	Problem with strainer	(1)	_____
		(2)	_____

(e) Report feedback loop

_____

_____

(f) Shade of dye

_____

_____

(g) Filter bed

_____

_____

(h) Depth of bore

_____

_____

(i) Weight of components

_____

_____

(j) Refrigerator temperature

_____

_____

4. How would you handle the following situations?

   (a) Sandy, an engineer, keeps saying that the problem is too technical for the group to work on and in general tries to make the team members feel incompetent.

   _____

   _____

   _____

   _____

   _____

   _____

(b) Bob has attended five meetings but has said very little. During the two brainstorm sessions, he said nothing but "Pass."

_____

_____

_____

_____

_____

(c) During a brainstorm, a team member resonds to the idea of "length of cure time" with the comment, "You're off track there. We solved that problem last August."

_____

_____

_____

_____

_____

_____

(d) The problem-solving group has concentrated on machine and on method as possible sources of trouble, but has not paid much attention to raw materials. What could you do to expand this brainstorm?

_____

_____

_____

_____

_____

_____

BRAINSTORMING: EXERCISES, SERIES 2

1. Here are some more topics for further brainstorming practice. Develop a brainstorm for each topic with at least 12 ideas per topic. Be sure to review the rules for brainstorming before you begin.

   - Uses for old shirts
   - Uses for leaves collected by the city
   - Reasons why the refrigerator isn't working
   - Causes for variation in waiting time at bank drive-through
   - Reasons why soup is served cold

2. This exercise gives you the chance to practice piggybacking. We have listed the main brainstorm topic and one possible cause in the table at the bottom of this page. Piggyback on each cause by offering two more ideas.

3. One way to prod a brainstorm session is by suggesting opposites. For the following ideas, give a pair of opposites. For example, oppostie suggestions for "tension on a line" could be "too tight" and "too slack."

   (a) Size of torque screw

   _____

   _____

   (b) Conveyor speed

   _____

   _____

   (c) Oven temperature

   _____

   _____

   (d) Depth of insulation

   _____

   _____

[Series 2] Brainstorm Topic	Possible Cause		Additional Cause
(a) Variation in coating thickness	Clogged applicator nozzle	(1)	_____
		(2)	_____
(b) Late deliveries	Routing sheets are incomplete	(1)	_____
		(2)	_____
(c) Misalignment of print	Wrong size print plates	(1)	_____
		(2)	_____
(d) Contaminant in bottles	Broken scrubbers	(1)	_____
		(2)	_____
(e) Malfunction of safety switch	Power surge	(1)	_____
		(2)	_____

(e) Number of bank tellers

_____

_____

(f) Proportion of weight of Component A to weight of Component B

_____

_____

(g) Banking time

_____

_____

(h) Coating thickness

_____

_____

(i) Die height

_____

_____

(j) Number of filters

_____

_____

4. How would you handle the following situations?

(a) During the brainstorm session, Chris offers two or three ideas per turn.

_____

_____

_____

(b) The brainstorm session has been going on for nearly five minutes, but now everyone is saying "Pass." You think the group could dig a little deeper. What can you do?

_____

_____

_____

_____

(c) Mike is new to the problem-solving group and tends to be quiet. The first time he contributes an idea, everybody laughs. What should you do?

_____

_____

_____

_____

_____

CAUSE AND EFFECT DIAGRAMS: REVIEW QUESTIONS

1. (a) Why does a brainstorm list need organizing?

_____

_____

(b) In what form does the cause and effect diagram organize the ideas in the brainstorm list?

_____

_____

2. What are the main headings under which you can organize the possible causes from a brainstorm?

(a) _____

(b) _____

(c) _____

(d) _____

(e) _____

WHY USE THE CAUSE AND EFFECT DIAGRAM?

1. What is the first reason for using the cause and effect (C and E) diagram?

_____

_____

_____

_____

2. The C and E diagram also shows relationships between ideas by grouping ideas under main headings. How can the use of the diagram help to fill gaps in the brainstorm?

_____

_____

_____

3. Because the C and E diagram serves as a record of the brainstorm, what does it help the team to do?

_____

_____

_____

HOW TO CONSTRUCT A CAUSE AND EFFECT DIAGRAM

Step 1. Gather the material.

What materials will you need to construct a C and E diagram?

(a) _____

(b) _____

(c) _____

(d) _____

Step 2. Call together everyone involved with the problem.

(a) Generally, who takes part in building the C and E diagram?

_____

_____

(b) Who else could participate?

_____

_____

(c) What does the recorder do?

_____

_____

Step 3. Begin to construct the diagram.

(a) Where do you write down the problem or effect?

_____

(b) Why should the problem be stated clearly?

_____

_____

(c) What do you do next? (See Figure 6-3 in the textbook.)

_____

_____

Step 4. Draw an arrow to the place where the effect is written.

What is another name for the arrow?

_____

Step 5. Add the main causes.

(a) What four main causes are used most often?

(1) _____

(2) _____

(3) _____

(4) _____

(b) What other possible causes might you use?

(1) _____

(2) _____

(3) _____

(4) _____

(5) _____

(6) _____

(7) _____

(8) _____

Step 6. Add the brainstorm ideas.

What do you do with your brainstorm ideas when you put them on the diagram?

_____

_____

THE PROCESS OF CONSTRUCTING THE CAUSE AND EFFECT DIAGRAM

1. (a) What are the two ways to generate ideas for the C and E diagrams?

(1) _____

(2) _____

(b) When is the process of building a C and E diagram like brainstorming?

_____

(c) What two responsibilities need to be filled?

(1) _____

(2) _____

(d) What rules apply? (List three).

(1) _____

(2) _____

(3) _____

2. (a) Why is guidance from the leader required for working out the diagram?

_____

_____

_____

_____

_____

_____

(b) Where must the emphasis always be?

_____

3. (a) What are the two ways to fill in the ideas under the causes?

(1) _____

_____

(2) _____

_____

(b) How can you handle an area that doesn't receive much attention?

_____

_____

(c) What do you do if an idea seems to fit under more than one heading?

_____

_____

TYPES OF CAUSE AND EFFECT DIAGRAMS

1. What is the most common type of C and E diagram?

_____

2. (a) What is another type of C and E diagram?

_____

 (b) How does this kind of diagram work?

_____

_____

_____

 (c) What does the team do at each stage of the production process?

_____

_____

_____

(d) How do you construct this kind of C and E diagram?

_____

_____

3. (a) What do brainstorming and cause and effect diagrams help you do?

_____

_____

 (b) Name two stages in the problem-solving process where you can use both methods.

 (1) _____

 (2) _____

CAUSE AND EFFECT DIAGRAMS: EXERCISES, SERIES 1

1. In Question 1, Series 1, of the brainstorming exercises, you generated a list of ideas for each brainstorm topic. Select two of these lists and build a cause and effect diagram for each list. Then answer the following questions.

 (a) What four main "bones" or causes are used most often?

 (1) _____
 (2) _____
 (3) _____
 (4) _____

 (b) What other possible main bones or causes could you use?

 (1) _____
 (2) _____
 (3) _____
 (4) _____
 (5) _____
 (6) _____
 (7) _____
 (8) _____

(c) What major bones or causes did you use for your C and E diagrams?

Diagram 1: _____

_____

Diagram 2: _____

_____

(d) Did the brainstorm cover all of these major causes?

Diagram 1: (yes/no) _____

Diagram 2: (yes/no) _____

(e) Are there other possible main causes you might want to consider? Write them here.

Diagram 1: _____

_____

Diagram 2: _____

_____

2. Review the piggyback ideas you developed for the causes in Question 2, Series 1, of the brainstorming exercises. Now decide under what main bones or headings you could list the piggyback ideas. Could a piggyback idea fall under more than one heading? If so, which headings? Write your answer in the space provided in the table below.

[Series 1] Possible Cause	Piggyback Ideas	Main Bone(s)
(a) Proportion of flour and eggs	(1) _____ (2) _____	(1) _____ (2) _____
(b) Thermometer in oven not always accurate	(1) _____ (2) _____	(1) _____ (2) _____
(c) Steel beams too short	(1) _____ (2) _____	(1) _____ (2) _____
(d) Speed of capper	(1) _____ (2) _____	(1) _____ (2) _____
(e) Problem with strainer	(1) _____ (2) _____	(1) _____ (2) _____

On separate sheets of paper, set up C and E diagrams. List the possible cause under the appropriate main bone or bones. Then write in the piggyback ideas. You will have only a partial diagram.

3. Refer to Figure 6-8 in the textbook. In this exercise, you are to set up simple process cause and effect diagrams using the process steps listed. Besides the four usual main bones, others may be appropriate. Write in all appropriate main bones for each step.

   Step 1. Goal: improve finishing of steel bars. Process steps: reheat, roll, condition, straighten, finish, inspect.

   Step 2. Goal: reduce damage to cereal boxes during filling. Process steps: set empties on conveyor, weigh cereal, fill boxes, seal inner liner, close top, stamp date, inspect.

   Step 3. Goal: reduce contamination in a dry mix operation. Process steps: weigh raw materials, clean mixer, load mixer, mix, check coolant.

   Step 4. Goal: Eliminate blisters in paint operation for auto bodies. Process steps: prep auto body, primer, dry, paint, dry, inspect/touch up.

CAUSE AND EFFECT DIAGRAMS: EXERCISES, SERIES 2

1. In Question 1, Series 2, of the brainstorming exercises, you generated a list of ideas for each brainstorm topic. Select two of these lists and build a cause and effect diagram for each list. Then answer the following questions.

   (a) What four main "bones" or causes are used most often?

   (1) _____

   (2) _____

   (3) _____

   (4) _____

   (b) What other possible main bones or causes could you use?

   (1) _____

   (2) _____

   (3) _____

   (4) _____

   (5) _____

   (6) _____

   (7) _____

   (8) _____

   (c) What major bones or causes did you use for your C and E diagrams?

   Diagram 1: _____

   _____

   Diagram 2: _____

   _____

   (d) Did the brainstorm cover all of these major causes?

   Diagram 1: (yes/no) _____

   Diagram 2: (yes/no) _____

   (e) Are there other possible main causes you might want to consider? Write them here.

   Diagram 1: _____

   _____

Diagram 2: _____

_____

2. Review the piggyback ideas you developed for the causes in Question 2, Series 2, of the brainstorming exercises. Now decide under what main bones or headings you could list the piggyback ideas. Could a piggyback idea fall under more than one heading? If so, which headings? Write your answer in the space provided in the table below.

   On separate sheets of paper, set up C and E diagrams. List the possible cause under the appropriate main bone or bones. Then write in the piggyback ideas. You will have only a partial diagram.

3. Refer to Figure 6-8 in the textbook. In this exercise, you are to set up simple process cause and effect diagrams using the process steps listed. Besides the four usual main bones, others may be appropriate. Write in all appropriate main bones for each step.

Step 1. Goal: reduce variation in machining operation. Process steps: bore, twist drill, core drill, ream, air clean, inspect.

Step 2. Goal: reduce spillage in crushing operation for ore. Process steps: receive crude ore, feed, crush, screen, convey to next process.

Step 3. Goal: decrease defects from welding damage. Process steps: main weld, first spot weld, second spot weld, third spot weld, CO_2 arc weld, inspect/repair.

Step 4. Goal: reduce time for purification of chemical. Process steps: add raw crystal, water, and activated charcoal to reaction vessel, dissolve, heat treat, filter, cool filtrate, centrifuge chemical.

[Series 2] Possible Cause	Piggyback Ideas	Main Bone(s)
(a) Clogged applicator nozzle	(1) _____ (2) _____	(1) _____ (2) _____
(b) Routing sheets incomplete	(1) _____ (2) _____	(1) _____ (2) _____
(c) Wrong print plates	(1) _____ (2) _____	(1) _____ (2) _____
(d) Scrubbers broken	(1) _____ (2) _____	(1) _____ (2) _____
(e) Power surge	(1) _____ (2) _____	(1) _____ (2) _____

PARETO ANALYSIS AND PARETO DIAGRAM: REVIEW QUESTIONS

1. (a) Why is Pareto analysis particularly useful in dealing with chronic problems?

   _____

   _____

   _____

   (b) How can you use Pareto analysis at the end of the problem-solving process?

   _____

   _____

2. How does Pareto analysis help you to be a more effective problem solver?

   _____

   _____

   _____

   _____

3. (a) Where can you see the idea behind Pareto analysis? Give an example.

   _____

   _____

   _____

   _____

   (b) Can you also sort a list of problems in this way?

   _____

4. What type of graph is a Pareto diagram?

   _____

5. (a) Of the problems listed on the Pareto diagram in Figure 6-9 in the textbook, which one does the text say is an obvious problem?

   _____

   (b) Which problem is the most frequent?

   _____

   (c) Which problem would you choose to work on?

   _____

   (d) Why?

   _____

6. (a) How does the Pareto diagram show the problem that occurs most frequently?

   _____

   _____

   _____

   (b) What could "frequency" mean?

   _____

   _____

7. In what ways does Pareto analysis help in problem solving?

   _____

   _____

   _____

   _____

HOW TO CONSTRUCT A PARETO DIAGRAM

Step 1. Specify the goal clearly.

Step 2. Collect data.

(a) If data are not already available, what must you do?

_____

(b) What is one place to look?

_____

_____

Step 3. Tally the data.

Step 4. Rank the categories of data by frequency.

(a) Which category should you list first?

_____

(b) Which should you list second?

_____

Step 5. Prepare the chart for the data.

(a) How do you mark the left-hand vertical scale?

_____

_____

_____

(b) How do you subdivide the horizontal scale?

_____

_____

_____

(c) Can you combine the smallest categories?

_____

(d) If so, how do you label the group of combined categories?

_____

(e) At most, what percentage of the overall total should this group include?

_____

Step 6. Draw in the bars. Label them.

(a) What size category does the first bar on the left represent?

_____

(b) What size category does the second bar from the left represent?

_____

Step 7. Make calculations based on the tallies.

(a) When you add frequencies, what is the name for the frequency you obtain as you add each entry?

_____

Continue adding frequencies until you reach the last entry.

(b) What should the total of the entries equal?

_____

_____

(c) Write (in words) the formula for finding the cumulative percentage:

_____

_____

_____

_____

In the following situation, suppose that the total number of defects is 56. The largest category of defects is poor solder joints, with 19 occurrences.

(d) What is the first cumulative frequency?

_____

(e) What is the first cumulative percentage?

_____

(f) If the second cumulative frequency is 26, what is the second cumulative percentage?

_____

(g) What is the last cumulative percentage?

_____

Step 8. Complete the Pareto diagram.

(a) Where do you draw the vertical scale for cumulative percentages?

_____

_____

(b) How many divisions do you mark off on this scale?

_____

(c) What do they represent?

_____

(d) What does the small circle over the first bar represent?

_____

_____

(e) What does the second small circle over the second bar represent?

_____

_____

(f) Why do you connect the circles?

_____

_____

Be sure to label your Pareto diagram.

HOW TO INTERPRET THE PARETO DIAGRAM

1. What are the advantages of using the Pareto diagram as a document of quality problems?

_____

_____

2. As a communication tool, what problem does the Pareto diagram help to avoid?

_____

_____

3. How does the Pareto diagram help to compare problems that exist before and after you work to improve the process?

_____

_____

_____

PARETO ANALYSIS AND PARETO DIAGRAM: EXERCISES, SERIES 1

For each of the following examples, you will construct a Pareto diagram. First, answer

Questions 1 through 3 and write your answers on the top part of the Pareto Diagram Worksheet. In Question 5, draw the Pareto diagram on the graph portion of the worksheet.

Set 1. Defects in a manual operation where wires are soldered to a blower motor: short circuit, 7; wire breaks, 28; commutator, 12; soldering, 63; excessive resistance, 17; dirt, 5.

Set 2. Defects in enameling of refrigerators: 17 dings, 6 nips, 19 scratches, 10 blisters, 7 runs, 6 "curtains," 5 chips.

1. Rank the categories of defects in order of frequency on the worksheet.

2. For each set, determine the cumulative frequencies and record them on the worksheet.

3. Once you have calculated the cumulative frequencies, you are ready to find the cumulative percentages for each example. Record your answers on the worksheet.

4. Write (in words) the formula for finding cumulative percentages:

_____

_____

_____

5. Using the tables you have developed, construct a Pareto diagram for each example. Use the graph portion of the worksheet.

PARETO ANALYSIS AND PARETO DIAGRAM: EXERCISES, SERIES 2

For each of the following examples, you will construct a Pareto diagram. First answer Questions 1 through 3 and write the answers on the top part of the Pareto Diagram Worksheet. In Question 5, draw the Pareto diagram on the graph portion of the worksheet.

Set 1. Waste from a cutting operation: winding on roller, 23 kg; first cut, 13 kg; tow piece take-up, 54 kg; incorrect cut, 19 kg; intermediate cut, 27 kg; break, 14 kg.

Set 2. Types of widget: 7 warbles, 6 tweets, 10 whiffles, 19 zerks, 12 thrims, 14 verts, 2 zoins, 3 turps.

1. Rank the categories of items in order of frequency on the worksheet.

2. For each set, determine the cumulative frequencies and record them on the worksheet.

3. Once you have calculated the cumulative frequencies, you are ready to find the cumulative percentages for each example. Record your answers on the worksheet.

4. Write (in words) the formula for finding cumulative percentages:

_____

_____

_____

5. Using the tablets you developed, construct a Pareto diagram for each example. Use the graph portion of the worksheet.

FLOW CHARTS: REVIEW QUESTIONS

1. What is a process flow chart?

_____

_____

2. What does the flow chart do?

_____

_____

_____

_____

3. The flow chart uses seven special symbols to describe process steps. Identify each symbol and explain what it is.

(a) _____

_____

(b) _____

_____

(c) _____

_____

(d) _____

_____

(e) _____

_____

(f) _____

_____

(g) _____

_____

CONSTRUCTING A PROCESS FLOW CHART

Step 1. Define the process.

(a) How do you define the beginning and end of the process?

_____

_____

Step 2. Identify the steps in the process.

(a) What is the easiest way to identify process steps?

_____

_____

(b) What are some other ways to identify process steps?

_____

_____

(c) When does a process step begin?

_____

(d) What is meant by the magnifying glass approach?

_____

_____

Step 3. Draw the flow chart.

(a) What information should be included for each process step along with its symbol?

_____

_____

(b) When should you use the connector symbol?

_____

_____

(c) Sometimes the flow chart may branch. What are three ways this can happen?

(1) _____

_____

(2) _____

_____

(3) _____

_____

Step 4. Determine the time or distance for each step.

(a) Why is it important to know the time for each process step?

_____

_____

(b) How do we determine how long a process step takes?

_____

_____

(c) Why might it be important to know the times for "storage" or a "delay?"

_____

_____

(d) Why might it be important to know the distance for a "move?"

_____

_____

Step 5. Assign a cost for each step.

(a) Why might cost information be important?

_____

_____

HOW TO USE THE PROCESS FLOW CHART

Two important uses of the completed process flow chart are for controlling the process and for improving the process.

1. (a) How can you use the flow chart to control a process?

_____

_____

_____

(b) What are some suggested tools you could use to control the process?

_____

_____

2. (a) How does the process flow chart help improve the process?

_____

_____

(b) What are some suggested tools you could use to improve the process?

_____

_____

3. The textbook mentions some other things to keep in mind when using a flow chart. What are they?

(a) _____

_____

(b) _____

_____

(c) _____

_____

(d) _____

_____

(e) _____

_____

FLOW CHARTS: EXERCISES, SERIES 1

Sometimes the flow chart may branch. To practice drawing branching operational steps, create flow charts using the steps described in the following examples.

Set 1. Start-up of envelope machine-web process—Regular sizes of envelopes, 6.5″ × 3.5″ to 9.5″ × 4.5″, are produced on a machine. A web of paper is fed into the machine, printed with the customer's return address and logo, cut to shape, has glue put on, is folded together, and put into a drying chain. In starting up the machine the associate goes through several steps: (1) bring the machine up to speed; (2) sample an envelope before the envelopes go onto the drying chain; (3) check the envelope to see if it is folded properly and the printing is in the correct position; (4) if correct, continue the run; (5) if slightly incorrect, adjust the machine while it runs, and go to step 3; (6) if badly folded or print for return address is way off, shut down machine; (7) readjust; (8) go to step 1.

Set 2. Steering wheel insert assembly operation—Steering wheel inserts are manufactured in just-in-time cells. Rims, cups, hubs, and spokes are brought to Cell A for welding operations, injection molding, inspection, and packing. The process steps are as follows: (1) wheel rims and spokes brought directly to arc welders "George" and Georgette" in Cell A; (2) cups and hubs brought to cup/hub weld operations; (3) cups and hubs welded; (4) cup/hub units moved to both arc weld operations; (5) rims, cups/hubs, and spokes loaded into either "George" or "Georgette;" (6) arc weld rims, cup/hubs, and spokes to form wheel insert; (7) wheel insert removed from arc welder and inspected; (8) wheel inserts moved to injection mold.

FLOW CHARTS: EXERCISES, SERIES 2

Construct a process flow chart for each of the following processes. Then, for each of the flow charts you construct, answer the provided questions.

Set 1. Preparing and assembling two metal parts—This process consists of preparing and assembling two metal parts. From the following operational information, construct a process flow chart.

1. Is there any branching in the flow chart?

_____

_____

_____

_____

2. Are there steps where statistical control charts could be used to monitor or control the process?

_____

_____

_____

_____

3. Which steps waste time? What could be done about the waste?

_____

_____

_____

_____

4. Are there potential bottlenecks in this process?

_____

_____

Step 1. Preparing and Assembling Two Metal Parts

Operation	Time (Minutes)	Distance (Feet)
1. Receive component A	5	—
2. Move to receiving dock	10	40
3. Store on receiving dock	50	—
4. Inspect	12	—
5. If acceptable, move to storage area	3	80
6. If not acceptable, stays on receiving dock for return to supplier	15	—
7. Store acceptable component A	2 days	—
8. Move to work area	5	120
9. Store in work area until component B arrives	(?)	—
10. Load components A and B onto conveyor	2	—
11. Move to workstation	2	12
12. Spray components with protective material	4	—
13. Load components A and B onto next conveyor	2	5
14. Components dry on conveyor	8	—
15. Components move to assembly area	23	180
16. Components stored in assembly area	—	—
17. Sample taken to lab	5	—
18. Wait for lab report	35 min–5 hrs	—
19. Lab report	—	—
20. If defective, scrap product	2	55
21. If OK, assemble	23	—
22. Move to table	2	25
23. Pack in shipping container	4	—
24. Move shipping container to storage area	2	—
25. Store for shipping	2 min–4.5 hrs	—

Set 2. This problem involves a chemical process that produces batches of elastomeric material. These batches are used in processes that form the material to the desired shape and then accelerate the chemical reaction to complete the vulcanization of the product.

A continuous improvement team is looking at the current process to determine if improvements can be made in the process. The team has studied the process and is now creating a process flow chart showing the mixing of the basic material. They have developed a sequence of activities required to mix a batch of elastomeric compound for producing products in various locations for different customers. Using the following information developed by the team, construct a process flow chart for producing the batches of material.

1. Is there any branching in the flow chart?

_____

_____

_____

_____

2. Are there steps where statistical control charts could be used to monitor or control the process?

_____

_____

_____

_____

3. Which steps waste time? What could be done about the waste?

_____

_____

_____

_____

4. Are there potential bottlenecks in this process?

_____

_____

Step 2. Rubber Mixing Process

Process Steps	Time (Minutes)	Distance (Feet)
1. Receive and store raw materials	120	30
2. Weigh material #4 and #5 on small scale and place in tub	5	15
3. Move in tub	2	15
4. Place material #6 in tub (vendor certified)	2	10
5. Place 50 lb. bag of carbon black #3 in tub. Place 16.8 lbs. of #3 loose in tub. Place 50 lb. bag of #8 with tub on belt	5	10
6. Weigh 191 lbs. of #1 and place on conveyor with tub	7	4
7. Move to mixer	2	25
8. Weigh #2 using computer operated scale and hold for addition to mixer	8	5
9. Weigh curative #7 manually from 55 gal. drum to bucket	5	5
10. Load mixer—all ingredients except #7	3	5
11. Mix two minutes—add #7	2	—
12. Mix to 210 degrees F	10	—
13. Dump batch from mixer to mill	2	5
14. Band on mill	5–10	—
15. Move to cooling tank	1	10
16. Cool	5–10	—
17. Load on pallet	1	5
18. Take lab sample * (lab technician)	2	
19. Test in lab * (lab technician)	20 min–12 hrs	—
20. Move to scales	1	10
21. Weigh and record	1	—
22. Move to storage	2	20
23. Store	—	—
24. Wait for lab approval	—	—
25. Release for shipment * (lab technician)	1	—
26. Package for shipment	5	—
27. Move to storage	5–10	100
28. Store for shipment	(?)	—

SCATTER DIAGRAMS: REVIEW QUESTIONS

1. What is the purpose of a scatter diagram?

_____

_____

2. When should you use a scatter diagram?

_____

_____

_____

_____

HOW TO CONSTRUCT A SCATTER DIAGRAM

3. In the scatter diagram, what does a plotted point represent?

_____

4. (a) What type of data should you use when constructing a scatter diagram?

_____

   (b) List some examples of this type of data.

_____

Step 1. Is the problem suitable for a scatter diagram?

What are the three criteria for a scatter diagram kind of problem?

(a) _____

_____

(b) _____

_____

(c) _____

_____

Step 2. Collect your data.

What should you do when collecting data?

_____

_____

Step 3. Determine the scales for the graph and plot the data.

(a) What do we mean by the term "dependent variable?"

_____

(b) On which axis do we plot the dependent variable?

_____

(c) How should you set the scales when plotting the dependent variable?

_____

(d) On which axis do we plot the other, or independent, variable?

_____

Step 4. Do the corner count test.

(a) After doing the corner count test a few times, you will be able to look at a new set of data and tell three things about these data at a glance. What are they?

(1) _____

_____

(2) _____

_____

(3) _____

_____

_____

(b) What do we mean by a straight-line relationship?

_____

_____

_____

_____

(c) If such a relationship does exist, what does it tell you?

_____

_____

(d) Why could this be important?

_____

_____

(e) What are the six steps to follow to do the corner count test?

(1) _____

(2) _____

(3) _____

(4) _____

(5) _____

(6) _____

(f) When doing the corner count, you will draw the two median lines on the scatter diagram. What is meant by the term "median?"

_____

_____

_____

(g) How do you draw the median for the dependent variable on the scatter diagram?

_____

_____

_____

_____

(h) How do you draw the median for the independent variable on the scatter diagram?

_____

_____

_____

_____

_____

(i) When drawing the medians on the scatter diagram:

(1) Where should you draw the median, if the number of points is odd?

_____

_____

(2) Where should you draw the median, if the number of points is even?

_____

_____

(3) What do you do if there is more than one point on a median line?

_____

_____

(j) The two median lines will have divided your scatter diagram into four parts, or quarters. How should you label each of the four quarters? Refer to Figure 6-20 in the textbook.

_____

_____

(k) (1) How do you do the corner counts of the plotted points?

_____

_____

_____

_____

(2) How do you assign a plus sign or a minus sign to the count of points?

_____

_____

(3) When do you stop counting points?

_____

_____

(l) How do you total the corner counts?

_____

_____

(m) What is the important thing to note about this total?

_____

_____

(n) Compare your result to the comparison number 11.

(1) What may it mean if your result is 11 or greater?

_____

_____

(2) What is the meaning of a result smaller than 11?

_____

_____

SCATTER DIAGRAMS: EXERCISES, SERIES 1

For each of the following sets of data, construct a scatter diagram.

SET 1.

Independent Variable	Dependent Variable
40	10
19	20
17	26
20	40
45	23
26	15
26	23
30	11
53	27
35	14
36	27
39	19

23	12
15	6
32	33

SET 2.

Independent Variable	Dependent Variable
10.8	55
11.0	60
11.0	65
11.2	68
11.4	64
11.5	70
11.8	67
11.9	65
12.2	76
12.3	71
12.4	62

12.6	74
12.7	70
13.0	7
13.0	85
13.2	80
13.7	84
13.8	80
13.8	88
14.1	92

SET 3.

Independent Variable	Dependent Variable
34	33
46	43
28	18
13	15
20	14
43	34
30	27
10	7
23	24
41	37
33	21
15	10

SET 4.

Independent Variable	Dependent Variable
8.7	32
12.7	14
7.5	3
6.8	40
10.8	25
10.0	20
7.6	36
7.8	41
8.2	30
11.5	22
9.0	36
8.9	19
8.2	36
11.8	12

9.6	24
9.2	26
10.6	22
11.6	17
10.9	29

1. What type of data are used in the scatter diagram?

_____

2. To prepare the scatter diagram in these exercises, first set up a graph for each data set. Then determine the scales. Find the largest and smallest values of the dependent variable. Circle the largest and draw a box around the smallest. Be sure the largest and smallest values fit inside the chart, not on the edges. On which axis do we usually plot the dependent variable?

_____

3. Now plot the data.

4. Do the corner count test for each set. What type of relationship between the variables are you looking for?

_____

5. Finding the medians for the two variables is part of doing the corner count test. For each data set find and draw the medians on your graph.

   (a) What do we mean by a median on a scatter diagram?

   _____

   _____

   _____

   (b) Look at the data for each exercise. Is the number of points to be plotted odd or even? Indicate your answer in the space provided.

   Set 1. _____

   Set 2. _____

   Set 3. _____

   Set 4. _____

(c) How do you determine the median when the number of points is odd?

_____

_____

6. Label each corner of the diagram. Refer to Figure 6-20 in the textbook.

7. (a) Do the corner counts. Record your corner counts for each set in the table provided.

Corner Count Table		Corner Count Table	
Series 1, Set 1		*Series 1, Set 2*	
Move Ruler	Count	Move Ruler	Count
from right	____	from right	____
from top	____	from top	____
from left	____	from left	____
from bottom	____	from bottom	____
Total	____	Total	____
Without sign	____	Without sign	____

Corner Count Table		Corner Count Table	
Series 1, Set 3		*Series 1, Set 4*	
Move Ruler	Count	Move Ruler	Count
from right	____	from right	____
from top	____	from top	____
from left	____	from left	____
from bottom	____	from bottom	____
Total	____	Total	____
Without sign	____	Without sign	____

(b) Remember that you remove the "+" or "–" sign from count total. Write the count total with the sign next to "Total" in the appropriate table for each set and write the total without the sign next to "Without sign" in the appropriate table for each set.

8. Next compare each set's count total (without the "+" or "–" sign) with the comparison number 11.

(a) Is the result equal to, or greater than, the comparison number? Write your answer in the space provided.

	Count total	Result greater/ less than comparison number
Set 1.	____	_____
Set 2.	____	_____
Set 3.	____	_____
Set 4.	____	_____

(b) If your result is 11 or higher, what kind of relationship between the two variables may be present?

_____

(c) Indicate for each set whether this type of relationshp could be present.

Set 1. _____

_____

Set 2. _____

_____

Set 3. _____

_____

Set 4. _____

_____

SCATTER DIAGRAMS: EXERCISES, SERIES 2

Construct a scatter diagram for each of the following sets of data.

SET 1.

Independent Variable	Dependent Variable
4.6	54
2.9	84
3.4	80
3.9	64
3.7	82
5.5	26
4.6	68
2.9	58
1.5	28
0.4	10
1.3	32
2.3	56
6.2	20
4.9	34
0.7	22
5.7	14
0.5	4
1.6	38
2.3	42
5.4	46
5.2	40

SET 2.

Independent Variable	Dependent Variable
13	80
20	63
16	67
14	74
19	71
28	60
30	70
23	75
27	65
35	57
30	74
40	63
26	69
23	64
33	68
32	64
20	79
23	68
40	58
35	74
37	65
35	62

SET 3.

Independent Variable	Dependent Variable
100	3.7
93	2.4
96	2.6
84	2.3
77	1.9
80	2.6
70	3.2
70	2.0
95	3.0
108	2.1
90	3.0
70	1.3
66	1.6
74	1.7
86	1.9
110	4.2
104	4.0
99	3.3

SET 4.

Independent Variable	Dependent Variable
−20	−5
−30	−19
−33	−16
−31	−11
−24	−12
−27	−6
−35	−7
−28	−24
−45	−8
−49	−26
−60	−30
−58	−20
−56	−25
−54	−28
−52	−13
−39	−11
−40	−23
−49	−21
−45	−17
−43	−23
−45	−28

1. What type of data are used in the scatter diagram?

   _____

2. To prepare the scatter diagrams in these exercises, first set up a graph for each data set. Then determine the scales. Find the largest and smallest values of the dependent variable. Circle the largest and draw a box around the smallest. Be sure the largest and smallest values fit inside the chart, not on the edges. On which axis do we usually plot the dependent variable?

   _____

3. Now plot the data.

4. Do the corner count test for each set. What type of relationship between the variables are you looking for?

   _____

5. Finding the medians for the two variables is part of doing the corner count test. For each data set find and draw the medians on your graph.

   (a) What do we mean by a median on a scatter diagram?

   _____

   _____

   _____

   (b) Look at the data for each exercise. Is the number of points to be plotted odd or even? Indicate your answer in the space provided.

   Set 1. _____

   Set 2. _____

   Set 3. _____

   Set 4. _____

   (c) How do you determine the median when the number of points is odd?

   _____

   _____

6. Label each corner of the diagram. Refer to Figure 6-20 in the textbook.

7. (a) Do the corner counts. Record your corner counts for each set in the table provided.

Corner Count Table		Corner Count Table	
Series 2, Set 1		*Series 2, Set 2*	
Move Ruler	Count	Move Ruler	Count
from right	____	from right	____
from top	____	from top	____
from left	____	from left	____
from bottom	____	from bottom	____
Total	____	Total	____
Without sign	____	Without sign	____

Corner Count Table		Corner Count Table	
Series 2, Set 3		*Series 2, Set 4*	
Move Ruler	Count	Move Ruler	Count
from right	___	from right	___
from top	___	from top	___
from left	___	from left	___
from bottom	___	from bottom	___
Total	___	Total	___
Without sign	___	Without sign	___

(b) Remember that you remove the "+" or "–" sign from count total. Write the count total with the sign next to "Total" in the appropriate table for each set and write the total without the sign next to "Without sign" in the appropriate table for each set.

8. Next compare each set's count total (without the "+" or "–" sign) with the comparison number 11.

(a) Is the result equal to, or greater than, the comparison number? Write your answer in the space provided.

	Count total	Result greater/ less than comparison number
Set 1.	___	___
Set 2.	___	___
Set 3.	___	___
Set 4.	___	___

(b) If your result is 11 or higher, what kind of relationship between the two variables may be present?

_____

(c) Indicate for each set whether this type of relationship could be present.

Set 1. _____

Set 2. _____

Set 3. _____

Set 4. _____

QUALITY PROBLEM-SOLVING TOOLS: CASE STUDIES

The following case studies come from real production situations. Use the problem-solving methods from Module 6 to analyze the cases. Data are given for each case. As you prepare each case, follow this procedure.

1. Determine the largest source of defects or errors. Prepare the appropriate chart or charts. Include forms or tables for recording data.

2. For each case, develop a list or lists of possible causes of the largest problem. What problem-solving tools would you use to develop your lists? Write out your answers.

3. Show how you would organize the list in order to find root causes and determine possible solutions.

CASE 6-1

The machining department of the Ridgely Engine Plant chronically has rejects of Z-7 engines from final start-up. The plant produces 300 to 325 of these engines a week. Problems seem to be caused by machining defects on main parts. Several people have said that the trouble is in the machining of the crankshafts.

You are part of a task team that has decided to look into this situation. You are responsible for coming up with data. Let's say you have found data describing defects over a six-week period from the week of February 5 through the week of March 12. Here are the data in raw form for you to analyze.

Week 1: cylinder head, 7; block, 8; camshaft, 5; #1 crankshaft, 6.

Week 2: block, 9; camshaft, 7; #2 crankshaft, 6; cylinder head, 6; manifold, 7.

Week 3: block, 10; camshaft, 7; #2 crankshaft, 5; #1 crankshaft, 6; cylinder head, 7; manifold, 1.

Week 4: manifold, 3; #1 crankshaft, 5; camshaft, 8; block, 9; cylinder head, 8.

Week 5: #1 crankshaft, 5; cylinder head, 8; block, 9; camshaft, 4.

Week 6: block, 4; cylinder head, 3; #2 crankshaft, 8; camshaft, 6; #1 crankshaft, 7.

CASE 6-2

VIV Manufacturing, Inc., produces epoxy-coated steel pipe for use in the chemical industry. Customer service has been receiving complaints from several customers. An initial summary shows that over the last six months, the following types of complaints have come in. There were 22 complaints about the quantity of pipe in the bundle; 8 order entry errors; 3 instances of damage in transit; 4 billing errors; 33 instances of misla-

beling; 2 order cancellations; 17 complaints about the quality of the pipe itself.

You are part of a task force that is trying to improve service. Show how your team could analyze this problem. Mention all supporting documents.

CASE 6-3

The management of Nike Trail Bikes is convinced that continuous improvement is the most effective way to maintain the company's position as a manufacturer of rugged, high-quality trail bikes. Consequently line workers, team leaders, and people in middle management have been taking classes in problem solving and in basic statistical techniques and thinking.

A work group from transmissions has chosen reduction in defects in the transmissions as its first quality improvement project. You and a workmate have collected data for one month. Your investigation reveals the following problems: 72 problems caused directly by suppliers; 113 from assembly of the transmissions; 60 in the grinding operation; 19 in gear cutting; 312 nicks; 3 scratches; 12 cracked transmissions; 2 cases of contamination from dirt. These problems mean that the transmissions must be either reworked or, in the worst case, scrapped. A management team wants to know what you find to be the biggest problem with the transmissions. Prepare a *short* report with supporting tables and diagrams.

After reviewing what you find, the management team encourages you to dig deeper and to see what you can do to reduce repair costs. Further investigation shows the following types of nicks: 12 in drive gear; 72 in clutch gear; 12 in idle; 108 in reverse gear; 43 in first gear; 27 in second gear; 38 in third gear. In preparing your findings, follow the procedure given in the introduction to the problem-solving case studies for Module 6.

CASE 6-4

Daggett Industries is a medium-sized producer of pharmaceuticals for the cosmetics industry. Research and development (R&D) wants to improve the performance of Pharmaceutical N-861006. This substance is produced in a batch operation that requires two to three weeks to manufacture from raw materials to finished product. Consequently, production runs for three shifts. An improvement team from R&D and engineering has been reviewing data gathered for the last year.

The team found that the following types of errors affected the yield. In 12 instances there were errors in weighing raw materials. The team also found 11 errors arising from poor maintenance of equipment and 3 cases of damaged or otherwise illegible labels on raw materials. When engineering reviewed the operating methods, they discovered that unclear operations standards caused errors on 43 occasions; missing operational steps resulted in 37 errors; workers' inexperience because of changeover from another process to N-861006 accounted for 29 errors.

Analyze this situation, following the procedure provided in the introduction to these case studies.

CASE 6-5

A small company has taken on the task of performing an assembly operation for a large customer. The task involves assembling a gasket to a mount housing device using an adhesive. The customer has agreed to deliver the components to the company's loading dock on a Just-In-Time basis.

The manager of the company and the associates who will be performing the operations on the new job have formed a team to determine the most efficient process sequence for the job. Because this job will operate on a Just-In-Time basis, the storage area and work-in-process will be minimized, along with the inspection of the incoming materials.

At first the team envisioned this job as a simple process with only four steps: receive components; apply adhesive; assemble gasket to housing; and pack and ship. However, after a thorough study of the requirements, the team identified all the individual steps necessary to accomplish the four main activities.

Using the following information developed by the team, construct a process flow chart for the assembly of the gasket and mount housing.

1a. Receive and inspect gaskets at loading dock and move to work area and store. (Inspection Instruction #101)
1b–3b. Receive adhesive and move to work area and store.
1c. Receive and store housings on dock. (Operation Instruction #103)
2c–3c. Move housings to work area and store.
4a. Operation #1—Load adhesive tank at gasket spray line.
4b. Operation #2—Load adhesive tank at housing spray line.
5a. Move gaskets from store area to workbench.
6a. Operation #3—Spray adhesive on gasket. (Operator Instruction #102)
7a. Move gasket to drying conveyor.
5b. Move housings to workbench.
6a. Operation #4—Spray adhesive on housing. (Operator Instruction #104)
7b. Move housing to drying conveyor.
8. Wait for adhesive to dry on conveyor.
9. Move gasket and housing to assembly press.
10. Operation #5—Assemble gasket to housing. (Operator Instruction #105)
11. Move assembly to table.
12. Inspect and pack assemblies. (Inspection Instruction #106)

13. Prepare shipping bins for shipment. (Operator Instruction #107)
14. Move shipping bins to shipping area.
15. Store shipping bins in shipping area.

CASE 6-6

You are a member of a continuous improvement team that has been formed to look into the process of a product your company makes and sells in large quantities. At one time, the scrap rate on this project was high, but a CI team was successful in reducing it, which helped get the cost of producing the product closer to the original estimated cost. However, if the company is to remain competitive, more must be done.

The first thing the team has decided to do is look at the total process, and they have put together the following list of activities that take place when producing the product you are studying.

1. Inspect incoming material.
2. Store incoming material in mill area.
3. Warm up stock on mill.
4. Prepare stock for mold line.
5. Inspect prepared stock for control chart.
6. Load stock racks.
7. Move stock to press line.
8. Store stock at press line.
9. Mold parts.
10. Inspect molded parts—X-R chart.
11. Load into tubs.
12. Move molded parts to lathe.
13. Store at lathe.
14. Cut to width on lathe.
15. Inspect width—X-R chart and Comp. Set.
16. Load pieces onto rack.
17. Move to inspect/pack area.
18. Store in inspect/pack area.
19. Inspect/pack—p-chart.
20. Move to audit area.
21. Outgoing audit.
22. Move finished stock.
23. Store.

Using these steps construct a flow chart that your team may use in identifying additional areas for improvement.

CASE 6-7A

The Trident Company manufactures steel piston rods that are part of shock absorber assemblies. The rods are chromium plated to reduce the wear on the diameter of the rods and thus increase the useful life of the product. Interested in extending the life of the rods, a continuous improvement team is examining the relationship of the plating cycle time to the thickness of the chromium plating.

By examining a production run of one batch of rods made from three different cycle time settings on the plater, the team members have found that the actual plating time varies from the time set on the plater's control panel. Therefore, the team members have recorded the actual plating cycle time as well as the thickness of the chromium on rods plated during the three different cycle time settings. The plating thickness is specified to be .0004 inches minimum. The three plating cycle time settings used were 45 seconds, 50 seconds, and 55 seconds.

The following actual plating times and the corresponding chromium thicknesses were recorded by the team. Use a scatter diagram to help the team determine if they can use the actual cycle time to predict the plating thickness with a relatively high degree of confidence.

CASE 6-7B

The team's decision may be different if a scatter diagram is created using only the three plating cycle time settings, instead of the actual plating times the team recorded. Create a scatter diagram to show how their decision would be affected.

Piston Rod Plating Thickness (Case 6-7A and B)		
Plating Cycle Time (seconds)	Chromium Thickness	Plater Cycle Time Setting (seconds)
42	.00062	40
40	.00060	40
43	.00058	40
42	.00056	40
44	.00054	40
42	.00052	40
46	.00062	45
48	.00066	45
48	.00070	45
50	.00070	45
52	.00072	45
46	.00064	45
55	.00078	50
54	.00076	50
56	.00074	50
53	.00072	50
54	.00070	50
55	.00068	50
56	.00066	50
54	.00064	50

CASE 6-8A

As a member of a continuous improvement team you have been working on an improvement project for a few months. As part of this project you need to determine whether or not to recommend the purchase of a new digital readout gage to replace one of the gages that is currently in use. The team must determine if the new digital readout gage is as good as the one in use. The question is whether new a type of gage changes the inspection results (i.e., do inspection results depend on the type of gage used).

In order to answer these questions, 20 parts were submitted to both the new digital readout gage and the gage currently in use on the job (Gage 6). The measurements were paired and recorded. Use the following data to create a scatter diagram for the team to use in addressing this problem.

Digital Gage Readings vs. Old Gage Readings (Case 6-8A)	
Gage 6	*Digital Gage*
.162	.161
.164	.165
.162	.165
.158	.159
.164	.162
.162	.164
.162	.163
.160	.164
.164	.163
.165	.167
.165	.167
.161	.165
.162	.166
.162	.164
.166	.167
.165	.165
.161	.164
.159	.161
.166	.166
.164	.164

CASE 6-8B

After analyzing these results, the CI team believes that they needed to look deeper into the factors affecting the use of gages. To determine whether people have an impact on the measurements the team has decided to examine the results of two different inspectors, each using the same gage to measure the same 20 parts. The results of the measurements are listed in the following chart. Prepare a scatter diagram and determine whether inspection results are dependent upon the inspectors who take the measurements.

Inspection Results (Case 6-8B)	
Inspector 1	Inspector 2
.161	.163
.166	.164
.165	.160
.159	.158
.162	.163
.164	.160
.163	.162
.164	.163
.163	.166
.167	.164
.167	.164
.165	.166
.163	.164
.164	.165
.167	.164
.165	.163
.164	.160
.161	.161
.166	.164
.164	.163

Elements of a Total Quality Management System

REVIEW QUESTIONS

WHAT IS TQM?

1. TQM differs from traditional management philosophies in what way?

_____

_____

_____

2. TQM companies have restructured their management and operations systems. Why?

_____

_____

_____

_____

3. Why does a TQM company work to continuously improve all of its processes, both manufacturing and organizational?

_____

_____

4. The term "customer" refers to more than one person or group of people. Who are they?

_____

_____

5. A TQM company integrates quality control into all the processes of the organization. How is this done?

(a) _____

(b) _____

6. TQM companies publish a vision or mission statement. What does it do?

_____

7. (a) What does the vision statement require of the employees to carry out TQM?

_____

_____

_____

(b) How is it accomplished?

_____

_____

_____

8. What is the business plan?

_____

9. (a) What are cross-functional activities?

_____

_____

(b) What do they do?

_____

_____

10. What are the two main functions of the TQM documentation system?

    (a) _____

    _____

    (b) _____

    _____

11. There are four key features in the business plan of a successful TQM effort. What are they?

    (a) _____

    _____

    (b) _____

    _____

    (c) _____

    _____

    (d) _____

    _____

12. The TQM documentation system contains four main levels. What are they?

    (a) _____

    (b) _____

    (c) _____

    (d) _____

KEYS TO TQM

1. Why does the customer drive everything in a successful TQM organization?

    _____

    _____

2. What or who are internal customers?

    _____

    _____

3. What or who are external customers?

    _____

    _____

4. TQM stresses the knowledge and skills of every member of the organization. How is this evident?

    (a) _____

    _____

    (b) _____

    _____

    _____

    (c) _____

5. What are the results of shifting from a detection mode of management to a prevention mode?

    _____

6. What is another driving force behind the success of TQM?

    _____

CONTINUOUS IMPROVEMENT

1. What is continuous improvement?

    _____

2. How is continuous improvement accomplished?

    _____

3. What does a steering committee do?

    _____

    _____

4. The problem-solving teams use a formalized approach based on the PDCA cycle.

    (a) What does PDCA represent?

    _____

    (b) How is it used?

    _____

PLAN

1. What is the purpose of the PLAN phase of a continuous improvement project?

   (a) _____

   (b) _____

   (c) _____

   (d) _____

2. What is the key to the success of the PLAN phase?

   _____

   _____

3. A CI team must first understand the processes around which the problem occurs. What is the tool the CI team can use to depict the relationships of all the activities in the process?

   _____

4. (a) What is the next step the CI team will take in solving a problem?

   _____

   (b) What are the elements of this step?

   (1) _____

   (2) _____

   (3) _____

   (4) _____

   (5) _____

5. How will the team identify possible causes of the problem?

   _____

6. How will the team determine the relationship of the causes to the problem?

   _____

7. How will the team decide on the main cause of the problem?

   _____

DO

1. What does the team do in the DO phase of their problem-solving activities?

   _____

   _____

CHECK

1. What are some of the SPC tools the team uses during the CHECK phase to analyze the process performance before and after the solution?

   (a) _____

   (b) _____

   (c) _____

ACT

1. What does the team do during the ACT phase of the problem-solving cycle?

   _____

   _____

2. What are the key elements of TQM?

   (a) _____

   (b) _____

   (c) _____

   (d) _____

   (e) _____

   (f) _____

   (g) _____

   (h) _____

3. How do we know that the concepts of TQM and CI are valid?

_____

_____

THE MALCOLM BALDRIGE NATIONAL QUALITY AWARD

1. Who is the presenter of the Malcolm Baldrige National Quality Award?

_____

_____

2. Who are the receivers of the Malcolm Baldrige National Quality Award?

_____

_____

3. In what ways do the Baldrige criteria benefit companies?

   (a) _____

   _____

   _____

   _____

   (b) _____

   _____

   _____

   _____

4. What are the categories for the Baldrige Awards?

   (a) _____

   (b) _____

   (c) _____

5. What are the seven areas that Baldrige Award winners are judged on?

   (a) _____

   (b) _____

   (c) _____

   (d) _____

   (e) _____

   (f) _____

   (g) _____

QUALITY MANAGEMENT STANDARDS

1. How do the standards differ from the Baldrige criteria?

_____

_____

_____

_____

2. What does certification to an ISO 9000 standard prove?

_____

_____

_____

_____

3. What is the quality management system standard published by the U.S. auto makers called?

_____

4. How do they differ from the ISO standards?

_____

_____

_____

_____

REVIEW QUESTIONS

1. Make variations between parts as small as possible.
2. (a) We can measure it.
   (b) Unless it is monitored, it tends to increase or worsen.
3. (a) According to a definite pattern.
   (b) Record measurements in tally format.
   (c) Frequency distribution.
   (d) There are more in the middle.
   (e) A bell.
4. (a) Around the middle.
   (b) 68
   (c) 4
   (d) The normal distribution curve.
5. (a) (1) Materials.
       (2) Machines.
       (3) Methods.
       (4) Environment.
       (5) Production associates.
   (b) (1) Chance causes (inherent variation).
       (2) Assignable causes (special causes).
   (c) Chance cause.
   (d) Inherent variation.
   (e) Assignable cause.
   (f) Special cause.
   (g) It will vary in a normal, predictable manner.
   (h) It's stable.
6. (a) Assignable causes.
   (b) The number of times each measurement occurred.
   (c) It helps show when only chance causes are present, and when assignable causes are present.
7. (a) When we're doing something we shouldn't.
   (b) When we're not doing something we should be doing.
   (c) When we're doing things right.

TOOLS OF QUALITY

1. (a) Are we doing something we shouldn't?
   (b) Are we not doing something we should?
   (c) Is the process operating OK, or has it gone wrong, requiring correction?
2. (a) Then only chance causes are at work. Only under this condition can we know with confidence what the quality level is.
   (b) It is consistent.

THE HISTOGRAM OR FREQUENCY DISTRIBUTION

1. Because it shows how a process is operating at a specific time.
2. (a) To the bell-shaped curve.
   (b) When the average and the midpoint of the specifications are close to each other.
   (c) When the histogram is well within the specifications.
3. (a) By comparing the curve of the process to the specifications.
   (b) How the measurements cluster around the middle of the curve.
4. (a) Evaluate or check the process.
   (b) Indicate when we need to take corrective action.
   (c) Measure the effects of corrective action.
   (d) Compare machine performances.
   (e) Compare materials.
   (f) Compare vendors.

THE CONTROL CHART

1. The frequency distribution is like a snapshot, whereas the control chart is like a movie.
2. (a) When it is running smoothly and when it needs attention.
   (b) Boundaries within which we can safely operate the process.
   (c) Past performances.
   (d) Then show what we can expect from the process as long as nothing is changed.
3. (a) When to take action.
   (b) When to leave the process alone.
4. (a) Variable control charts.
   (b) Attribute control charts.

Variables Charts: Average and Range Charts

1. The average and range chart.
2. It greatly simplifies the arithmetic.
3. (a) Add them up and divide this total by the sample size.
   (b) The mean.
4. Find the largest and smallest, then subtract the smallest from the largest.
5. (a) To keep the process centered on the specified dimension.
   (b) To monitor the spread of the measurements around the average.

6. (a) Inside the control limits.
   (b) The job is "out of control."

Attribute Charts

1. "Go/no-go" or "good/bad" inspection results.
2. (a) That the process is satisfactory.
   (b) That correction is needed.

SUMMARY

1. To show that a process is in control but still producing parts out of specs.
2. (a) Chance causes.
   (b) By making a basic change in the process.
   (c) A management team.
3. (a) An assignable cause.
   (b) A floor-solvable problem.

FREQUENCY HISTOGRAMS: REVIEW QUESTIONS

1. It doesn't show any variation.
2. A series of measurements.

FREQUENCY HISTOGRAMS

1. (a) Helps to keep track of variation.
   (b) (1) The spread.
       (2) How many there are of each measurement (the frequencies).
2. (a) Horizontal scale.
   (b) Records the distances (measurements) between rivet holes.
   (c) Records how often each measurement occurred (frequency).
3. (a) Shortest to longest measurements.
   (b) Most frequent measurements.
   (c) The center of the measurements.
4. (a) Does *not* tell if the variation is caused by one machine or more than one.
   (b) Does *not* show patterns over time.

CONSTRUCTING A FREQUENCY HISTOGRAM

Step 1. Into fairly small groups.
Step 2. Circle the largest and box the smallest.
Step 3. Double circle the vary largest and double box the very smallest.
Step 4. Subtract the very smallest from the very largest.
Step 5. (a) Divide it into smaller intervals of equal widths.
   (b) Use about 10 intervals.
   (c) It hides information.
   (d) It makes the histogram too flat, thus we miss something.
   (e) It makes the information in the data show up on the histogram.
Step 6. (a) Divide the range by the desired number of intervals.
   (b) $5\frac{5}{8}$
   (c) 6
   (d) 8
   (e) 6

(f) Determine intervals, boundaries, and midpoints.
(g) *Between*, not *on* boundaries.
(h) 38
(i) 38
(j) 44
(k) We don't know which interval it belongs in.
(l) Use boundaries.
(m) Add or subtract a decimal place to or from the endpoints.
(n) 49.5
(o) 55.5
(p) 55.5 to 61.5
(q) At 58.5, the center of the interval.
(r) 6 units.
(s) 64.5

Step 7. (a) Put a check (tally mark) for each measurement in the corresponding interval. Then check the tallies, add them, and write the totals under "Frequency." Add all the numbers in the "Frequency" column as a last check.
   (b) (1) Do a tally check by repeating all the tallies.
       (2) Count the frequencies to see if the total is correct.
Step 8. (a) (1) Tell the story of the data, no more and no less.
       (2) Be neat and make it easy to read.
   (b) (1) Mark and label the vertical scale.
       (2) Mark and label the horizontal scale.
       (3) Draw in bars according to the tallies.
       (4) Label the histogram.
   (c) Use the midpoints.
   (d) (1) Paste graph paper onto a white background and write on the background.
       (2) Make the frequencies and midpoints easy to read.
       (3) Don't make it too tall, too short, too wide, or too narrow.
       (4) Keep it simple. Don't include extra information or superimpose another histogram.

SOME CAUTIONS

1. Unequal ones tend to be confusing.
2. (a) No
   (b) With open intervals we may not know where the midpoints are. We can't tell how large the largest measurement in the interval is or how small the smallest measurement is.

3. They may be overlooked.
4. Too few may hide a single high or low reading. Too many may make it so flat that it's hard to see any patterns.
5. It may be confusing.
6. It may not be understandable.

WHAT FREQUENCY HISTOGRAMS TELL YOU ABOUT UNDERLYING FREQUENCY DISTRIBUTIONS

1. They may look different because the samples they are based on are different.
2. (a) The underlying frequency distribution.
   (b) It includes *all* of the items, not just a sample.
3. (a) They don't give a clear picture of the underlying frequency distribution.
   (b) The small samples are probably different from each other so the histograms will be different.
4. (a) To get a good idea of what the underlying frequency distribution looks like.
   (b) 100

FREQUENCY HISTOGRAMS IN PRODUCTION SITUATIONS

1. (a) When the amount of variation is so small that all measurements fit inside the specifications and the center of the histogram is at the center of the specifications.
   (b) Even if all measurements fall inside the specifications, a small percentage may actually be outside.
2. It doesn't tell us what happened over time.
3. (a) Even more measurements would be out of spec.
   (b) A management team.
   (c) (1) Reduce the variation.
       (2) Widen the specs.
       (3) Live with it.
4. (a) Make a simple adjustment to center the process halfway between the specs.
   (b) You must know how to make the adjustment.
   (c) A small portion may fall out of spec.
5. (a) There are *two* underlying frequency distributions, not one.
   (b) (1) Two machines feeding into the same bin of parts.
       (2) Two heads on one machine.
       (3) Two batches of material.
       (4) Two shifts performing differently.
   (c) If two machines are causing the two histograms, get histograms from each machine *separately*. Then adjust either, or both, to bring them into focus.

FREQUENCY HISTOGRAMS: EXERCISES, SERIES 1

1. **Set 1.** (smallest, largest)

(a) 68, 76	(h) 75, 80	(o) 74, 82
(b) 62, 82	(i) 73, 78	(p) 75, 83
(c) 76, 84	(j) 68, 80	(q) 74, 83
(d) 76, 83	(k) 71, 80	(r) 72, 78
(e) 72, 77	(l) 72, 80	(s) 70, 78
(f) 66, 81	(m) 71, 80	(t) 61, 80
(g) 70, 75	(n) 61, 78	

Set 2.

(a) .888, .986	(h) .901, .977	(o) .898, .935
(b) .884, .979	(i) .886, .949	(p) .925, .968
(c) .887, .984	(j) .871, .969	(q) .872, .984
(d) .884, .899	(k) .821, .948	(r) .858, .928
(e) .883, .986	(l) .885, .968	(s) .872, .970
(f) .893, .977	(m) .885, .948	(t) .883, 938
(g) .893, .949	(n) .884, .955	

Set 3.

(a) 26, 41	(h) 34, 42	(o) 30, 35
(b) 29, 43	(i) 32, 40	(p) 35, 40
(c) 29, 43	(j) 31, 40	(q) 21, 38
(d) 34, 42	(k) 32, 38	(r) 35, 43
(e) 27, 37	(l) 26, 41	(s) 28, 40
(f) 31, 40	(m) 34, 43	(t) 33, 38
(g) 21, 40	(n) 30, 38	

Set 4.

(a) 30, 50	(h) 16, 30	(o) 11, 49
(b) 23, 37	(i) 16, 45	(p) 26, 41
(c) 19, 52	(j) 21, 31	(q) 21, 33
(d) 24, 38	(k) 15, 44	(r) 10, 35
(e) 10, 44	(l) 13, 34	(s) 24, 38
(f) 21, 30	(m) 9, 50	(t) 16, 44
(g) 11, 27	(n) 16, 37	

2. *See the answer charts.*
3. *See the answer charts.*
4. (a) Divide the large interval into smaller ones.
   (b) 8
   (c) For convenience.
   (d) *See the answer charts.*
   (e) *See the answer charts.*
5. (a) To avoid guess work about which interval the reading falls into.
   (b) Use one more decimal place in the boundaries than in the readings.
6. Divide the width by 2, then add the result to the lower boundary.

7. (a) For each observation or reading, determine which interval it lies within and make a tally mark there.
    (b) Do a tally check—repeat the tallies, then total the frequencies to see if that equals the total sample size.
8. *See the answer charts.*
9. (a) Set 1. Small.
    Set 2. Small.
    Set 3. Large
    Set 4. Looks OK at first glance, but be careful! The variation uses nearly the entire width of the specifications. This could mean that product occasionally will be outside specs.
    (b) Set 1. No.
    Set 2. Yes.
    Set 3. No.
    Set 4. Yes.
    (c) Set 1. Adjust the center of the process
    Set 3. The process variation is too large for the specs.
    (d) Set 1. The production associate on site.
    Set 3. The management team.
    (e) Set 1. About 74
    Set 2. At 0.93
    Set 3. About 36
    Set 4. About 30
    (f) Set 1. Yes
    Set 2. Yes
    Set 3. No
    Set 4. Yes, but remember that the variation uses nearly the entire specification width. Product could occasionally be outside specs.
    (g) Set 1. For this case, no product would be outside spec.
    Set 2. For this case, no product would be outside spec.
    Set 3. A management team.
    Set 4. The production associate—if he or she can adjust and hold the center exactly where it should be. A management team should be aware that the variation in the process uses nearly the entire width of the specifications and should work with the associate(s) to reduce this variation.

FREQUENCY HISTOGRAMS: EXERCISES, SERIES 2

1. **Set 1.** (smallest, largest)

(a) 53, 61	(h) 48, 55	(o) 55, 61
(b) 50, 57	(i) 50, 57	(p) 52, 57
(c) 52, 58	(j) 52, 57	(q) 51, 59
(d) 48, 58	(k) 55, 59	(r) 52, 58
(e) 54, 62	(l) 52, 59	(s) 49, 55
(f) 50, 59	(m) 52, 56	(t) 55, 60
(g) 51, 57	(n) 53, 60	

Set 2.

(a) .107, .149	(h) .119, .144	(o) .111, .143
(b) .122, .148	(i) .112, .140	(p) .122, .140
(c) .107, .137	(j) .114, .145	(q) .133, .141
(d) .121, .177	(k) .123, .135	(r) .126, .146
(e) .110, .133	(l) .117, .133	(s) .126, .148
(f) .120, .151	(m) .130, .154	(t) .120, .150
(g) .107, .130	(n) .117, .140	

Set 3.

(a) 73, 81	(h) 68, 75	(o) 72, 80
(b) 68, 78	(i) 70, 82	(p) 69, 81
(c) 70, 83	(j) 70, 80	(q) 69, 77
(d) 70, 77	(k) 68, 83	(r) 70, 82
(e) 70, 77	(l) 67, 75	(s) 70, 73
(f) 67, 73	(m) 66, 78	(t) 74, 78
(g) 68, 75	(n) 70, 76	

Set 4.

(a) −5, 10	(h) −19, 13	(o) −16, 15
(b) 3, 11	(i) −8, 21	(p) −20, 3
(c) −4, 16	(j) −13, 10	(q) −23, 10
(d) −4, 18	(k) −10, 21	(r) −8, 7
(e) −10, 3	(l) −22, 0	(s) −8, 18
(f) −13, 16	(m) −11, 14	(t) −23, 13
(g) −1, 24	(n) −18, 6	

2. *See the answer charts.*
3. *See the answer charts.*
4. (a) Divide the large interval into smaller ones.
    (b) 8
    (c) For convenience.
    (d) *See the answer charts.*
    (e) *See the answer charts.*
5. (a) To avoid guess work about which interval the reading falls into.
    (b) Use one more decimal place for the boundaries than for the readings.
6. Divide the interval width by 2, then add the result to the lower boundary.
7. (a) For each observation or reading, determine which interval it lies within and make a tally mark there.
    (b) Do a tally check—repeat the tallies
8. *See the answer charts.*
9. (a) Set 1. Large.
    Set 2. Small.
    Set 3. Looks OK at first glance, but be cautious. The variation uses nearly the entire width of the specifications. This could mean that pieces will occasionally be produced out of spec.
    Set 4. Small.
    (b) Set 1. No.
    Set 2. No.
    Set 3. Yes.
    Set 4. Yes.

(c) Set 1. Process can't make all parts within specifications.
   Set 2. Must adjust the center.
(d) Set 1. Management team.
   Set 2. Production associate.
(e) Set 1. About 54.5
   Set 2. About 0.135
   Set 3. About 73.5
   Set 4. About 2
(f) Set 1. No.
   Set 2. Yes.

Set 3. Yes, probably.
Set 4. Yes.
(g) Set 1. Management team.
   Set 2. In this case, no product should be outside spec.
   Set 3. The associate on the floor should be able to center this process, but because the variation uses nearly the entire specification width, a management team should work with the associate to reduce the variation.
   Set 4. In this case, no product should be outside spec.

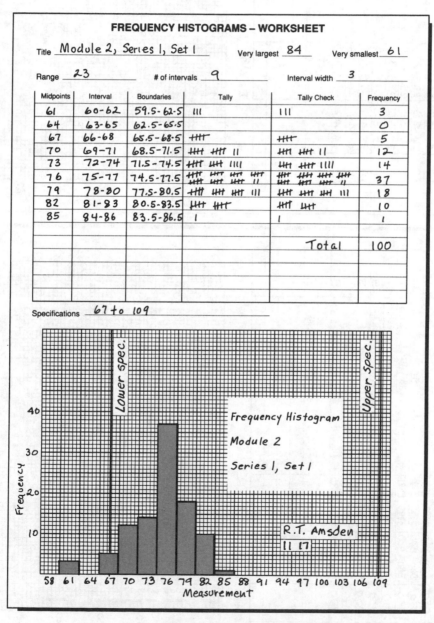

Module 2, Series 1, Set 1. Frequency histogram worksheet.

FREQUENCY HISTOGRAMS – WORKSHEET

Title _Module 2, Series 1, Set 3_   Very largest _43_   Very smallest _21_

Range _22_   # of intervals _8_   Interval width _3_

Midpoints	Interval	Boundaries	Tally	Tally Check	Frequency
21	20-22	19.5-22.5	11	11	2
24	23-25	22.5-25.5			0
27	26-28	25.5-28.5	卌	卌	5
30	29-31	28.5-31.5	卌 卌 卌 II	卌 卌 卌 II	17
33	32-34	31.5-34.5	卌 卌 卌	卌 卌 卌	15
36	35-37	34.5-37.5	卌 卌 卌 卌 卌 ,	卌 卌 卌 卌 卌 ,	31
39	38-40	37.5-40.5	卌 卌 卌 卌	卌 卌 卌 卌	20
42	41-43	40.5-43.5	卌 卌	卌 卌	10
45	44-46	43.5-46.5			0
				Total	100

Specifications _30 to 42_

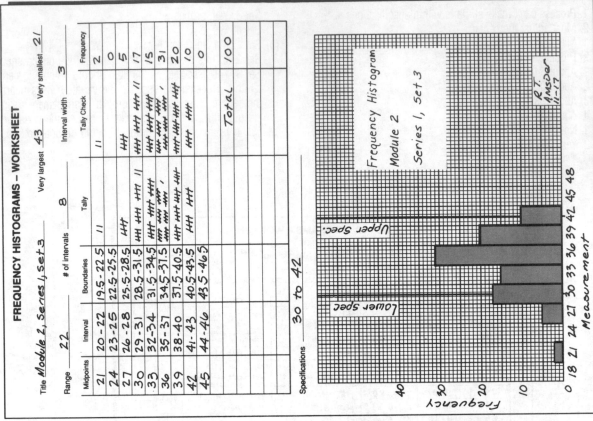

Frequency Histogram
Module 2
Series 1, Set 3

R.T. Amsder 11-17

Module 2, Series 1, Set 3. Frequency histogram worksheet.

FREQUENCY HISTOGRAMS – WORKSHEET

Title _Module 2, Series 1, Set 2_   Very largest _.986_   Very smallest _.82l_

Range _0.165_   # of intervals _9_   Interval width _.020_

Midpoints	Interval	Boundaries	Tally	Tally Check	Frequency
.830	.820-.840	.8195-.8395	I	I	1
.850	.840-.860	.8395-.8595	I	I	1
.870	.860-.880	.8595-.8795	III	III	3
.890	.880-.900	.8795-.8995	卌 卌 卌 卌 卌 卌 I	卌 卌 卌 卌 卌 卌 I	31
.910	.900-.920	.8995-.9195	卌	卌	5
.930	.920-.940	.9195-.9395	卌 卌 卌 卌 卌	卌 卌 卌 卌 卌	25
.950	.940-.960	.9395-.9595	卌 卌 卌 I	卌 卌 卌 I	15
.970	.960-.980	.9595-.9795	卌 卌 I	卌 卌 I	11
.990	.980-1.000	.9795-.9995	卌 III	卌 III	8
				Total	100

Specifications _.77 To 1.07_

Frequency Histogram
Module 2
Series 1, Set 2

R.T. Amsden 11-17

Module 2, Series 1, Set 2. Frequency histogram worksheet.

FREQUENCY HISTOGRAMS – WORKSHEET

Title _Module 2, Series 2, Set 1_

Range _14_   # of intervals _8_   Interval width _2_

Very largest _62_   Very smallest _48_

Midpoints	Interval	Boundaries	Tally	Tally Check	Frequency
48.5	48-49	47.5-49.5	111	111	3
50.5	50-51	49.5-51.5	5++ 111	5++ 111	8
52.5	52-53	51.5-53.5	5++ 5++ 5++ 5++ 1111	5++ 5++ 5++ 5++ 1111	24
54.5	54-55	53.5-55.5	5++ 5++ 5++ 5++ 111	5++ 5++ 5++ 5++ 111	23
56.5	56-57	55.5-57.5	5++ 5++ 5++ 5++ 1111	5++ 5++ 5++ 5++ 1111	24
58.5	58-59	57.5-59.5	5++ 5++ 1	5++ 5++ 1	11
60.5	60-61	59.5-61.5	5++ 1	5++ 1	6
62.5	62-63	61.5-63.5	1	1	1
			Total		100

Specifications _50.5 to 58.5_

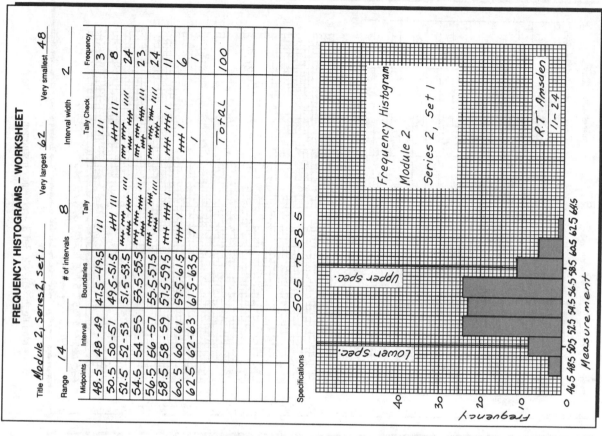

Module 2, Series 2, Set 1. Frequency histogram worksheet.

FREQUENCY HISTOGRAMS – WORKSHEET

Title _Module 2, Series 1, Set 4_

Range _43_   # of intervals _9_   Interval width _5_

Very largest _52_   Very smallest _9_

Midpoints	Interval	Boundaries	Tally	Tally Check	Frequency
10	8-12	7.5-12.5	5++	5++	5
15	13-17	12.5-17.5	5++ 11	5++ 11	7
20	18-22	17.5-22.5	5++ 5++	5++ 5++	10
25	23-27	22.5-27.5	5++ 5++ 5++ 1	5++ 5++ 5++ 1	16
30	28-32	27.5-32.5	5++ 5++ 5++ 5++ 5++ 111	5++ 5++ 5++ 5++ 5++ 111	28
35	33-37	32.5-37.5	5++ 5++ 5++ 11	5++ 5++ 5++ 11	17
40	38-42	37.5-42.5	5++ 11	5++ 11	7
45	43-47	42.5-47.5	5++ 1	5++ 1	6
50	48-52	47.5-52.5	1111	1111	4
			Total		100

Specifications _5 to 55_

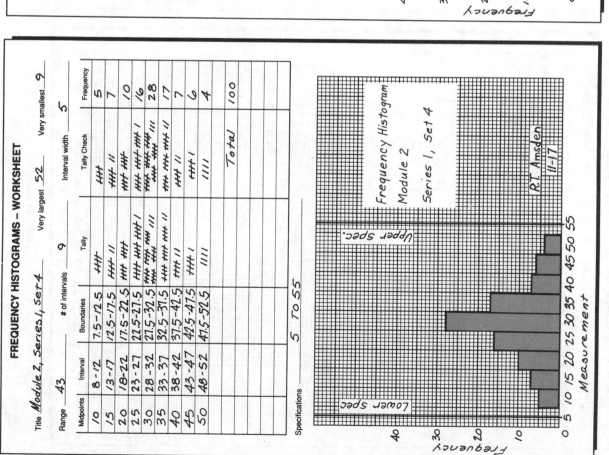

Module 2, Series 1, Set 4. Frequency histogram worksheet.

FREQUENCY HISTOGRAMS – WORKSHEET

Title _Module 2, Series 2, Set 3_   Very largest _83_   Very smallest _66_

Range _17_   # of intervals _9_   Interval width _2_

Midpoints	Interval	Boundaries	Tally	Tally Check	Frequency
66.5	66-67	65.5-67.5	///	///	3
68.5	68-69	67.5-69.5	++++ ////	++++ ////	9
70.5	70-71	69.5-71.5	++++ ++++ ++++ /	++++ ++++ ++++ /	16
72.5	72-73	71.5-73.5	++++ ++++ ++++ ++++ //	++++ ++++ ++++ ++++ //	22
74.5	74-75	73.5-75.5	++++ ++++ ++++ ++++ /	++++ ++++ ++++ ++++ /	21
76.5	76-77	75.5-77.5	++++ ++++ ++++	++++ ++++ ++++	15
78.5	78-79	77.5-79.5	++++ /	++++ /	6
80.5	80-81	79.5-81.5	////	////	4
82.5	82-83	81.5-83.5	////	////	4
				Total	100

Specifications _64.5 to 84.5_

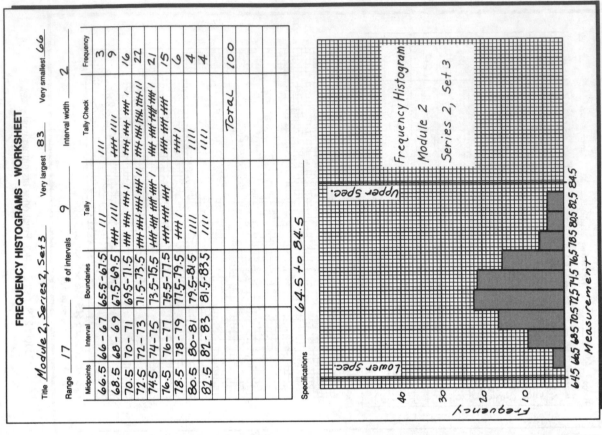

Module 2, Series 2, Set 3. Frequency histogram worksheet.

FREQUENCY HISTOGRAMS – WORKSHEET

Title _Module 2, Series 2, Set 2_   Very largest _0.07_   Very smallest _0.01_

Range _0.070_   # of intervals _8_   Interval width _0.11_

Midpoints	Interval	Boundaries	Tally	Tally Check	Frequency
.105	.100-.110	.1005-.1105	++++	++++	5
.115	.110-.120	.1105-.1205	++++ ++++ /	++++ ++++ /	11
.125	.120-.130	.1205-.1305	++++ ++++ ++++ ++++ ++++ ++++	++++ ++++ ++++ ++++ ++++ ++++	30
.135	.130-.140	.1305-.1405	++++ ++++ ++++ ++++ ++++ ++++ ++++	++++ ++++ ++++ ++++ ++++ ++++ ++++	35
.145	.140-.150	.1405-.1505	++++ ++++ ++++	++++ ++++ ++++	15
.155	.150-.160	.1505-.1605	///	///	3
.165	.160-.170	.1605-.1705			0
.175	.170-.180	.1705-.1805	/	/	1
				Total	100

Specifications _.115 to .245_

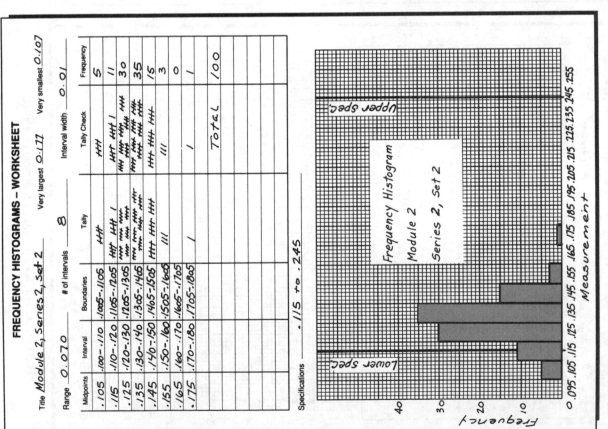

Module 2, Series 2, Set 2. Frequency histogram worksheet.

FREQUENCY HISTOGRAMS – WORKSHEET

Title _Module 2, Series 2, Set 4_   Very largest _24_   Very smallest _−23_

Range _47_   # of intervals _9_   Interval width _6_

Midpoints	Interval	Boundaries	Tally	Tally Check	Frequency
−22	−24, −19	−24.5, −18.5	＋＋＋	＋＋＋	5
−16	−18, −13	−18.5, −12.5	＋＋＋	＋＋＋	5
−10	−12, −7	−12.5, −6.5	＋＋＋ ＋＋＋ /	＋＋＋ ＋＋＋ /	11
−4	−6, −1	−6.5, −0.5	＋＋＋ ＋＋＋ ////	＋＋＋ ＋＋＋ ////	14
2	0, 5	−0.5, 5.5	＋＋＋ ＋＋＋ ＋＋＋ //	＋＋＋ ＋＋＋ ＋＋＋ //	17
8	6, 11	5.5, 11.5	＋＋＋ ＋＋＋ ///	＋＋＋ ＋＋＋ ///	13
14	12, 17	11.5, 17.5	＋＋＋ ＋＋＋	＋＋＋ ＋＋＋	10
20	18, 23	17.5, 23.5	////	////	4
26	24, 29	23.5, 29.5	/	/	1
				Total	80

Specifications _−46 to 44_

Module 2, Series 2, Set 4. Frequency histogram worksheet.

CHECKSHEETS: REVIEW QUESTIONS

1. Data that come from things you can measure, such as weight, time, or distance.
2. The checklist helps collect and analyze non-variable data easily in an organized manner.
3. (a) The frequency histogram checksheet.
   (b) The checklist checksheet.
   (c) The item checksheet.
   (d) The location checksheet.
   (e) The matrix checksheet.

THE FREQUENCY HISTOGRAM CHECKSHEET

1. Where the data are centered, the amount of variation, and the distribution of the data.
2. Data are handled only once because each observation is recorded directly on the checksheet allowing for fewer opportunities for errors that occur when transferring data. You may also spend less time.
3. When you already have some familiarity with the data and the time or order of the data is not important.
4. When the time or order of the data is important. By plotting the data on a frequency histogram checksheet, you lose the time component, or the order, of the data.

THE CHECKLIST CHECKSHEET

1. Use this type of checksheet to check off a list of items or tasks as they are completed.
2. You will find that there are many opportunities for using the type of checksheet in your work situation. For example, you can make a list of:
   (a) Steps in a process;
   (b) Ingredients in a chemical product;
   (c) Steps in a die changeover.

THE ITEM CHECKSHEET

1. This type of checksheet counts the number of times an item occurs.
2. (a) It serves as a partial analysis of the data because it is easy to see the size of each category of items.
   (b) We can easily use the data from the item checksheet in constructing a Pareto diagram.
3. Here are some possible checksheets:
   (a) Reasons for warranty repairs.
   (b) Types of defects in an enameling operation.
   (c) Types of customer complaints.

THE LOCATION CHECKSHEET

1. To show visually the location of the data you are collecting.
2. Here are some possible checksheets:
   (a) Location of defects on a classroom chalkboard.
   (b) Location of leaks in the seal of aquariums.
   (c) Location of soldering defects on a circuit board.

THE MATRIX CHECKSHEET

1. Two or more attributes of each observation.
2. Here are some possible examples:
   (a) Shutdowns of stamping presses by shifts.
   (b) Types of warranty claims by region.
   (c) Types of printing defects by types of print job.

CHECKSHEETS: EXERCISES, SERIES 1

FREQUENCY HISTOGRAM CHECKSHEET

The frequency histogram checksheets you have created give you a good idea of where the data are centered, the amount of variation in the process, and the distribution of the data. However, it may be difficult to determine from these checksheets how many of the measurements are out of specification. Use a probability plot, which is described in Module 5, if you need to determine the percentage of measurements that do not fall within the specification limits.

1. *See the answer checksheets.*
2. *See the answer checksheets.*
3. *See the answer checksheets.*
4. *See the answer checksheets.*
5. *See the answer checksheets.*
6. *See the answer checksheets.*
7. (a) Set 1. Small.
       Set 2. Small.
       Set 3. Large.
       Set 4. The variation is such that it uses almost all of the specification width.
   (b) Set 1. No.
       Set 2. Yes.
       Set 3. No.
       Set 4. Yes.
   (c) Set 1. About 76
       Set 2. About 0.93
       Set 3. About 36
       Set 4. About 30

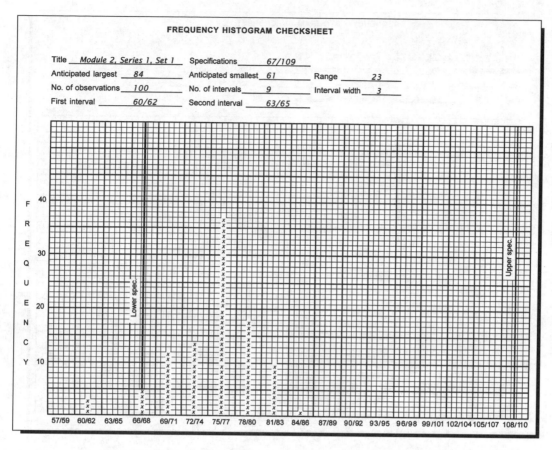

Module 2, Series 1, Set 1. Frequency histogram checksheet.

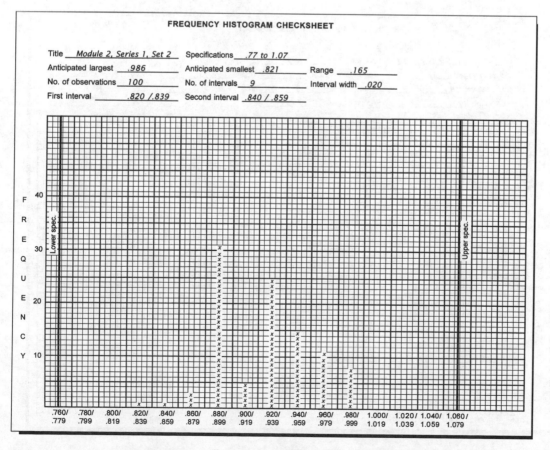

Module 2, Series 1, Set 2. Frequency histogram checksheet.

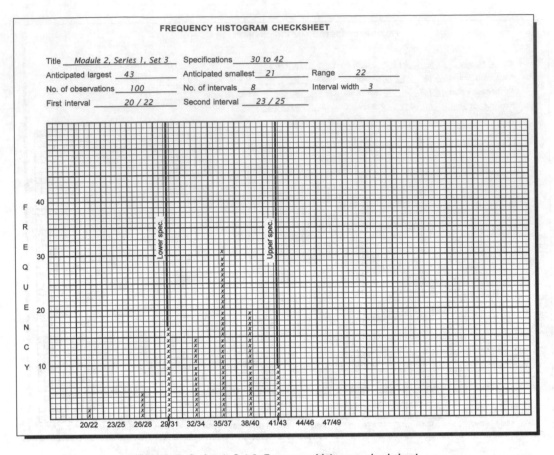

Module 2, Series 1, Set 3. Frequency histogram checksheet.

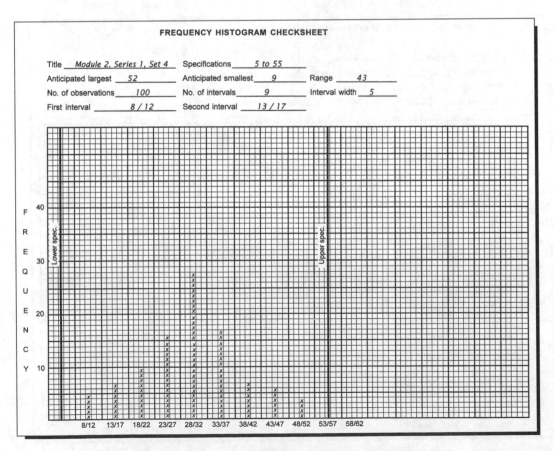

Module 2, Series 1, Set 4. Frequency histogram checksheet.

Checklist Checksheet for Starting Up a Die-Cut Envelope Operation	
1. Is work area around the die-cut press: Clean? Free of loose tools? Well lighted?	
2. Do we have correct paper: Weight? Color? Quantity?	
3. Is the paper placed correctly?	
4. Is the correct die ready and in place?	
5. Is machine maintenance up to date?	
6. Are the safety "Begin Cycle" buttons operating correctly?	
7. Turn on the press.	
8. Load paper onto press bed	
9. Position the die	
10. Activate press with two-hand "Begin Cycle" buttons	

Module 2, Series 1, Question 1. Checklist checksheet.

CHECKLIST CHECKSHEET

1. Because the checklist checksheet for an example from your workplace depends on your specific situation, we will illustrate how it might look for the startup of a die-cut envelope operation.
2. Here is our checklist checksheet for changing an automobile tire. How does yours compare?

ITEM CHECKSHEET

1. Here is the item checksheet for defects in the plastic parts. How does yours compare? Did you remember to make a label for the date, part number, and notes for future reference? Did you leave extra space for other defect types you may discover?
2. Here is the item checksheet we designed for the labeling operation. How does yours compare? Did you remember to make a place for the date, shift, which labeling machine, and notes? Did you leave extra space for other things you may find?

LOCATION CHECKSHEETS

1 & 2. Location checksheets are very specific to your workplace. Therefore, ask yourself the following questions.
   1. Do your location checksheets clearly show the location of whatever you are investigating? Could anyone easily locate the actual items?
   2. Is the date recorded?
   3. Is your name recorded?
   4. Have you made a space for any notes on the checksheet?
   5. If it is important to record the number of incidences per location, have you left enough room for it on your checksheet?

MATRIX CHECKSHEET

1. Here is our matrix checksheet for Tasty Pastry Bakery. How does the one you developed compare?
2. This is our matrix checksheet for heat treat processes and times. How does yours compare?

Checklist Checksheet for Changing an Automobile Tire	
1. Be sure car and you are safely out of traffic	
2. Set parking brakes firmly and put transmission into "Park"	
3. Set up warning devices (flare, etc.) to warn traffic	
4. Check to make sure tire is flat and not bulging because it rests on a stone or curb	
5. Consult owner's manual to see where to place car jack underneath car	
6. Remove spare tie, jack, jack handle, and lugnut wrench	
7. Check wheel at end of car opposite flat	
8. Place jack in prescribed position; raise car so that flat tire is almost free to rotate, but not quite.	
9. Remove hub cap Loosen and remove lugnuts	
10. Raise car and wheel more than enough to be able to remove flat tire	
11. Remove flat tire and wheel from car	
12. Put spare tire and wheel on the car	
13. Manually replace all lugnuts and hand tighten	
14. Lower spare tire and car just enough so that the spare tire won't turn when wrenching the lugnuts	
15. Using lugnut wrench, tighten lugnuts firmly. You may need to use your foot on the wrench	
16. Lower car and wheel so that jack can be removed	
17. Replace hub cap	
18. Put flat tire into spare tire well and lock in place. Replace jack, jack handle, and lugnut wrench	
19. Retrieve emergency warning devices	
20. Say "thanks!" and drive to a service station to have tire repaired	

Module 2, Series 1, Question 2. Checklist checksheet.

Item Checksheet for Defects in Plastic Parts	
Defect Type	*Number*
Excess flashing	
Torn	
Cracked	
Discoloration	
Too Soft	
Too Hard	
Holes	
Breaks	
Part No.: Date: Shift:	
Associate:	
Notes:	

Module 2, Series 1, Question 1. Item checksheet.

Item Checksheet for Labeling Operation	
Mislabeling	*Number*
Labels misprinted	
Labels unclear/smudged	
Labeling machine not working properly	
Problem with glue	
Torn labels	
Wrong labels	
Not enough labels	
No labels	
Date: Shift: Machine:	
Associate:	
Notes:	

Module 2, Series 1, Question 2. Item checksheet.

Matrix Checksheet for
Tasty Pastry Bakery

	Machine A	*Machine B*	*Machine C*
Mixer sticks			
Mixer not clean			
Oil leak			
Motor overheats			
Speed too fast			
Speed too slow			
Date:	Shift:		Associate:
Notes:			

Module 2, Series 1, Question 1. Matrix checksheet.

Matrix Checksheet for
Heat Treat Process

Heat treat	*Time*			
	T1	T2	T3	T4
H1				
H2				
Date:	Associate:			
Notes:				

Module 2, Series 1, Question 2. Matrix checksheet.

CHECKSHEETS: EXERCISES, SERIES 2

FREQUENCY HISTOGRAM CHECKSHEET

The frequency histogram checksheets you have created give you a good idea of where the data are centered, the amount of variation in the process, and the distribution of the data. However, it may be difficult to determine from these checksheets how many of the measurements are out of specification. Use a probability plot, which is described in Module 5, if you need to determine the percentage of measurements that do not fall within the specification limits.

1. *See the answer checksheets.*
2. *See the answer checksheets.*
3. *See the answer checksheets.*
4. *See the answer checksheets.*
5. *See the answer checksheets.*
6. *See the answer checksheets.*
7. (a) Set 1. Large.
    Set 2. Small.
    Set 3. The variation is such that it uses almost all of the specification width.
    Set 4. Small.
   (b) Set 1. No.
    Set 2. No.

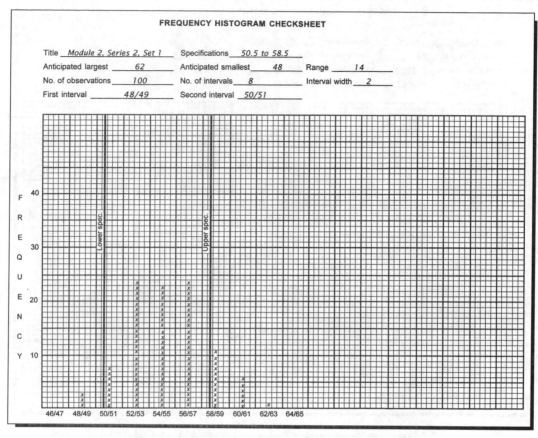

Module 2, Series 2, Set 1. Frequency histogram checksheet.

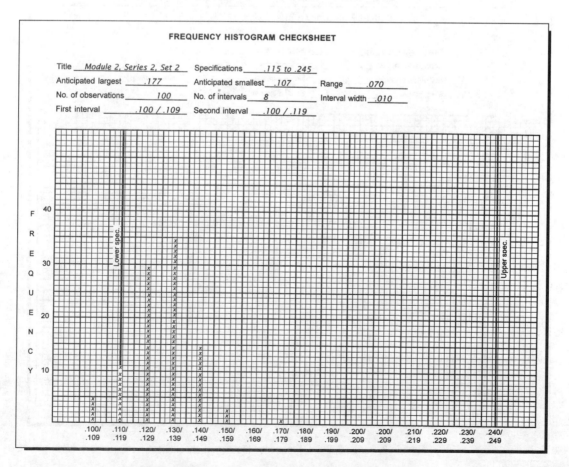

Module 2, Series 2, Set 2. Frequency histogram checksheet.

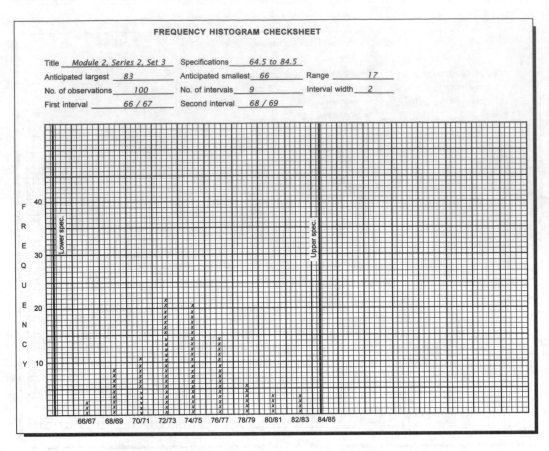

Module 2, Series 2, Set 3. Frequency histogram checksheet.

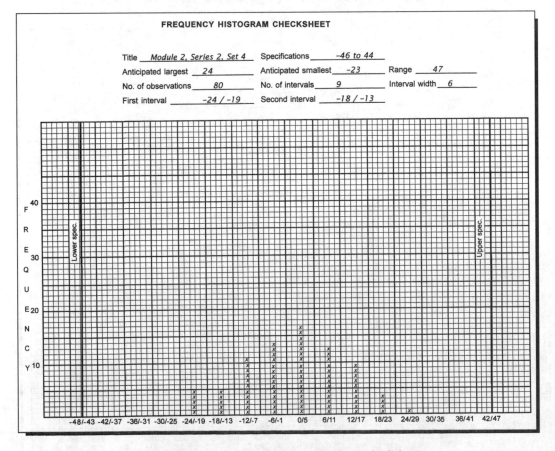

Module 2, Series 2, Set 4. Frequency histogram checksheet.

Set 3. Yes.
Set 4. Yes.
(c) Set 1. About 54.5
Set 2. About 0.134
Set 3. About 74.5
Set 4. About 2.5

CHECKLIST CHECKSHEET

1. This is one possible list of emergency items. How does your list compare? Note that we have left space to write in additional items as we think of them.
2. The following is an example of a checklist checksheet for the operation of two injection molds.

ITEM CHECKSHEET

1. This is the item checksheet we developed for defects in a soldering process. How does it compare to the one you created? What other defects can you think of?
2. Here is the item checksheet we developed. How does yours compare? If there are warranty problems with several models of the filtration units, you would probably want to keep a record on each model, so include a space for recording the model number.

LOCATION CHECKSHEET

1 & 2. Location checksheets are very specific to your workplace. Therefore, ask yourself the following questions:
1. Does your location checksheet clearly show where the baskets are situated, for example, so that someone could easily locate them on the plant floor?
2. Is the date recorded?
3. Is your name recorded?
4. Have you made a space for any notes on the checksheet?
5. If it is important to record the number of incidences per location, have you left enough room for it on your checksheet?

MATRIX CHECKSHEET

1. The matrix checksheet shown is one way you could have set up the matrix. There are 12 spaces beneath each class for the name of the participants. Doing it this way gives the instructor a rough idea who will be in the class. Other information you could include would be the times when the classes are to be offered. How does the matrix checksheet you prepared compare to this one?
2. This is the matrix checksheet for the audit inspections at E.M. Envelope Company. How does yours compare to this one? What label information did you include?

Checklist Checksheet for a Home Emergency Kit	
Flashlight with batteries Tweezers with fine points Scissors Jack knife Safety pins, assorted sizes Rubber gloves Rubbing alcohol Hydrogen peroxide 3% Household ammonia Mild soap Baking soda Table salt Activated charcoal Petroleum jelly	Band-Aids Adhesive tape Plain sterile gauze Sterile gauze pads Cloth bandage (assorted sizes) Large sanitary pads Sterile cotton Q-Tips Heating pad Blanket

Module 2, Series 2, Question 1. Matrix checksheet.

Checklist Checksheet for New Associate Learning Operation of Two Simultaneous Injection Molds	
1. Check supply of vinyl pellets in supply tank	
2. Check temperature of mold, machine #1	
3. Visually inspect condition of mold, machine #1	
4. Check temperature of mold, machine #2	
5. Visually inspect condition of mold, machine #2	
6. Place metal insert into mold, machine #1	
7. Close guard gate	
8. Press "Cycle Begin" button	
9. Move to machine #2	
10. Place metal insert into mold, machine #2	
11. Close guard gate	
12. Press "Cycle Begin" button	
13. Return to machine #1	
14. When machine cycle ends, open gate, remove product	
15. Inspect product. Remove flashing. Place product on hanger on dolly.	
16. Place metal insert into mold	
17. (Continue operations above, going back and forth between the two machines)	

Module 2, Series 2, Question 2. Checklist checksheet.

Item Checksheet for Defects in Soldering Process			
Defect Type	*Number of Occurrences*		
Commutator			
Wire breaks			
Short circuits			
Dirt			
Resistance			
Solder			
Other			
Date:	Shift:	Associate:	
Notes:			

Module 2, Series 2, Question 1. Item checksheet.

Item Checksheet for Warranty Claims on Filter Unit	
Defect Type	*Number of Defects*
Scratches on filter tank	
Filter motor is noisy	
Motor won't function or sticks	
Component missing	
Electrical short	
Defective return tube	
Other	
Date:	Model No.: Associate:
Notes:	

Module 2, Series 2, Question 2. Item checksheet.

	Class A	Class B	Class C	Class D	Class E	Class F	Class G	Class H
Matrix Checksheet for Training Sessions—Merrimac Plant								
1								
2								
3								
4								
5								
6								
7								
8								
9								
10								
11								
12								

Module 2, Series 2, Question 1. Matrix checksheet.

Matrix Checksheet for Envelope Inspections									
		Machine							
		1	*2*	*3*	*4*	*5*	*6*	*7*	*Total*
Shift 1	Reject								
	OK								
Shift 2	Reject								
	OK								
Shift 3	Reject								
	OK								
Totals	Reject								
	OK								

Directions: Enter 1 tally mark for each sample of 100 envelopes audited. If 8 or more envelopes defective, tally as "Reject." If 7 or less defective, tally as "OK."

Notes:

Date:

Module 2, Series 2, Question 2. Matrix checksheet.

FREQUENCY HISTOGRAMS: ANALYSIS AND DISCUSSION OF CASE STUDIES

CASE 2-1

When constructing a frequency histogram you must determine the range of the values in the data. The data in this problem are listed such that you can identify the largest and the smallest values in each group of five values or in each column of values. From these values you can easily determine the very largest and the very smallest values in the manner described in the textbook.

The total number of measurements recorded is 125. The range of these values is determined to be 804 minus 741, or 63. By referring to Table 2-4 in the textbook, we see that seven to 12 class intervals are best for developing a frequency histogram when there are more than 100 measurements in the data. When the range (63) is divided by 12, we arrive at a class interval size of 5.25; when we divide by 10, we arrive at 6.3. Dividing the range by 7, the smallest number of intervals shown in the guidelines in Table 2-4, we arrive at a class interval of 9.0. It is reasonable to choose a class interval of either 5.0 or 6.0 when developing a frequency histogram based on this amount of data (125 measure-

ments). A class interval of 9 may cause the frequency histogram to be too narrow to detect variation in the output of the operation. We will show and discuss frequency histograms developed using all three values, so you can compare your graph with ours if you used 5.0, 6.0, or 9.0.

The 5.25 was rounded off to 5.0, so each class interval for this graph is five gram values wide. In other words, the measurements are grouped into about 12 intervals, each five gram values wide. There is an interval containing only one value at the far left end of the graph, which will be discussed later. The frequency histogram work sheet (Figure 2-A) used for this problem shows the class intervals to be 738/742, 743/747, 748/752, 753/757, and so on up to 803/807. (All numbers are expressed in grams.)

In each class the boundaries are set at five-tenths of a gram below the lower value and five-tenths of a gram above the upper value of the class interval. As you can see on the graph, the upper boundary of one class interval and the lower boundary of the next class interval are the same value. The boundary is the line or value separating the intervals; none of the measurements can fall on it.

The midpoints are 740, 745, 750, 755, 760, 765, and so on up to 805 grams. These are the middle values between each pair of boundaries;

they represent all of the measurements that fall within the boundaries of each class interval.

The longest bar on the graph shows a frequency of 22 at the class interval that has a midpoint of 780. The rest of the stock preparation weights are distributed on either side of that class interval. The last bar on the right-hand side of the graph is at the class interval that has a midpoint of 805. The bar is one-fourth the height of the heavy horizontal line, which represents a frequency of four. This means that one piece of material was weighed and found to be within the class interval of 803/807. That piece did not necessarily weigh 805 grams; it could have been any weight from 803 to 807 grams.

The last bar on the left-hand side of the graph is at the class interval that has a midpoint of 740. This bar shows that there is one piece in this class interval; there is an empty class interval between it and the rest of the measurements. Closer examination of the graph shows that the measurements tail off farther to the left of the middle of the graph than to the right. The overall shape of the graph approaches the shape of the bell-shaped curve, which indicates a normal distribution, but it is not a perfect fit. This lack of fit, along with the one measurement that is separated from the rest of the data, could be an indication that things were not normal, that is, bell-shaped, at all times when the measurements were taken.

Keep in mind that the frequency histogram is useful for giving you an overall picture of the average output of a process and showing the shape of the distribution of the measurements about that average. It is not a precise tool, however. It cannot signal precisely when something non-normal is happening in the process.

When the specification limits are drawn on the histogram, you can see that none of the bars of the graph is near the lower specification limit of 730 grams. This shows that we should not expect any individual pieces of stock to be at or below 730 grams. Therefore we can conclude that the stock preparation operation is set up to assure that all cavities in the molding operation will be filled completely.

You were also asked to state whether the operation is set up to assure that all cavities would be filled and that the use of material would be minimized. The position of the graph relative to the specification limits shows that if the average weight of the pieces coming from the operation was reduced slightly, the left-hand end of the graph might still be above the lower specification limit. This step would reduce the amount of material used in the molding of parts, but you must remember that this frequency histogram provides only a general view of the output of the operation. As a result, we cannot answer this question with a high degree of confidence. We can only make a guess, and say that the average weight of the pieces coming from the stock preparation operation could be adjusted downward slightly to minimize the use of material. There are more precise statistical tools that we can use to answer this question.

If you used a class interval of 6.0, the frequency histogram you developed will have 11 class intervals. (See Figure 2-B.) The class intervals shown on this histogram are 740/745, 746/751, 752/757, 758/763, and so on up to 800/805. The boundaries are five-tenths of a gram above and below the limits of the class intervals. The midpoints of the

class intervals are 742, 748, 754, 760, 766, and so on up to 802. Note that these values are not exactly the midpoints of the class intervals. The true midpoint of the interval 740/745 is 742.5, but it is easier simply to call it 742 and not to bother with the decimal because the midpoint represents all numbers from 740 to 745 anyway.

You will note that this histogram is "bunched up" slightly more than the histogram in Figure 2-A because there are fewer class intervals. The longest bar on this histogram is at interval 778, whereas in Figure 2-A it is at interval 780. The longest bar contains 27 measurements. The bar farthest to the right is at the 802 interval, and contains four measurements. The bars to the left of the bar at interval 778 are spread out more widely than those to the right.

The two frequency histograms in Figures 2-A and 2-B show essentially the same characteristics. The shapes of both histograms are somewhat like a bell-shaped curve. They both tend to tail off to the left; the bar at the left end is close to the lower specification limit but not outside it. Either frequency histogram would be equally useful in this case.

The frequency histogram shown in Figure 2-C was constructed with a class interval of 9.0, resulting in a graph that is narrower than the two discussed before. This frequency histogram shows almost as much about the output of the stock preparation operation as the other two. The possibility that something non-normal was occurring when the measurements were taken is not nearly so apparent. This frequency histogram appears to fit the bell-shaped curve more closely than the other two because when a large class interval is used, the chart will be narrower. As a result, non-normal variations in the data will be hidden.

It is a good idea to construct more than one frequency histogram from the same data if you have trouble making a decision on the basis of your first histogram. When two frequency histograms tell you the same story, as do Figures 2-A and 2-B, you may want to take additional measurements and develop another histogram to confirm or deny what the first ones told you. Frequency histograms can be developed quickly and easily, often with small numbers of measurements, so you can use them to build confidence in decisions made at production operations.

CASE 2-2

This problem asks you to recommend which of two production setups should be run to fill current orders. A frequency histogram often can quickly provide the information necessary to make the best decision.

The two production setups are identified as Hammer #2—Die #1 and Hammer #3—Die #2. If you constructed the frequency histograms using the measurements from each production setup and followed the general rules for constructing frequency histograms, you should have made two graphs similar to those shown in Figures 2-D and 2-E. The range of values for Figure 2-D is .030 because the smallest measurement is .000 and the largest is .030. When you divide this range by 10 (the number of class intervals desired), you will obtain a class interval of .003. As can be seen, the class intervals for the graph are .000/.002, .003/.005, .006/.008, and so on up to .030/.032. The midpoints for these class intervals are .001, .004, .007, .010, and so on up to .031.

FREQUENCY HISTOGRAMS – WORKSHEET

Title: STOCK PREPARATION Very largest: 804 Very smallest: 74L

Range: 63 # of intervals: 11 Interval width: 6

Midpoints	Interval	Boundaries	Tally	Tally Check	Frequency
742	740 – 745	739.5/745.5	I	I	1
748	746 – 751	745.5/751.5	IIII	IIII	4
754	752 – 757	751.5/757.5	ĦĦ IIII	ĦĦ IIII	9
760	758 – 763	757.5/763.5	ĦĦ IIII	ĦĦ IIII	9
766	764 – 769	763.5/769.5	ĦĦ ĦĦ I	ĦĦ ĦĦ I	11
772	770 – 775	769.5/775.5	ĦĦ ĦĦ I	ĦĦ ĦĦ I	11
778	776 – 781	775.5/781.5	ĦĦ ĦĦ ĦĦ ĦĦ ĦĦ II	ĦĦ ĦĦ ĦĦ ĦĦ ĦĦ II	27
784	782 – 787	781.5/787.5	ĦĦ ĦĦ ĦĦ ĦĦ IIII	ĦĦ ĦĦ ĦĦ ĦĦ IIII	24
790	788 – 793	787.5/793.5	ĦĦ ĦĦ IIII	ĦĦ ĦĦ IIII	14
796	794 – 799	793.5/799.5	ĦĦ ĦĦ I	ĦĦ ĦĦ I	11
802	800 – 805	799.5/805.5	IIII	IIII	4
808	806 – 811	805.5/811.5			

Total 125

Specifications: 730 to 790 GM

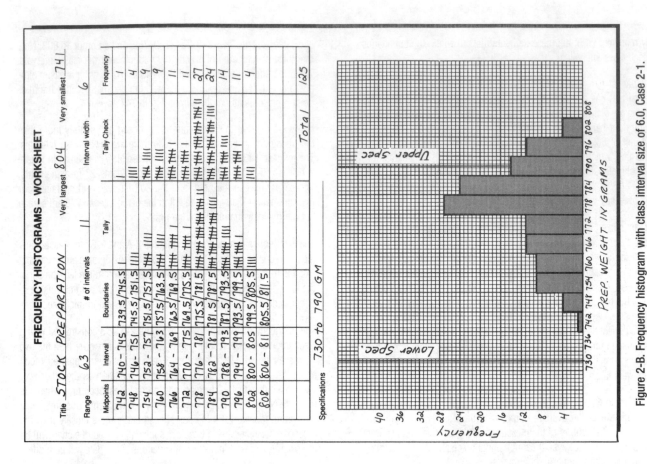

Figure 2-B. Frequency histogram with class interval size of 6.0, Case 2-1.

FREQUENCY HISTOGRAMS – WORKSHEET

Title: STOCK PREPARATION Very largest: 804 Very smallest: 74L

Range: 63 # of intervals: 14 Interval width: 5

Midpoints	Interval	Boundaries	Tally	Tally Check	Frequency
740	738 – 742	737.5/742.5	I	I	1
745	743 – 747	742.5/747.5	ĦĦ	ĦĦ	5
750	748 – 752	747.5/752.5	ĦĦ III	ĦĦ III	8
755	753 – 757	752.5/757.5	ĦĦ II	ĦĦ II	7
760	758 – 762	757.5/762.5	ĦĦ ĦĦ I	ĦĦ ĦĦ I	11
765	763 – 767	762.5/767.5	ĦĦ II	ĦĦ II	7
770	768 – 772	767.5/772.5	ĦĦ ĦĦ IIII	ĦĦ ĦĦ IIII	14
775	773 – 777	772.5/777.5	ĦĦ ĦĦ ĦĦ ĦĦ II	ĦĦ ĦĦ ĦĦ ĦĦ II	22
780	778 – 782	777.5/782.5	ĦĦ ĦĦ ĦĦ ĦĦ I	ĦĦ ĦĦ ĦĦ ĦĦ I	21
785	783 – 787	782.5/787.5	ĦĦ ĦĦ II	ĦĦ ĦĦ II	12
790	788 – 792	787.5/792.5	ĦĦ IIII	ĦĦ IIII	9
795	793 – 797	792.5/797.5	ĦĦ II	ĦĦ II	7
800	798 – 802	797.5/802.5	I	I	1
805	803 – 807	802.5/807.5			

Total 125

Specifications: 730 to 790 GM

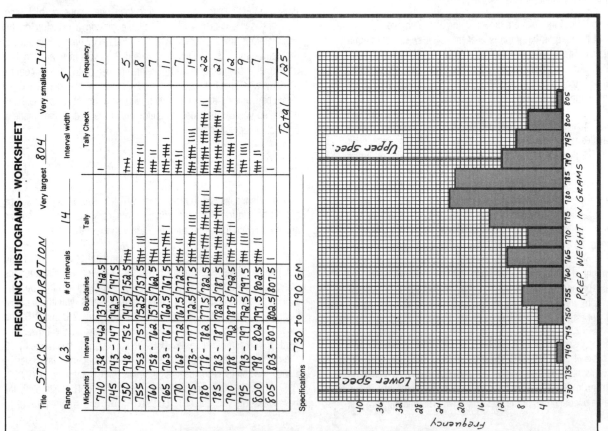

Figure 2-A. Frequency histogram with class interval size of 5.0, Case 2-1.

FREQUENCY HISTOGRAMS – WORKSHEET

Title **HAMMER #2 – DIE #1**

Range __.030__   Very largest __.030__   Very smallest __.003__

# of intervals __11__   Interval width __.003__

Midpoints	Interval	Boundaries	Tally	Tally Check	Frequency
.001	0 – .002	0 / .0025	IIII	IIII	4
.004	.003 – .005	.0025/.0055			10
.007	.006 – .008	.0055/.0085			10
.010	.009 – .011	.0085/.0115			15
.013	.012 – .014	.0115/.0145			14
.016	.015 – .017	.0145/.0175			20
.019	.018 – .020	.0175/.0205			13
.022	.021 – .023	.0205/.0235			8
.025	.024 – .026	.0235/.0265			5
.028	.027 – .029	.0265/.0295			
.031	.030 – .032	.0295/.0325	I	I	1
.034	.033 – .035	.0325/.0355			
.037	.036 – .038	.0355/.0385			
.040	.039 – .041	.0385/.0415			
				Total	100

Specifications __.000 to .040__

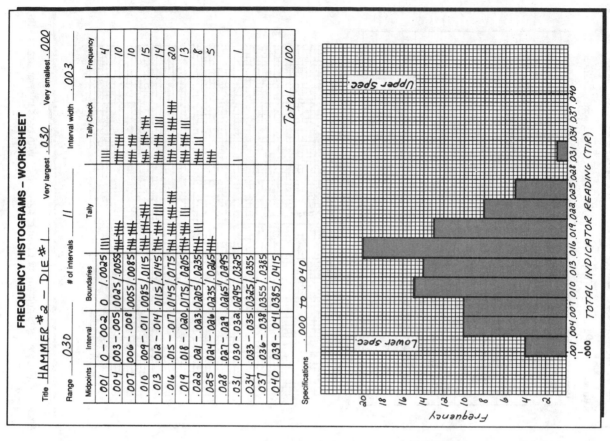

Figure 2-D. Frequency histogram for Hammer #2—Die #1 with class interval size of .003, Case 2-2.

FREQUENCY HISTOGRAMS – WORKSHEET

Title __STOCK PREPARATION__   Very largest __804__   Very smallest __741__

Range __63__   # of intervals __8__   Interval width __9__

Midpoints	Interval	Boundaries	Tally	Tally Check	Frequency
732	728 – 736	727.5/736.5	I		1
741	737 – 745	736.5/745.5			6
750	746 – 754	745.5/754.5			16
759	755 – 763	754.5/763.5			16
768	764 – 772	763.5/772.5			33
777	773 – 781	772.5/781.5			33
786	782 – 790	781.5/790.5			16
795	791 – 799	790.5/799.5			4
804	800 – 808	799.5/808.5			
813	809 – 817	808.5/817.5			
				Total	125

Specifications __730 to 790 GM__

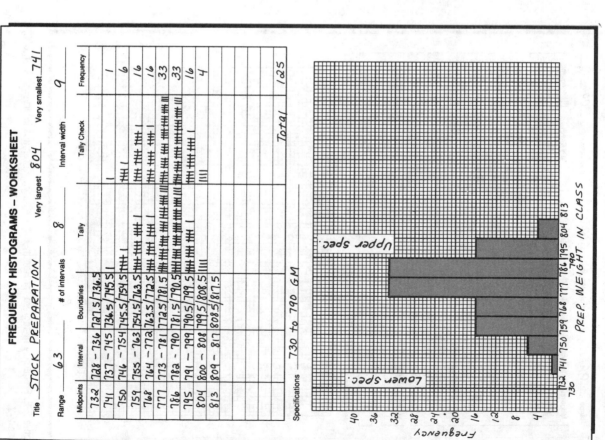

Figure 2-C. Frequency histogram with class interval size of 9.0, Case 2-1.

FREQUENCY HISTOGRAMS – WORKSHEET

Title __HAMMER #2 – DIE #1__

Range __.030__   # of intervals __6__   Very largest __.030__   Very smallest __.000__   Interval width __.006__

Midpoints	Interval	Boundaries	Tally	Tally Check	Frequency
.002	0 - .005	0 / .0055	ҵ ҵ ҵ IIII	ҵ ҵ IIII	14
.008	.006 - .011	.0055 / .0115	ҵ ҵ ҵ ҵ ҵ	ҵ ҵ ҵ ҵ ҵ	25
.014	.012 - .017	.0115 / .0175	ҵ ҵ ҵ ҵ ҵ ҵ IIII	ҵ ҵ ҵ ҵ ҵ ҵ IIII	34
.020	.018 - .023	.0175 / .0235	ҵ ҵ ҵ ҵ I	ҵ ҵ ҵ ҵ I	21
.026	.024 - .029	.0235 / .0295	ҵ	ҵ	5
.032	.030 - .035	.0295 / .0355	I	I	1
.038	.036 - .041	.0355 / .0415			
.044	.042 - .047	.0415 / .0475			
.050	.048 - .053	.0475 / .0535			
.056	.054 - .059	.0535 / .0595			
.062	.060 - .065	.0595 / .0655			
.068	.066 - .071	.0655 / .0715		Total	100

Specifications __.000 to .040__

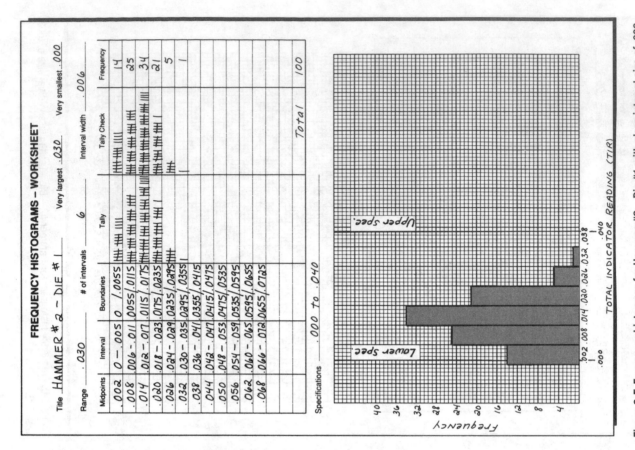

Figure 2-F. Frequency histogram for Hammer #2—Die #1 with class interval size of .006, Case 2-2.

FREQUENCY HISTOGRAMS – WORKSHEET

Title __HAMMER #3 – DIE #2__

Range __.065__   # of intervals __12__   Very largest __.066__   Very smallest __.001__   Interval width __.006__

Midpoints	Interval	Boundaries	Tally	Tally Check	Frequency
.002	0 - .005	0 / .0055	ҵ I	ҵ I	6
.008	.006 - .011	.0055 / .0115	ҵ ҵ ҵ ҵ I	ҵ ҵ ҵ ҵ I	21
.014	.012 - .017	.0115 / .0175	ҵ ҵ ҵ ҵ ҵ ҵ	ҵ ҵ ҵ ҵ ҵ ҵ	30
.020	.018 - .023	.0175 / .0235	ҵ ҵ ҵ ҵ I	ҵ ҵ ҵ ҵ I	21
.026	.024 - .029	.0235 / .0295	ҵ IIII	ҵ IIII	9
.032	.030 - .035	.0295 / .0355	ҵ I	ҵ I	6
.038	.036 - .041	.0355 / .0415	II	II	2
.044	.042 - .047	.0415 / .0475	I	I	1
.050	.048 - .053	.0475 / .0535	III	III	3
.056	.054 - .059	.0535 / .0595			
.062	.060 - .065	.0595 / .0655			
.068	.066 - .071	.0655 / .0715	I	Total	100

Specifications __.000 to .040__

Figure 2-E. Frequency histogram for Hammer #3—Die #2 with class interval size of .006, Case 2-2.

In developing the frequency histogram for the set of measurements from Hammer #3—Die #2, as shown in Figure 2-E, we find the range for the measurements to be .065 because the smallest measurement is .001 and the largest is .066. Dividing this range by 10, we obtain .0065, so we establish a class interval of .006 for the graph. These intervals are .000/.005, .006/.011, .012/.017, .018/.023, and so on up to .066/.071. Here again, we have designated the midpoints to be numbers that are easy to handle. Instead of calling the midpoint for the first class interval .0025, we call it .002. The next midpoint is .008, the next .014, and so on.

The tolerance lines are placed on these two frequency histograms to show how measurements from each production setup relate to the specification of a total indicator reading of .040. That is, any individual part in which the concentricity of the two cylindrical sections is not more than .040 is considered acceptable.

In selecting the production setup that should be used for current orders, you should compare the two frequency histograms for the shape of the graph and to see how each one fits to the specification lines. When looking at the shape of the graph, note that this dimension under consideration is somewhat different from most dimensions analyzed with a frequency histogram. Concentricity is considered to be best when the measured value is zero. Normally we look at a frequency histogram to see how well it would fit a bell-shaped curve, but this is not always the case in working with concentricity measurements. The operations producing the best concentricity dimension will turn out parts with measurements that are close to zero. Most of the measurements will be at or near zero, and the rest will tail off to the right on a graph. The frequency histograms of such an operation would look like half a bell-shaped curve with the peak at or near zero and tailing off to the right.

Neither the graph in Figure 2-D nor in Figure 2-E shows a tendency to peak at or near zero. Therefore you should look for the peak or the highest bar of each graph to see which has the peak closer to zero and how far each set of measurements tails off to the right. When making this comparison, keep in mind that the two graphs are constructed on the basis of two different scales: the class interval is .003 for Figure 2-D and .006 for Figure 2-E. This difference would cause the two graphs to look different even if the measurements were exactly alike. In addition, the frequency scale (the scale used to determine how tall the bar will be to represent a given number of parts) is different for the two graphs.

For ease of comparison, it is a good idea to use the same class interval and frequency scales for both frequency histograms. Figure 2-F is a frequency histogram constructed with the measurements from Hammer #2—Die #1 but with the same class interval and frequency scale as in Figure 2-E. These two frequency histograms can be compared more easily than Figures 2-D and 2-E. It can be estimated that the two production setups are set at about the same average. The spreads of the two graphs are seen to be different. The frequency histogram for Hammer #2—Die #1 shows that all the bars of the graph are inside the specification lines. The frequency histogram for Hammer #3—Die #2 shows that some of the measurements are outside the specification limit. The shape of this graph shows a greater tendency to extend to the right than does the graph for Hammer #2—Die #1. This may be a signal that something was not normal during the production run. Keep in mind, however, that we cannot confidently make any estimates about

the relative stability of the two operations from the analysis of the frequency histograms.

When comparing the two frequency histograms constructed with the same scale and class interval, it is relatively easy to recommend that Hammer #2—Die #1 be used to run current orders. Do you agree?

CASE 2-3

In taking measurements for statistical analysis of a manufacturing operation, it is important that the data be in a form that will be most usable for the analysis. The dimension under consideration must be measured with a degree of precision that will show the variation present in the operation. The dimension that concerns us in this problem is 323.0 ± 3.2 millimeters. The lower limit is 319.8 mm and the upper limit is 326.2 mm. The measurements should have been taken and recorded to at least the nearest tenth of a millimeter because the dimension is specified to that degree. You will find that sometimes the measurements have been taken before you are asked to analyze them. This is the situation in this problem; the analysis has been made and the frequency histogram is shown in Figure 2-G.

The measurements in this problem contain only five measurement values, which vary from 321.0 mm to 325.0 mm. The best frequency histogram that can be constructed with this data will have only five class intervals.

This frequency histogram is centered between the specification lines. Therefore we can say that the process is centered on the specified dimension. The graph does not contain enough class intervals to enable us to make a judgment about the normality or stability of the process. We cannot say that the graph fits the bell-shaped curve, which would be an indication of process stability. Neither can we say that it does not fit the bell-shaped curve, which would be an indication of assignable causes.

CASE 2-4

The frequency histogram generated by the first set of measurements is shown in Figure 2-H. As in Case 2-3, the graph shows that the process may be centered on the specification; it has only six class intervals, however, and two of the bars are longer than the bars in the other class intervals. It is difficult to decide whether the distribution of the measurements actually is shaped like the normal (bell-shaped) curve, which would be a sign of stability. We can say only that all measurements were within the specification limits.

The frequency histogram constructed with the measurement data recorded to the nearest tenth of a millimeter is shown in Figure 2-I. Did your graph contain 12 class intervals such as the one shown? As you can see, the histogram is spread out much more than the histogram in Figure 2-H. That histogram was constructed from the same measurements, but they were recorded to the nearest whole millimeter. The histogram in Figure 2-I shows that the process is probably centered on the specification, but in addition it gives a somewhat clearer picture of the variation of the operation. At first glance, you might be inclined to say that the measurements take the shape of a normal curve, but look at the two short bars near the middle of the graph. They show frequen-

FREQUENCY HISTOGRAMS – WORKSHEET

Title _R.H. STATIONARY SNAP_   Very largest _325_   Very smallest _320_

Range _5_   # of intervals _6_   Interval width _1_

Midpoints	Interval	Boundaries	Tally	Tally Check	Frequency
320	320	319.5/320.5			7
321	321	320.5/321.5			14
322	322	321.5/322.5			31
323	323	322.5/323.5			13
324	324	323.5/324.5			24
325	325	324.5/325.5			11
				Total	100

Specifications _319.8 to 326.2 mm_

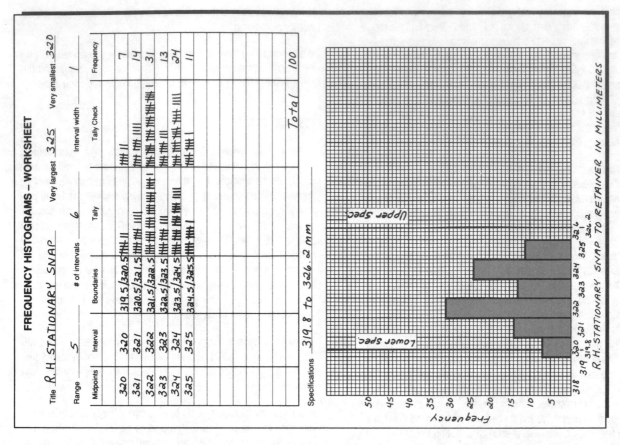

R.H. STATIONARY SNAP TO RETAINER IN MILLIMETERS

Figure 2-H. Frequency histogram with six class intervals, Case 2-4.

FREQUENCY HISTOGRAMS – WORKSHEET

Title _L.H. STATIONARY SNAP_   Very largest _325_   Very smallest _321_

Range _4_   # of intervals _5_   Interval width _1_

Midpoints	Interval	Boundaries	Tally	Tally Check	Frequency
321	321	320.5/321.5			10
322	322	321.5/322.5			12
323	323	322.5/323.5			35
324	324	323.5/324.5			35
325	325	324.5/325.5			8
				Total	100

Specifications _319.8 to 326.2 mm_

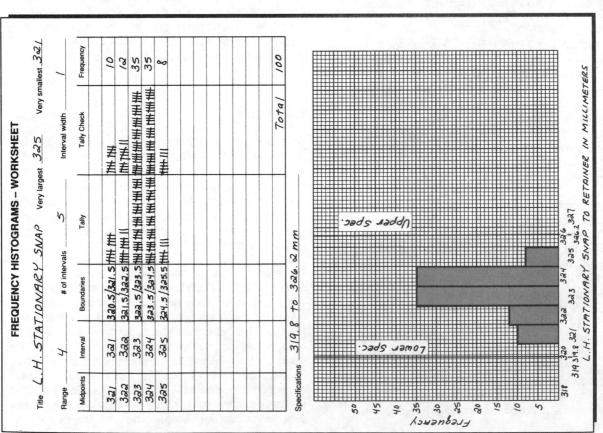

L.H. STATIONARY SNAP TO RETAINER IN MILLIMETERS

Figure 2-G. Frequency histogram, Case 2-3.

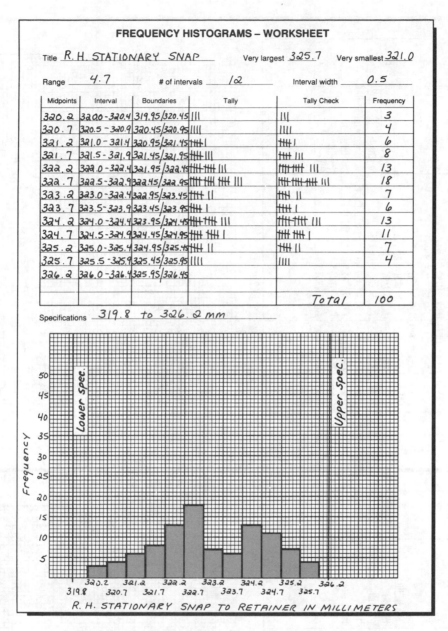

FREQUENCY HISTOGRAMS – WORKSHEET

Title R.H. STATIONARY SNAP   Very largest 325.7   Very smallest 321.0

Range 4.7   # of intervals 12   Interval width 0.5

Midpoints	Interval	Boundaries	Tally	Tally Check	Frequency
320.2	320.0 - 320.4	319.95/320.45	III	III	3
320.7	320.5 - 320.9	320.45/320.95	IIII	IIII	4
321.2	321.0 - 321.4	320.95/321.45	HHI	HHI	6
321.7	321.5 - 321.9	321.45/321.95	HH III	HH III	8
322.2	322.0 - 322.4	321.95/322.45	HH HH III	HH HH III	13
322.7	322.5 - 322.9	322.45/322.95	HH HH HH III	HH HH HH III	18
323.2	323.0 - 323.4	322.95/323.45	HH II	HH II	7
323.7	323.5 - 323.9	323.45/323.95	HH I	HH I	6
324.2	324.0 - 324.4	323.95/324.45	HH HH III	HH HH III	13
324.7	324.5 - 324.9	324.45/324.95	HH HH I	HH HH I	11
325.2	325.0 - 325.4	324.95/325.45	HH II	HH II	7
325.7	325.5 - 325.9	325.45/325.95	IIII	IIII	4
326.2	326.0 - 326.4	325.95/326.45			
				Total	100

Specifications 319.8 to 326.2 mm

Figure 2-I. Frequency histogram with 12 class intervals, Case 2-4.

cies of six and seven measurements in these two class interval. The bar in the class interval immediately to the left shows a frequency of 18; the bar in the class interval immediately to the right shows a frequency of 13. It would be fairly rare to find such a condition near the middle of the graph if these measurements came from a stable operation, stable meaning that no assignable causes were present.

The shape we see in this graph could be the result of the measurements being made up of two distributions with different averages. This situation could be caused by a shift in the process average during the time when the measurements were being obtained. Such a condition is generally due to an assignable cause and not to chance variation in the process. We can say only that there is probably a reason for the distortion in the shape of this frequency histogram. We cannot say anything about when it may have occurred or what it might be.

The use of more precise measurements enables us to create a clearer picture of the operation. The frequency histogram shown in Figure 2-H exhibits very little of value in analyzing the operation. The frequency histogram in Figure 2-I shows a fairly strong possibility of an unstable operation.

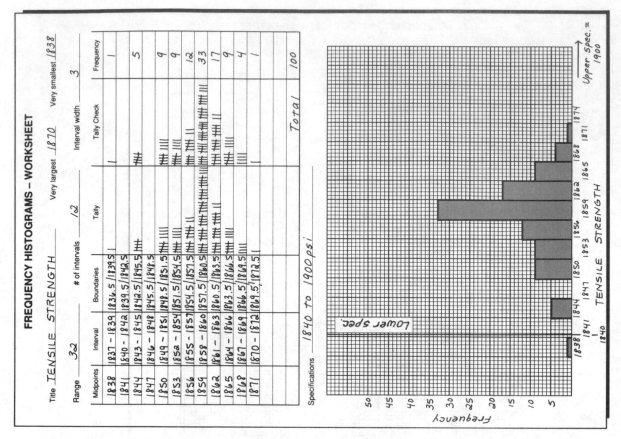

Figure 2-K. Frequency histogram with class interval size of 3, Case 2-5.

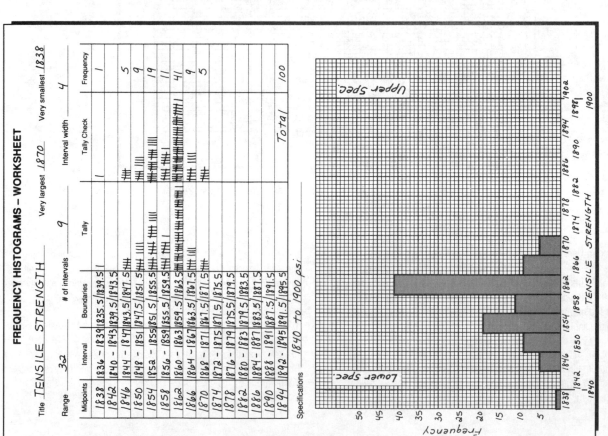

Figure 2-J. Frequency histogram with class interval size of 4, Case 2-5.

CASE 2-5

The range of the 100 values is 1870 - 1838 = 32. Table 2-4 in the textbook suggests establishing six to ten class intervals when 100 values are used in constructing a frequency histogram. If we select eight class intervals and divide the range by that number, the class interval value is 4. The lower limit of the specification is 1840 psi, so if we establish that value as the lower value of a class interval, that interval would contain the tensile values 1840, 1841, 1842, and 1843.

In determining the range of values to be entered on the graph, we see that the smallest value is 1838 psi; therefore there must be a class interval that contains that value. That class interval will contain the values 1836, 1837, 1838, and 1839. A frequency histogram constructed in this way is shown in Figure 2-J. The shape of this graph shows a distribution that tails off to the left, or to the lower tensile values. A large number of the tensile values are grouped in one class interval. This could be due to the way in which the class intervals were selected or to the size of the class interval, but the fact that the rest of the values tail off to the left shows that the true distribution of the tensile values is not normal and is not bell-shaped.

The frequency histogram shown in Figure 2-K was constructed with twelve class intervals, resulting in a class interval value of 3. The intervals in this case were established to be 1837/1839, 1840/1842, 1843/1845, and so on.

At first examination, this graph may appear to be more bell-shaped than the other. The tendency of the tensile values to tail off to the left is less evident. This graph also has one class interval that contains a large number of the tensile values, but two of the class intervals contain no values. This is an indication that the values tail off to the left.

Both of these frequency histograms should have led you to the same conclusions: it is probable that the mixing process is not stable, and assignable causes are present. One batch was produced out of specification; if the assignable cause or causes are not found and corrected, more batches will be produced out of specification.

CHECKSHEETS: ANALYSIS AND DISCUSSION OF CASE STUDIES

CASE 2-6

This problem asks you to create a checksheet of the causes of rejected parts by type of cause and cavity number. The checksheet you created should look similar to the one shown in Figure 2-L.

The title of the checksheet should clearly identify its purpose. The heading also should contain information relating to the time span covered and the total shown in the body of the checksheet.

In Figure 2-L the cavity numbers are shown across the top of the checksheet, and dimensions, or causes, appear down the left side of

the sheet. The totals along the bottom of the checksheet represent the sum for each cavity of all causes and the total down the right side of the checksheet are the sums for each cause of rejection for all cavitites.

A review of the completed checksheet reveals some facts about the performance of this job not readily apparent before the information was put in this form. First, we find 277 parts have been rejected out of 5,577 parts inspected. This 5% rejection rate indicates that there certainly is cause for concern about the quality of this job.

One thing that stands out is that all of the rejections are from five of the nine dimensions inspected. Of those five causes for rejection, by far most of them are from two causes, shelf height and TIR.

These two account for 236 of the total 277 rejections. Elimination of these two causes of rejection would decrease the rejection rate to 0.7%.

This checksheet makes it easy to see that the main causes of the quality problem are found in only some of the cavities. Although the mold contains 15 cavities, 267 of the total 277 rejections came from just seven of the 15 cavities. In fact, 148 of the rejections came from cavities 7 and 11 alone. Correcting these two cavities would drop the rejection rate to 2.3%—more than a 50% reduction. Cavities 1, 13, 14, and 15 produced no rejections and cavities 3 and 12 produced only one each. The CI team may conclude that, as a temporary measure, cavities 7 and 11 should be blocked off and not used until they can be corrected.

The information easily obtained from this checksheet presents the CI team with many paths of investigation that will result in great improvements in the quality of the product.

CASE 2-7

This problem deals with five different causes of the loss of production, or downtime. These causes, along with the days of the week, are depicted in a checksheet showing the amount of production time lost by cause and by day of the week. The lost time is indicated by tally marks placed opposite the cause of the lost time and under the column headed by the day the lost time occurred. Each tally mark represents five minutes of downtime of the operation. The production associates were instructed to determine the downtime to the nearest five minutes when recording the data. The amount of error introduced into the data by tallying five-minute intervals will not be great enough to affect the analysis the CI team will make using the data.

Using the data generated, the team that originally attacked this problem created a checksheet that looks like the one in Figure 2-M. The heading at the top of the checksheet contains the title of the activity, along with the time period of the data and a notation that each tally represents a five-minute time period. The columns across the checksheet are headed by the days of the week—Monday through Friday—covered by the data. The rows of the checksheet are labeled with the causes of the downtimes noted on the checksheet. The columns are totalled across the bottom and the rows are totalled down the right side.

SCRAP BY CAUSE AND CAVITY — PART NO. 3201450

Date __10/3 to 10/7__   Shift__ All__   Total Inspected __5577__   Total Rejects _2 77 = 5.0%_

Cavity / Dimension	1	2	3	4	5	6	7	8	9	10	11	12	13	14	15	Total
Diameter																
Ovality				1	2	3	11		4	2	1					24
Squareness																
Shelf Height					2	14	48		8	14	18	1				105
Parallelism								1		1	1					3
Outside Diameter																
TIR		6	1	1	2	3	28	15	23	12	40					131
Overall Height																
Bent Insert					6	4	1		3							14
Total by Cavity		6	1	2	12	24	88	16	38	29	30	1				277

Figure 2-L. Scrap by cause and cavity checksheet, Case 2-6.

A member of the CI team created the finished checksheet for the CI team to use in analyzing the problem of downtime. The checksheet enables the team to determine which area of investigation would be most fruitful for them to pursue.

A review of the completed checksheet reveals that 4 hours and 35 minutes of the total downtime recorded is due to no stock on hand. This is slightly more than half of the total downtime. Unless there are other areas more easily and quickly improved, the focus of the CI team should be on reducing the downtime due to no stock on hand.

The checksheet also provides thought provoking clues to the no stock situation. The checksheet shows there was no downtime for lack of stock on the day just before the worst day of the week and only one five-minute interval of downtime for no stock on the day just after the worst day. Questions the team should pursue arise from this observation. For example: Is the production of stock by the supplying department coordinated with the team's needs? Is it sporadic or continuous? Do you have a "feast or famine" situation that needs correcting?

The no stock on hand problem seems to be worse on some days than others. The other causes of downtime seem to be fairly consistent from day to day. The overage stock cause may be related to the inconsistencies of the no stock cause. This is further evidence that the no stock on hand cause should be thoroughly investigated.

The broken tool cause may or may not be related to the overage stock cause. The team should schedule a collection of paired data and develop a scatter diagram to see if this looks like a candidate for a more intensive study.

MACHINE DOWNTIME

Date 4/15 to 4/19   Shift All Three   (Times are to the nearest 5 minutes)

Cause \ Day	Monday	Tuesday	Wednesday	Thursday	Friday	Total
No Stock on Hand	‖‖‖ ‖‖‖ ‖‖‖ ‖‖‖ (90 minutes)	‖‖‖ ‖ (30 minutes)		‖‖‖ ‖‖‖ ‖‖‖ ‖‖‖ ‖‖‖ ‖‖‖ (150 minutes)	‖ (5 minutes)	55 (4 hours, 35 minutes)
Overage Stock	‖ (10 minutes)	‖‖‖ ‖ (30 minutes)	‖‖‖ ‖‖‖ (40 minutes)		‖‖‖ ‖‖‖ (50 minutes)	26 (2 hours, 10 minutes)
Machine Maintenance		‖ (5 minutes)			‖ (5 minutes)	2 (10 minutes)
Broken Tool	‖ (5 minutes)	‖‖‖‖ (20 minutes)	‖‖‖ ‖‖ (35 minutes)		‖‖‖ ‖‖‖ (40 minutes)	20 (1 hour, 40 minutes)
Miscellaneous	‖ (10 minutes)		‖‖‖ (15 minutes)	‖ (5 minutes)		6 (30 minutes)
Total Count by Day (Total Time)	23 (1 hour, 55 minutes)	17 (1 hour, 25 minutes)	18 (1 hour, 30 minutes)	31 (2 hours, 35 minutes)	20 (1 hour, 40 minutes)	109 (9 hours, 5 minutes)

Figure 2-M. Checksheet for machine downtime, Case 2-7.

AVERAGE AND RANGE CHARTS: REVIEW QUESTIONS

1. $\overline{X}$-R control chart.
2. (a) (1) Mean.
    (2) X-bar ($\overline{X}$)
   (b) Add the numbers, then divide by the number of numbers.
3. (a) First, find the largest number and draw a circle around it; then find the smallest number and draw a box around it.
   (b) Subtract the smallest number from the largest.
4. (a) Upper control limit.
   (b) Lower control limit.
5. (a) The process is OK, or in statistical control.
   (b) Nothing; keep the process running as is.
   (c) Find the cause and remove it.
6. (a) Because of inherent variation.
   (b) Chance causes or system causes.
   (c) No.
   (d) They are in the system, the raw materials, the machines, the method, or the production associate. By and large they are not under the associate's control.
7. (a) Find the cause and remove it, so that the process is back to where it was before the point went out of control.
   (b) It has shifted or changed.
   (c) There is one or more assignable cause(s) at work.
   (d) It is changing the overall average.
   (e) No.
8. (a) Person.
   (b) Machine.
   (c) Method.
   (d) Material.
   (e) Environment.
9. (a) Is the inherent variation under the associate's control?
   (b) No, not usually.
   (c) It usually means the process itself has gone haywire.
10. (a) Control.
    (b) Analysis.
    (c) Education.
    (d) Communication.
    (e) Documentation.

SETTING UP AVERAGE AND RANGE CHARTS

Step 1. (a) Select something important, and control that.
        (b) If you can't measure it directly, then measure something that, when controlled, will control that important thing.
Step 2. (a) It consists of several measurements.
        (b) Only inherent variation.
        (c) So that we see only inherent variation within samples.
        (d) A short period of time.
        (e) A single source (one machine, one machine head, one operator, etc.).
Step 4. Record them in the order of production.
Step 5. (a) Total the sample, then divide by the number of measurements in the sample.
        (b) In the row marked "Average, $\overline{X}$."
Step 6. (a) Overall mean.
        (b) $\overline{\overline{X}}$
        (c) Add up all the averages, then divide by the number of averages.
Step 7. (a) The largest and the smallest.
        (b) Subtract the smallest from the largest.
Step 8. (a) Add up all the ranges, then divide by the number of ranges.
        (b) $\overline{R}$
Step 9. (a) So that the largest and smallest fit comfortably, leaving extra room for the control limits.
        (b) At zero.
        (c) The control limits, which we hope are farther out than all the plot points.
Step 10. (a) We need to see whether the variation itself is stable or not.
         (b) D_4
         (c) Yes.
         (d) $D_4 = 2.114$
         (e) $D_4 = 2.282$
         (f) $UCL_R = D_4 \times \overline{R}$
         (g) Whenever the sample size is six or less.
Step 11. (a) All the ranges are inside the control limits.
         (b) One or two ranges are outside the control limits.
         (c) Three or more ranges are outside the control limits.
         (d) When all the ranges are inside the control limits.
         (e) It is stable.
         (f) There are none for ranges.
         (g) Throw out these one or two samples, including both the ranges and means, then recalculate.

(h) Refigure $\overline{R}$, the upper control limit for ranges. and $\overline{\overline{X}}$.

(i) No.

(j) The process is out of statistical control.

(k) Find and remove the assignable causes. Collect new data and set up a new chart.

(l) Use these new control limits for production.

(m) The process is out of statistical control.

(n) It is *not* stable.

(o) There are assignable causes upsetting the ranges.

(p) Find and remove the assignable causes. Then collect new data and set up new charts.

Step 12. (a) The ranges must be in statistical control first.

(b) A_2

(c) 0.577

(d) 0.729

(e) $UCL_{\overline{x}} = \overline{\overline{X}} + (A_2 \times \overline{R})$

(Be sure to multiply A_2 by $\overline{R}$ first, then add the result to $\overline{\overline{X}}$.)

(f) $LCL_{\overline{x}} = \overline{\overline{X}} - (A_2 \times \overline{R})$

Step 13. (a) (1) All the averages are inside the control limits.

(2) One or two averages are outside the control limits.

(3) Three or more averages are outside the control limits.

(b) When all the averages are inside the control limits.

(c) It is stable.

(d) There are none for averages.

(e) Both the averages and ranges must be in statistical control.

(f) Throw out these one or two (*not* the ranges) and recalculate.

(g) No.

(h) The process is out of statistical control.

(i) Clean up the process, collect new data, and redo the control charts.

(j) Use the control charts in production, but be careful.

(k) The process is out of statistical control.

(l) There are assignable causes in addition to inherent variation.

(m) Find and remove the assignable causes. Then collect new data and set up new control charts.

HOW TO USE CONTROL CHARTS IN CONTINUED PRODUCTION

1. (a) When all the ranges and averages are inside the control limits.

(b) Only inherent variation.

(c) Because of chance causes.

(d) The inherent variation is stable.

2. (a) It is smooth and consistent.

(b) Consistent ones are being produced.

(c) You may make many products outside of specifications.

3. (a) Specifications are designers' hopes and wishes. Control limits are based on actual variation in the process.

(b) No, definitely not.

4. It will change the control limits for the averages and affect the percentage that falls within specification. (It probably will have no effect on the ranges.)

AVERAGE AND RANGE CHARTS: EXERCISES, SERIES 1

1. *See the answer charts.*

2. *See the answer charts.*

3. *See the answer charts.*

4. (a) D_4

(b) 5

(c) 2.114

(d) $UCL_R = D_4 \times \overline{R}$

(e) For sample sizes of six or less.)

5. *See the answer charts.*

6. (a) Sets 1–4: No.

(b) Sets 1–4: Go ahead and set up the $\overline{X}$ chart.

7. (a) A_2

(b) 5

(c) 0.577

(d) $UCL_{\overline{x}} = \overline{\overline{X}} + (A_2 \times \overline{R})$

(e) $LCL_{\overline{x}} = \overline{\overline{X}} - (A_2 \times \overline{R})$

8–9. *See the answer charts.*

10. (a) Sets 1–4: No

(b) Sets 1:4 Use the chart to control and monitor the process; make no adjustments.

AVERAGE AND RANGE CHARTS: EXERCISES, SERIES 2

1. *See the answer charts.*

2. *See the answer charts.*

3. *See the answer charts.*

4. (a) D_4

(b) 2.114

(c) 2.282

(d) $UCL_R = D_4 \times \overline{R}$

(e) For sample sizes of six or less.

5. *See the answer charts.*

6. (a) Sets 1–4: No.

(b) Sets 1–4: Nothing; go ahead and set up the $\overline{X}$ chart.

7. (a) A_2

(b) 0.577

(c) 0.729

(d) $UCL_{\overline{x}} = \overline{\overline{X}} + (A_2 \times \overline{R})$

(e) $LCL_{\overline{x}} = \overline{\overline{X}} - (A_2 \times \overline{R})$

8–9. *See the answer charts.*

10. (a) Set 1: No.
      Set 2: No.
      Set 3: Yes, one.
      Set 4: No.

  (b) Set 1: Use the control charts in production.

      Set 2: Use the control charts in production.

      Set 3: Remove the one point; recalculate the control limits for X̄'s.

      Set 4: Use the control charts in production.

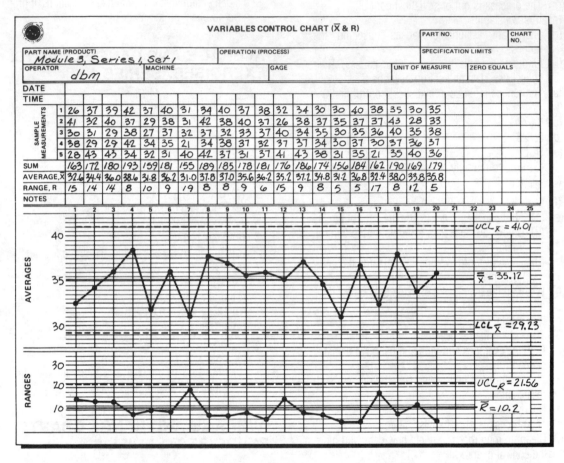

Module 3, Series 1, Set 1. Average and range chart.

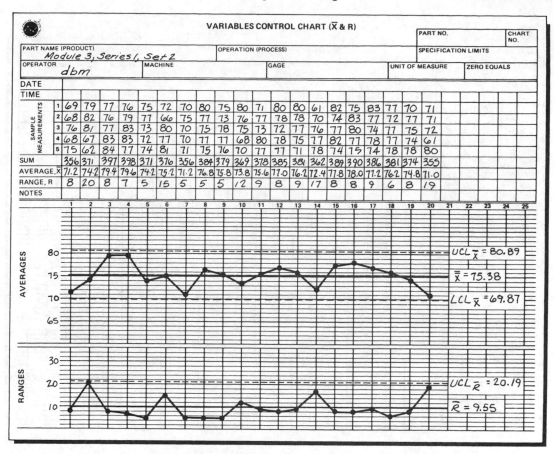

VARIABLES CONTROL CHART (X̄ & R)

PART NAME (PRODUCT)	OPERATION (PROCESS)		SPECIFICATION LIMITS	
Module 3, Series 1, Set 2				

OPERATOR: dbm

	1	2	3	4	5	6	7	8	9	10	11	12	13	14	15	16	17	18	19	20
1	69	79	77	76	75	72	70	80	75	80	71	80	80	61	82	75	83	77	70	71
2	68	82	76	79	77	66	75	77	73	76	77	78	78	70	74	83	77	72	77	71
3	76	81	77	83	73	80	70	75	78	75	73	72	77	76	77	80	74	77	75	72
4	68	67	83	83	72	77	70	77	77	68	80	78	75	77	82	77	78	77	74	61
5	75	62	84	77	74	81	71	75	76	70	77	77	71	78	74	75	74	78	78	80
SUM	356	371	397	398	371	376	356	384	379	369	378	385	381	362	389	390	386	381	374	355
AVERAGE, X̄	71.2	74.2	79.4	79.6	74.2	75.2	71.2	76.8	75.8	73.8	75.6	77.0	76.2	72.4	77.8	78.0	77.2	76.2	74.8	71.0
RANGE, R	8	20	8	7	5	15	5	5	5	12	9	8	9	17	8	8	9	6	8	19

$UCL_{\bar{X}} = 80.89$

$\bar{\bar{X}} = 75.38$

$LCL_{\bar{X}} = 69.87$

$UCL_{\bar{R}} = 20.19$

$\bar{R} = 9.55$

Module 3, Series 1, Set 2. Average and range chart.

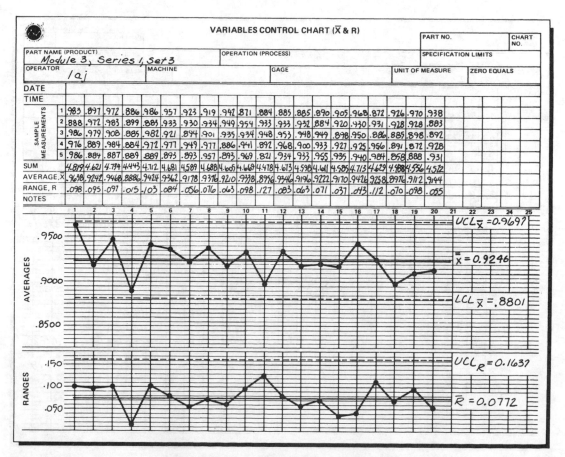

VARIABLES CONTROL CHART (X̄ & R)

PART NAME (PRODUCT)	OPERATION (PROCESS)		SPECIFICATION LIMITS	
Module 3, Series 1, Set 3				

OPERATOR: laj

	1	2	3	4	5	6	7	8	9	10	11	12	13	14	15	16	17	18	19	20
1	.983	.897	.972	.886	.986	.957	.923	.919	.942	.871	.884	.885	.885	.890	.905	.968	.872	.926	.970	.938
2	.888	.972	.983	.899	.883	.933	.930	.934	.949	.954	.933	.933	.932	.884	.920	.930	.931	.928	.928	.883
3	.986	.979	.908	.885	.982	.921	.894	.901	.935	.934	.948	.953	.948	.949	.898	.950	.886	.885	.898	.892
4	.976	.889	.984	.884	.972	.977	.949	.977	.886	.941	.892	.968	.900	.933	.927	.925	.956	.891	.872	.928
5	.986	.884	.887	.889	.889	.893	.893	.957	.893	.969	.821	.934	.933	.955	.935	.940	.984	.858	.888	.931
SUM	4.819	4.621	4.734	4.443	4.712	4.681	4.589	4.688	4.605	4.669	4.478	4.613	4.598	4.611	4.585	4.713	4.629	4.488	4.556	4.572
AVERAGE, X̄	.9638	.9242	.9468	.8886	.9424	.9362	.9178	.9376	.9210	.9338	.8956	.9226	.9196	.9222	.9170	.9426	.9258	.8976	.9112	.9144
RANGE, R	.098	.095	.097	.015	.103	.084	.056	.076	.063	.098	.127	.083	.063	.071	.037	.043	.112	.070	.098	.055

$UCL_{\bar{X}} = 0.9697$

$\bar{\bar{X}} = 0.9246$

$LCL_{\bar{X}} = .8801$

$UCL_{R} = 0.1637$

$\bar{R} = 0.0772$

Module 3, Series 1, Set 3. Average and range chart.

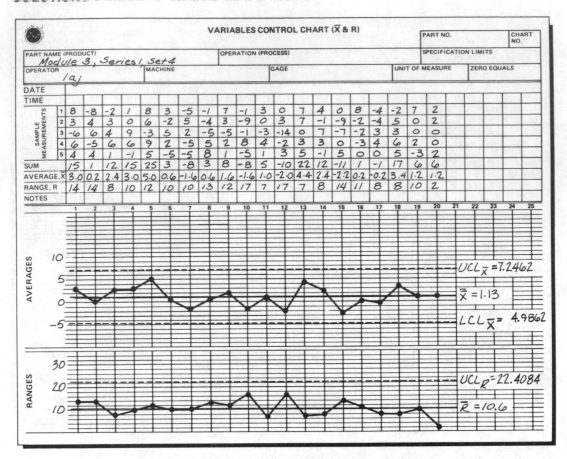

Module 3, Series 1, Set 4. Average and range chart.

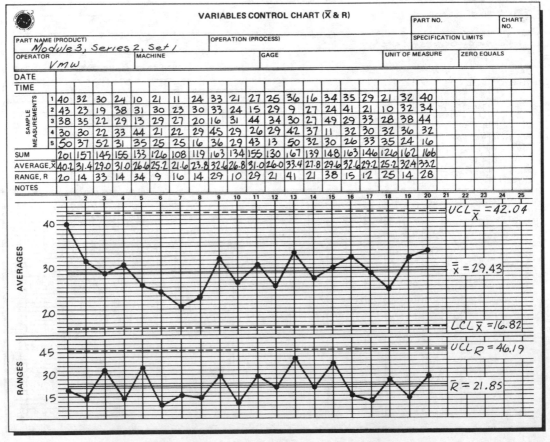

Module 3, Series 2, Set 1. Average and range chart.

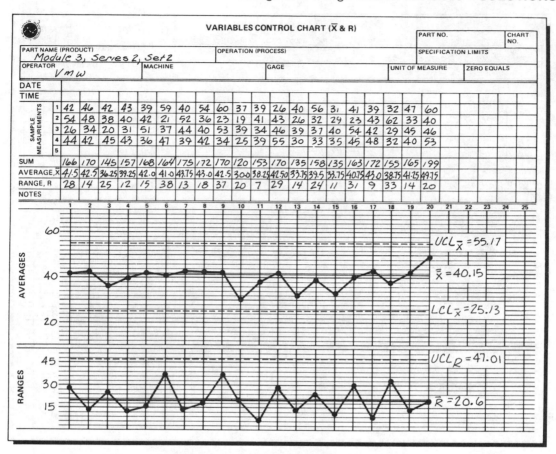

Module 3, Series 2, Set 2. Average and range chart.

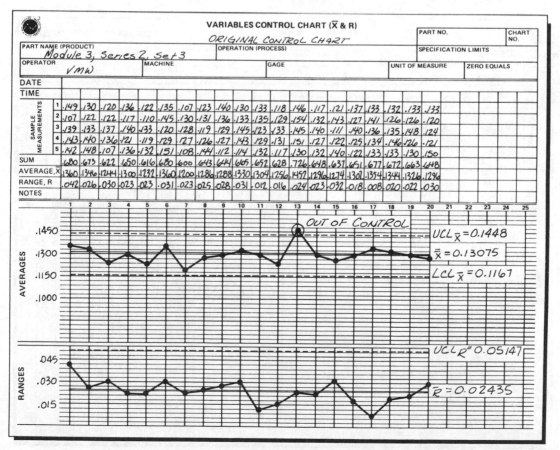

Module 3, Series 2, Set 3. Original average and range chart.

VARIABLES CONTROL CHART (X̄ & R)

CONTROL CHART WITH NEW X̿ AND CONTROL LIMITS

PART NAME (PRODUCT): Module 3, Series 2, Set 3
OPERATOR: VMW

	1	2	3	4	5	6	7	8	9	10	11	12	13	14	15	16	17	18	19	20
1	.149	.130	.120	.136	.122	.135	.107	.123	.140	.130	.133	.118	.146	.117	.121	.137	.133	.132	.133	.133
2	.107	.122	.122	.117	.110	.145	.130	.131	.136	.133	.135	.129	.154	.132	.143	.127	.141	.126	.126	.120
3	.139	.133	.137	.140	.133	.120	.128	.119	.129	.145	.123	.133	.145	.140	.111	.140	.136	.135	.148	.124
4	.143	.140	.136	.121	.119	.129	.127	.126	.127	.143	.129	.131	.151	.127	.122	.125	.134	.146	.126	.121
5	.142	.148	.107	.136	.132	.151	.108	.144	.112	.114	.132	.117	.130	.132	.140	.122	.133	.133	.130	.150
SUM	.680	.673	.622	.650	.616	.680	.600	.643	.644	.665	.652	.628	.726	.648	.637	.651	.677	.672	.663	.648
AVERAGE, X̄	.1360	.1346	.1244	.1300	.1232	.1360	.1200	.1286	.1288	.1330	.1304	.1256	.1452	.1296	.1274	.1302	.1354	.1344	.1326	.1296
RANGE, R	.042	.026	.030	.023	.023	.031	.023	.025	.028	.031	.012	.016	.024	.023	.032	.018	.008	.020	.022	.030

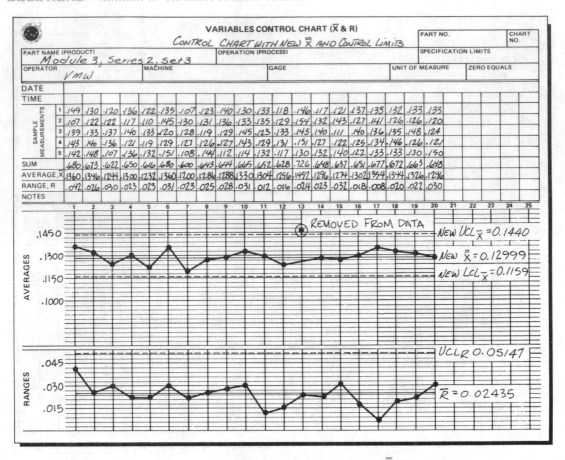

REMOVED FROM DATA

NEW $UCL_{\bar{X}} = 0.1440$

NEW $\bar{\bar{X}} = 0.12999$

NEW $LCL_{\bar{X}} = 0.1159$

$UCL_R\ 0.05147$

$\bar{R} = 0.02435$

Module 3, Series 2, Set 3. Average and range chart with new X̿ and control limits.

VARIABLES CONTROL CHART (X̄ & R)

PART NAME (PRODUCT): Module 3, Series 2, Set 4
OPERATOR: VMW

	1	2	3	4	5	6	7	8	9	10	11	12	13	14	15	16	17	18	19	20
1	7	3	2	3	3	-9	13	-19	-8	10	21	-22	14	-18	-16	2	-23	6	18	12
2	-3	11	-4	-4	-10	-13	2	10	-3	2	-1	-3	-4	-3	13	-11	-9	6	10	13
3	10	6	5	18	-6	16	24	13	21	0	-10	-2	-11	-1	15	3	10	7	3	9
4	-5	4	16	-4	-9	-12	-1	3	1	-13	15	0	1	6	3	-20	-13	-8	-8	-23
5																				
SUM	9	24	19	13	-22	-18	38	7	11	-1	25	-27	0.0	-16	15	-26	-35	11	23	11
AVERAGE, X̄	2.25	6	4.75	3.25	-5.5	-4.5	9.5	1.75	2.75	-0.25	6.25	-6.75	0.0	-4.0	3.75	-6.5	-8.75	2.75	5.75	2.75
RANGE, R	15	8	20	22	13	29	25	32	29	23	31	22	25	24	31	23	33	15	26	36

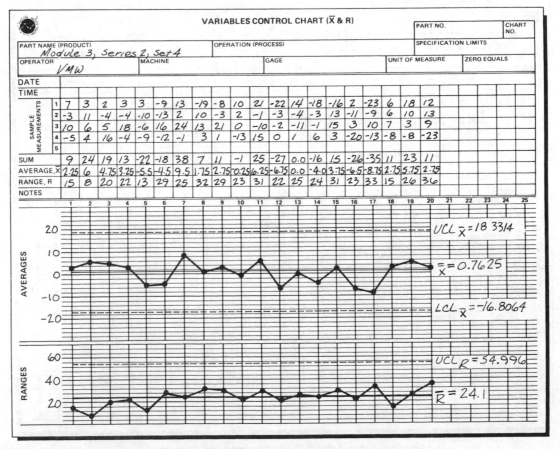

$UCL_{\bar{X}} = 18.3314$

$\bar{\bar{X}} = 0.7625$

$LCL_{\bar{X}} = -16.8064$

$UCL_R = 54.996$

$\bar{R} = 24.1$

Module 3, Series 2, Set 4. Average and range chart.

MEDIAN AND RANGE CHARTS: REVIEW QUESTIONS

1. (a) When the process is (1) known to be normal, (2) not often disturbed by assignable causes, and (3) easily adjusted by the production associate.
   (b) $\overline{X}$-R chart.
2. (a) Work with samples of size two to ten.
   (b) Three or five are the easiest.

DEVELOPING THE MEDIAN AND RANGE CHART

Step 1. Use a short time frame.
Step 2. In the "Sample Measurements" columns.
Step 3. (a) The middle measurement.
   (b) Count from the smallest to the largest and pick the middle one as the median.
   (c) The one between the smallest and the largest.
   (d) It is the third measurement which lies between the two largest and the two smallest.
   (e) It is halfway between the two middle measurements.
   (f) In the "Median" row.
   (g) The median is the middle measurement and the mean is the average.
   (h) 44.6
   (i) Order the measurements, then pick the middle one.
   (j) 46
Step 4. (a) The same as for the $\overline{X}$-R charts.
   (b) In the "Range" row.
   (c) 12, 15, 17
   (d) 17
   (e) 12
   (f) 15
   (g) 5
Step 5. (a) Order the 15 medians and pick the middle one, the 8th largest (or 8th smallest).
   (b) $\widetilde{\overline{X}}$
   (c) Order the ranges and pick the 8th largest (or 8th smallest).
   (d) $\widetilde{R}$
Step 6. It should use one-half to three-fourths of the chart space.
Step 7. Do it the same way as for the medians chart.
Step 8. (a) Yes.
   (b) Plot the median as a point or dot on the median chart and circle it.
   (c) Helps to spot trends.
   (d) The same way as for $\overline{X}$-R charts.
Step 9. (a) No.

(b) $\widetilde{D}_4$
(c) 2.75
(d) 2.18
(e) $UCL_R = \widetilde{D}_4 \times \widetilde{R}$
(f) Zero.
(g) Throw out those one or two samples including *both* the range and median. Then recalculate the control limits.
(h) Find and remove the assignable causes. Then collect new data and set up new control charts.
(i) Only if the ranges are in statistical control.
(j) $\widetilde{A}_2$
(k) 1.26
(l) 0.71
(m) $UCL_{\widetilde{X}} = \widetilde{\overline{X}} + (\widetilde{A}_2 \times \widetilde{R})$
(n) $LCL_{\widetilde{X}} = \widetilde{\overline{X}} - (\widetilde{A}_2 \times \widetilde{R})$
(o) Remove those one or two medians (leave their ranges). Recalculate the control limits.
(p) Recalculate the $\widetilde{\overline{X}}$ and control limits for $\widetilde{X}$'s.
(q) The medians are *not* in statistical control.
(r) Find and remove the assignable causes. Then collect new data and set up new charts.
(s) The medians are out of statistical control.
(t) Find and remove the assignable causes. Collect new data and set up new charts.

HOW TO USE MEDIAN AND RANGE CHARTS IN CONTINUED PRODUCTION

(a) The medians, the ranges, *and* the individual measurements themselves.
(b) Yes.
(c) Only when the ranges or medians go outside the control limits. Do not correct if individual points go outside the control limits or even if individuals go outside the specs.
(d) Yes.
(e) No.
(f) Only when the medians or ranges go outside the control limits.

MEDIAN AND RANGE CHARTS: EXERCISES, SERIES 1

1. (a) 44
   (b) 20
   (c) 63
   (d) 77
   (e) 34
   (f) 30
   (g) 76
   (h) 11
   (i) 63
   (j) 24
   (k) 16.5

(l) 55.5
(m) 97.5
(n) 31.5
(o) 62.5
(p) 56
(q) 6
(r) 44.5
(s) 85
(t) 1.59

2. *See the answer charts.*
3. *See the answer charts.*
4. *See the answer charts.*
5. *See the answer charts.*
6. (a) $\widetilde{D}_4$
    (b) 5
    (c) 2.18
    (d) 4
    (e) 2.38
    (f) 3
    (g) 2.75
    (h) $UCL_R = \widetilde{D}_4 \times \widetilde{R}$
    (i) Zero.
7. *See the answer charts.*
8. (a) Sets 1–3. No.
    (b) Sets 1–3. Determine the limits for the medians.
9. (a) $\widetilde{A}_2$
    (b) 5
    (c) 0.71
    (d) 4
    (e) 0.83
    (f) 3
    (g) 1.26
    (h) $UCL_{\widetilde{X}} = \widetilde{\overline{X}} + (A_2 \times \widetilde{R})$
         (Be sure to multiply $\widetilde{A}_2$ by $\widetilde{R}$ first, then add the result to $\widetilde{\overline{X}}$.)
    (i) $LCL_{\widetilde{X}} = \widetilde{\overline{X}} - (\widetilde{A}_2 \times \widetilde{R})$
10–11. *See the answer charts.*
12. (a) Sets 1–3. No.
     (b) Sets 1–3. You may use the charts in continued production.
     (c) Set 1. Yes.
          Set 2. Yes.
          Set 3. No.
          Sets 1–3. Make no adjustments.

MEDIAN AND RANGE CHARTS: EXERCISES, SERIES 2

1. (a) 40
    (b) 32
    (c) 162
    (d) 15
    (e) 76
    (f) 49
    (g) 87

(h) 7
(i) 71
(j) 27
(k) 16
(l) 67
(m) 193
(n) 51.5
(o) 20.5
(p) 36
(q) 0.72
(r) 10
(s) −13
(t) 131

2. *See the answer charts.*
3. *See the answer charts.*
4. *See the answer charts.*
5. *See the answer charts.*
6. (a) $\widetilde{D}_4$
    (b) 4
    (c) 2.38
    (d) 3
    (e) 2.75
    (f) 5
    (g) 2.18
    (h) $UCL_R = \widetilde{D}_4 \times \widetilde{R}$
    (i) Zero.
7. *See the answer charts.*
8. (a) Sets 1–3. No.
    (b) Sets 1–3. Determine the limits for the medians.
9. (a) $\widetilde{A}_2$
    (b) 4
    (c) 0.83
    (d) 3
    (e) 1.26
    (f) 5
    (g) 0.71
    (h) $UCL_{\widetilde{X}} = \widetilde{\overline{X}} + (\widetilde{A}_2 \times \widetilde{R})$
         (Be sure to multiply $\widetilde{A}_2$ by $\widetilde{R}$ first, then add the result to $\widetilde{\overline{X}}$.)
    (i) $LCL_{\widetilde{X}} = \widetilde{\overline{X}} - (\widetilde{A}_2 \times \widetilde{R})$
10–11. *See the answer charts.*
12. (a) Set 1. No.
          Set 2. Yes, two.
          Set 3. No.
     (b) Set 1. Use the charts in continued production.
          Set 2. Remove these two medians. Recalculate the control limits for medians. If all medians are then inside the limits, you may use the charts in continued production.
          Set 3. Use the charts in continued production
     (c) Sets 1–3. Yes.
     (d) Sets 1–3. Adjust *only* if the medians are outside the control limits.

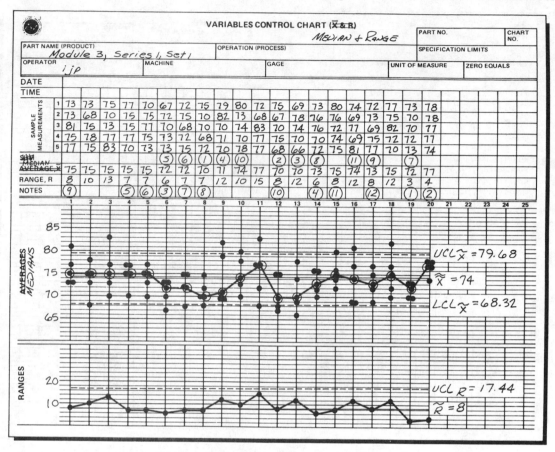

Module 3, Series 1, Set 1. Median and range chart.

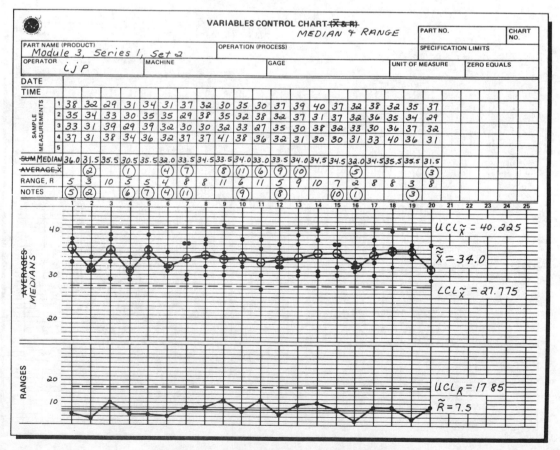

Module 3, Series 1, Set 2. Median and range chart.

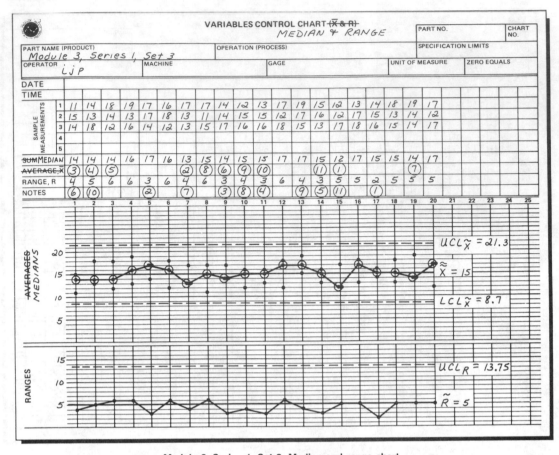

Module 3, Series 1, Set 3. Median and range chart.

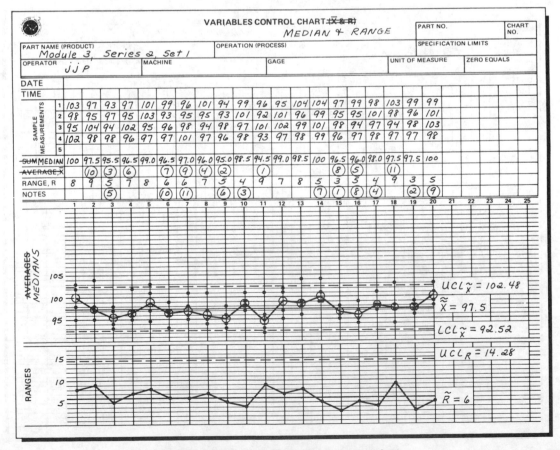

Module 3, Series 2, Set 1. Median and range chart.

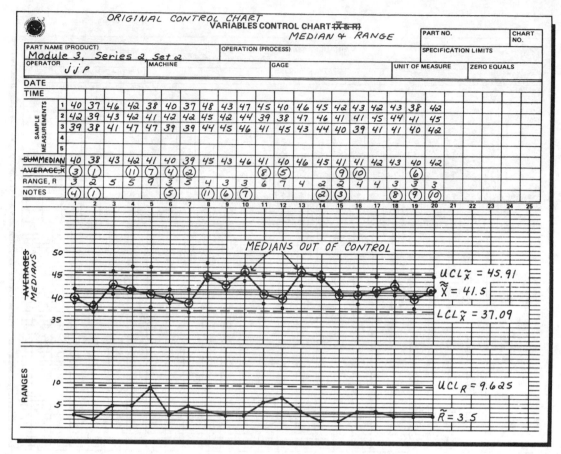

Module 3, Series 2, Set 2. Original median and range chart.

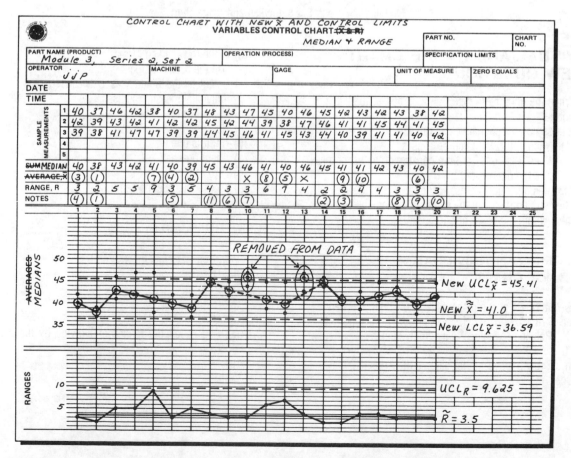

Module 3, Series 2, Set 2. Median and range chart with new $\tilde{X}$ and control limits.

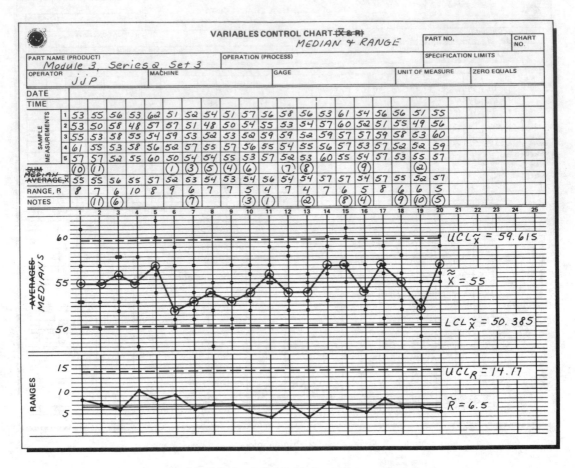

Module 3, Series 2, Set 3. Median and range chart.

INDIVIDUAL AND RANGE CHARTS: REVIEW QUESTIONS

1. (a) When the underlying distribution is bell-shaped, that is, normal.
   (b) It does not detect changes as quickly.
2. (a) (1) When you have batch processes.
       (2) When it is costly or time-consuming to test or measure the dimension.
   (b) Mixtures, chemical baths, coatings.
   (c) They should be about the same no matter where we take them within the batch or bath.

DEVELOPING AN INDIVIDUAL AND RANGE CHART

1. Cross out "$\overline{X}$-R" and replace with "Individual and Range." Replace "Time" with "Batch." Cross out "Sum" and "Average, $\overline{X}$." Replace "Averages" with "Individuals."
2. (a) 20
   (b) In the row marked "1" for sample measurements.
   (c) One.
   (d) In the row marked "Time."
   (e) Use the batch numbers.
3. (a) Calculate the differences between successive pairs of individual measurements.
   (b) In the "Range" row.
   (c) No.
   (d) No, it is one less.
4. (a) About one-half.
   (b) Zero.
   (c) They should be the same.

CONTROL LIMITS

1. In the same way as for $\overline{X}$'s and R's.
2. (a) D_4
   (b) 2
   (c) 3.268
   (d) $UCL_R = D_4 \times \overline{R}$
3. (a) Add up all the ranges and divide by the number of ranges.
   (b) No.
4. Zero.

5. (a) The process is out of statistical control.
  (b) Find and remove the assignable causes. Collect new data and make a new chart.
  (c) Throw out those one or two.
  (d) Yes.
  (e) Yes.
6. (a) The process is out of statistical control.
  (b) Find and remove the assignable causes. Collect new data and set up new charts.
  (c) Proceed to calculate control limits for the individuals.
7. They must be in statistical control.
8. (a) Add up all the individual measurements and divide by the number of individual measurements.
  (b) One.
  (c) 2.66
  (d) $UCL_X = \bar{\bar{X}} + (2.66 \times \bar{R})$
    (Be sure to multiply 2.66 by $\bar{R}$ first, then add the result to $\bar{\bar{X}}$.)
9. (a) The process is out of statistical control.
  (b) Find and remove the assignable causes. Collect new data and set up new charts.
  (c) Throw out those one or two individuals (not their ranges). Recalculate the control limits for individuals.
  (d) The process is out of control.
  (e) Find and remove the assignable causes. Then collect new data and set up new charts.
10. (a) Once you have established the individual and range chart with proper control limits.
  (b) Yes.
  (c) Individual measurements.
11. (a) Yes.
  (b) It is a floor-solvable problem.
  (c) Floor personnel.
  (d) Find the assignable causes and remove them.
  (e) It is a management-team-solvable problem.
  (f) A management-team.
  (g) Correct the plans, instructions, or process.
  (h) The process will produce some parts outside of specifications.
  (i) Recalculate the control limits once you have obtained more measurements.

INDIVIDUAL AND RANGE CHARTS: EXERCISES, SERIES 1

1. Practice Set 1.

(a) —	(h) 5	(o) 0
(b) 5	(i) 12	(p) 7
(c) 2	(j) 9	(q) 4
(d) 5	(k) 5	(r) 2
(e) 0	(l) 1	(s) 5
(f) 3	(m) 11	(t) 8
(g) 3	(n) 2	

Practice Set 2.

(a) —	(h) .001	(o) .001
(b) .015	(i) .005	(p) .016
(c) .000	(j) .003	(q) .014
(d) .020	(k) .002	(r) .015
(e) .09	(l) .006	(s) .000
(f) .012	(m) .025	(t) .006
(g) .015	(n) .022	

2. *See the answer charts.*
3. *See the answer charts.*
4. *See the answer charts.*
5. *See the answer charts.*
6. (a) D_4
  (b) 2
  (c) 3.268
  (d) $UCL_R = D_4 \times \bar{R}$
  (e) At zero.
7. *See the answer charts.*
8. (a) Sets 1–4. No.
  (b) Sets 1–4. Set up the individuals portion of the individual and range chart.
9. (a) 1
  (b) 2.66
  (c) $UCL_X = \bar{\bar{X}} + (A_2 \times \bar{R})$
  (d) $LCL_X = \bar{\bar{X}} - (A_2 \times \bar{R})$
10–11. *See the answer charts.*
12. (a) Sets 1–4. No.
  (b) Sets 1–4. Use the chart to monitor and control the process.

INDIVIDUAL AND RANGE CHARTS: EXERCISES, SERIES 2

1. Practice Set 1.

(a) —	(h) 0.4	(o) 1.5
(b) 0.4	(i) 2.3	(p) 6.3
(c) 1.5	(j) 7.1	(q) 9.6
(d) 9.6	(k) 1.3	(r) 5.4
(e) 10.0	(l) 0.1	(s) 4.4
(f) 2.9	(m) 0.1	(t) 3.2
(g) 3.4	(n) 0.6	

Practice Set 2.

(a) —	(h) 0	(o) 0
(b) 6	(i) 4	(p) 1
(c) 7	(j) 3	(q) 2
(d) 4	(k) 2	(r) 7
(e) 2	(l) 4	(s) 4
(f) 4	(m) 1	(t) 5
(g) 5	(n) 1	

2. *See the answer charts.*
3. *See the answer charts.*
4. *See the answer charts.*
5. *See the answer charts.*
6. (a) D_4

(b) 2

(c) 3.268

(d) $UCL_R = D_4 \times \bar{R}$

(e) Zero.

7. *See the answer charts.*

8. (a) Sets 1–4. No.

(b) Sets 1–4. Calculate limits for the individuals.

9. (a) 1

(b) 2.66

(c) $UCL_X = \bar{\bar{X}} + (A_2 \times \bar{R})$

(d) $LCL_X = \bar{\bar{X}} - (A_2 \times \bar{R})$

10–11. *See the answer charts.*

12. (a) Sets 1–4. No.

(b) Sets 1–4. Use these charts in production.

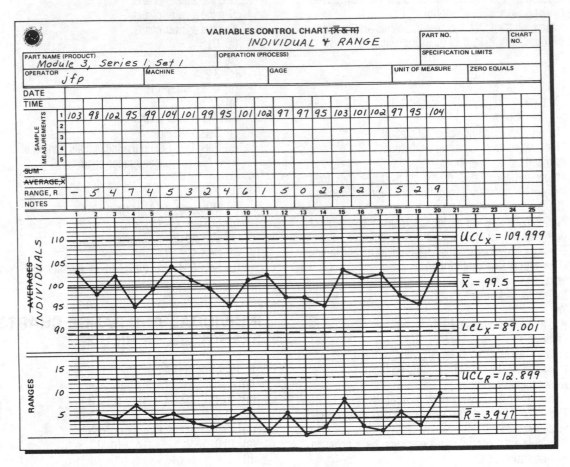

Module 3, Series 1, Set 1. Individual and range chart.

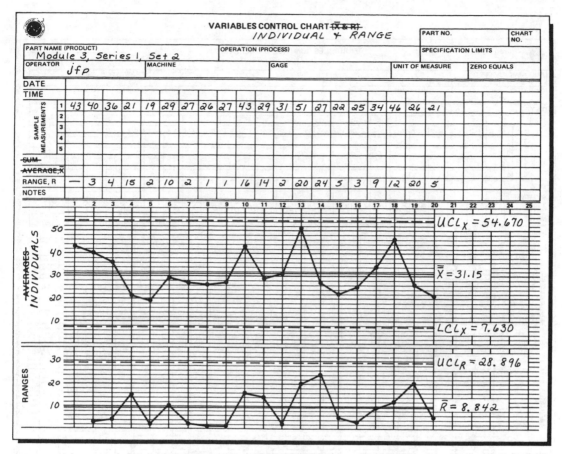

Module 3, Series 1, Set 2. Individual and range chart.

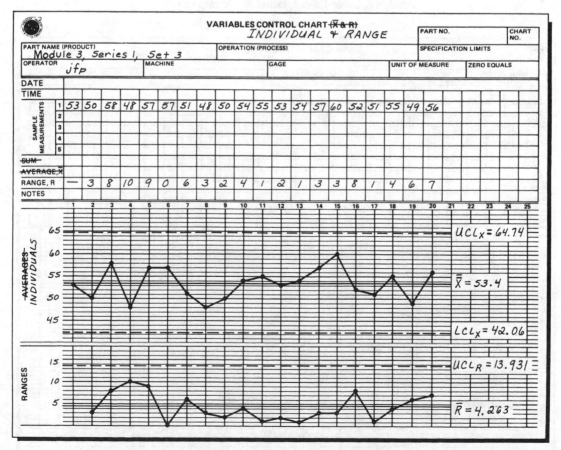

Module 3, Series 1, Set 3. Individual and range chart.

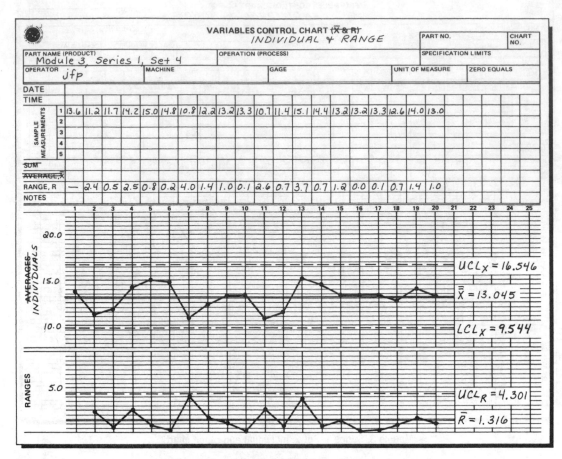

Module 3, Series 1, Set 4. Individual and range chart.

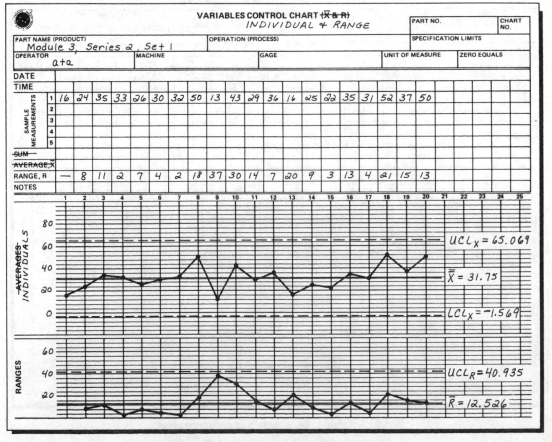

Module 3, Series 2, Set 1. Individual and range chart.

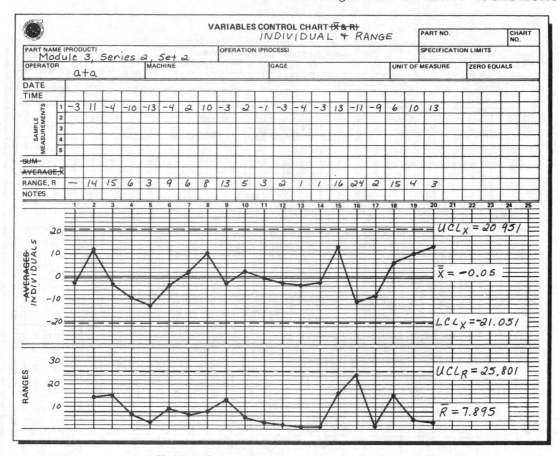

VARIABLES CONTROL CHART (X̄ & R)
INDIVIDUAL + RANGE

PART NAME (PRODUCT)	OPERATION (PROCESS)		SPECIFICATION LIMITS
Module 3, Series 2, Set 2			

OPERATOR	MACHINE	GAGE	UNIT OF MEASURE	ZERO EQUALS
a+a				

	1	-3	11	-4	-10	-13	-4	2	10	-3	2	-1	-3	-4	-3	13	-11	-9	6	10	13

RANGE, R: — 14 15 6 3 9 6 8 13 5 3 2 1 1 16 24 2 15 4 3

$UCL_X = 20.951$

$\bar{\bar{X}} = -0.05$

$LCL_X = -21.051$

$UCL_R = 25.801$

$\bar{R} = 7.895$

Module 3, Series 2, Set 2. Individual and range chart.

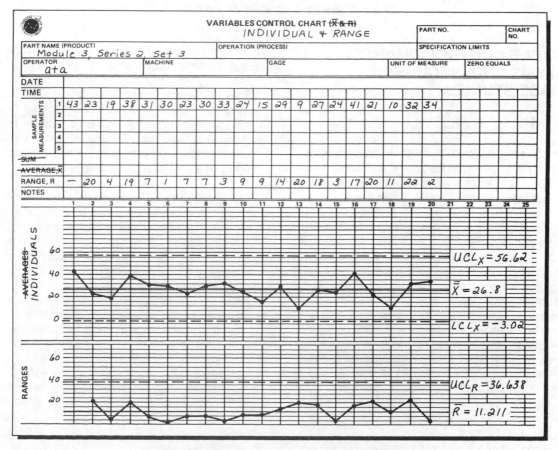

VARIABLES CONTROL CHART (X̄ & R)
INDIVIDUAL + RANGE

PART NAME (PRODUCT)	OPERATION (PROCESS)		SPECIFICATION LIMITS
Module 3, Series 2, Set 3			

OPERATOR	MACHINE	GAGE	UNIT OF MEASURE	ZERO EQUALS
a+a				

	1	43	23	19	38	31	30	23	30	33	24	15	29	9	27	24	41	21	10	32	34

RANGE, R: — 20 4 19 7 1 7 7 3 9 9 14 20 18 3 17 20 11 22 2

$UCL_X = 56.62$

$\bar{\bar{X}} = 26.8$

$LCL_X = -3.02$

$UCL_R = 36.638$

$\bar{R} = 11.211$

Module 3, Series 2, Set 3. Individual and range chart.

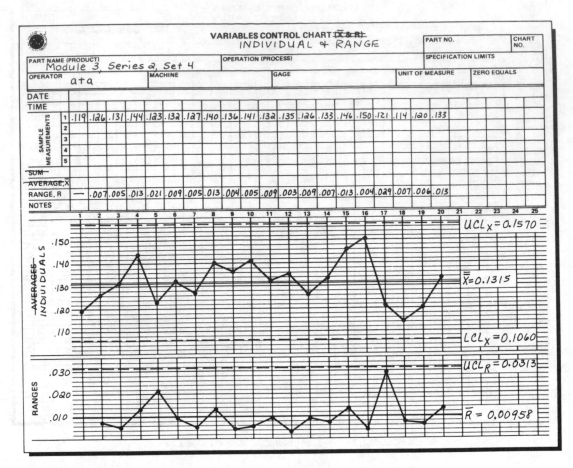

Module 3, Series 2, Set 4. Individual and range chart.

VARIABLE CONTROL CHARTS: ANALYSIS AND DISCUSSION OF CASE STUDIES

CASE 3-1

The best variable control chart for the stock preparation operation described in this problem is an average and range chart ($\overline{X}$-R), as shown in Figure 3-A. A median and range chart also could be developed and used effectively in an operation such as this.

You should decide early in the development of the control chart whether the chart will be simplified if the recorded weights are coded. The block in the upper right-hand section of the chart form titled "Zero Equals" should show that zero equals 700 grams. This means that we have subtracted 700 grams from each weight measurement listed; thus the first sample of five weights—listed as 765, 760, 748, 749, and 756—is recorded on the control chart as 65, 60, 48, 49, and 56. This step simplifies the job of finding the averages and the ranges of the samples. Simply keep in mind that the averages plotted on the chart are actually 700 grams greater than the number recorded on the chart. This rule does not apply to the range values, however. The range values plotted on the chart are the true ranges of the samples.

Remember to calculate the average range and the upper control limit first. The average range is used in calculating the control limits for the averages. If the range is shown to be too far out of control, the averages and the control limits for the averages need not be calculated. (See Figure 3-16 in the textbook.) The calculation of the upper control limit for ranges shows that all 25 range values are below the upper control limit. (See Figure 3-B.) Calculate the overall average ($\overline{\overline{X}}$). Then determine the upper and the lower control limits around that average, using the average range ($\overline{R}$), as noted previously.

Before drawing the control limits and the overall average lines on the chart, look at each sample average ($\overline{X}$) value and compare it to the upper and lower control limits you just calculated. Using the "Decision Chart for Working with Averages" (Figure 3-19 in the textbook), determine whether this job is well enough in control to allow you to continue using this chart for control of the operation.

When you compare the averages to the control limits, you should find that the values ($\overline{X}$) for Sample 1 (55.6) and for Sample 3 (60.4) are used outside the lower control limit. All of the other averages are within the control limits.

Eliminate Samples 1 and 3 from the values used; make new calculations for the ranges and the averages and for their control limits.

Record all of the calculations for the original 25 samples or subgroups and for the 23 remaining samples on the calculation work sheet on the back of the control chart. (See Figure 3-B). In this way you have a permanent record of the development of the control chart. Now you can complete the control chart by establishing a value scale for averages that allows room for the upper and the lower control limits, plus a little extra space in case an average value must be plotted outside a control limit at a later time. The overall average ($\overline{X}$) value should be located at or near the darker line on the middle of the chart. Then set the scale value to accommodate the upper and lower control limits.

The average range ($\overline{R}$) value is usually placed at or near the lowest of the three darker lines on the chart. The upper control limit for ranges (UCL_R) is located on the basis of the scale values established in this way; the bottom of the chart always has the value of zero.

The average lines, both the $\overline{X}$ and the $\overline{R}$, are drawn on the chart as solid lines. The control limit lines are drawn on the chart as dotted or broken lines.

This chart is the development chart. The control limits and average lines calculated on this chart can now be placed on a blank chart to be used as an ongoing control for the stock preparation operation for this part. It is important to enter all pertinent information on this chart. The chart heading should be filled out; the date and the time when the measurements were taken should be recorded. The control limit values should be noted.

CASE 3-2

You were asked to recommend which of two production setups should be run to fill current orders. Using measurements obtained from 100 parts per setup, you should have developed an average and range chart for each setup. (See Figures 3-C and 3-E.) The calculation work sheets for the two charts are shown in Figures 3-D and 3-F.

The calculation work sheet (Figure 3-D) and the control chart (Figure 3-C) for the production setup using Hammer #2—Die #1 show that this job set was very stable during the trial run of 100 parts. It was not necessary to eliminate any averages or ranges from the calculations of the control limits.

The calculation work sheet (Figure 3-F) and the control chart (Figure 3-E) for the production setup using Hammer #3—Die #2 show that the process had variation due to assignable causes. Samples 8 and 15 were eliminated from the calculations of the control limits, but this is not an important consideration in recommending which setup to run. Assignable causes can show up in either or both production setups.

The fact that there were points out of control on one chart but not on the other should not influence your recommendation.

The average range is the feature that you should compare on the charts. This is an indicator of the inherent variation in the process. Control charts are completed in order to determine the average range under stable conditions. The production setup with the smallest average range should make products with the least piece-to-piece variation.

Hammer #3—Die #2 showed an average range of .02122 inch. Hammer #2—Die #1 showed an average range of .01515 inch.

Did you recommend the setup using Hammer #2—Die #1?

CASE 3-3

All of the data for this chart are found to be in the range of 321.0 to 325.0 mm. The calculations involved in developing the chart are greatly simplified if the measurements are coded using 320.0 millimeters as zero. (See Figure 3-G.) The measurements then can be recorded on the chart as very small numbers.

The average range is calculated and is found to be 2.65. (See Figure 3-H.) The upper control limit for the range (UCL_R) is calculated to be 5.60. We can see that none of the individual range values is greater than 4, so none will be outside the UCL. The overall average now can be calculated. We find that it is 3.19. This value is equal to 323.19 mm when we reference it to the zero value of 320.0.

The specified dimension for this assembly operation is 323.0 ± 3.2 mm. One reason for developing this chart was to determine whether the process was set up at or near the center of the specification. To do this, we must determine first whether the operation is stable and free from assignable causes. If assignable causes are present, they must be removed before we can be confident of any decisions made on the basis of this control chart.

The upper control limit is calculated to be 4.72; the lower control limit is calculated to be 1.66. A review shows that all of the sample averages are within the upper and lower control limits. This means that no assignable causes are present in the process; the variation in the measurements is that variation that is built into the process. Therefore it is reasonable to assume that the overall average calculated is a good estimate of the process average. In this case the overall average is 3.19, which is equal to 323.19 mm. The specified dimension for this operation is 323.0 mm. Thus we can say with a high degree of confidence that the process is set up very nearly on the middle of the specification.

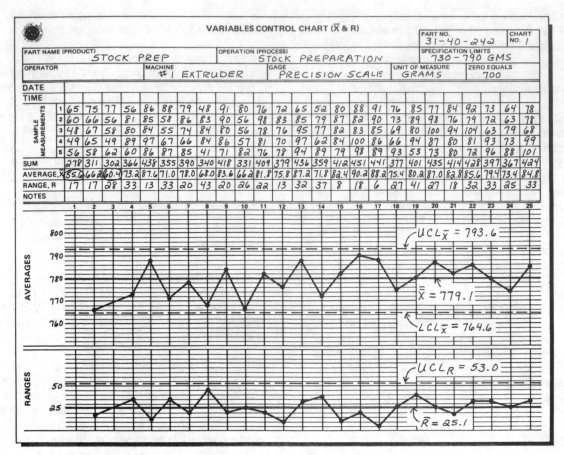

Figure 3-A. Average and range chart, Case 3-1.

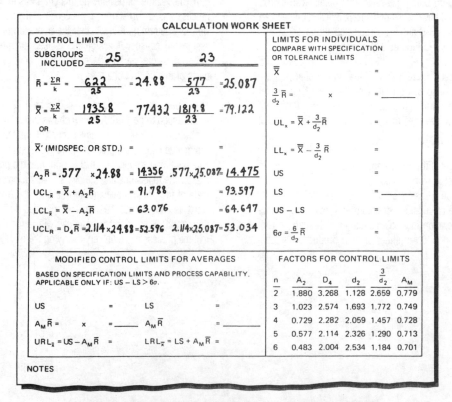

Figure 3-B. Calculation work sheet for chart in Figure 3-A, Case 3-1.

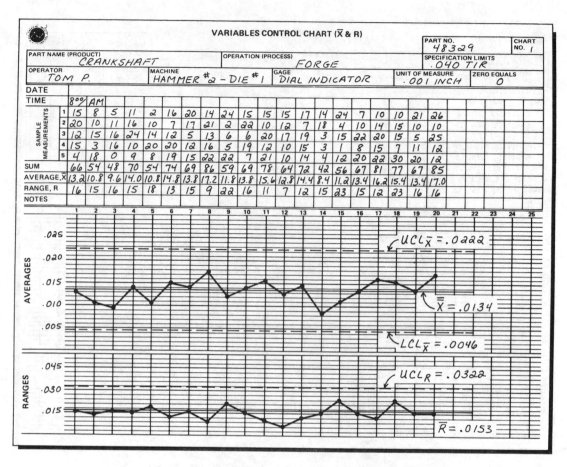

Figure 3-C. Average and range chart for Hammer #2—Die #1, Case 3-2.

CALCULATION WORK SHEET

CONTROL LIMITS

SUBGROUPS INCLUDED _____ 20 _____

$\bar{R} = \dfrac{\Sigma R}{k} = \dfrac{305}{20} = 15.25$ _____ =

$\bar{\bar{X}} = \dfrac{\Sigma \bar{X}}{k} = \dfrac{267.6}{20} = 13.38$ _____ =

OR

$\bar{X}'$ (MIDSPEC. OR STD.) = _____ =

$A_2\bar{R} = .577 \times 15.25 = \underline{8.80}$ x _____ =

$UCL_{\bar{x}} = \bar{\bar{X}} + A_2\bar{R} = 22.18$ _____ =

$LCL_{\bar{x}} = \bar{\bar{X}} - A_2\bar{R} = 4.58$ _____ =

$UCL_R = D_4\bar{R} = 2.114 \times 15.25 = 32.239$ x _____ =

LIMITS FOR INDIVIDUALS
COMPARE WITH SPECIFICATION OR TOLERANCE LIMITS

$\bar{\bar{X}}$ =

$\dfrac{3}{d_2}\bar{R} =$ x = _____

$UL_x = \bar{\bar{X}} + \dfrac{3}{d_2}\bar{R}$ =

$LL_x = \bar{\bar{X}} - \dfrac{3}{d_2}\bar{R}$ =

US =

LS =

US − LS =

$6\sigma = \dfrac{6}{d_2}\bar{R}$ =

MODIFIED CONTROL LIMITS FOR AVERAGES

BASED ON SPECIFICATION LIMITS AND PROCESS CAPABILITY. APPLICABLE ONLY IF: US − LS > 6σ.

US = _____ LS =

$A_M\bar{R} =$ x _____ $A_M\bar{R} =$ _____ =

$URL_{\bar{x}} = US - A_M\bar{R} =$ _____ $LRL_{\bar{x}} = LS + A_M\bar{R} =$

FACTORS FOR CONTROL LIMITS

n	A_2	D_4	d_2	$\dfrac{3}{d_2}$	A_M
2	1.880	3.268	1.128	2.659	0.779
3	1.023	2.574	1.693	1.772	0.749
4	0.729	2.282	2.059	1.457	0.728
5	0.577	2.114	2.326	1.290	0.713
6	0.483	2.004	2.534	1.184	0.701

NOTES

Figure 3-D. Calculation work sheet for chart in Figure 3-C, Case 3-2.

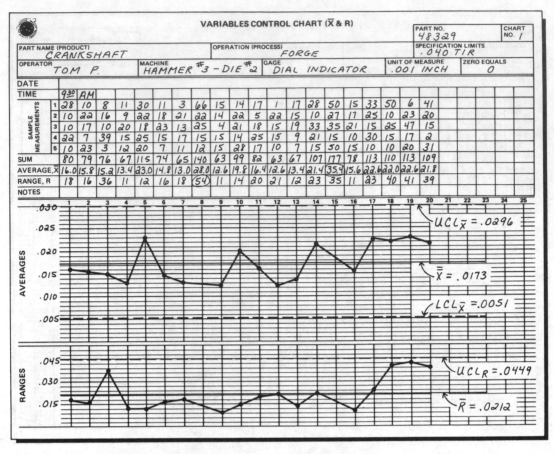

Figure 3-E. Average and range chart for Hammer #3—Die #2, Case 3-2.

CALCULATION WORK SHEET

CONTROL LIMITS

SUBGROUPS INCLUDED   **20**   **19**

$\bar{R} = \dfrac{\Sigma R}{k} = \dfrac{471}{20} = 23.55$ $\dfrac{417}{19} = 21.95$

$\bar{\bar{X}} = \dfrac{\Sigma \bar{X}}{k} =$ $\dfrac{347.4}{19} = 18.28$

OR

$\bar{X}'$ (MIDSPEC. OR STD.) =

$A_2 \bar{R} =$ $\times$ $.577 \times 21.95 = 12.67$

$UCL_{\bar{x}} = \bar{\bar{X}} + A_2 \bar{R} =$ $= 30.95$

$LCL_{\bar{x}} = \bar{\bar{X}} - A_2 \bar{R} =$ $= 5.61$

$UCL_R = D_4 \bar{R} = 2.114 \times 23.55 = 49.78$ $2.114 \times 21.95 = 46.40$

LIMITS FOR INDIVIDUALS
COMPARE WITH SPECIFICATION OR TOLERANCE LIMITS

$\bar{\bar{X}}$ =

$3\dfrac{\bar{R}}{d_2}$ = $\times$

$UL_x = \bar{\bar{X}} + \dfrac{3\bar{R}}{d_2}$ =

$LL_x = \bar{\bar{X}} - \dfrac{3\bar{R}}{d_2}$ =

US =

LS =

US − LS =

$6\sigma = \dfrac{6\bar{R}}{d_2}$ =

MODIFIED CONTROL LIMITS FOR AVERAGES
BASED ON SPECIFICATION LIMITS AND PROCESS CAPABILITY. APPLICABLE ONLY IF: US − LS > 6σ.

US   =   LS

$A_M \bar{R} =$ $\times$ $A_M \bar{R}$

$URL_{\bar{x}} = US - A_M \bar{R} =$ $LRL_{\bar{x}} = LS + A_M \bar{R}$

FACTORS FOR CONTROL LIMITS

n	A_2	D_4	d_2	$\dfrac{3}{d_2}$	A_M
2	1.880	3.268	1.128	2.659	0.779
3	1.023	2.574	1.693	1.772	0.749
4	0.729	2.282	2.059	1.457	0.728
5	0.577	2.114	2.326	1.290	0.713
6	0.483	2.004	2.534	1.184	0.701

NOTES   *Subgroups 8 ἰ 15 deleted*

$\bar{R} = 392/18 = 21.22$

$UCL_R = 2.114 \times 21.22 = 44.86$

$\bar{\bar{X}} = 312/18 = 17.33$

$A_2 \bar{R} = .577 \times 21.22 = 12.24$

$UCL_{\bar{x}} = 29.57$

$LCL_{\bar{x}} = 5.09$

Figure 3-F. Calculation work sheet for chart in Figure 3-E, Case 3-2.

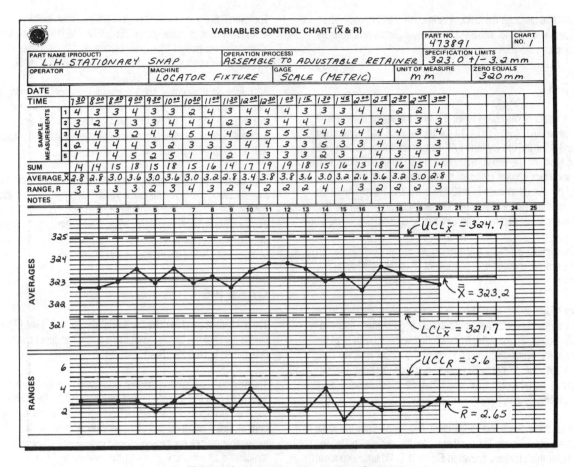

Figure 3-G. Average and range chart, Case 3-3.

CALCULATION WORK SHEET

CONTROL LIMITS

SUBGROUPS INCLUDED _____ 20 _____ _____

$\bar{R} = \dfrac{\Sigma R}{k} = \dfrac{53}{20} = 2.65$ _____ =

$\bar{\bar{X}} = \dfrac{\Sigma \bar{X}}{k} = \dfrac{63.8}{20} = 3.19$ _____ =

OR

$\bar{X}'$ (MIDSPEC. OR STD.) = _____ =

$A_2 \bar{R} = .577 \times 2.65 = 1.53$ _____ x _____ = _____

$UCL_{\bar{x}} = \bar{\bar{X}} + A_2\bar{R} = 4.72$ _____ =

$LCL_{\bar{x}} = \bar{\bar{X}} - A_2\bar{R} = 1.66$ _____ =

$UCL_R = D_4\bar{R} = 2.114 \times 2.65 = 5.60$ _____ x _____ =

LIMITS FOR INDIVIDUALS
COMPARE WITH SPECIFICATION OR TOLERANCE LIMITS

$\bar{\bar{X}}$ = _____

$\dfrac{3}{d_2}\bar{R} =$ _____ x _____ = _____

$UL_x = \bar{\bar{X}} + \dfrac{3}{d_2}\bar{R}$ = _____

$LL_x = \bar{\bar{X}} - \dfrac{3}{d_2}\bar{R}$ = _____

US _____ =

LS _____ =

US − LS _____ =

$6\sigma = \dfrac{6}{d_2}\bar{R}$ _____ =

MODIFIED CONTROL LIMITS FOR AVERAGES

BASED ON SPECIFICATION LIMITS AND PROCESS CAPABILITY. APPLICABLE ONLY IF: US − LS > 6σ.

US _____ = LS _____ =

$A_M \bar{R} =$ _____ x _____ = _____ $A_M \bar{R} =$ _____ = _____

$URL_{\bar{x}} = US - A_M\bar{R} =$ _____ $LRL_{\bar{x}} = LS + A_M\bar{R} =$

FACTORS FOR CONTROL LIMITS

n	A_2	D_4	d_2	$\dfrac{3}{d_2}$	A_M
2	1.880	3.268	1.128	2.659	0.779
3	1.023	2.574	1.693	1.772	0.749
4	0.729	2.282	2.059	1.457	0.728
5	0.577	2.114	2.326	1.290	0.713
6	0.483	2.004	2.534	1.184	0.701

NOTES

Figure 3-H. Calculation work sheet for chart in Figure 3-G, Case 3-3.

Keep in mind that although the process is in control and is centered on the specification, we do not know yet whether all pieces produced are in specification.

CASE 3-4

The average range is calculated to be 3.6 and the upper control limit for the range is 7.61. (See Figure 3-I for the average and range chart and Figure 3-J for the calculations.) All ranges are found to be inside the control limit, so the overall average can be calculated along with the upper and lower control limits for the averages. When this is done, we see that the overall average is 3.10 (equal to 323.1 mm). All of the sample average values are within the control limits, so we can say that the operation is stable and free from assignable causes.

Because the sample averages and the ranges are in control, we can estimate the process average with confidence. It is estimated to be 3.1, or 323.1 mm.

The pattern of the points plotted on the average chart appears to be almost as we would expect. We would expect slightly more than two-thirds of the points, or about 14, to be plotted within one-third of the distance from the overall average ($\overline{\overline{X}}$) line to the upper or lower control limit. In this case, 17 of the 20 points are within that area. This difference cannot be attributed to the fact that the measurements were recorded to tenths of a millimeter.

Figure 3-K is the average and range chart developed from the same measurements but ignoring the numbers after the decimal point. The calculations for this chart are shown in Figure 3-L. When we compare this chart with the one shown in Figure 3-I, we see that the patterns formed by the subgroup averages and the ranges on each chart are very much alike. The overall average is slightly less in Figure 3-K, but the average range is almost the same for both charts. Ignoring the numbers after the decimal point does not reduce the efficiency of the average and range chart nearly as much as in the frequency histogram.

CASE 3-5

Because the production associate has several machines to keep running and several control charts to maintain, it is much easier to record only one number of each measurement taken. The sleeves in this operation are cut to a length of about 615 mm, and it is easy to see that the variation in the measurements is found in the last number of the measurement. The measurements actually run from 612.0 to 618.0, so if 610.0 is subtracted from each measurement, we have only small numbers to work with. (See Figure 3-M.)

The average range is calculated to be 3.25; the upper control limit for ranges is 6.87. All of the range values fall below the upper control limit, so the chart for the sample averages can be developed.

The overall average or the average of the averages is determined to be 4.18. (This value is actually 614.18 because 610.0 was subtracted from all the measurements.) The upper control limit is calculated to be 6.06 and the lower control limit is determined to be 2.30. (See Figure 3-N.)

All points on the control chart are within the control limits, and the overall average is 614.18. The machine is set up to produce sleeves that average slightly below the mean of the specified length, and no assignable causes are present. The cutoff operation is running about as well as could be expected.

This case, however, includes a problem that is not uncommon in a manufacturing plant. The measuring and recording of the lengths of the samples take a significant amount of time, and the operator must do this for several machines. When an operation shows good stability, as this one does, it is often possible to use a different control chart to monitor and control the operation. (See Case 3-6.)

CASE 3-6

The median range of the chart is determined to be 3. (See Figure 3-O.) On the basis of the factors given in the book, the upper control limit is determined to be 8.25. (See Figure 3-P.)

The median of medians is determined to be 614, with an upper control limit of 617.78 and a lower control limit of 610.22. The calculations for these control limits are shown in Figure 3-P. All points fall within the control limits, showing that the operation is very stable and that no assignable causes are present. (See Figure 3-O.) These are the same indications as we obtained using the average and range chart. When you compare the pattern of the points on the average and range chart with the pattern of the points on the median and range chart, you will see that they are very similar.

We have recorded the actual value of the measurements on the median and range chart because the calculations involved in plotting the chart are minimal. All three values in each sample are recorded on the chart; the median of the three is identified with a circle. If the dot with the circle around it is outside the control limits, an assignable cause is present. An individual value outside a control limit does not indicate an assignable cause, but it can tell the associate when an individual piece is outside the specified limit.

The median and range chart may be used on operations that are not often subject to assignable causes. This type of chart will not detect the presence of an assignable cause as quickly as the average and range chart, but it works well for manufacturing operations that are easy to adjust and are fast-operating.

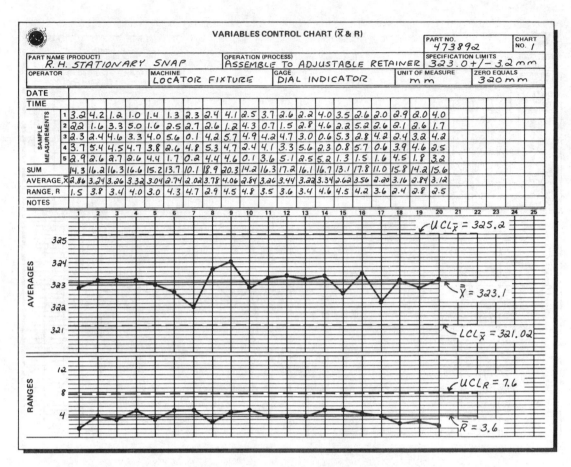

Figure 3-I. Average and range chart including numbers after decimal point, Case 3-4.

CALCULATION WORK SHEET

CONTROL LIMITS

SUBGROUPS INCLUDED ___20___

$\bar{R} = \dfrac{\Sigma R}{k} = \dfrac{72}{20} = 3.6$

$\bar{\bar{X}} = \dfrac{\Sigma \bar{X}}{k} = \dfrac{61.92}{20} = 3.10$

OR

$\bar{X}'$ (MIDSPEC. OR STD.) =

$A_2 \bar{R} = .577 \times 3.6 = 2.08$

$UCL_{\bar{x}} = \bar{\bar{X}} + A_2 \bar{R} = 5.18$

$LCL_{\bar{x}} = \bar{\bar{X}} - A_2 \bar{R} = 1.02$

$UCL_R = D_4 \bar{R} = 2.114 \times 3.6 = 7.61$

LIMITS FOR INDIVIDUALS
COMPARE WITH SPECIFICATION OR TOLERANCE LIMITS

$\bar{\bar{X}}$ =

$\dfrac{3}{d_2} \bar{R} = \qquad \times \qquad =$ _____

$UL_x = \bar{\bar{X}} + \dfrac{3}{d_2} \bar{R} =$

$LL_x = \bar{\bar{X}} - \dfrac{3}{d_2} \bar{R} =$

US =

LS = _____

US − LS =

$6\sigma = \dfrac{6}{d_2} \bar{R} =$

MODIFIED CONTROL LIMITS FOR AVERAGES

BASED ON SPECIFICATION LIMITS AND PROCESS CAPABILITY. APPLICABLE ONLY IF: US − LS > 6σ.

US = ____ LS =

$A_M \bar{R} = \qquad \times \qquad = \qquad A_M \bar{R} =$

$URL_{\bar{x}} = US - A_M \bar{R} = \qquad LRL_{\bar{x}} = LS + A_M \bar{R} =$

NOTES

FACTORS FOR CONTROL LIMITS

n	A_2	D_4	d_2	$\dfrac{3}{d_2}$	A_M
2	1.880	3.268	1.128	2.659	0.779
3	1.023	2.574	1.693	1.772	0.749
4	0.729	2.282	2.059	1.457	0.728
5	0.577	2.114	2.326	1.290	0.713
6	0.483	2.004	2.534	1.184	0.701

Figure 3-J. Calculation work sheet for chart in Figure 3-I, Case 3-4.

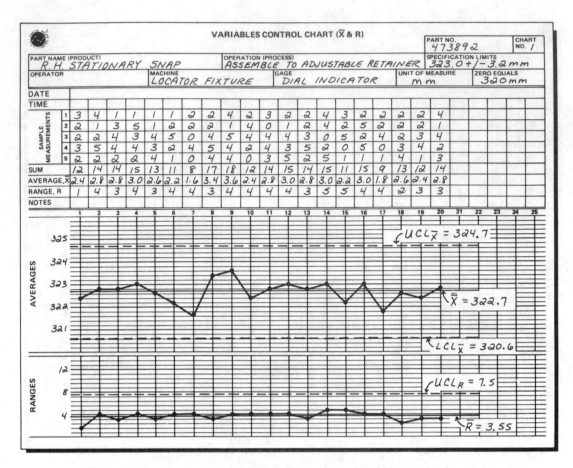

Figure 3-K. Average and range chart ignoring numbers after decimal point, Case 3-4.

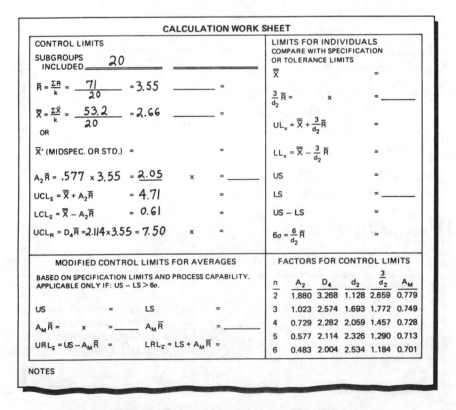

Figure 3-L. Calculation work sheet for chart in Figure 3-K, Case 3-4.

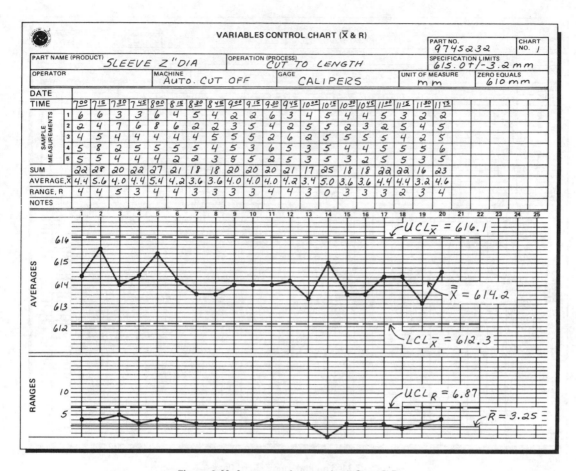

Figure 3-M. Average and range chart, Case 3-5.

CALCULATION WORK SHEET

CONTROL LIMITS

SUBGROUPS
INCLUDED ___20___

$\bar{R} = \frac{\Sigma R}{k} = \frac{65}{20} = 3.25$ _____ =

$\bar{\bar{X}} = \frac{\Sigma \bar{X}}{k} = \frac{83.6}{20} = 4.18 \ (614.18 \text{ mm}) =$

OR

$\bar{X}'$ (MIDSPEC. OR STD.) = _____ =

$A_2\bar{R} = .577 \times 3.25 = \underline{1.88}$ x _____

$UCL_{\bar{x}} = \bar{\bar{X}} + A_2\bar{R} = 6.06 \ (616.06 \text{ mm}) =$

$LCL_{\bar{x}} = \bar{\bar{X}} - A_2\bar{R} = 2.30 \ (612.30 \text{ mm}) =$

$UCL_R = D_4\bar{R} = 2.114 \times 3.25 = 6.87$ x =

LIMITS FOR INDIVIDUALS
COMPARE WITH SPECIFICATION
OR TOLERANCE LIMITS

$\bar{\bar{X}}$ =

$\frac{3}{d_2}\bar{R} =$ x =

$UL_x = \bar{\bar{X}} + \frac{3}{d_2}\bar{R}$ =

$LL_x = \bar{\bar{X}} - \frac{3}{d_2}\bar{R}$ =

US =

LS = _____

US − LS =

$6\sigma = \frac{6}{d_2}\bar{R}$ =

MODIFIED CONTROL LIMITS FOR AVERAGES		
BASED ON SPECIFICATION LIMITS AND PROCESS CAPABILITY. APPLICABLE ONLY IF: US − LS > 6σ.		

US = LS =

$A_M\bar{R} =$ x = _____ $A_M\bar{R} =$ = _____

$URL_{\bar{x}} = US - A_M\bar{R}$ = $LRL_{\bar{x}} = LS + A_M\bar{R} =$

NOTES

FACTORS FOR CONTROL LIMITS

n	A_2	D_4	d_2	$\frac{3}{d_2}$	A_M
2	1.880	3.268	1.128	2.659	0.779
3	1.023	2.574	1.693	1.772	0.749
4	0.729	2.282	2.059	1.457	0.728
5	0.577	2.114	2.326	1.290	0.713
6	0.483	2.004	2.534	1.184	0.701

Figure 3-N. Calculation work sheet for chart in Figure 3-M, Case 3-5.

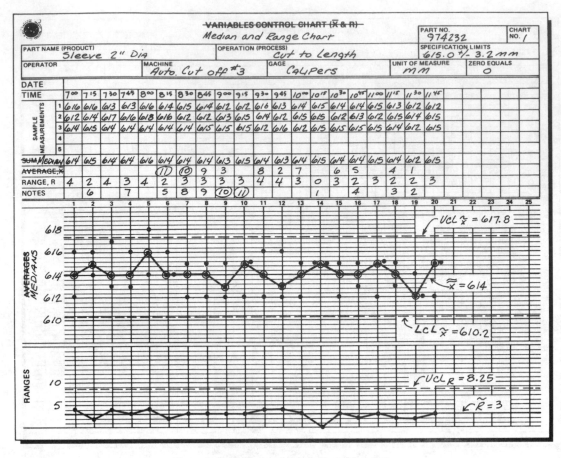

Figure 3-O. Median and range chart, Case 3-6.

CALCULATION WORK SHEET

CONTROL LIMITS

SUBGROUPS
INCLUDED

$\bar{R} = \dfrac{\Sigma R}{k}$ =

$\bar{\bar{x}} = \dfrac{\Sigma \bar{x}}{k}$ =

OR

$\tilde{\bar{X}}$ (MIDSPEC. OR STD.) =

$A_2\bar{R}$ =

$UCL_{\bar{x}} = \bar{\bar{x}} + A_2\bar{R}$ =

$LCL_{\bar{x}} = \bar{\bar{x}} - A_2\bar{R}$ =

$UCL_R = D_4\bar{R}$ =

LIMITS FOR INDIVIDUALS
COMPARE WITH SPECIFICATION
OR TOLERANCE LIMITS

$\bar{\bar{x}}$ =

$\dfrac{3\,\bar{R}}{d_2}$ =

$UL_x = \bar{\bar{x}} + \dfrac{3}{d_2}\bar{R}$ =

$LL_x = \bar{\bar{x}} - \dfrac{3}{d_2}\bar{R}$ =

US =

LS =

US − LS =

$6\sigma = \dfrac{6\,\bar{R}}{d_2}$ =

FACTORS FOR CONTROL LIMITS

n	A_2	D_4	d_2	$\dfrac{3}{d_2}$	A_M
2	1.880	3.268	1.128	2.659	0.779
3	1.023	2.574	1.693	1.772	0.749
4	0.729	2.282	2.059	1.457	0.728
5	0.577	2.114	2.326	1.290	0.713
6	0.483	2.004	2.534	1.184	0.701

MODIFIED CONTROL LIMITS FOR AVERAGES

BASED ON SPECIFICATION LIMITS AND PROCESS CAPABILITY.
APPLICABLE ONLY IF: US − LS > 6σ.

US =   LS =

$A_M\bar{R}$ =   × $A_M\bar{R}$ =

$URL_{\bar{x}} = US - A_M\bar{R}$ = $LRL_{\bar{x}} = LS + A_M\bar{R}$ =

NOTES

$\tilde{R} = 3$

$UCL_R = 2.75 \times 3 = 8.25$

$\tilde{\tilde{X}} = 614$

$UCL_{\tilde{x}} = 614 + (1.26 \times 3)$

$= 614 + 3.78$

$= 617.78$

$LCL_{\tilde{x}} = 614 - 3.78$

$= 610.22$

CASE 3-7

As indicated by the data, three pieces were measured and recorded over a fairly long period of time. (See Figure 3-Q.) You can construct an average and range chart using a three-piece sample, but you must be careful to use the proper factors when calculating the control limits for the charts. (See Figure 3-R.)

When the range chart upper control limit is calculated, the range for Sample 16 is determined to be outside the control limit of .0121. We will wait to perform the calculation of control limits for the averages. (See Figures 3-Q and 3-R.) The decision tree in Figure 3-16 of the textbook shows that when one or two ranges are outside the control limits, we can eliminate that sample and recalculate the control limits. If the remaining range values are inside the new control limits, then we can proceed to calculate the control limits for the averages.

The new range control limit is calculated to be .0108. All range values are below this value, so the control limits for the averages can be calculated. These values are .8029 for the upper control limit and .7943 for the lower control limit. Comparing the sample averages with these limits, we find that Samples 11, 12, 15, 17, and 20 are above the upper control limit. According to the decision tree for averages in Figure 3-19 of the textbook, the averages are out of control. Therefore we should find and remove the assignable causes and then obtain more measurements and establish control limits. In this problem, however, it is not practical to obtain more measurements to answer the question about the stability of the operation and to determine whether it would be safe to ignore the operation.

The plotted averages fall roughly into two groups of 10 values each, which apparently are at different levels. This could be an indication that something happened in the process that caused average value of the dimension to change on June 1. The calculations work sheet (Figure 3-R) shows the calculation of the average range and the overall average, along with their control limits, using the first 10 samples to make the calculations. These control limits show the first 10 samples to be stable, but the second 10 samples are definitely at a different process average. We can draw the conclusion that the operation has an inherent ability to be stable but also can be subject to changes in the level of operation. Therefore the operation should not be ignored, but the output must be monitored periodically with a control chart.

CASE 3-8

Figure 3-S shows the calculation of the median range and the control limit. The first calculation using median range for all 20 samples shows an upper control limit of .011. The range for Sample 16 is outisde this limit. If we delete this sample and recalculate the upper control limit, we obtain the same range as before, so the upper control limit of .011 is the same as we obtained using all 20 samples. All of the range values are now within the upper control limit, so we can

make the calculations to determine the median of the medians and the upper and lower control limits. The median of the medians is determined to be .799, the upper control limit is calculated to be .804, and the lower control limit is .794, as shown in Figure 3-S. When the medians are compared to the control limits, we find that Samples 7 and 10 are below the lower control limit and Samples 12 and 17 are above the upper control limit.

According to the rules given in Figure 3-19 of the textbook, we cannot use this data to establish a control chart for use on the job. Yet in order to compare the median and range chart to the average and range chart, we must look at the pattern of the plotted points and also must calculate the control limits using the first 10 subgroups of the data, as in Case 3-7.This calculation is shown in Figure 3-S.

When we compare the median values with the control limits, we see that the medians for Samples 11, 12, 15, 17, and 20 are outside the upper control limit. (See Figure 3-T.) The average and range chart developed in Case 3-7 from the same measurements showed the same condition. The average and range chart and the median and range chart both showed the range for Sample 16 to be outside the upper control limit.

The median for Sample 16 is shown to be outside the lower control limit in Figure 3-T, but this point on the average and range chart (Figure 3-Q) is within the control limits. This could have happened because we are using a very small sample. The median and range chart is more likely than the average and range chart to miss an out-of-control signal and to give an out-of-control signal when no assignable cause is present. The average and range chart is more sensitive than the median and range chart to variations in a process.

When a sample size as small as three is used, the chart may give a signal that an assignable cause is present when actually there is none. Likewise, sometimes it will not detect the presence of an assignable cause when one is present. This is a risk we take in exchange for the benefit of using a small sample and an easy plotting procedure, with the median and range chart.

The median and range chart exhibits the same pattern of variation as does the average and range chart. (See Figure 3-T.) When the control limits are constructed from the same 10 samples as used in the average and range chart, the two control charts tell the same story. Therefore, when we are taking samples as small as three pieces, we might as well use the median and range chart because it is easier and faster than the average and range chart.

CASE 3-9

The first 25 batches are used to develop Chart 1. (See the calculations in Figure 3-U.) All individual values and ranges are within the control limits, as shown in Figure 3-V, indicating a stable process. The calculated control limits can be used for the succeeding batches.

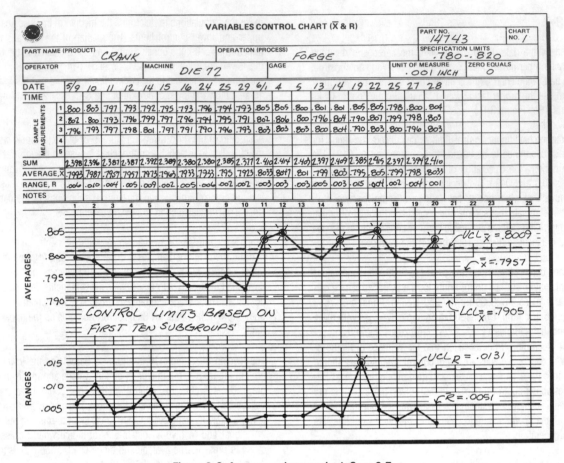

Figure 3-Q. Average and range chart, Case 3-7.

Figure 3-R. Calculation work sheet for chart in Figure 3-Q, Case 3-7.

The lower limit of the specifications is 1840 psi. The lower control limit is calculated to be 1840.05. (See Figure 3-U.) This means that as long as the process operates normally (with no assignable causes present), we can expect all batches to be above 1840.05 psi. This chart plots individual batch values, so the values plotted can be compared to the specification.

Figure 3-W, Chart 2 (Batches 26 through 50), shows that Batch 39 is outside the lower control limit. This indicates that an assignable cause was present when the batch was processed and that Batch 39 is different from the others. In regular use, the assignable cause would be sought out and corrected. The control chart shows that this was done, because the following batches are inside the control limits.

The tensile value for Batch 39 is not used to determine the range value for Batch 40. Batch 39 is eliminated from the data, so the next range value is the difference between Batch 38 and Batch 40. Figure 3-X shows the notation that was recorded on the calculation work sheet side of the control chart shown in Figure 3-W.

Figure 3-Y, Chart 3 (Batches 51 through 75), continues to show process stability. All points are inside the control limits; they appear to be centered around the overall average line and the average range line.

Figure 3-Z, Chart 4 (Batches 76 through 100), shows all points to be within the control limits. The pattern of the range values, however (17 of 25 below the average range line), shows that the process now may be operating with less batch-to-batch variation. The individuals chart shows that 17 of 25 individual measurements are above the overall average and that eight batches in a row (88 through 95) are also above the overall average. This pattern indicates a change in the process average. It would be proper to use the values in Chart 4 to recalculate the average range and the overall average and to establish new control limits for this process. The new control limits are shown on Chart 4, Figure 3-Z; the calculations are shown in Figure 3-AA.

The new control limit for the range shows that the batch-to batch variation has decreased. This change is reflected in the new control limits for the individuals, which are closer together than before.

CALCULATION WORK SHEET

CONTROL LIMITS

SUBGROUPS INCLUDED

$\bar{R} = \dfrac{\Sigma R}{k} =$

$\bar{\bar{X}} = \dfrac{\Sigma \bar{X}}{k} =$

OR

$\tilde{\bar{X}}$ (MIDSPEC. OR STD.) =

$A_2\bar{R} = \times =$

$UCL_{\bar{X}} = \bar{\bar{X}} + A_2\bar{R} =$

$LCL_{\bar{X}} = \bar{\bar{X}} - A_2\bar{R} =$

$UCL_R = D_4\bar{R} = \times =$

LIMITS FOR INDIVIDUALS
COMPARE WITH SPECIFICATION OR TOLERANCE LIMITS

$\bar{\bar{X}} =$

$\dfrac{3\bar{R}}{d_2} = =$

$UL_x = \bar{\bar{X}} + \dfrac{3\bar{R}}{d_2} =$

$LL_x = \bar{\bar{X}} - \dfrac{3\bar{R}}{d_2} =$

$US =$

$LS =$

$US - LS =$

$6\sigma = \dfrac{6\bar{R}}{d_2} =$

MODIFIED CONTROL LIMITS FOR AVERAGES
BASED ON SPECIFICATION LIMITS AND PROCESS CAPABILITY. APPLICABLE ONLY IF: US − LS > 6σ.

$US = LS =$

$A_M\bar{R} = A_M\bar{R} =$

$URL_{\bar{x}} = US - A_M\bar{R} =$ $LRL_{\bar{x}} = LS + A_M\bar{R} =$

FACTORS FOR CONTROL LIMITS

n	A_2	D_4	d_2	$\dfrac{3}{d_2}$	A_M
2	1.880	3.268	1.128	2.659	0.779
3	1.023	2.574	1.693	1.772	0.749
4	0.729	2.282	2.059	1.457	0.728
5	0.577	2.114	2.326	1.290	0.713
6	0.483	2.004	2.534	1.184	0.701

First ten subgroups

$\tilde{R} = .005$

$UCL_R = 2.75 \times .005 = .01375$

$\tilde{\tilde{X}} = .7965$

$UCL_{\tilde{x}} = .7965 + (1.26 \times .005)$
$= .8028$

$LCL_{\tilde{x}} = .7965 - (1.26 \times .005)$
$= .7902$

NOTES

$\tilde{R} = .004$

$UCL_R = \tilde{D}_4 \times \tilde{R}$

$UCL_R = 2.75 \times .004 = .011$

Delete #16

$\tilde{R} = .004$

$UCL_R = 2.75 \times .004 = .011$

$\tilde{\tilde{X}} = .799$

$\tilde{A}_2\tilde{R} = 1.26 \times .004 = .005$

$UCL_{\tilde{x}} = .799 + .005 = .804$

$LCL_{\tilde{x}} = .799 - .005 = .794$

Figure 3-S. Calculation work sheet for chart in Figure 3-T, Case 3-8.

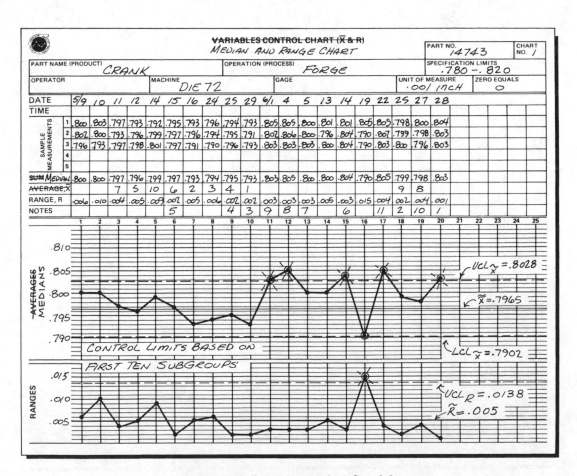

Figure 3-T. Median and range chart, Case 3-8.

CALCULATION WORK SHEET

CONTROL LIMITS

SUBGROUPS INCLUDED _____

$\bar{R} = \dfrac{\Sigma R}{k} =$

$\bar{\bar{X}} = \dfrac{\Sigma \bar{X}}{k} =$

OR

$\bar{X}'$ (MIDSPEC. OR STD.) =

$A_2 \bar{R} = \quad \times \quad =$

$UCL_{\bar{x}} = \bar{\bar{X}} + A_2\bar{R} =$

$LCL_{\bar{x}} = \bar{\bar{X}} - A_2\bar{R} =$

$UCL_R = D_4\bar{R} = \quad \times \quad =$

LIMITS FOR INDIVIDUALS
COMPARE WITH SPECIFICATION OR TOLERANCE LIMITS

$\bar{\bar{X}} =$

$\dfrac{3\bar{R}}{d_2} =$

$UL_x = \bar{\bar{X}} + \dfrac{3\bar{R}}{d_2} =$

$LL_x = \bar{\bar{X}} - \dfrac{3\bar{R}}{d_2} =$

$US =$

$LS =$

$US - LS =$

$6\sigma = \dfrac{6\bar{R}}{d_2} =$

FACTORS FOR CONTROL LIMITS

n	A_2	D_4	d_2	$\dfrac{3}{d_2}$	A_M
2	1.880	3.268	1.128	2.659	0.779
3	1.023	2.574	1.693	1.772	0.749
4	0.729	2.282	2.059	1.457	0.728
5	0.577	2.114	2.326	1.290	0.713
6	0.483	2.004	2.534	1.184	0.701

MODIFIED CONTROL LIMITS FOR AVERAGES
BASED ON SPECIFICATION LIMITS AND PROCESS CAPABILITY.
APPLICABLE ONLY IF: US − LS > 6σ.

$US = \qquad LS =$

$A_M\bar{R} = \quad \times \quad = \qquad A_M\bar{R} =$

$URL_{\bar{x}} = US - A_M\bar{R} = \qquad LRL_{\bar{x}} = LS + A_M\bar{R} =$

NOTES *Control limits calculated using batches 1 through 25*

$\Sigma R = 162$

$\bar{R} = 162/24 = 6.75$

$UCL_R = D_4\bar{R} = 3.268 \times 6.75$
$\qquad = 22.06$

$\bar{\bar{X}} = \Sigma X/25 = 1451/25 = 58.04$

$UCL_X = \bar{\bar{X}} + 2.66\bar{R} = 58.04 + (2.66 \times 6.75)$
$\qquad = 76.0$

$LCL_X = 58.04 - (2.66 \times 6.75)$
$\qquad = 40.09$

Figure 3-U. Calculation work sheet for chart in Figure 3-V, Case 3-9.

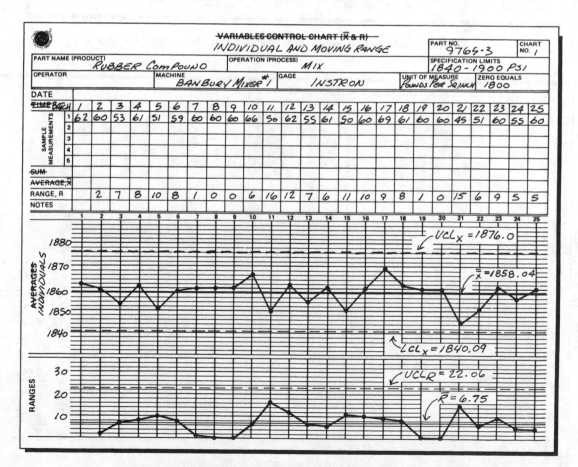

Figure 3-V. Individual and range chart, Chart 1, Batches 1-25, Case 3-9.

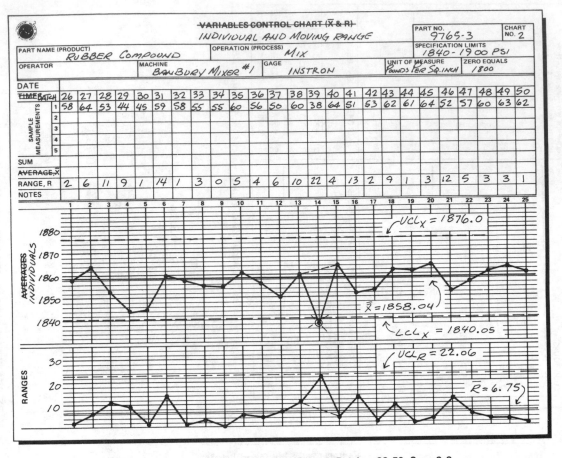

Figure 3-W. Individual and range chart, Chart 2, Batches 26-50, Case 3-9.

NOTES

#1 - Batch #39 is outside the lower control limit. This indicates an assignable cause was present when the batch was processed, and batch #39 is different from the others. The variation in the tensile strength is not due to chance causes. The tensile strength in this batch is, in fact, below the specification limit of 1840 psi. The tensile value for batch #39 should not be used to determine the range plotted for batch #40. The range value to be used is the difference between batch #38 and batch #40.

Figure 3-X. Calculation work sheet for chart in Figure 3-W, Case 3-9.

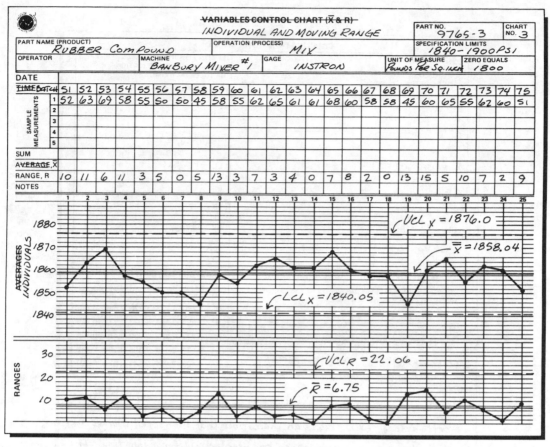

Figure 3-Y. Individual and range chart, Chart 3, Batches 51-75, Case 3-9.

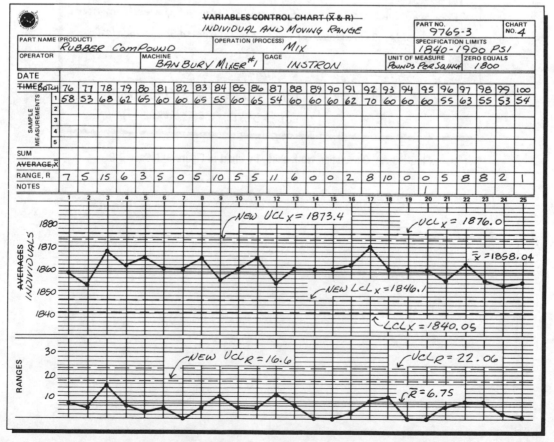

Figure 3-Z. Individual and range chart, Chart 4, Batches 76-100, Case 3-9.

CALCULATION WORK SHEET

CONTROL LIMITS	LIMITS FOR INDIVIDUALS COMPARE WITH SPECIFICATION OR TOLERANCE LIMITS

SUBGROUPS
  INCLUDED _____   _____

$\bar{R} = \frac{\Sigma R}{k}$ = _____ = _____ =

$\bar{\bar{X}} = \frac{\Sigma \bar{X}}{k}$ = _____ = _____ =

  OR

$\bar{X}'$ (MIDSPEC. OR STD.) =   =

$A_2\bar{R}$ =   x   = _____   x   = _____

$UCL_{\bar{x}} = \bar{\bar{X}} + A_2\bar{R}$ =   =

$LCL_{\bar{x}} = \bar{\bar{X}} - A_2\bar{R}$ =   =

$UCL_R = D_4\bar{R}$ =   x   =   x   =

$\bar{\bar{X}}$ =

$\frac{3}{d_2}\bar{R}$ =   x   =

$UL_x = \bar{\bar{X}} + \frac{3}{d_2}\bar{R}$ =

$LL_x = \bar{\bar{X}} - \frac{3}{d_2}\bar{R}$ =

US

LS   = _____

US – LS   =

$6\sigma = \frac{6}{d_2}\bar{R}$ =

MODIFIED CONTROL LIMITS FOR AVERAGES	FACTORS FOR CONTROL LIMITS				
BASED ON SPECIFICATION LIMITS AND PROCESS CAPABILITY. APPLICABLE ONLY IF: US – LS > 6σ.	n	A_2	D_4	d_2	$\frac{3}{d_2}$	A_M

n	A_2	D_4	d_2	$\frac{3}{d_2}$	A_M
2	1.880	3.268	1.128	2.659	0.779
3	1.023	2.574	1.693	1.772	0.749
4	0.729	2.282	2.059	1.457	0.728
5	0.577	2.114	2.326	1.290	0.713
6	0.483	2.004	2.534	1.184	0.701

US   =   LS   =

$A_M\bar{R}$ =   x   = _____ $A_M\bar{R}$ = _____

$URL_{\bar{x}} = US - A_M\bar{R}$ = $LRL_{\bar{x}} = LS + A_M\bar{R}$ =

NOTES

#1 – The tensile values for batches #88 through #95 are all above the overall average ($\bar{\bar{X}}$). This is an indication that the overall average has increased or an assignable cause has been present for a long time. If the assignable cause can be found and made a permanent part of the process, the overall average would be closer to the specification mean. There would be less chance of making a batch out of specification on the low side. If new control limits are calculated using the last 25 batches:

$\bar{R} = 127/25 = 5.08$ $\bar{\bar{X}} = 1497/25 = 59.88$

$UCL_R = 3.268 \times 5.08$ $UCL_x = 59.88 + (2.66 \times 5.08) = 73.4$

$= 16.6$ $LCL_x = 59.88 - (2.66 \times 5.08) = 46.4$

Figure 3-AA. Calculation work sheet for chart in Figure 3-Z, Case 3-9.

p-CONTROL CHARTS: REVIEW QUESTIONS

1. (a) Variable data.
   (b) From things you can measure such as end play, inside diameter, or resistance.
2. (a) Attribute data.
   (b) They provide attribute or counting data.
3. (a) p-chart.
   (b) np-chart.
   (c) c-chart.
   (d) p-charts monitor *percentage* of defective pieces.
   (e) np-charts monitor *number* of defective pieces.
   (f) c-charts monitor number of defects.
   (g) *Percentage.*
   (h) *Number* of defective *parts.*
   (i) *Count.*
4. (a) A bad piece or unit.
   (b) A defect is something wrong in a piece. The presence of one or more defects in a single piece makes that piece defective or unacceptable.

PERCENT DEFECTIVE p-CHARTS

1. (a) The number of units defective in 100 units.
   (b) A percent defective p-chart.
2. (a) p = number of defective pieces divided by sample size. Multiply the result by 100%.
   (b) p = six percent.
   (c) p = eight percent.
3. (a) Yes.
   (b) Upper control limit.
   (c) Lower control limit.
4. (a) The process is in statistical control.
   (b) Continue to run the process *without* any adjustments.
   (c) If the point is inside the control limit, keep running the process without adjustment. If outside, then find the assignable cause and remove it.
5. (a) Probably, *only* inherent variation that is also called system causes, common causes, or natural variation.
   (b) System causes, common causes, natural variation, or random variation.
   (c) Chance causes are the result of variations in raw materials, machine performance, method, environment, people, etc.
   (d) The production associate can usually do little, if anything, about it.

6. (a) The process is out of statistical control. There are one or more special causes at work.
   (b) An assignable or special cause is present.
   (c) *Immediately* identify the cause and remove it.
7. (a) Machine.
   (b) Raw materials.
   (c) Method.
   (d) Environment.
   (e) The production associate.

SETTING UP PERCENT DEFECTIVE p-CHARTS

1. (a) For control.
   (b) For analysis.
   (c) For communication.
2. They help focus attention on consistent quality.
Step 1   (a) (1) At least fifty.
             (2) Four or more.
             (3) Very large samples over a long time.
             (4) Break them into smaller samples over shorter time spans.
             (5) Calculate separate control limits for these samples.
         (b) *Only* inherent variation, i.e., system causes.
         (c) They appear at random; they are completely unpredictable.
         (d) Over a short period from a single source of production. Take them from one machine, one machine head, one associate, one batch of materials.
         (e) About five defectives.
         (f) Yes.
Step 3. (a) The date and time.
         (b) The number inspected in each sample.
         (c) The number of defectives in each sample.
Step 4. p = number of defectives divided by number inspected times 100 percent.
Step 5. (a) Add all the numbers of defective pieces. Divide this total by the total number of pieces inspected. Multiply by 100%.
         (b) 1,000 ($20 \times 50 = 1,000$).
Step 6. (a) Set the vertical scale so that the largest and smallest p's fit easily on the graph.
         (b) For the upper control limit.
         (c) Plot the p's and connect the plot points.
         (d) The average percent defective, which is designated as $\bar{p}$.

Step 7. (a) Square root.
(b) ×
(c) The sample size, or number of pieces in each sample.
(d) The average of the p's.

(e) $UCL_p = \bar{p} + 3\sqrt{\dfrac{\bar{p} \times (100\% - \bar{p})}{n}}$

(f) Subtract $\bar{p}$ from 100%.
(g) 78.7%
(h) Divide by the sample size n, which is 50.
(i) 33.5262
(j) Take the square root of 33.5262.
(k) 5.790%
(l) 3
(m) 17.37%
(n) Add this to the average percent defective, $\bar{p}$.
(o) 38.67%
(p) 50
(q) 11.6% defective.

(r) $UCL_p = \bar{p} + 3\sqrt{\dfrac{\bar{p} \times (100\% - \bar{p})}{n}}$

$= 11.6 + 3\sqrt{\dfrac{11.6 \times (100 - 11.6)}{50}}$

$= 11.6 + 3\sqrt{20.5088}$
$= 11.6 + (3 \times 4.529)$
$= 25.186\%$

(s) $LCL_p = \bar{p} - 3\sqrt{\dfrac{\bar{p} \times (100\% - \bar{p})}{n}}$

(t) For the upper control limit, we *add* the quantity three times the square root. For the lower control limit, we subtract three times the square root.
(u) At zero.

FRACTION DEFECTIVE p-CHARTS

(a) The fraction defective p-chart.
(b) Fractions *not* percentages. That is, it shows the result of dividing the number of defective pieces in a sample by the sample size.
(c) A fraction, which may be in decimal form.
(d) p equals the result of dividing the number of defective pieces by the sample size.
(e) Definitely *not*.
(f) A fraction.
(g) At the left-most side of the number. It would be two places to the left of the corresponding percentage.
(h) Add up all the numbers of defective pieces. Divide this by the total of all the samples.

(i) $UCL_p = \bar{p} + 3\sqrt{\dfrac{\bar{p} \times (1 - \bar{p})}{n}}$

(j) $LCL_p = \bar{p} - 3\sqrt{\dfrac{\bar{p} \times (1 - \bar{p})}{n}}$

(k) (1) We use the average fraction defective, not the average percentage defective.

(2) We use "1" instead of "100%."

(l) Yes, except for the two differences described before.
(m) In decimal form, not in percentages.

Step 8. 1. (a) The process is in statistical control.
(b) Only inherent variation.
2. (a) Throw out those one or two p's and recalculate.
(b) Refigure the average percent defective, $\bar{p}$. Then refigure the control limits.
(c) It is out of statistical control.
(d) Find the special causes, remove them, take new data, and set up the chart again.
(e) Go ahead and run the process.
(f) There may be some assignable causes still present.
3. (a) It is out of statistical control.
(b) Find the special causes, remove them, collect new data, and prepare a new p-chart.

Step 9. (a) Yes.
(b) Yes, it can have any number of defects.

HOW TO USE THE p-CHART IN CONTINUED PRODUCTION

1. (a) If all the p's are in control.
(b) Apparently only inherent variation is at work.
2. (a) To make sure the process is where you think it is; to confirm whether a change may have occurred.
(b) Take ten new p's. Calculate a new $\bar{p}$ based on those ten p's.
(c) Compare the new $\bar{p}$ with the old $\bar{p}$.

p-CONTROL CHARTS: EXERCISES, SERIES 1, A

1. **Practice Set.**

(a) 20%	(h) 16%	(o) 10%
(b) 6%	(i) 14%	(p) 16%
(c) 12%	(j) 12%	(q) 14%
(d) 6%	(k) 22%	(r) 18%
(e) 16%	(l) 12%	(s) 16%
(f) 6%	(m) 8%	(t) 20%
(g) 18%	(n) 6%	

2. *See the answer charts.*
3. *See the answer charts.*

4. $UCL_p = \bar{p} + 3\sqrt{\dfrac{\bar{p} \times (100\% - \bar{p})}{n}}$

5. *See the answer charts.*
Example calculations for Set 1:

$$UCL_p = \bar{p} + 3\sqrt{\frac{\bar{p} \times (100\% - \bar{p})}{n}}$$

$$= 11.3 + 3\sqrt{\frac{11.3 \times (100 - 11.3)}{50}}$$

$$= 11.3 + 3\sqrt{20.0462}$$
$$= 11.3 + (3 \times 4.4772)$$
$$= 11.3 + 13.4319$$
$$= 24.73\%$$

6. (a) $LCL_p = \bar{p} - 3\sqrt{\frac{\bar{p} \times (100\% - \bar{p})}{n}}$

  (b) For the upper limit, we are *adding* three times the square root term to $\bar{p}$. For the lower control limit we *subtract* three times the square root term.
  (c) Set the lower control limit at zero.

7. *See the answer charts.*
Example calculations for Set 1:

$$LCL_p = \bar{p} - 3\sqrt{\frac{\bar{p} \times (100\% - \bar{p})}{n}}$$

$$= 11.3 - 3\sqrt{\frac{11.3 \times (100 - 11.3)}{50}}$$

$$= 11.3 - \sqrt{20.0462}$$
$$= 11.3 - (3 \times 4.4772)$$
$$= 11.3 - 13.4319$$
$$= -2.13$$

Set $LCL_p = 0.00$

6. (a) Sets 1–4. No.
  (b) Sets 1–4. Since all the p's are in control, use the chart to control and monitor the process.

p-CONTROL CHARTS: EXERCISES, SERIES 1, B

1. **Practice Set.**

(a) 0.32	(h) 0.24	(o) 0.16
(b) 0.10	(i) 0.18	(p) 0.24
(c) 0.14	(j) 0.20	(q) 0.22
(d) 0.12	(k) 0.28	(r) 0.24
(e) 0.24	(l) 0.18	(s) 0.28
(f) 0.18	(m) 0.10	(t) 0.22
(g) 0.26	(n) 0.10	

2. (a) p = the number of defective pieces divided by the sample size.
  (b) No.
  (c) A decimal fraction.
3. *See the answer charts.*

4. $UCL_p = \bar{p} + 3\sqrt{\frac{\bar{p} \times (1 - \bar{p})}{n}}$

5. *See the answer charts.*
Example calculations for Set 1:

$$UCL_p = \bar{p} + 3\sqrt{\frac{\bar{p} \times (1 - \bar{p})}{n}}$$

$$= 0.195 + 3\sqrt{\frac{0.195 \times (1 - 0.195)}{50}}$$

$$= 0.195 + 3\sqrt{0.0031395}$$
$$= 0.195 + (3 \times 0.05603)$$
$$= 0.195 + 0.16809$$
$$= 0.3631$$

6. (a) $LCL_p = \bar{p} - 3\sqrt{\frac{\bar{p} \times (1 - \bar{p})}{n}}$

  (b) The upper control limit for fractions defective *adds* the square root term, $3\sqrt{\bar{p}(1 - \bar{p})/n}$, whereas the lower control limit subtracts the same term.
  (c) Set the lower control limit at zero.

7. *See the answer charts.*
Example calculations for Set 1:

$$LCL_p = \bar{p} - 3\sqrt{\frac{\bar{p} \times (1 - \bar{p})}{n}}$$

$$= 0.195 - 3\sqrt{\frac{0.195 \times (1 - 0.195)}{50}}$$

$$= 0.195 - 3\sqrt{0.0031395}$$
$$= 0.195 - (3 \times 0.05603)$$
$$= 0.195 - 0.16809$$
$$= 0.02691$$

8. (a) Sets 1–2. No.
  (b) Sets 1–2. Since all the p's are in control, you may use the chart to run the job and monitor the process.

p-CONTROL CHARTS: EXERCISES, SERIES 2, A

1. **Practice Set.**

(a) 14%	(h) 14%	(o) 10%
(b) 16%	(i) 14%	(p) 6%
(c) 8%	(j) 8%	(q) 8%
(d) 10%	(k) 8%	(r) 12%
(e) 12%	(l) 8%	(s) 18%
(f) 18%	(m) 14%	(t) 12%
(g) 16%	(n) 14%	

2. *See the answer charts.*
3. *See the answer charts.*

4. $UCL_p = \bar{p} + 3\sqrt{\frac{\bar{p} \times (100\% - \bar{p})}{n}}$

5. *See the answer charts.*
Example calculations for Set 1:

$$UCL_p = \bar{p} + 3\sqrt{\frac{\bar{p} \times (100\% - \bar{p})}{n}}$$

$$= 27.7 + 3\sqrt{\frac{27.7 \times (100 - 27.7)}{50}}$$

$$= 27.7 + 3\sqrt{40.0542}$$
$$= 27.7 + (3 \times 6.3288)$$
$$= 27.7 + 18.9865$$
$$= 46.7\%$$

6. (a) $LCL_p = \bar{p} - 3\sqrt{\dfrac{\bar{p} \times (100\% - \bar{p})}{n}}$

(b) For the upper limit, we are *adding* three times the square root term to $\bar{p}$. For the lower control limit we *subtract* three times the square root term.

(c) Set it at zero.

7. *See the answer charts.*
Example calculations for Set 1:

$$LCL_p = \bar{p} - 3\sqrt{\frac{\bar{p} \times (100\% - \bar{p})}{n}}$$

$$= 27.7 - 3\sqrt{\frac{27.7 \times (100 - 27.7)}{50}}$$

$$= 27.7\% - 3\sqrt{40.0542}$$
$$= 27.7\% - (3 \times 6.3288)$$
$$= 27.7\% - 18.9865$$
$$= 8.7\%$$

8. (a) Sets 1–4. No.

(b) Sets 1–4. Since all the p's are in control, you may use the chart to run the job and monitor the process.

p-CONTROL CHARTS: EXERCISES, SERIES 2, B

1. **Practice Set.**

(a) 0.14	(h) 0.16	(o) 0.14
(b) 0.18	(i) 0.16	(p) 0.6
(c) 0.10	(j) 0.10	(q) 0.10
(d) 0.12	(k) 0.12	(r) 0.12
(e) 0.14	(l) 0.16	(s) 0.18
(f) 0.18	(m) 0.16	(t) 0.12
(g) 0.20	(n) 0.16	

2. (a) p = the number of defective pieces divided by the sample size.
   (b) No.
   (c) A decimal fraction.

3. *See the answer charts.*

4. $UCL_p = \bar{p} + 3\sqrt{\dfrac{\bar{p} \times (1 - \bar{p})}{n}}$

5. *See the answer charts.*
Example calculations for Set 1:

$$UCL_p = \bar{p} + 3\sqrt{\frac{\bar{p} \times (1 - \bar{p})}{n}}$$

$$= 0.181 + 3\sqrt{\frac{0.181 \times (1 - 0.181)}{50}}$$

$$= 0.181 + 3\sqrt{0.00296}$$
$$= 0.181 + (3 \times 0.054)$$
$$= 0.181 + 0.163$$
$$= 0.344$$

6. (a) $LCL_p = \bar{p} - 3\sqrt{\dfrac{\bar{p} \times (1 - \bar{p})}{n}}$

(b) The upper control limit for fractions defective *adds* the square root term to $\bar{p}$, $3\sqrt{\bar{p}(1 - \bar{p})}/n$, whereas the lower control limit *subtracts* the same term.

(c) Set the lower control limit at zero.

7. *See the answer charts.*
Example calculations for Set 1:

$$LCL_p = \bar{p} - 3\sqrt{\frac{\bar{p} \times (1 - \bar{p})}{n}}$$

$$= 0.181 - 3\sqrt{\frac{0.181 \times (1 - 0.181)}{50}}$$

$$= 0.181 - 3\sqrt{0.00296}$$
$$= 0.181 - (3 \times 0.054)$$
$$= 0.181 - 0.163$$
$$= 0.018$$

8. (a) Sets 1–2. No.

(b) Sets 1–2. Make *no* adjustments at all. All p's are in control.

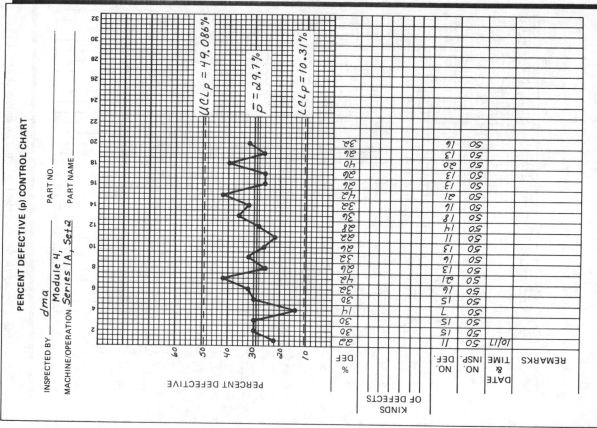

Module 4, Series 1A, Set 2. Percent defective (p) control chart.

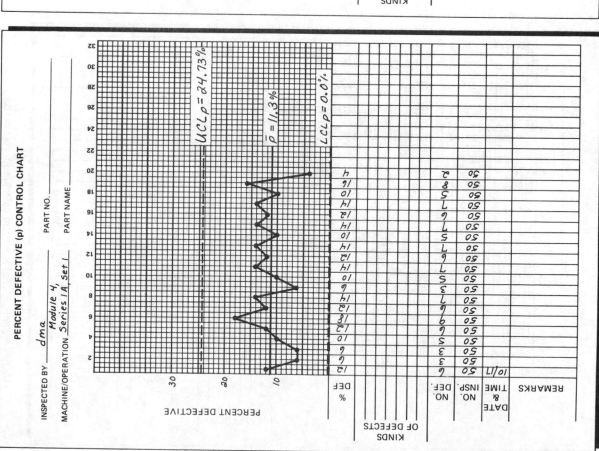

Module 4, Series 1A, Set 1. Percent defective (p) control chart.

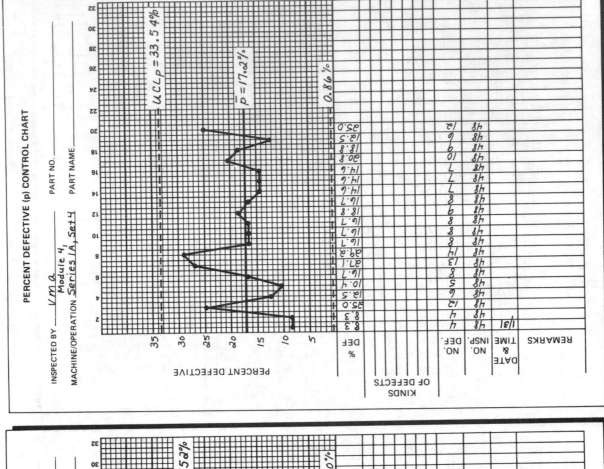

Module 4, Series 1A, Set 4. Percent defective (p) control chart.

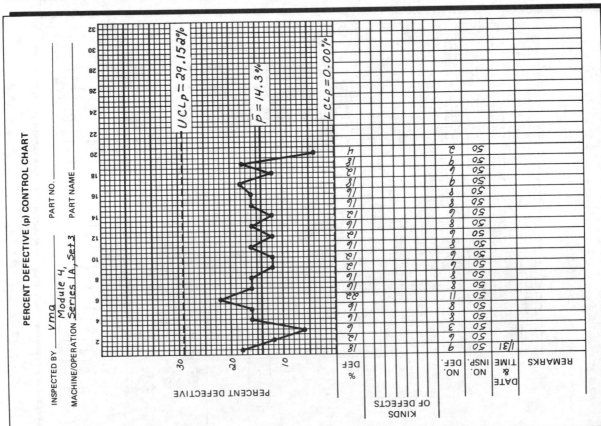

Module 4, Series 1A, Set 3. Percent defective (p) control chart.

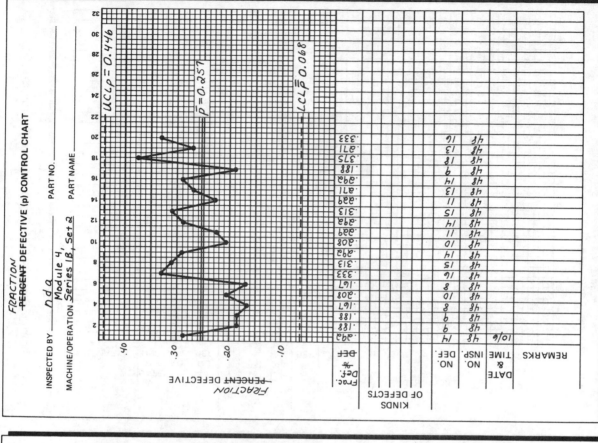

Module 4, Series 1B, Set 2. Fraction defective (p) control chart.

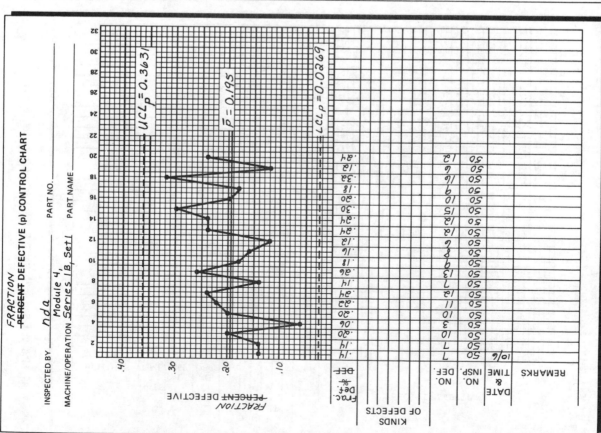

Module 4, Series 1B, Set 1. Fraction defective (p) control chart.

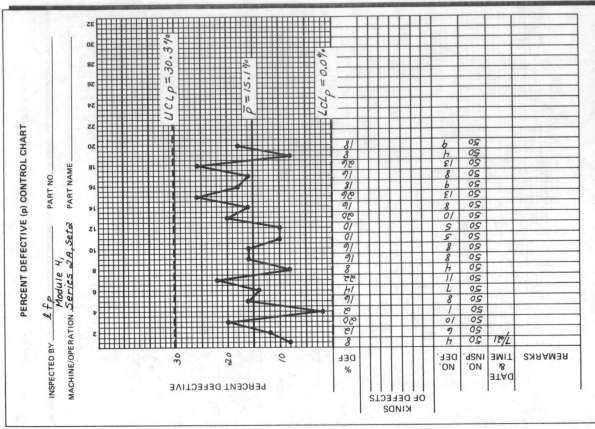

Module 4, Series 2A, Set 2. Percent defective (p) control chart.

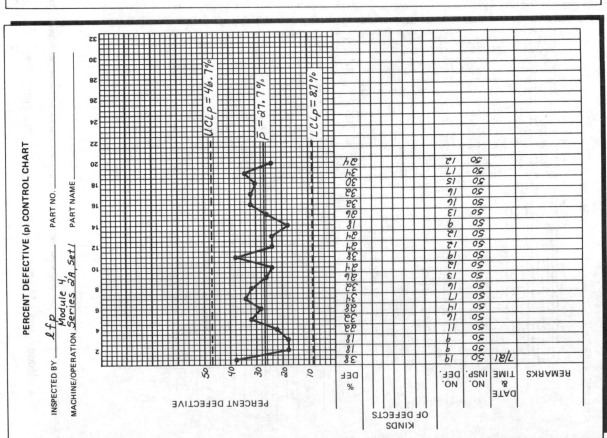

Module 4, Series 2A, Set 1. Percent defective (p) control chart.

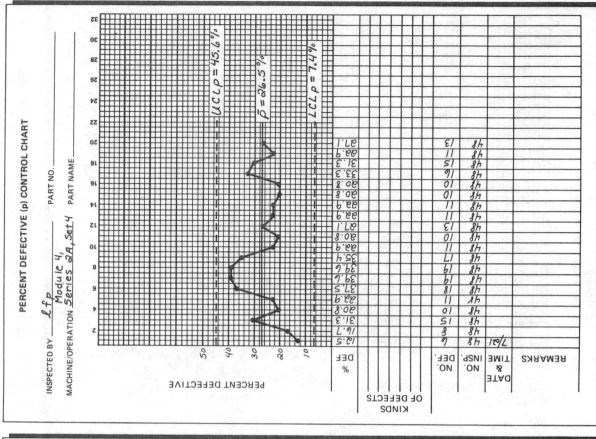

Module 4, Series 2A, Set 4. Percent defective (p) control chart.

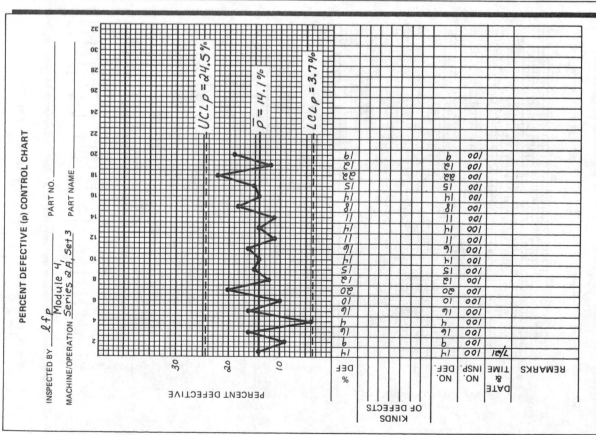

Module 4, Series 2A, Set 3. Percent defective (p) control chart.

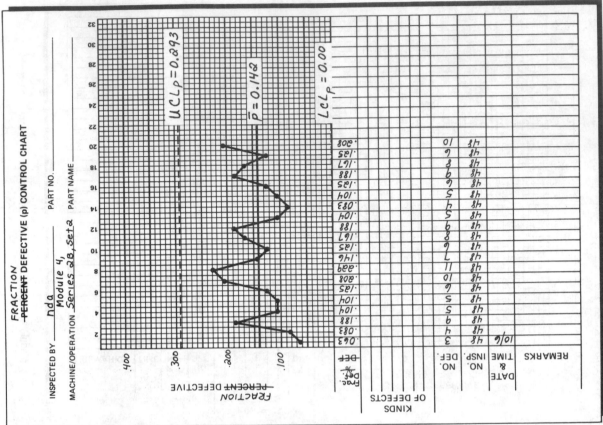

Module 4, Series 2B, Set 2. Fraction defective (p) control chart.

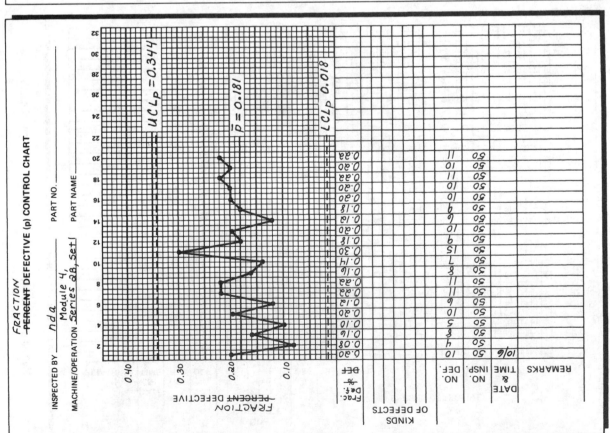

Module 4, Series 2B, Set 1. Fraction defective (p) control chart.

np-CONTROL CHARTS: REVIEW QUESTIONS

1. The np-chart plots the number of defectives instead of the percentage defective in a sample.
2. Yes.

SETTING UP THE np-CHART

1. You record the number of defectives instead of the percentage of defectives.

Step 1. (a) Large enough so that you average four or more defectives per sample.
   (b) The same way as for percentage defectives. (Refer to page 92 in the textbook, *SPC Simplified*.)
   (c) As frequently as for the percentage defectives. (Refer to page 92 in the textbook, *SPC simplified*.)

Step 2. (a) Yes.
   (b) "NUMBER DEFECTIVE." Do not write anything under "% DEF."

Step 3. (a) Yes.
   (b) Yes. It is very important to keep this point in mind.
   (c) The number of defective parts, not the percentage.

Step 4. (a) The average number of defectives for the process.
   (b) Add up the total number of defectives in all the samples and divide the total by the number of samples.
   (c) Yes.
   (d) No, it is not.
   (e) Divide 176 by 20.
   (f) 8.8

Step 5. (a) Set the scale so that the smallest and largest np's will fit comfortably, leaving enough extra room for the upper control limit. Also, choose a scale that makes it easy to plot the points.
   (b) Zero.

Step 6. (a) To the one for p's, percentages defective.
   (b) $UCL_{np} = 3\sqrt{n\overline{p} \times (1 - n\overline{p}/n)}$
   (c) Square root.
   (d) $\times$
   (e) The sample size.
   (f) The average number of defectives for the process.
   (g) Divide the $n\overline{p}$ in the parentheses by the sample size, n.
   (h) 0.118
   (i) Multiply this result by $n\overline{p}$.
   (j) 5.2038
   (k) Take the square root of this last result.
   (l) 2.281
   (m) 3
   (n) 6.844
   (o) Add the result to $n\overline{p}$.
   (p) 12.74
   (q) 50
   (r) 7.2

(s) $UCL_{np} = n\overline{p} + 3\sqrt{n\overline{p} \times (1 - n\overline{p}/n)}$
$$= 7.2 + 3\sqrt{7.2 \times (1 - 7.2/50)}$$
$$= 7.2 + 3\sqrt{7.2 \times (1 - 0.144)}$$
$$= 7.2 + 3\sqrt{7.2 \times 0.856}$$
$$= 7.2 + 3\sqrt{6.1632}$$
$$= 7.2 + (3 \times 2.4826)$$
$$= 7.2 + 7.4477$$
$$= 14.6477 = 14.648$$
(t) $LCL_{np} = n\overline{p} - 3\sqrt{n\overline{p} \times (1 - n\overline{p}/n)}$
(u) Set the lower control limit at zero.

Step 7. 1. (a) It is in statistical control.
   (b) Only inherent variation (common causes, chance variation).
2. (a) Throw out those one or two samples and recalculate the $n\overline{p}$ and the control limts.
   (b) Recalculate $n\overline{p}$, then recalculate the control limits.
   (c) It is out of statistical control.
   (d) Find and remove any and all assignable causes, then gather new data and set up a new control chart.
   (e) You may continue to use the chart with its $n\overline{p}$ and control limits.
   (f) Assignable causes.
   (g) There may still be some present.
3. (a) It is out of statistical control
   (b) Find and remove the assignable causes, then collect new data and set up a new control chart.

np-CONTROL CHARTS: EXERCISES, SERIES 1

1. (a) No
   (b) You use 20, the number of samples, when you calculate $n\overline{p}$.
   (c) 7.1
2. *See the answer charts.*
3. *See the answer charts.*
4. (a) $UCL_{np} = n\overline{p} + 3\sqrt{n\overline{p} \times (1 - n\overline{p}/n)}$
   (b) $LCL_{np} = n\overline{p} - 3\sqrt{n\overline{p} \times (1 - n\overline{p}/n)}$
   (c) Set the lower control limit to zero.
5. *See the answer charts.*
   Example calculations for Set 1:
   $UCL_{np} = n\overline{p} + 3\sqrt{n\overline{p} \times (1 - n\overline{p}/n)}$
$$= 8.6 + 3\sqrt{8.6 \times (1 - 0.172)}$$
$$= 8.6 + 3\sqrt{8.6 \times 0.828}$$
$$= 8.6 + 3\sqrt{7.1208}$$
$$= 8.6 + (3 \times 2.6685)$$
$$= 8.6 + 8.0054$$
$$= 16.6054$$
   $LCL_{np} = n\overline{p} - 3\sqrt{n\overline{p} \times (1 - n\overline{p}/n)}$
$$= 8.6 - 3\sqrt{8.6 \times (1 - 8.6/50)}$$
$$= 8.6 - 8.0054$$
$$= 0.5946$$

6. (a) Set 1. No.
   Set 2. No.
   Set 3. Yes, 2.
   Set 4. No.

   (b) Set 1. Nothing. You may use the np-chart in running the job.
   Set 2. Nothing. You may use the np-chart in running the job.
   Set 3. Throw out these two samples. Recalculate $n\overline{p}$ and control limits.
   Set 4. Nothing. You may use the np-chart in running the job.

np-CONTROL CHARTS: EXERCISES, SERIES 2

1. (a) No
   (b) You use 20, the number of samples, when you calculate $n\overline{p}$.
   (c) 7.5
2. *See the answer charts.*
3. *See the answer charts.*
4. (a) $UCL_{np} = n\overline{p} + 3\sqrt{n\overline{p} \times (1 - n\overline{p}/n)}$
   (b) $LCL_{np} = n\overline{p} - 3\sqrt{n\overline{p} \times (1 - n\overline{p}/n)}$
   (c) Set the lower control limit to zero.
5. *See the answer charts.*
   Example calculations for Set 1:
   Original control limit calculations:

$n\overline{p} = 168/20 = 8.4$
$UCL_{np} = n\overline{p} + 3\sqrt{n\overline{p} \times (1 - n\overline{p}/n)}$
$= 8.4 + 3\sqrt{8.4 \times (1 - 8.4/50)}$
$= 8.4 + 3\sqrt{8.4 \times (1 - 0.168)}$
$= 8.4 + 3\sqrt{8.4 \times 0.832}$
$= 8.4 + 3\sqrt{6.9888}$
$= 8.4 + (3 \times 2.64363)$
$= 8.4 + 7.9309$
$= 16.3309$
$LCL_{np} = n\overline{p} - 3\sqrt{n\overline{p} \times (1 - n\overline{p}/n)}$
$= 8.4 - 3\sqrt{8.4 \times (1 - 0.168)}$
$= 8.4 - 7.9309$
$= 0.4691$

Recalculated control limits:
$n\overline{p} = 150/19 = 7.89$
$UCL_{np} = 7.89 + 3\sqrt{7.89 \times (1 - 7.89/50)}$
$= 7.89 + 7.73$
$= 15.62$
$LCL_{np} = 7.89 - 7.73$
$= 0.16$

6. (a) Set 1. Yes, 1.
   Set 2. No.
   Set 3. No.
   Set 4. No.

   (b) Set 1. Throw out the one out of control sample. Recalculate $n\overline{p}$ and control limits.
   Set 2. Use the np chart to monitor the process.
   Set 3. Use the chart to monitor the process.
   Set 4. Use the chart to monitor the process.

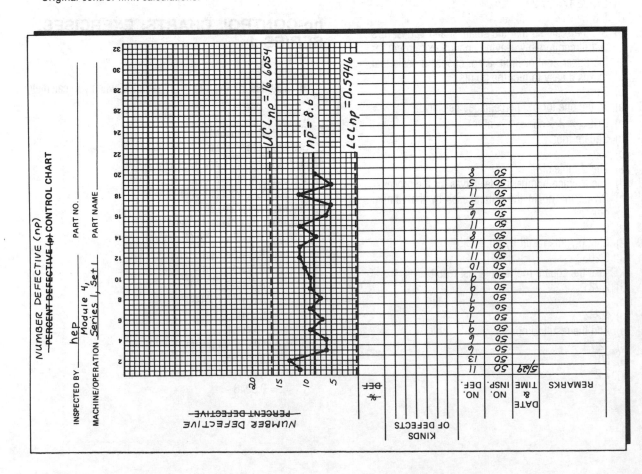

Module 4, Series 1, Set 1. Number defective (np) control chart.

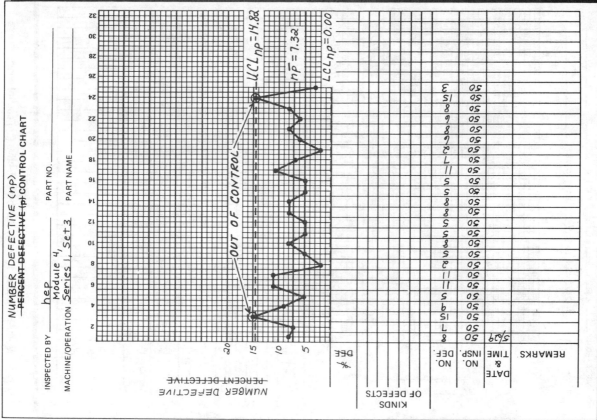

Module 4, Series 1, Set 3. Number defective (np) control chart.

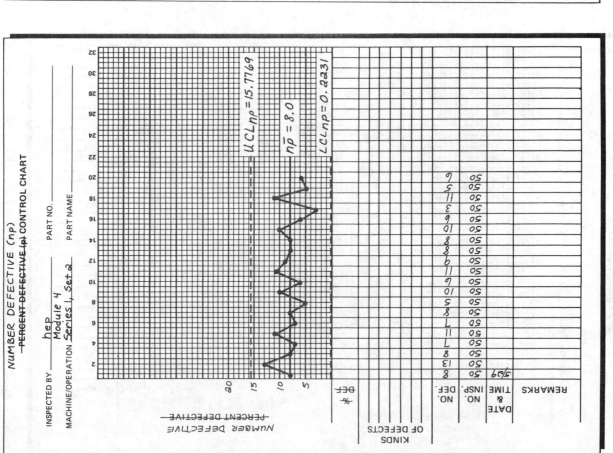

Module 4, Series 1, Set 2. Number defective (np) control chart.

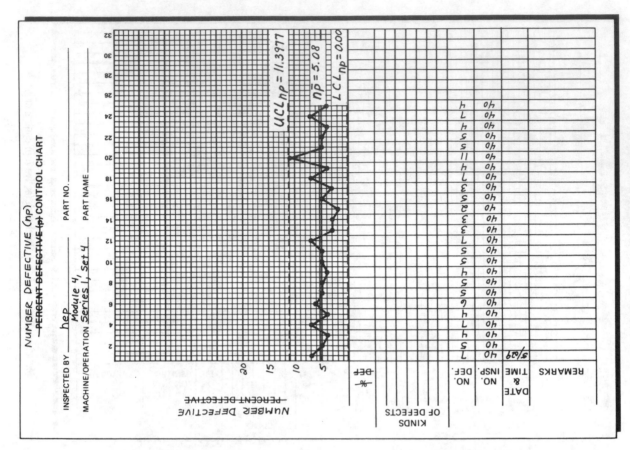

Module 4, Series 1, Set 4. Number defective (np) control chart.

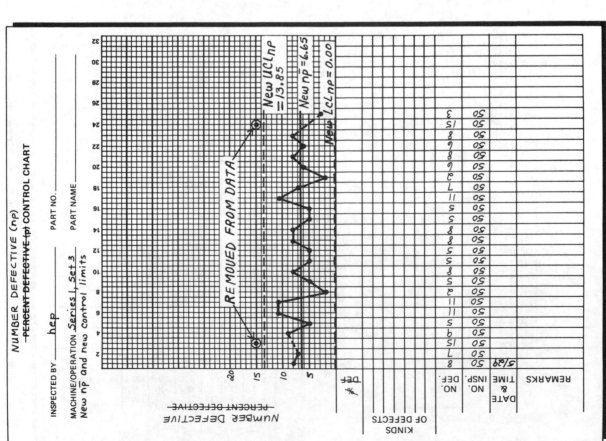

Module 4, Series 1, Set 3. Number defective (np) control chart with new npw and control limits.

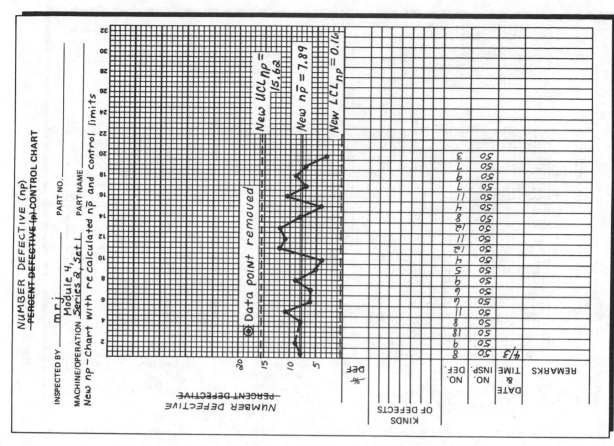

Module 4, Series 2, Set 1. Number defective (np) control chart with recalculated npw and control limits.

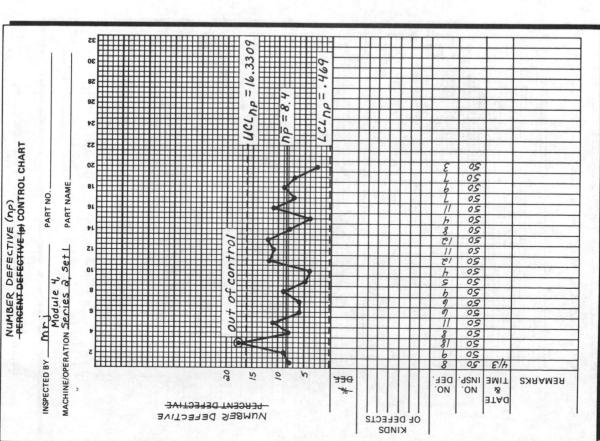

Module 4, Series 2, Set 1. Number defective (np) control chart.

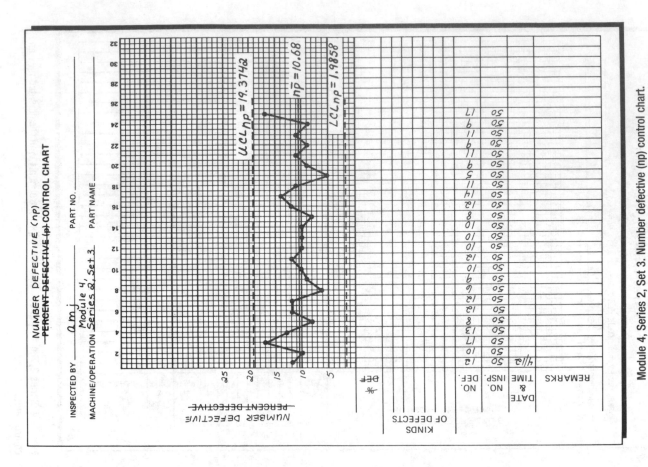

Module 4, Series 2, Set 3. Number defective (np) control chart.

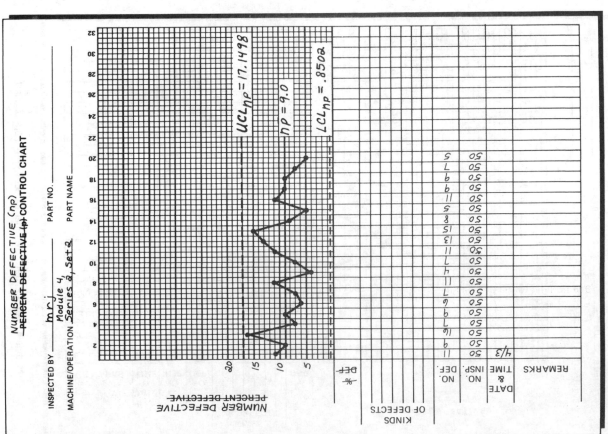

Module 4, Series 2, Set 2. Number defective (np) control chart.

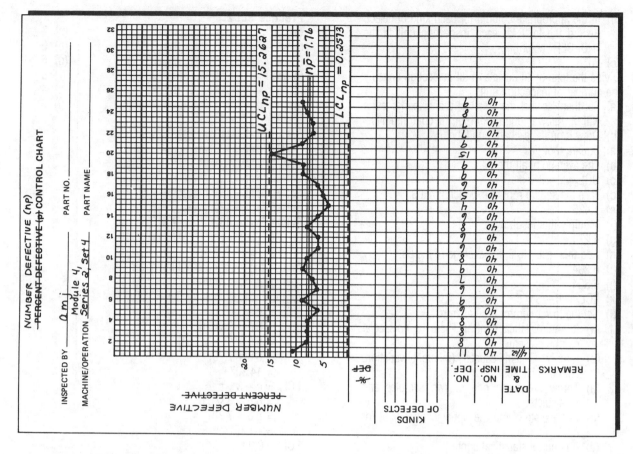

Module 4, Series 2, Set 4. Number defective (np) control chart.

c-CONTROL CHARTS: REVIEW QUESTIONS

1. (a) An attribute chart.
   (b) Percentages defective.
   (c) Counts of defectives.
   (d) Numbers of defects.
   (e) When there can be one or more defects in a single unit.
2. (a) The numbers of defective pieces per sample of pieces.
   (b) The numbers of defects in each piece.
3. (a) They all use attribute, or counting, data.
   (b) They count the number of defective pieces (units) in the sample and then plot the number, the percentage, or the fraction defective.
   (c) The number of defects in each piece (unit). It then plots these numbers (counts).
   (d) It could be a single part or unit or a collection of parts such as a printed circuit board.
   (e) There is no limit to the possible number of defects per unit.
   (f) Count the number of defects in the individual inspection unit.
4. Because each unit may have several different kinds of defects. We record the types for problem-solving purposes. For percent defective charts (p-charts), we say a part is either acceptable or not acceptable. (We still might want to record why a part is not acceptable.)

INTERPRETING c-CHARTS

1. (a) Yes.
   (b) It is in statistical control.
   (c) Yes, as long as the c's stay within the control limits.
   (d) (1) Whether the c's are in statistical control, or not.
       (2) Whether only inherent variation (common causes) is at work.
       (3) Whether special (assignable) causes are present.
   (e) Find the special (assignable) cause, remove it, thus returning the process to a control state.
   (f) There are several major categories: machine, method, materials, environment, and people.

SETTING UP c-CHARTS

1. (a) Monitor the process.
   (b) Keep track of numbers and kinds of defects.
   (c) Document and communicate what is happening.
Step 1. (a) It should show *only* inherent variation.
        (b) It should represent only *one* source of data.
        (c) Take it from *one* machine, *one* associate, *one* batch of raw materials, over a short time, etc.
        (d) Yes.
Step 2. Yes, it is quite similar, but not identical.
Step 3. (a) Count the numbers by type of defect in each inspection unit.

(b) In the appropriate column for each kind of defect. Record the total for each inspection unit in the "NO. DEF." column.

(c) 20

Step 4. Divide the total of all defects in all inspection units by the number of inspection units.

Step 5. (a) Set them so that the smallest c and the largest c will fit. Allow enough room for the control limits.

(b) Draw it on the c-chart, and label it.

Step 6. (a) Square root.

(b) The average of all the c's.

(c) $UCL_c = \bar{c} + 3\sqrt{\bar{c}}$

(d) Take the square root of $\bar{c}$, which is 2.03.

(e) 1.425

(f) Multiply this result by 3.

(g) 4.274

(h) Add this result to $\bar{c}$, the average of the c's.

(i) 6.304

(j) 6.304

(k) $LCL_c = \bar{c} - 3\sqrt{\bar{c}}$

(l) Set the lower control limit at zero.

Step 7. 1. (a) It is in statistical control. There are *no* special causes present.

(b) Simply system causes (inherent variation, common causes).

2. (a) Throw out these one or two samples and recalculate.

(b) Recalculate $\bar{c}$ and the upper control limit for c's.

(c) It is out of statistical control.

(d) Find the assignable causes, remove them, thus returning to the control condition.

(e) Go ahead and run the process using the new control limits.

(f) There may be assignable causes present. Look for them.

3. (a) It is out of statistical control.

(b) Find and remove the assignable causes, collect new data, and set up a new chart.

c-CONTROL CHARTS: EXERCISES, SERIES 1

1. **Practice Set 1.**

(a)	3	(h)	5	(o)	7
(b)	4	(i)	2	(p)	7
(c)	6	(j)	4	(q)	5
(d)	5	(k)	6	(r)	3
(e)	9	(l)	7	(s)	6
(f)	8	(m)	5	(t)	12
(g)	10	(n)	4		

Practice Set 2.

(a)	6	(h)	10	(o)	7
(b)	6	(i)	7	(p)	5
(c)	4	(j)	7	(q)	6
(d)	6	(k)	3	(r)	8
(e)	6	(l)	8	(s)	4
(f)	3	(m)	9	(t)	6
(g)	9	(n)	5		

2. Set 1. Total = 118; average = 5.9
   Set 2. Total = 125; average = 6.25

3. *See the answer charts.*

4. Set 1. Total = 132; average = 6.6
   Set 2. Total = 153; average = 7.65
   Set 3. Total = 139; average = 6.95
   Set 4. Total = 132; average = 6.6

5. (a) $UCL_c = \bar{c} + 3\sqrt{\bar{c}}$
   (b) $LCL_c = \bar{c} - 3\sqrt{\bar{c}}$
   (c) Set the lower control limit at zero.

6. *See the answer charts.*
   Example calculations for Set 1:
   $$UCL_c = \bar{c} + 3\sqrt{\bar{c}}$$
   $$= 6.6 + 3\sqrt{6.6}$$
   $$= 6.6 + (3 \times 2.569)$$
   $$= 6.6 + 7.707$$
   $$= 14.307$$
   $$LCL_c = c - 3\sqrt{\bar{c}}$$
   $$= 6.6 - 3\sqrt{6.6}$$
   $$= 6.6 - 7.707$$
   $$= -1.107$$
   $$LCL_c = 0.00$$

7. (a) Sets 1–4. No.
   (b) Sets 1–4. Since all the c's are in control, run the job and use the chart to monitor the process.

c-CONTROL CHARTS: EXERCISES, SERIES 2

1. **Practice Set 1.**

(a)	5	(h)	8	(o)	7
(b)	7	(i)	8	(p)	6
(c)	10	(j)	4	(q)	8
(d)	6	(k)	8	(r)	10
(e)	16	(l)	3	(s)	8
(f)	10	(m)	10	(t)	10
(g)	7	(n)	9		

Practice Set 2.

(a)	12	(h)	11	(o)	7
(b)	3	(i)	5	(p)	4
(c)	7	(j)	9	(q)	9
(d)	8	(k)	8	(r)	8
(e)	12	(l)	7	(s)	9
(f)	10	(m)	11	(t)	12
(g)	7	(n)	7		

2. Set 1. Total = 160; average = 8.0
   Set 2. Total = 166; average = 8.3
3. *See the answer charts.*
4. Set 1. Total = 157; average = 7.85
   Set 2. Total = 152; average = 7.6
   Set 3. Total = 152; average = 7.6
   Set 4. Total = 168; average = 8.4
5. (a) $UCL_c = \bar{c} + 3\sqrt{\bar{c}}$
   (b) $LCL_c = \bar{c} - 3\sqrt{\bar{c}}$
   (c) Set the lower control limit at zero.
6. *See the answer charts.*
   Example calculations for Set 1:
   $$UCL_c = \bar{c} + 3\sqrt{\bar{c}}$$
   $$= 7.85 + 3\sqrt{7.85}$$
   $$= 7.85 + (3 \times 2.8018)$$
   $$= 7.85 + 8.4054$$
   $$= 16.2554$$
   $$LCL_c = \bar{c} - 3\sqrt{\bar{c}}$$
   $$= 7.85 - 3\sqrt{7.85}$$
   $$= 7.85 - 8.4054$$
   $$= -0.5554$$
   $$LCL_c = 0.00$$

7. (a) Set 1. No.
   Set 2. No.
   Set 3. Yes, 1.
   Set 4. No.
   (b) Set 1. Since all the c's are in control, use the c-chart to continue running the process.
   Set 2. Since all the c's are in control, use the c-chart to continue running the process.
   Set 3. Remove the one sample, then recalculate $\bar{c}$ and control limits.
   Set 4. Since all the c's are in control, use the c-chart to continue running the process.

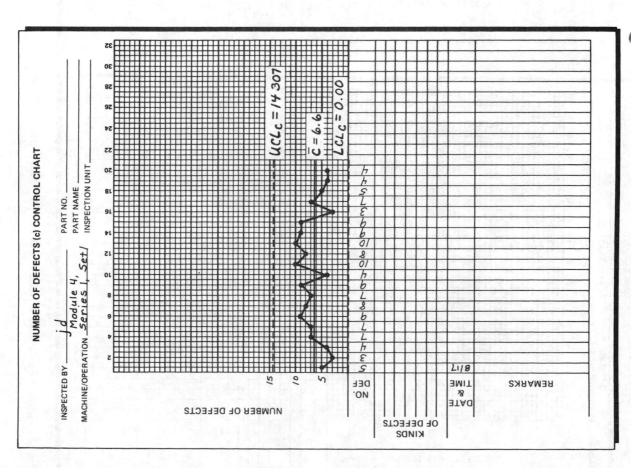

Module 4, Series 1, Set 1. Number of defects (c) control chart.

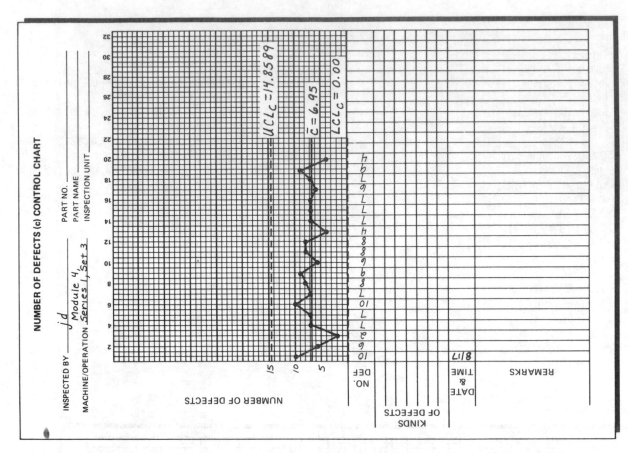

Module 4, Series 1, Set 3. Number of defects (c) control chart.

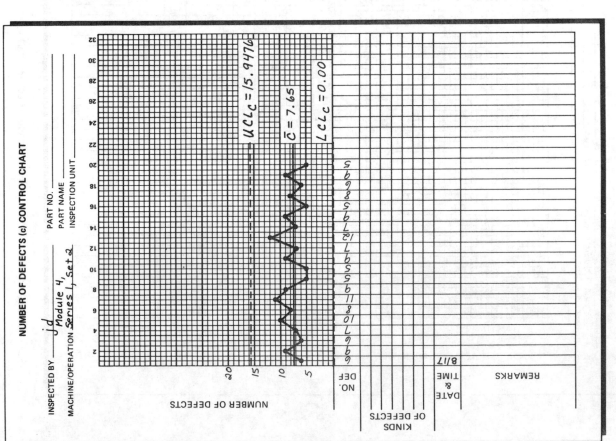

Module 4, Series 1, Set 2. Number of defects (c) control chart.

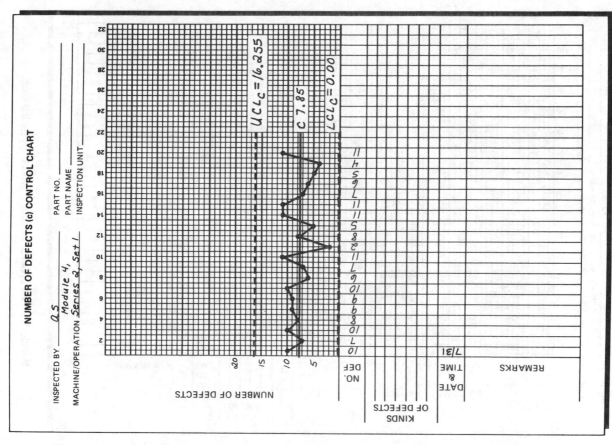

Module 4, Series 2, Set 1. Number of defects (c) control chart.

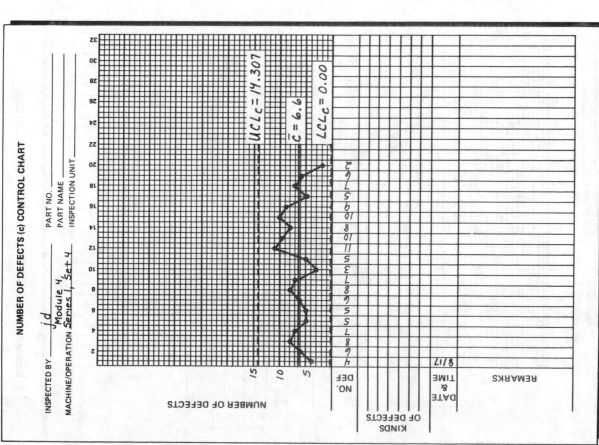

Module 4, Series 1, Set 4. Number of defects (c) control chart.

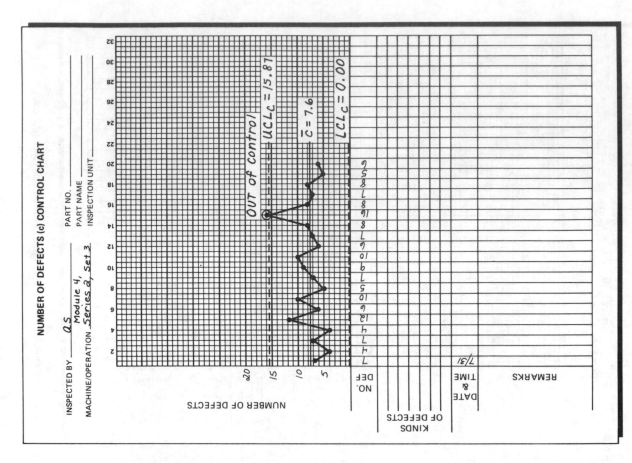

Module 4, Series 2, Set 3. Number of defects (c) control chart.

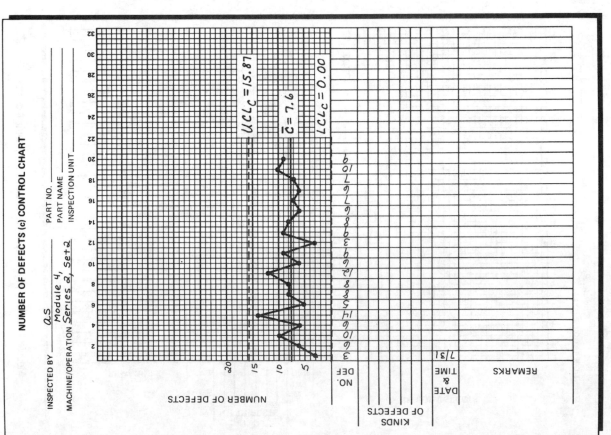

Module 4, Series 2, Set 2. Number of defects (c) control chart.

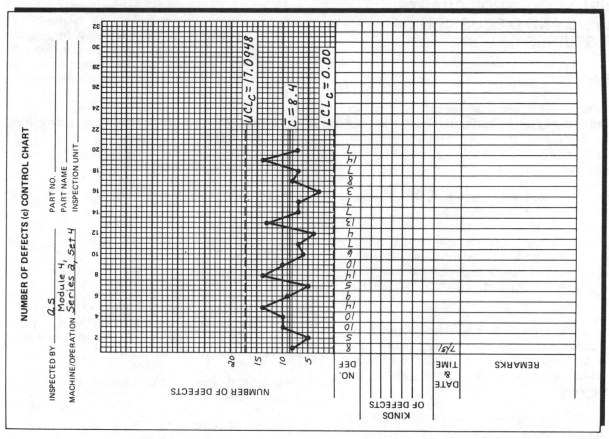

Module 4, Series 2, Set 4. Number of defects (c) control chart.

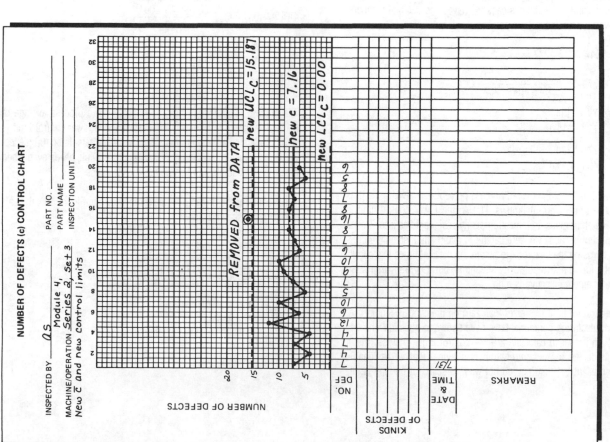

Module 4, Series 2, Set 3. Number of defects (c) control chart with new cw and new control limits.

ATTRIBUTE CONTROL CHARTS: ANALYSIS AND DISCUSSION OF CASE STUDIES

CASE 4-1

You were asked to construct percent defective charts using data that you obtained by drawing samples from a box of beads. Most of the beads were natural in color, but the remaining beads were red, white, brown, blue, or yellow. Each color was to be considered as a different type of defect in the product.

When a p-chart is constructed on the basis of the combined total of colored beads in the sample, we do not know anything about the variability of the individual colors. This is often the situation in a manufacturing process. The output of the process is sampled and the defectives are recorded. A p-chart is constructed showing the stability of the process as a whole, but we cannot easily identify which individual defect is responsible when the p-chart shows that an assignable cause is present.

In this case study we have used the fraction defective formula to calculate the control limits, and then show them as percentages to demonstrate that using either the fraction defective or the percent defective formula will give you the same values. The student may find this approach easier.

The p-chart using all colors is shown in Figure 4–A. The calculations of the overall process average, $\bar{p}$, and of the control limits are shown below. To make the calculations easy, we have used decimal numbers. The answer in parentheses is a percent.

$$\bar{p} = 554/2000 = .277 \ (27.7\%)$$

$$UCL_p = .277 + 3\sqrt{\frac{.277 \times (1 - .277)}{100}}$$

$UCL_p = .277 + .134$
$UCL_p = .411 \ (41.1\%)$

$LCL_p = .277 - .134$
$LCL_p = .143 \ (14.3\%)$

This chart shows that the overall process percent defective, or the $\bar{p}$, is 27.7%. The upper control limit is 41.1%; the lower control limit is 14.3%. The chart gives no indication of any assignable causes. This is to be expected because we were careful to avoid any instability in this problem by using the bead box to obtain the data. At times this condition can be found in actual factory situations, but it is rarely true when the overall percent defective is high.

The lower control limit is greater than zero on the chart in Figure 4-A. Some manufacturing personnel have been known to question why one should even bother to calculate a lower control limit. They say that a point outside the lower control limit is a signal that an assignable cause is present but that they do not want to search it out and elimi-

nate it. In that case, why bother with the lower control limit? It is true that a point outside the lower control limit shows that something not normal to the process has happened. In such a case, the quality level has been improved. This is why we would want to know about it. The assignable cause should be searched out and, if possible, made a permanent part of the process, thereby improving the performance of the process.

The p-chart based on the data for the red bead defect is shown in Figure 4-B; the calculations are shown below.

$$\bar{p} = 264/2000 = .132 \ (13.2\%)$$

$$UCL_p = .132 + 3\sqrt{\frac{.132 \times (1 - .132)}{100}}$$

$UCL_p = .132 + .102$
$UCL_p = .234 \ (23.4\%)$

$LCL_p = .132 - .102$
$UCL_p = .030 \ (3.0\%)$

Again, the chart shows a stable process. It has a much lower $\bar{p}$ than the chart in Figure 4-A, and the control limits are closer to the process average line. The $\bar{p}$ in this case is 13.2%. The upper control limit is 23.4% and the lower control limit is 3.0%.

The p-chart for the white bead defect is shown in Figure 4-C; the calculations are shown below.

$$\bar{p} = 162/2000 = .081 \ (8.1\%)$$

$$UCL_p = .081 + 3\sqrt{\frac{.081 \times (1 - .081)}{100}}$$

$UCL_p = .081 + .082$
$UCL_p = .163 \ (16.3\%)$

$LCL_p = 0$

The process for the white beads is stable, with a process average of 8.1%. The upper control limit is 16.3% and the lower control limit is zero. The $\bar{p}$ is small enough that when we take a sample of 100 pieces, we would expect to see samples containing no white beads even when the process is stable and has no assignable causes.

The p-chart for the brown bead defect is shown in Figure 4-D; the calculations are shown below.

$$\bar{p} = 85/2000 = .0425 \ (4.25\%)$$

$$UCL_p = .0425 + 3\sqrt{\frac{.0425 \times (1 - .0425)}{100}}$$

$UCL_p = .0425 + .0605$
$UCL_p = .103 \ (10.3\%)$

$LCL_p = 0$

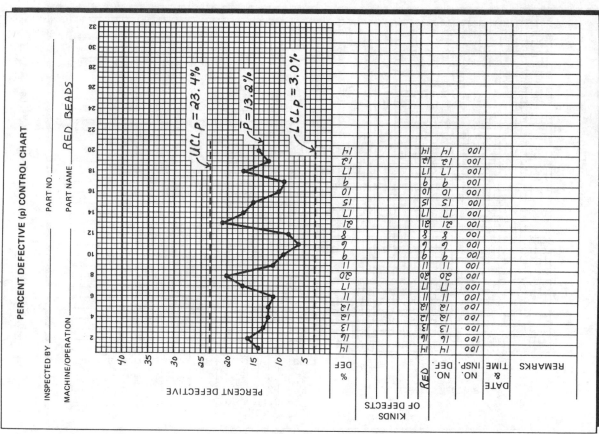

Figure 4-B. Percent defective chart, red bead defects, Case 4-1.

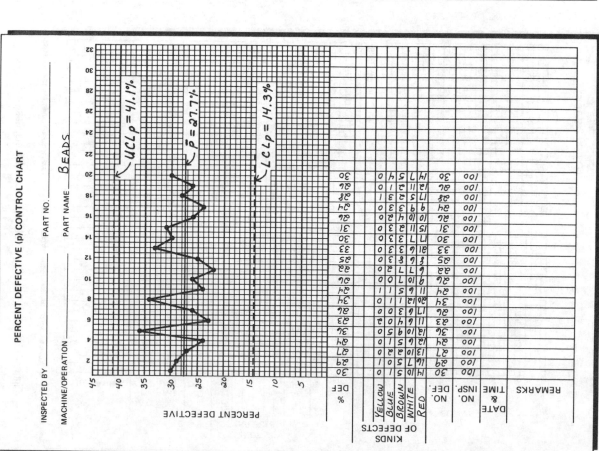

Figure 4-A. Percent defective chart, all colored bead defects, Case 4-1.

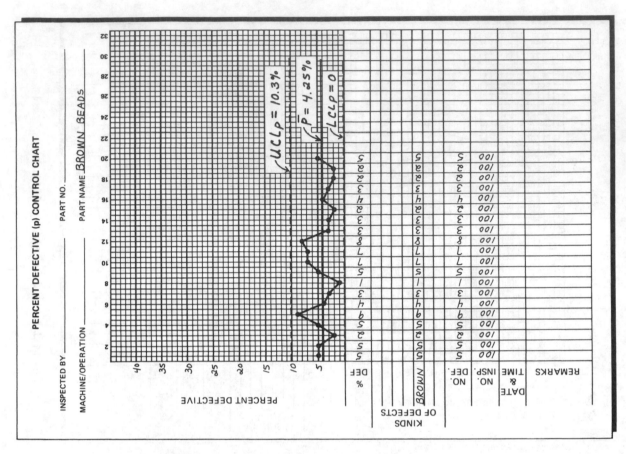

Figure 4-D. Percent defective chart, brown bead defects, Case 4-1.

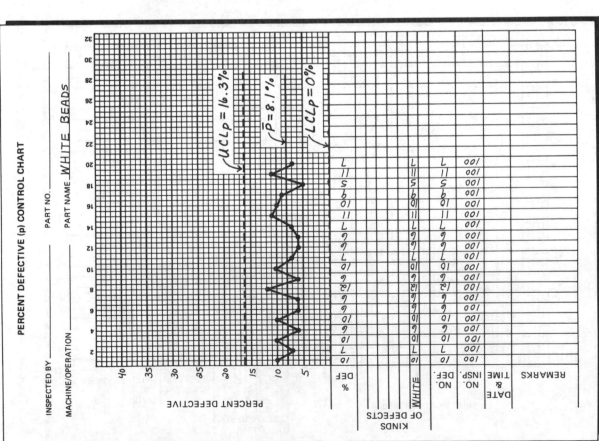

Figure 4-C. Percent defective chart, white bead defects, Case 4-1.

The control chart shows the brown bead defect to be stable, as expected. This defect shows a smaller process percent defective than did the two previous defects.

The p-chart for the blue bead defect is shown in Figure 4-E; the calculations are shown below.

$$\bar{p} = 38/2000 = .019 \ (1.9\%)$$

$$UCL_p = .019 + 3\sqrt{\frac{.019}{100}}$$

$$UCL_p = .019 + .0414$$
$$UCL_p = .0604 \ (6.04\%)$$

$$LCL_p = 0$$

When the expected number of defects in each sample is four or less, the calculations for the control limits may be simplified. The upper control limit is the process fraction defective plus three times the square root of the value obtained by dividing the process fraction defective by the sample size. When using this simpler calculation, you will find that the control limit value differs insignificantly from the control limit value calculated in the normal way.

The blue bead defect percent defective is 1.9%. The sample size is 100 pieces. When sampling a process that is 1.9% defective, we would expect the percent defective of the sample to vary about 1.9% and to average 1.9% in the long run. This means that we expect 1.9 defectives per 100 pieces sampled. Obviously we cannot have something less than a whole defective, but we expect the average to be 1.9.

The chart in Figure 4-E shows that the process produces a small percentage of blue bead defects but is stable at that level.

The p-chart for yellow bead defects is shown in Figure 4-F; the calculations are shown below.

$$\bar{p} = 5/2000 = .0025 \ (.25\%)$$

$$UCL_p = .0025 + 3\sqrt{\frac{.0025}{100}}$$

$$UCL_p = .0025 + .015$$
$$UCL_p = .0175 \ (1.75\%)$$

$$LCL_p = 0$$

This p-chart shows Sample 6 to be above the upper control limit. Sample 6 contained two yellow bead defectives and is 2% defective; the upper control limit is 1.75%.

When you use percent defective control charts for processes that have a very low process percent defective, the chart sometimes will show a point outside the control limit when no assignable cause exists. If the defect is critical to the performance of the product, a larger sample size must be used to overcome the problem. Often a different technique for calculating the control limits must be used when the sample size becomes very large. (This is an advanced technique that is not covered in this book.)

In this problem we asked you to construct a control chart using all colors of beads combined and then to construct individual control charts for each color bead defect. Now that you have done this, you can see that each color defect contributes to the total variation of the process, as shown in Figure 4-A (the p-chart constructed from all colors of bead defects). In fact, when the process percents defective ($\bar{p}$) of all the charts are added together, you can see readily that they equal the $\bar{p}$ for all colors combined.

Examination of the individual charts shows that the red bead defects contributed about half of the total variation of the chart in Figure 4-A. If an assignable cause occurred in one of the other defect types, it may be hidden by the normal variation in the red bead defects or in a combination of the others. The defect types that occur at a higher average sometimes can "overpower" a signal of an assignable cause coming from one of the defect types that has a lower process percent defective. For this reason it is recommended that when you first develop a control chart that contains multiple defects, you chart the individual defects for a period of time.

Charting the defect types individually will show which defects are most likely to be due to assignable causes, and will identify the defects that have the highest process percent defective. This procedure can be the basis for determining which defect types can be combined safely into one chart and which ones must be maintained and controlled separately.

This approach to attribute control chart development is recommended for c-charts and np-charts as well as for p-charts.

CASE 4-2

This problem concerns scratches on an assembly. The customer has complained about them; you are asked to determine the size of the problem and whether it is inherent in the process or whether the scratches are caused by some action not usually a part of the process.

The number of scratches found on the assemblies as they are packed has been recorded for each container load of 80 assemblies. You should have constructed a number defective chart ($n\bar{p}$) based on these

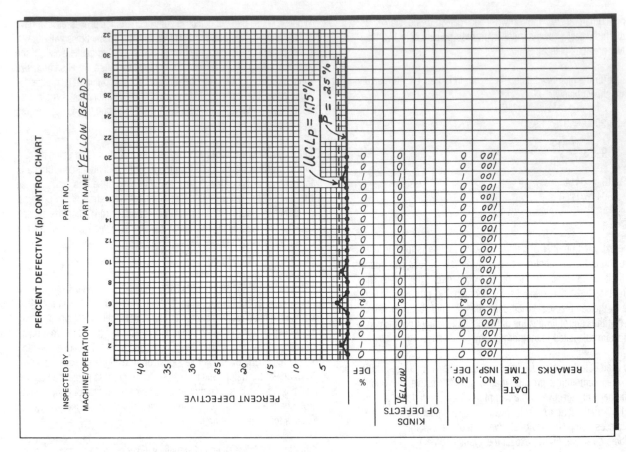

Figure 4-F. Percent defective chart, yellow bead defects, Case 4-1.

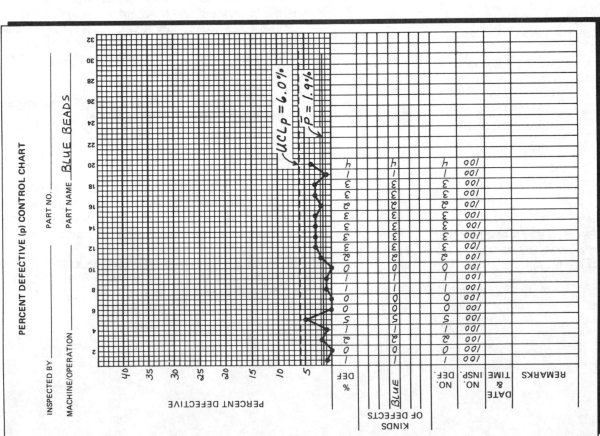

Figure 4-E. Percent defective chart, blue bead defects, Case 4-1.

data. Your chart should be similar to the one shown in Figure 4-G. The calculations for this control chart are shown below.

$$n\overline{p} = 158/20 = 7.9$$

$$UCL_{np} = 7.9 + 3\sqrt{7.9[1 - (7.9/80)]}$$
$$UCL_{np} = 7.9 + 8.0$$
$$UCL_{np} = 15.9$$

$$LCL_{np} = 0$$

Delete Sample 11

$$n\overline{p} = 141/19 = 7.42$$

$$UCL_{np} = 7.42 + 3\sqrt{7.42[1 - (7.42/80)]}$$
$$UCL_{np} = 7.42 + 7.78$$
$$UCL_{np} = 15.2$$

$$LCL_{np} = 0$$

Examination of the control chart reveals that the average number of scratches per container is estimated to be 7.42. The people in this company who are responsible for making a product that meets the customer's expectations may or may not have been aware of this number. This control chart presents documentary evidence of the size of the problem. It provides a starting point for finding the cause of the problem and then correcting it.

You were asked to determine whether the causes of the scratches were a part of the process or whether they were due to something that did not usually occur in the course of producing the assemblies. The control chart will help in making this determination. If the chart shows the process to be in control—that is, if all the points on the chart are normally distributed around the process average ($n\overline{p}$)—it can be said that the causes of the scratches are inherent in the process. If the control chart shows the process to be unstable—that is, if it shows a lot of out-of-control points—then it can be said that the scratches are due to assignable causes. These causes can be found and corrective action can be taken to prevent them from occurring in the future.

The control chart shown in Figure 4-G was developed by eliminating Sample 11 from the data used to calculate the average number defective and the upper and lower control limits. The first calculations showed this sample to be above the upper control limit. When it was eliminated and the new calculations were completed, the process was shown to be stable.

We can conclude from this control chart that an indication of an assignable cause is present but the process is generally stable. Some processes are found to be so unstable that a usable control chart cannot be developed until the assignable causes are eliminated. This is not the case in this problem; the chart shows a slight instability, but the calculated $n\overline{p}$ of 7.42 is to be considered an accurate estimate of the average number defective for this process. Any major reduction in the number of scratches must be achieved by making changes in the process. Continued use of the control chart will show when such changes have been effective.

CASE 4-3

This problem involves the defects in an epoxy coating on a tubing assembly. Five different defects are considered in the inspection operation; each of these defects may occur more than once in any assembly. The inspection data have been recorded to show the results of the inspection of 20 tubing assemblies. A number of defects chart, or c-chart, is appropriate for monitoring and analyzing the quality of the coating process.

The c-chart constructed from the inspection data is shown in Figure 4-H; the calculations for the average number of defects ($\overline{c}$) are shown below.

$$\overline{c} = 51/20 = 2.55$$
$$UCL_c = 2.55 + 3\sqrt{2.55}$$
$$UCL_c = 7.34$$

$$LCL_c = 0$$

A review of the control chart shows the process to be stable. There are no points outside the upper control limit, and the points are distributed very normally around the average number of defects ($\overline{c}$) line. This chart should be maintained for a longer time to confirm the stability of the process.

No assignable causes are present in the process; therefore the process is producing the best-quality tubing assemblies it can be expected to produce as long as it is operated with the current methods, people, tooling, equipment, and materials, and as long as the current environment is maintained. The associates can do no better than an average of 2.55 defects per tubing assembly. Any improvement in the quality of the coating on the assemblies must be accomplished by making changes in the process. The defects appearing on the tubing assemblies produced by the present process are created by random causes that are inherent in the process. A management team must implement changes in the ways in which the product is manufactured if such defects are to be eliminated.

In using a number of defects chart, the sample size must be maintained at all times. The $\overline{c}$ and the control limits are based on a sample that contains a certain number of chances for defects to occur. If that sample size is changed, the $\overline{c}$ and the control limits may no longer be valid. This also is true for the number of defect types that are included on the control chart. If one or more defect types are added to those used to develop the c-chart, the $\overline{c}$ and the control limits may no longer be valid.

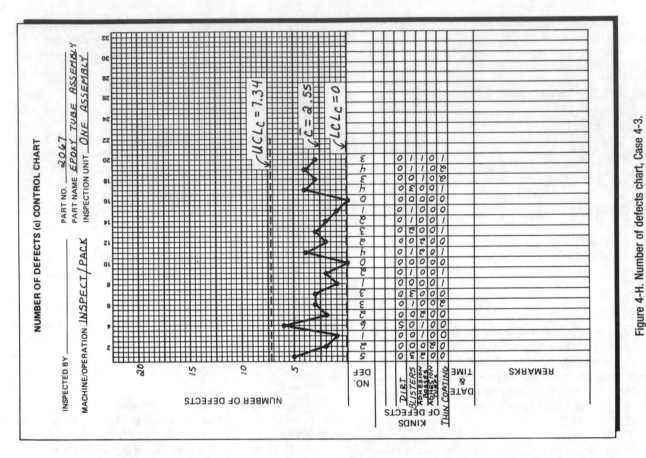

Figure 4-H. Number of defects chart, Case 4-3.

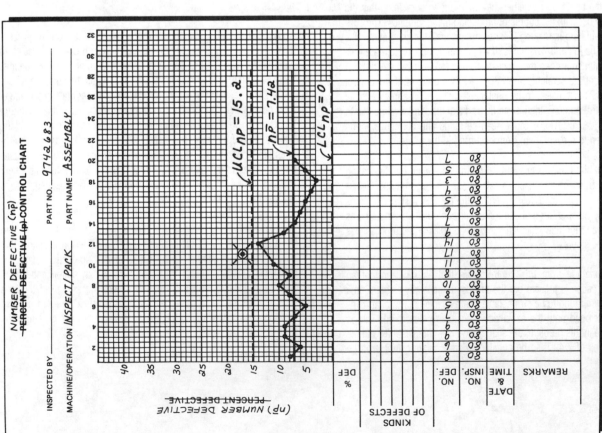

Figure 4-G. Number defective chart, Case 4-2.

When the conditions used to develop the control chart are changed, a new control chart must be developed.

CASE 4-4

This problem requires the development of control charts that a management team can use to monitor the quality performance of a manufacturing process and that production floor associates can use to determine when to take corrective action. The product is an assembly in which there are five different defects of concern. The control chart that a team would use to monitor the performance of the process is not necessarily the same chart that would be used on the production floor to detect the presence of assignable causes calling for corrective action. Although a team will or should review some of the control charts from the production floor, they are generally interested in the overall performance of the manufacturing operation. A control chart showing the number of defects found in the assemblies, without regard to the type of defect, would serve this purpose. Control charts for individual defects in the assemblies are needed to monitor the stability of the process. When different types of defects are combined into one chart, there is a risk that one of the defects will be out of control but will not be detected.

Figure 4-I shows the number of defects control chart ($\bar{c}$) that a manager could use to monitor the performance of the process. The calculations for that control chart are shown below.

$$\bar{c} = 498/20 = 24.9$$

$$UCL_c = 24.9 + 3\sqrt{24.9}$$
$$UCL_c = 24.9 + 15.0$$
$$UCL_c = 39.9$$

$$LCL_c = 24.9 - 15.0$$
$$LCL_c = 9.9$$

This control chart will show the team how the process is performing and whether any projects aimed at improving quality are effective. It also will tell them who in the organization should be working to achieve improvement in quality. If the control chart shows instability in the process by showing points out of control, the most effective corrective action can be taken by people on the production floor. On the other hand, if the control chart shows the process to be stable or free of indications of assignable causes, the people who should be working to improve product quality are those who are responsible for the design and specification of the process or for the materials.

The associates on the production floor need to know when a nonnormal event takes place in the process. This event would be an assignable cause. Such a cause can affect one or more of the characteristics that are being tested on the finished assemblies. Development and use of control charts for each defect type can identify which defect type is affected by some cause. Problem-solving groups can

make good use of such a situation by examining the control charts for this evidence when attempting to solve quality problems or when trying to locate and correct assignable causes. For these reasons it is a good idea to develop and maintain individual control charts on those dimensions or characteristics that are considered to be important to the function of the product.

Figure 4-J shows the number of defects ($\bar{c}$) control chart for Defect 1. Shown below are the calculations of the average number of defects and the upper and lower control limits.

$$\bar{c} = 244/20 = 12.2$$

$$UCL_c = 12.2 + 3\sqrt{12.2}$$
$$UCL_c = 12.2 + 10.48$$
$$UCL_c = 22.7$$

$$LCL_c = 12.2 - 10.48$$
$$LCL_c = 1.7$$

This control chart shows a $\bar{c}$ of 12.2, the amount that this type of defect contributes to the overall quality problem. This statement can be made with confidence because the control chart shows the process to be stable around that average number of defects.

Figure 4-K shows the number of defects ($\bar{c}$) control chart for Defect 2. Shown below are the calculations of the average number of defects and the upper and lower control limits.

$$\bar{c} = 139/20 = 6.95$$

$$UCL_c = 6.95 + 3\sqrt{6.95}$$
$$UCL_c = 6.95 + 7.91$$
$$UCL_c = 14.86$$

$$LCL_c = 0$$

This control chart shows that Defect 2 is stable around an average of 6.95 defects.

The control chart for Defect 3 is shown in Figure 4-L. The calculations for the average number of defects and the upper and lower control limits are shown below.

$$\bar{c} = 64/20 = 3.2$$

$$UCL_c = 3.2 + 3\sqrt{3.2}$$
$$UCL_c = 3.2 + 5.37$$
$$UCL_c = 8.57$$

$$LCL_c = 0$$

This control chart shows a lower $\bar{c}$ than the charts for Defects 1 and 2. No signals of assignable causes are evident.

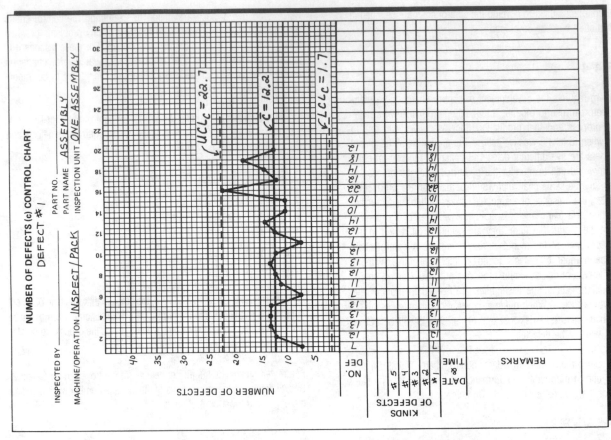

Figure 4-J. Number of defects chart, Defect 1, Case 4-4.

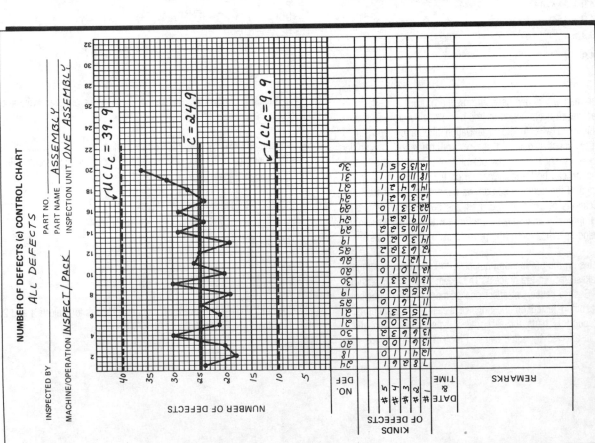

Figure 4-I. Number defective chart, assemblies, all defects, Case 4-4.

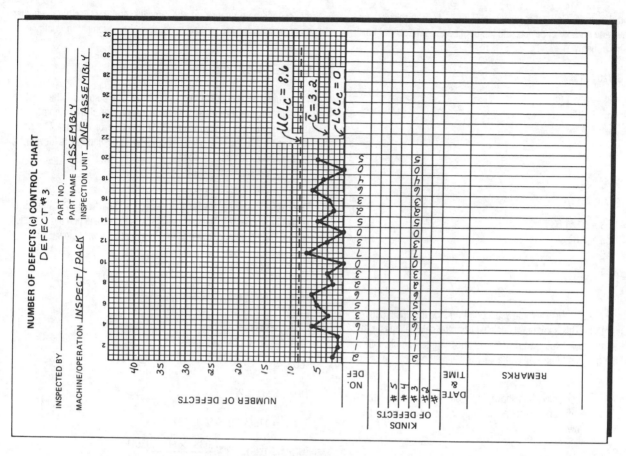

Figure 4-L. Number of defects chart, Defect 3, Case 4-4.

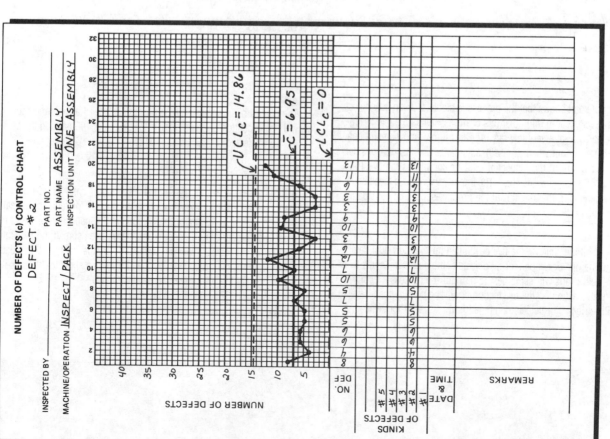

Figure 4-K. Number of defects chart, Defect 2, Case 4-4.

The control chart for Defect 4 is shown in Figure 4-M. The calculations for the average number of defects and the upper and lower control limits are shown below.

$$\bar{c} = 37/20 = 1.85$$

$$UCL_c = 1.85 + 3\sqrt{1.85}$$
$$UCL_c = 1.85 + 4.08$$
$$UCL_c = 5.93$$

$$LCL_c = 0$$

Delete Sample 1

$$\bar{c} = 31/19 = 1.63$$

$$UCL_c = 1.63 + 3\sqrt{1.63}$$
$$UCL_c = 1.63 + 3.83$$
$$UCL_c = 5.46$$

$$LCL_c = 0$$

The control chart for Defect 4 showed a point outside the upper control limit (Sample 1). This sample was deleted from the calculations for the average number of defects and for the control limits. The chart then showed the process to be stable at a very low defect rate.

The control chart for Defect 5 is shown in Figure 4-N. The calculations for the average number of defects and for upper and lower control limits are shown below.

$$\bar{c} = 14/20 = .7$$

$$UCL_c = .7 + 3\sqrt{.7}$$
$$UCL_c = .7 + 2.51$$
$$UCL_c = 3.21$$

$$LCL_c = 0$$

This control chart shows that the process is stable at a very low defect rate. It must be kept in mind that this chart, as well as the one in Figure 4-M, has a $\bar{c}$ at a very low rate. At times it may show a point outside the control limit when no assignable cause is present. Consider increasing the size of the inspection unit or combining the two low-level types of defect into one chart. The importance of the dimension or the characteristic to the function of the product should be considered in taking such action.

A review of all the charts—the five developed for the individual defect types and the one developed for all defects combined—will show that the individual charts will serve best to monitor the process for control and corrective action on the production floor. The control chart developed with all types of defects combined is most useful for evaluating the overall performance of the process and for deciding whether process revisions are needed to cause an improvement in quality.

CASE 4-5

The proper control chart for monitoring the output of the coating operation in this problem is a percent defective chart (p-chart). The results of inspection are recorded by the type of defects. The sample size is 100 pieces, which should be large enough to develop a usable control chart.

The p-chart developed with the inspection data from 32 samples is shown in Figure 4-0. The calculations for the average percent defective and for the upper and lower control limits are shown below.

$$\bar{p} = 138/3200 = 0.0431 \ (4.31\%)$$

$$UCL_p = .0431 + 3\sqrt{\frac{.0431 \times (1 - .0431)}{100}}$$

$$UCL_p = .0431 + .0609$$
$$UCL_p = .1040 \ (10.4\%)$$

$$LCL_p = 0$$

Delete Sample 26

$$\bar{p} = 118/3100 = .0381 \ (3.81\%)$$

$$UCL_p = .0381 + 3\sqrt{\frac{.0381 \times (1 - .0381)}{100}}$$

$$UCL_p = .0381 + .0574$$
$$UCL_p = .0955 \ (9.55\%)$$

$$LCL_p = 0$$

The control chart shows that the process is free of assignable causes, with the exception of Sample 26, when 20 of the 100 parts in the sample were rejected because of thin coating.

At first glance it would appear that this control chart is adequate to meet the need. Closer examination of the causes for rejection reveals that thin coating is the major defect found in the inspection of the samples. The number of defects found may have been spread more evenly among all the defect types at some time in the past, but the data obtained in the period covered by the 32 samples show that thin coating accounted for 106 of the 138 defects found.

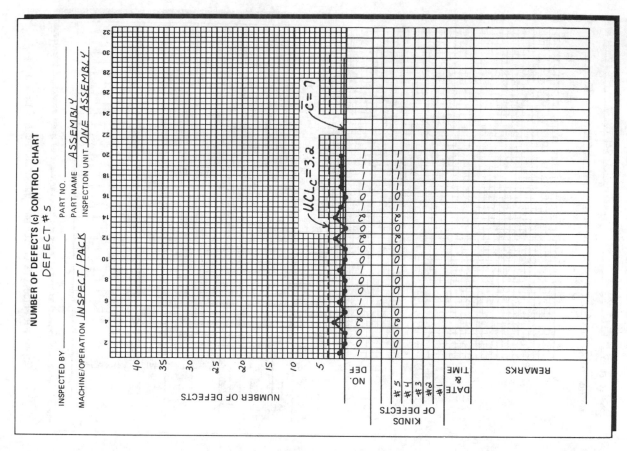

Figure 4-N. Number of defects chart, Defect 5, Case 4-4.

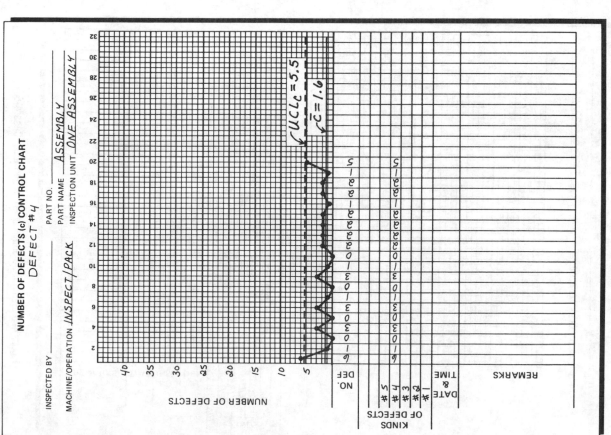

Figure 4-M. Number of defects chart, Defect 4, Case 4-4.

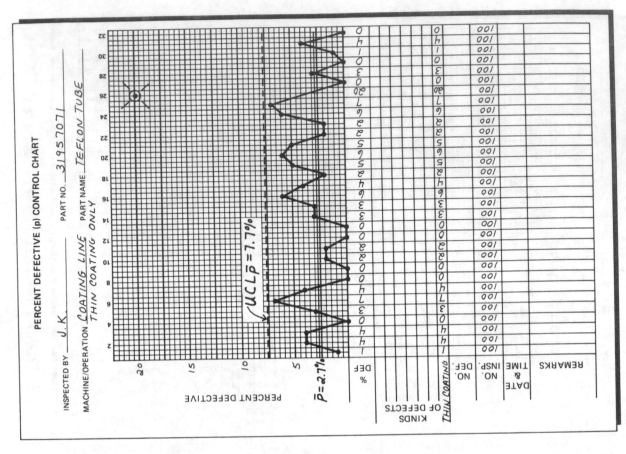

Figure 4-P. Percent defective chart, thin coating only, Case 4-5.

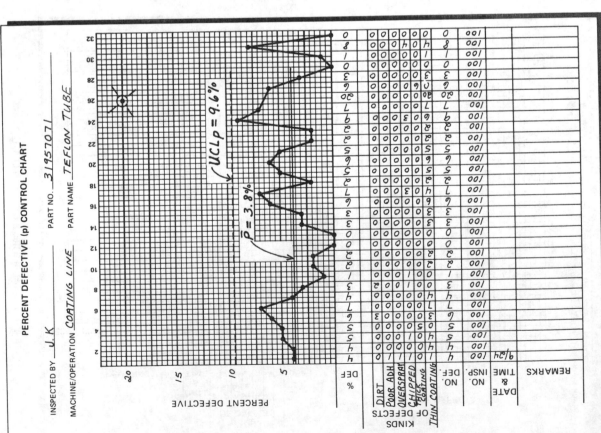

Figure 4-O. Percent defective chart, Teflon tube, Case 4-5.

When the data show such a condition as we find in this problem, it is best that the predominant defect be monitored separately from the other defect types. A p-chart for monitoring thin coating only should be developed. When you have completed such a chart, compare it with the one shown in Figure 4-P. The calculations are shown below.

$$\bar{p} = 106/3200 = .033 \ (3.3\%)$$

$$UCL_p = .033 + 3\sqrt{\frac{.033 \times (1 - .033)}{100}}$$

$$UCL_p = .033 + .054$$
$$UCL_p = .087 \ (8.7\%)$$

$$LCL_p = 0$$

Delete Sample 26

$$\bar{p} = 86/3100 = .0277 \ (2.8\%)$$

$$UCL_p = .0277 + 3\sqrt{\frac{.0277 \times (1 - .0277)}{100}}$$

$$UCL_p = .0277 + .0492$$
$$UCL_p = .077 \ (7.7\%)$$

$$LCL_p = 0$$

The greatest reduction in the overall rejection rate may be attained by using the p-chart developed for thin coating only. The remaining defect types could be combined properly into a single p-chart until that control chart shows evidence that one or more of those defect types is increasing. At that time it would be a good idea to develop another p-chart for that defect only.

CASE 4-6

This problem requires you to develop a p-chart using inspection data obtained from sampling parts as they were inspected before being packed. Samples of 100 parts were obtained by collecting consecutive parts as they moved down an inspection conveyor belt. You were asked to determine whether the process is in control by examining the p-chart.

A p-chart similar to the one you have developed is shown in Figure 4-Q. The calculations for the overall average percent defective ($\bar{p}$) and for the upper and lower control limits are shown below.

$$\bar{p} = 204/3200 = .0638 \ (6.38\%)$$

$$UCL_p = .0638 + 3\sqrt{\frac{.0638 \times (1 - .0638)}{100}}$$

$$UCL_p = .0638 + .0733$$
$$UCL_p = .1371 \ (13.71\%)$$

$$LCL_p = 0$$

Delete Sample 22

$$\bar{p} = 188/3100 = .0606 \ (6.06\%)$$

$$UCL_p = .0606 + 3\sqrt{\frac{.0606 \times (1 - .0606)}{100}}$$

$$UCL_p = .0606 + .0716$$
$$UCL_p = .1322 \ (13.22\%)$$

$$LCL_p = 0$$

Examination of the completed p-chart shows that with the exception of Sample 22, all the points are within the control limits. This one point outside the upper control limit would not normally mean that the process should be declared out of control; it would, however, call for a closer examination of the p-chart. We should look at the chart to see how well the points are distributed around the overall percent defective ($\bar{p}$) line. We should see about one-half of the points on each side of the $\bar{p}$. This seems to be what we find on this chart: there are 14 points below 6%, 14 points above 6%, and three points at 6%. This is a reasonable distribution of points above and below the average.

Another way of examining a p-chart is to see how many points are close to the average and how many are nearer the control limit. This type of check is made on the half of the chart above the $\bar{p}$. If there are 14 points above the $\bar{p}$, we would expect about two-thirds of that number, or about nine, to fall between the average line and one-third of the distance to the upper control limit, which is at about 8.5%. This would leave about five points between 8.5% and 13.2%, the upper control limit.

We see that there are five points between the average line and 8.5% and nine points between 8.5% and the upper control limit. This is not to be expected if the process is operating normally. Remember that this chart was developed using the combined variation of four defect types. Each of these defects could vary independently of the others. Therefore it is possible that some of the defect types are not in control.

It cannot be said with confidence that this process is in control. More study or analysis is needed before a decision can be reached.

CASE 4-7

In this problem you are asked to determine which defect group you would recommend that a quality improvement team start first to improve.

The p-chart developed from the inspection data in Case 4-6 showed an overall percent defective of 6.06% for all defect types. In most cases, the defect type that contributes most to this overall percent defective should be recommended as the one in which the greatest improvement could be attained most easily. This defect type can be determined by constructing individual p-charts for each of the four defect types.

Charts similar to those that you should have constructed are shown in Figures 4-R, 4-S, 4-T, and 4-U. Examination of the overall percent defective ($\bar{p}$) of each defect type shows that bad trim accounts for most of the defectives because it has a $\bar{p}$ of 3.31%. Blisters has a $\bar{p}$ of 1.4%, non-fills and foreign material defect types are both at about .3%. Thus it is very probable that the team will attain the greatest improvement if it concentrates on bad trim defects.

The second question asked in this problem is whether the team should look to the production floor for the improvements or to requests for management action. This can be answered most accurately by examining the control charts constructed for each defect type. Points outside the control limits indicate the presence of assignable causes. There are actions or activities in the process that are not a normal part of the process, and these activities are causing defects. If this is the case, the causes can be found on the production floor.

When the assignable causes are eliminated, the quality will improve. If the process still generates defects, they are due to causes built into the process and can be eliminated only by management action.

Examination of the four p-charts shows that all four have points out of control. The quality improvement team should be able to improve the quality of the parts by searching out the causes on the production floor.

Upon completing this problem, you may have detected what would seem to be a contradictory situation. When the inspection data for all four defect types are plotted together, as in Figure 4-Q, a fairly stable process is indicated. Only Sample 22 was deleted in the calculations of the $\bar{p}$ and of the upper and lower control limits. When the four defect types are charted separately, however, they all show points outside the control limits.

This situation comes about in part because the p-chart is showing the combined effect of more than one defect type, each one varying independently of the others. The individual variable, or defect, sometimes must send a clearer signal if the remaining defect types, by chance, were less than the average at the time when the sample was selected.

Another factor in such a chart is the situation in which one defect type dominates the total. In this problem, bad trim is responsible for more than half of the defects (106 of 204) that go to determine the average percent defective and the control limits for the control chart. When one or two defect types dominate the defectives recorded in a p-chart, the user must be aware that this situation exists. The chart must be watched closely for other signals of assignable causes in addition to points outside the control limits. Close examination of the chart in Figure 4-Q, shows that bad trim and blisters dominate. In addition, there are five points plotted near the upper control limit, more than we would expect if no assignable causes were present. This signal should lead to the analysis discussed in Case 4-6.

When such conditions are seen in control charts that are newly developed or currently in use, p-charts for individual defect types should be constructed. The stability of each defect type then can be estimated, as in this problem.

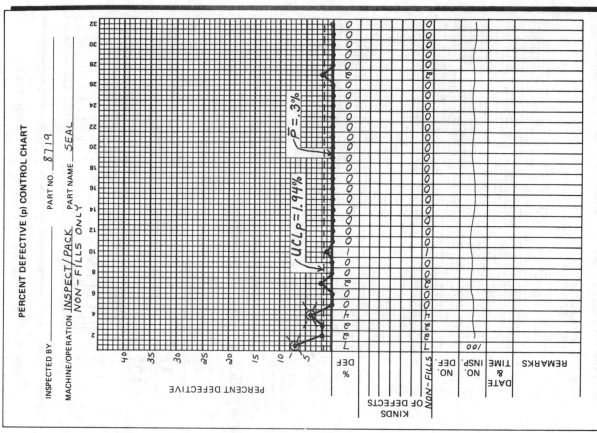

Figure 4-R. Percent defective chart, non-fills only, Case 4-7.

Figure 4-Q. Percent defective chart, rubber parts, all defects, Case 4-6.

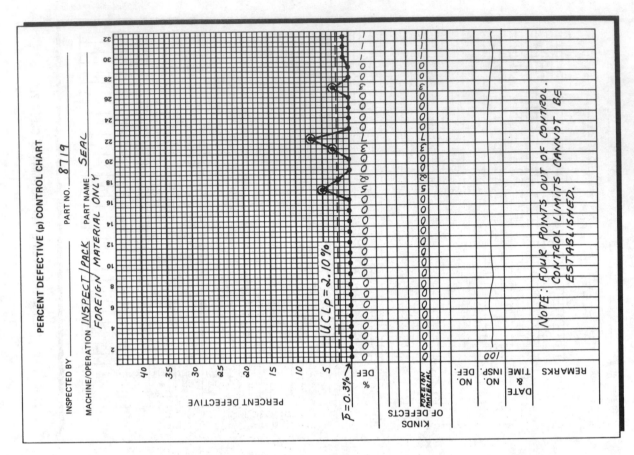

Figure 4-T. Percent defective chart, foreign material only, Case 4-7.

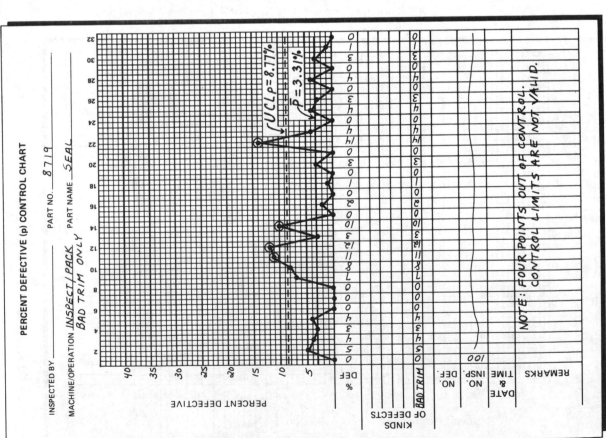

Figure 4-S. Percent defective chart, bad trim only, Case 4-7.

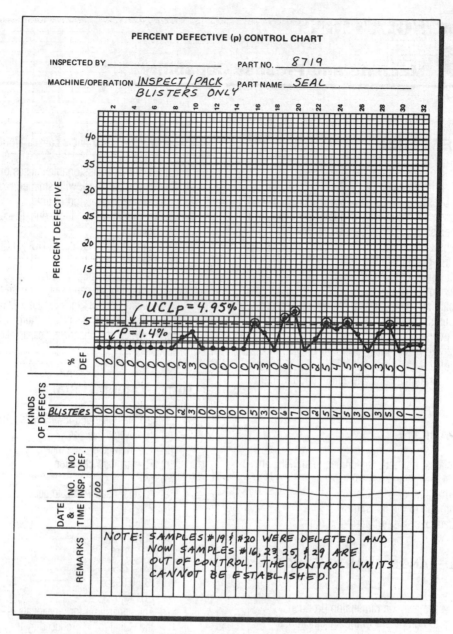

Figure 4-U. Percent defective chart, blisters only, Case 4-7.

REVIEW QUESTIONS

1. (a) When assignable causes have been removed.
   (b) The stability of the process.
2. (a) Has this process or machine been designed and installed in such a manner that no quality problems will arise once the assignable causes are removed?
   (b) A management team.
3. (a) (1) $\overline{X}$-R control chart method.
   (2) Probability plot method.
   (b) Use both methods.
4. (a) Process capability includes variations of machines, people, suppliers, methods, and environment. Machine capability is only a part of this.
   (b) When you want to determine effects of changes in tools, methods, or materials.
   (c) To study the operation as a whole after the job is in production.

MACHINE CAPABILITY

1. Production associates, methods, machines, materials, environment, etc.
2. (a) On a single machine or operation.
   (b) Only variation due to the machine.
   (c) Collect the data over a short period of time.

AVERAGE AND RANGE CHART METHOD

1. (a) One.
   (b) To determine the average dimension produced.
   (c) We will want to compare it to the specifications.
2. To determine the process spread.
3. (a) The measurements based on parts produced.
   (b) We need to know the stability of the operation.
   (c) On the statistics of the operation when *all* conditions are normal and stable.
4. (a) Use the $\overline{X}$-R control chart.
   (b) We can see if points are outside the control limits, indicating the presence of assignable causes.
5. (a) The histogram.
   (b) Put specs on it.
   (c) As a quick check when we are sure there are no assignable causes present.
   (d) The $\overline{X}$-R control chart method.

6. (a) When *all* assignable causes are identified and elmininated.
   (b) Stability (*no* assignable causes present).
7. (a) So you can work with smaller, easier numbers.
8. (a) Over a short period of time.
   (b) To minimize variation due to causes other than the machine.
9. (a) Sum, $\overline{X}$, R, $\overline{R}$, UCL_R, $\overline{\overline{X}}$, $UCL_{\overline{x}}$, $LCL_{\overline{x}}$
   (b) The range chart.
   (c) We must determine whether the variation is stable or not. If it is, then we can use the $\overline{R}$ from the range chart for calculating control limits for the $\overline{X}$ part of the control chart.
10. Assignable causes distort the normal frequency distribution curve. When this happens, capability predictions are less accurate.

LIMITS FOR INDIVIDUALS

1. Estimate the upper and lower limits for individuals.
2. (a) The overall average.
   (b) The average of the ranges.
   (c) The standard deviation.
   (d) σ
   (e) A factor used with $\overline{R}$ to get σ.
   (f) 2.326
   (g) 2.059
   (h) $3\overline{R}/d_2$
   (i) (1) 13.16
       (2) 12.32
       (3) 0.09957
       (4) 13.67
   (j) The upper limit for individuals. It is the estimated largest individual to be produced by the operation.
   (k) $UL_X = \overline{\overline{X}} + 3\overline{R}/d_2$
   (l) (1) 48.28
       (2) 87.70
       (3) 1.02421
       (4) 14.80
   (m) The lower limit for individuals. It is the estimated smallest part to be produced by the operation.
   (n) $LL_X = \overline{\overline{X}} + 3\overline{R}/d_2$
   (o) (1) 21.96
       (2) 63.06
       (3) 0.82507
       (4) −12.54
   (p) Upper specification limit.

(q) Lower specification limit.
(r) US – LS
(s) 14.41
(t) Specification limit.
(u) $6\sigma = 6\bar{R}/d_2$
(v) 18.09

3. (a) When the UL_X is less than US *and* LL_X is greater than LS.
   (b) The process must be stable and normal.
4. (a) Capable.
   (b) $UL_X = US$, $LL_X = LS$.
   (c) We lost capability, i.e., if the operation worsens, parts will be made outside of the specs.
5. (a) The process spread is greater than the spec limits.
   (b) Yes.
6. (a) $\bar{\bar{X}}$ is too high.
   (b) Yes.
   (c) Move $\bar{\bar{X}}$ to halfway between US and LS.
7. (a) On the specification.
   (b) The process spread is considerably less than the difference between the specs.
   (c) Good. The process can change a bit and parts will still be inside the specs.
8. They will cause the process spread to be greater than that caused by the machine alone.
9. The variability built into the machine must be small enough to allow for other sources of variation to enter the process and still keep the process output with 3σ above and 3σ below the mean.
10. The chart shows whether the process is stable or not.

THE PROBABILITY PLOT

1. (a) Use a probability plot.
   (b) Plot them in a different way.
2. (a) Center.
   (b) Spread.
   (c) General shape of the frequency distribution curve.
   (d) Percentage outside of specs.
Step 1. (a) 100
   (b) Your estimate could be wrong.
Step 2 (a) The frequency tally.
   (b) 10

(c) The coded ones.
(d) In the appropriate section above the "VALUE" row.
Step 3 (a) Transform the frequency of each measurement value to EAF's and then to percentages.
   (b) *E*stimated *a*ccumulated *f*requency.
   (c) To put them into a form we can use to estimate how normally the measurements are distributed around the average.
   (d) Transfer the first frequency to the EAF space or cell two rows below.
   (e) Start with the first EAF just entered, add to it the frequency directly above it, add the frequency directly to the right of the first frequency, and put the total in the EAF row.
   (f) Do these in the same manner as the first EAF.
   (g) The final, or highest, EAF should be exactly twice the sample size.
   (h) EAF's: 2, 14, 53, 105, 134, 151, 177, 194, 198, 200. *(See the answer chart.)*
   (i) 100
   (j) Yes.
Step 4. (a) Convert the EAF's to percentages.
   (b) Plot point = (EAF/2N) × 100%
   (c) Plot points (%): 1, 7, 26.5, 52.5, 67, 75.5, 88.5, 97, 99, —. *(See the answer chart)*
   (d) "% UNDER."
   (e) Plot points.
   (f) 1.0
   (g) Find 1.0 on the "% UNDER" (left-hand edge) and follow the corresponding line to the heavy line that runs up to the "PLOT POINTS" box that has 1.0 in it. Draw a point or small circle where the vertical and horizontal lines meet.
Step 5. (a) The distribution of measurements from this process is normal (bell-shaped).
   (b) The normal distribution is distorted.
   (c) If the points fall on the line, or very close to it, then the $\bar{X}$ and σ from the $\bar{X}$-R chart method are accurate, if not, then we have less confidence in our $\bar{X}$ and σ.
Step 6. (a) The lowest value we can expect from the operation or process.
   (b) The largest value we can expect.

FREQUENCY				2	10	29	23	6	11	15	2	2								
Follow arrows and perform additions as shown (N ≥ 25)																				
EST. ACCUM. FREQ. (EAF)				2	14	53	105	134	151	177	194	198	200								
PLOT POINTS (%) (EAF/2N) × 100				1	7	26.5	52.5	67	75.5	88.5	97	99	X								

Module 5, Review Questions, The Probability Plot, Step 3 (h) and Step 4 (c).

(c) The spread of the measurements from the operation.

(d) The expected spread of measurements from the operation when no assignable causes are present. It equals 6σ.

ESTIMATING THE PROPORTION OF PARTS OUT OF SPECIFICATION

1. (a) To estimate the percent outside the upper spec.
   (b) To estimate the percent outside the lower spec.
   (c) You can still use them, but the estimates will not be as good.
2. (a) It's well centered.
   (b) 6σ (0.0122) is less than the tolerance of 0.018.
   (c) UL_X is less than US.
   (d) LL_X is greater than LS.
3. (a) It crosses the US *before* it crosses the top of the graph.
   (b) Some will be above the US.
   (c) No.
   (d) Even if we centered the process between the specs, we would continue to produce parts out of spec.
4. That you need more data and information before a decision can be made with confidence.

PROCESS CAPABILITY

1. Machine capability is concerned with variability from *only* one machine or operation. Process capability is concerned with variation caused by *all* sources of variation: machine, people, materials, methods, and environment.
2. (a) Variation from *all* sources.
   (b) Variation built into the process which occurs *only* over a long time period, changes in incoming shipments of material, shifts in temperature, etc.
3. A fairly long one.
4. (a) Develop an $\overline{X}$-R control chart.
   (b) 30 days.
5. (a) Identify and note all assignable causes, especially those affecting the ranges.
   (b) Make a probability plot.
   (c) Estimate process spread from the probability plot and evaluate it by comparing it with the spec limits.
6. (a) To see if the process is stable.
   (b) (1) The process spread when the sample was taken.
       (2) It reflects the machine capability.
   (c) It tells us about variation from sources other than the machine.
7. (a) It should be constant.
   (b) It may move up or down with new shipments of materials, as weather changes, as tools wear, etc.

8. Because the average is affected by variation from all sources.
9. (a) Shape of distribution.
   (b) Process average.
   (c) Process spread.
10. (a) Yes.
    (b) All the points are inside the control limits.
11. (a) Yes.
    (b) $\overline{R}$, which reflects mainly machine variation.
12. Yes.
13. It's the value where the line of best fit crosses the horizontal 50% line on the chart.
14. (a) Less.
    (b) By looking at the graph we see that the line of best fit crosses the upper and lower edges of the graph *before* it crosses the spec lines.
15. (a) It is well centered between the specs.
    (b) Process spread is less than tolerance.
    (c) UL_X is less than US.
    (d) LL_X is greater than LS.

CAPABILITY INDEX

1. (a) A number expressing capability.
   (b) Compare the process spread to the spec spread and express this in terms of σ's
2. (a) Capability index.
   (b) The machine or process is capable.
   (c) 1.0.
   (d) C_P = tolerance/6s of the machine or process.
3. (a) C_P = 0.93/0.77 = 1.21
   (b) Yes.
4. (a) Yes.
   (b) Where the process is centered.
5. (a) C_{pk}
   (b) The process average is outside of the specification tolerance.
   (c) It's noncapable.
   (d) (1) $C_{pk} = (US - \overline{\overline{X}})/3\sigma$
       (2) $C_{pk} = (\overline{\overline{X}} - LS)/3\sigma$
   (e) The smaller of the two values.
6. (a) 6σ
   (b) On one side of the process average.

CAPABILITY RATIO

1. (a) It expresses machine or process capability.
   (b) $CR = (6\sigma/tolerance) \times 100\%$
2. A noncapable machine or process.
3. It tells us nothing about the process average.
4. It describes the capability of the process when the average is centered on the specification mean.

CAPABILITY STUDIES: EXERCISES, SERIES 1

1. *See the answer charts.*
2. Set 1. 30
   Set 2. 31 (0.231 for uncoded data)
   Set 3. 2.95
   Set 4. 97
3. Set 1. Yes.
   Set 2. Yes.
   Set 3. No.
   Set 4. No.
4. Set 1. Yes.
   Set 2. No.
   Set 3. No.
   Set 4. Yes.
5. (a) Range chart.
   (b) We need to know whether the inherent variation is stable.
6. Set 1. Stable.
   Set 2. Stable.
   Set 3. Stable, once one $\overline{X}$ is removed.
   Set 4. Stable, once one range and the accompanying $\overline{X}$ are removed.
7. (a) The overall average or mean.
   (b) Average range.
   (c) Standard deviation.
   (d) σ
   (e) Factor we use with $\overline{R}$ to determine σ.
   (f) 2.326
   (g) 2.059
   (h) $3\sigma = 3\overline{R}/d_2$
   (i) Upper limit for individuals (the estimated largest individual part to be produced by the operation).
   (j) $UL_X = \overline{\overline{X}} + 3\overline{R}/d_2$
   (k) Lower limit for individuals (the estimated smallest individual part to be produced by the operation).
   (l) $LL_X = \overline{\overline{X}} - 3\overline{R}/d_2$
8. Set 1. $UL_X = 62.964$, $LL_X = -2.684$
   Example calculations for Set 1:
   $UL_X = \overline{\overline{X}} + 3\overline{R}/d_2$
   $= 30.14 + 3(25.45)/2.326$
   $= 30.14 + 76.35/2.326$
   $= 30.14 + 32.824$
   $= 62.964$
   $LL_X = \overline{\overline{X}} - 3\overline{R}/d_2$
   $= 30.14 - 3(25.45)/2.326$
   $= 30.14 - 32.824$
   $= -2.684$
   Set 2. $UL_X = 61.68$ (uncoded: 0.26168), $LL_X = 0.68$ (uncoded: 0.20068)
   Set 3. $UL_X = 5.579$, $LL_X = 0.318$ (with recalculated $\overline{X}$: $UL_X = 5.512$, $LL_X = 0.252$)
   Set 4. $UL_X = 170.594$, $LL_X = 8.626$
9. (a) Upper specification.
   (b) Lower specification.

(c) Tolerance = upper spec − lower spec
   Set 1. $65 -(-10) = 75$
   Set 2. $50 - 5 = 45$ (for uncoded data: $0.250 - 0.205 = 0.045$)
   Set 3. $4.0 - 0.0 = 4.0$
   Set 4. $250 - 10 = 240$
10. (a) $6\sigma = 6\overline{R}/d_2$
    (b) Set 1. 65.649
       Example calculations for Set 1:
       $6\sigma = 6\overline{R}/d_2$
       $= 6(25.45)/2.326$
       $= 152.7/2.326$
       $= 65.649$
       Set 2. 61.01 (for uncoded data: 0.26101)
       Set 3. 5.262
       Set 4. 161.969
11. Set 1. tolerance = 75, process spread = 65.649, capable? Yes.
    Set 2. tolerance = 45, process spread = 61.01, capable? No.
    Set 3. tolerance = 4.0, process spread = 5.262, capable? No.
    Set 4. tolerance = 240, process spread = 161.969, capable? Yes.
12–15. *See the answer charts*
16. (a) Yes.
    (b) Sets 1–4. Yes.
17. (a) Set 1. −2.5, 59.5
       Set 2. −0.5, 58.5 (uncoded: 0.1995, 0.2585)
       Set 3. 0.35, 5.40
       Set 4. 10, 179
    (b) Subtract the lowest value you can expect from the operation from the highest value.
    (c) Set 1. 62.0
       Example calculations for Set 1:
       Process spread = highest value − lowest value = $59.5 - (-2.5) = 62.0$
       Set 2. 59 (uncoded: 0.259)
       Set 3. 5.05
       Set 4. 169
18. Set 1. tolerance = 75, process spread = 62.0, capable? Yes.
    Set 2. tolerance = 45, process spread = 59.0, capable? No.
    Set 3. tolerance = 4.0, process spread = 5.05, capable? No.
    Set 4. tolerance = 240, process spread = 169, capable? Yes.
19. Set 1. No
    Set 2. Yes, crosses both.
    Set 3. Yes, crosses upper spec limit.
    Set 4. No.
20. Set 1. 0% above, 0% below
    Set 2. 18% above, 0.8% below
    Set 3. 0.0% above, 9.0% below
    Set 4. 0.0% above, 0.0% below

21. (a) It's the point where the line of best fit crosses the 50% line on the probability chart.
    (b) Set 1. $\overline{\overline{X}}$ = 29.0
        Set 2. $\overline{\overline{X}}$ = 29.0 (uncoded: 0.229)
        Set 3. $\overline{\overline{X}}$ = 2.8
        Set 4. $\overline{\overline{X}}$ = 93
    (c) Set 1. Yes.
        Set 2. Yes.
        Set 3. Yes.
        Set 4. No.

22. (a) C_p = tolerance/6σ
    (b) Set 1. 1.21
        Example calculations for Set 1:
        C_p = tolerance/6σ
        = 75/62 = 1.21
        Set 2. 0.76
        Set 3. 0.792
        Set 4. 1.42

23. Set 1. Yes.
    Set 2. No.
    Set 3. No.
    Set 4. Yes.

24. (a) C_{pk} = smaller result of (USL − $\overline{\overline{X}}$)/3σ or ($\overline{\overline{X}}$ − LSL)/3σ
    (b) Set 1. 1.161
        Example calculations for Set 1:
        USL − $\overline{\overline{X}}$ = (65 − 29)/31
        = 36/31 = **1.161**
        $\overline{\overline{X}}$ − LSL = [29 − (−10)]/31
        = 39/31 = 1.258
        Set 2. 0.712
        Set 3. 0.474
        Set 4. 0.98

25. Sets 1–4. Inside.

26. Set 1. Capable.
    Set 2. Not capable.
    Set 3. Not capable.
    Set 4. Probably not.

27. (a) ($6/\sigma$ tolerance) × 100%
    (b) Set 1. 82%
        Set 2. 131%
        Set 3. 126%
        Set 4. 70.4%

28. Set 1. Capable.
    Set 2. Not capable.
    Set 3. Not capable.
    Set 4. Capable.

CAPABILITY STUDIES: EXERCISES, SERIES 2

1. *See the answer charts.*
   Set 1. 80
   Set 2. 0.290
   Set 3. 430
   Set 4. 30

3. Set 1. No. Operation average is on high side.
   Set 2. Yes.
   Set 3. A little off toward low side, but close.
   Set 4. Yes.

4. Set 1. Yes, if centered properly.
   Set 2. No.
   Set 3. Yes.
   Set 4. Yes.

5. (a) Range chart.
   (b) We need to know whether the inherent variation is stable.

6. Set 1. Stable.
   Set 2. Stable.
   Set 3. Stable.
   Set 4. Stable.

7. (a) The overall average or mean.
   (b) Average range.
   (c) Standard deviation.
   (d) σ
   (e) Factor we use with $\overline{R}$ to determine σ.
   (f) 2.326
   (g) 2.059
   (h) $3\sigma = 3\overline{R}/d_2$
   (i) Upper limit for individuals (the estimated largest individual part to be produced by the operation).
   (j) $UL_X = \overline{X} + 3\overline{R}/d_2$
   (k) Lower limit for individuals (the estimated smallest individual part to be produced by the operation).
   (l) $LL_X = \overline{X} − 3\overline{R}/d_2$

8. Set 1. UL_X = 112.06, LL_X = 51.699
   Example calculations for Set 1:
   $UL_X = \overline{X} + 3\overline{R}/d_2$
   = 81.88 + 3(23.4)/2.326
   = 81.88 + 70.2/2.326
   = 81.88 + 30.181
   = 112.06
   LL_X = 81.88 − 3(23.4)/2.236
   = 81.88 − 30.181
   = 51.699
   Set 2. UL_X = 0.579, LL_X = 0.027
   Set 3. UL_X = 56.307, LL_X = 3.813
   Set 4. UL_X = 57.61, LL_X = 1.25

9. (a) Upper specification.
   (b) Lower specification.
   (c) Tolerance = upper spec − lower spec
   Set 1. 90 − 10 = 80
   Set 2. 0.470 − 0.100 = 0.370
   Set 3. 470 − 400 = 70
   Set 4. 55 − 5 = 50

10. (a) $6\sigma = 6\overline{R}/d_2$
    (b) Set 1. 60.361
    Example calculations for Set 1:
    $6\sigma = 6\overline{R}/d_2$
    = 6(23.4)/2.326
    = 140.4/2.326
    = 60.361

Set 2. 0.552
Set 3. 52.494
Set 4. 56.363

11. Set 1. tolerance = 80, process spread = 60.361, capable? Yes.

Set 2. tolerance = 0.370, process spread = 0.552, capable? No.

Set 3. tolerance = 70, process spread = 52.494, capable? Yes.

Set 4. tolerance = 50, process spread = 56.363, capable? No.

12–15. *See the answer charts.*

16. (a) Yes.
   (b) Set 1. Yes.
       Set 2. No.
       Set 3. Probably.
       Set 4. Yes.

17. (a) Set 1. 50, 113
       Set 2. 0.043, 0.579
       Set 3. 403, 462
       Set 4. 0, 60
   (b) Subtract the lowest value you can expect from the operation from the highest value.
   (c) Set 1. 63
       Example calculations for Set 1:
       Process spread = highest value − lowest value
       $$= 113 - 50 = 63$$
       Set 2. 0.536
       Set 3. 59
       Set 4. 60

18. Set 1. tolerance = 80, process spread = 63, capable? Yes.

Set 2. tolerance = 0.370, process spread = 0.536, capable? No.

Set 3. tolerance = 70, process spread = 59, capable? Yes.

Set 4. tolerance = 50, process spread = 60, capable? No.

19. Set 1. Yes, crosses upper spec limit.
Set 2. Yes, crosses both.
Set 3. No.
Set 4. Yes, crosses both.

20. Set 1. 22.0% above, 0.0% below
Set 2. 3.5% above, 0.9% below
Set 3. 0.0% above, 0.0% below
Set 4. 0.7% above, 0.7% below

21. (a) It's the point where the line of best fit crosses the 50% line on the probability chart.
   (b) Set 1. $\overline{\overline{X}} = 82$
       Set 2. $\overline{\overline{X}} = 0.307$
       Set 3. $\overline{\overline{X}} = 432$
       Set 4. $\overline{\overline{X}} = 30$
   (c) Set 1. No.
       Set 2. No.
       Set 3. Yes.
       Set 4. Somewhat.

22. (a) $C_p = \text{tolerance}/6\sigma$
   (b) Set 1. 1.27
       Example calculations for Set 1:
       $C_p = \text{tolerance}/6\sigma$
       $$= 80/63 = 1.27$$
       Set 2. 0.69
       Set 3. 1.186
       Set 4. 0.83

23. Set 1. Capable.
Set 2. Not capable.
Set 3. Capable.
Set 4. Not capable.

24. (a) $C_{pk} = \text{smaller result of } (USL - \overline{\overline{X}})/3\sigma \text{ or } (\overline{\overline{X}} - LSL)/3\sigma$
   (b) Set 1. 0.25
       Example calculations for Set 1:
       $USL - \overline{X} = (90 - 82)/32 = 8/32 = \textbf{0.25}$
       $\overline{X} - LSL = (82 - 10)/32 = 72/32 = 2.25$
       Set 2. 0.608
       Set 3. 1.085
       Set 4. 0.833

25. Sets 1–4. Inside.

26. Set 1. No.
Set 2. No.
Set 3. Yes.
Set 4. No.

27. (a) $(6\sigma/\text{tolerance}) \times 100\%$
   (b) Set 1. 78.75%.
       Set 2. 144.86%.
       Set 3. 84.29%
       Set 4. 120%

28. Set 1. Capable.
Set 2. Not capable.
Set 3. Capable.
Set 4. Not capable.

Part No. & Name	12-1 (Series 1)												Char. Measured					
Operation No. & Desc.													Spec.					
VALUE																		
FREQUENCY			3	0	5	12	14	37	18	10	1							
Follow arrows and perform additions as shown (N ≥ 25)																		
EST. ACCUM. FREQ. (EAF)			3	6	11	28	54	105	160	188	199	200						
PLOT POINTS (%) (EAF/2N) X 100			1.5	3	5.5	14	27	52.5	80	94	99.5	X						

Module 5, Series 1. Practice chart for EAF's and plot points (12-1).

Part No. & Name	12-2 (Series 1)												Char. Measured					
Operation No. & Desc.													Spec.					
VALUE																		
FREQUENCY			1	1	3	31	5	25	15	11	8							
Follow arrows and perform additions as shown (N ≥ 25)																		
EST. ACCUM. FREQ. (EAF)			1	3	7	41	77	107	147	173	192	200						
PLOT POINTS (%) (EAF/2N) X 100			0.5	1.5	3.5	20.5	38.5	53.5	73.5	86.5	96	X						

Module 5, Series 1. Practice chart for EAF's and plot points (12-2).

Part No. & Name: 12-3 (Series 1)

Char. Measured:

Operation No. & Desc.:

Spec.:

VALUE											
FREQUENCY		2	0	5	17	15	31	20	10	0	
Follow arrows and perform additions as shown (N ≥ 25)											
EST. ACCUM. FREQ. (EAF)		2	4	9	31	63	109	160	190	200	
PLOT POINTS (%) (EAF/2N) × 100		1	2	4.5	15.5	31.5	54.5	80	95	X	

Module 5, Series 1. Practice chart for EAF's and plot points (12-3).

Part No. & Name: 12-4 (Series 1)

Char. Measured:

Operation No. & Desc.:

Spec.:

VALUE											
FREQUENCY		5	5	9	16	27	16	7	6	4	
Follow arrows and perform additions as shown (N ≥ 25)											
EST. ACCUM. FREQ. (EAF)		5	15	29	54	97	140	163	176	186	190
PLOT POINTS (%) (EAF/2N) × 100		2.6	7.9	15.3	28.4	51.1	73.7	85.8	92.6	97.9	X

Module 5, Series 1. Practice chart for EAF's and plot points (12-4).

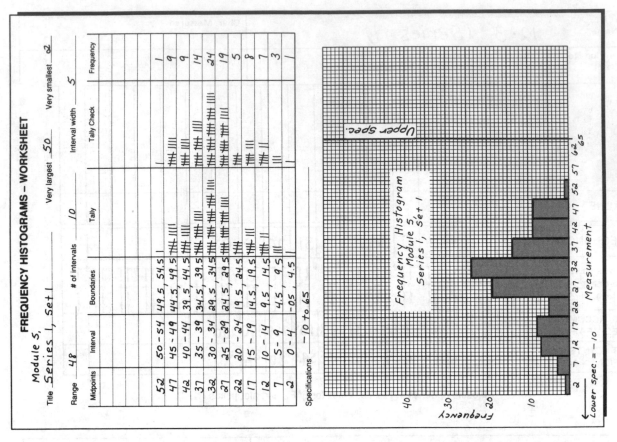

FREQUENCY HISTOGRAMS – WORKSHEET

Module 5,
Title **Series 1, Set 1**

Range **48**   # of intervals **10**   Very largest **50**   Very smallest **2**   Interval width **5**

Midpoints	Interval	Boundaries	Tally	Tally Check	Frequency
52	50 – 54	49.5, 54.5			1
47	45 – 49	44.5, 49.5			9
42	40 – 44	39.5, 44.5			9
37	35 – 39	34.5, 39.5			14
32	30 – 34	29.5, 34.5			24
27	25 – 29	24.5, 29.5			19
22	20 – 24	19.5, 24.5			5
17	15 – 19	14.5, 19.5			8
12	10 – 14	9.5, 14.5			7
7	5 – 9	4.5, 9.5			3
2	0 – 4	-0.5, 4.5			1

Specifications ———— **-10 to 65**

Module 5, Series 1, Set 1. Frequency histogram worksheet.

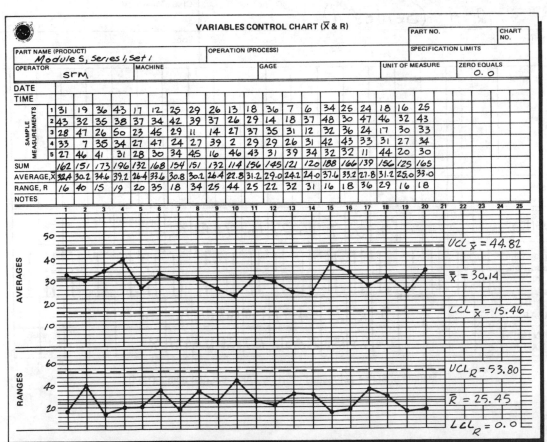

Module 5, Series 1, Set 1. Average and range chart.

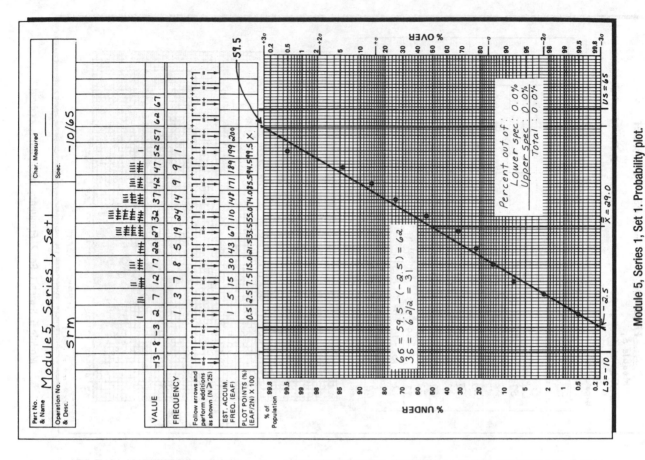

Module 5, Series 1, Set 1. Probability plot.

Module 5, Series 1, Set 1. Process capability study. Average and range chart method.

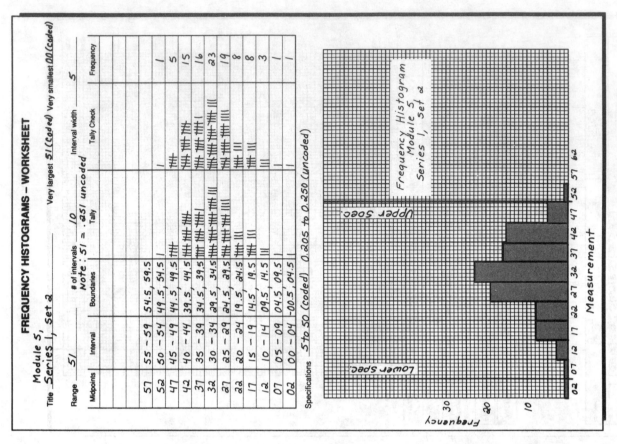

Module 5, Series 1, Set 2. Frequency histogram worksheet.

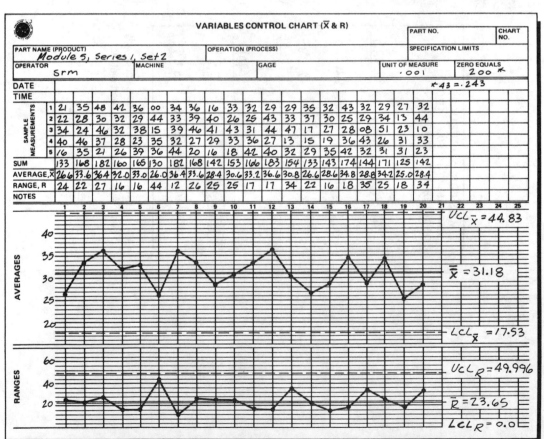

Module 5, Series 1, Set 2. Average and range chart.

Part No. & Name	Module 5, Series 1, Set 2	Char. Measured	
Operation No. & Desc.	Srm	Spec.	5/50

VALUE	02	07	12	17	22	27	32	37	42	47	52	57	62	67
FREQUENCY		1	3	8	19	23	16	15	5	1				
EST. ACCUM. FREQ. (EAF)		1	3	7	18	34	61	103	142	173	193	199	200	
PLOT POINTS (%) (EAF/2N) X 100		0.5	1.5	3.5	9.0	17.0	30.5	51.5	71.0	86.5	96.5	99.5		

Follow arrows and perform additions as shown (N ≥ 25)

58.5

X

% Above U.S. is 1.8%

$6\sigma = 58.5 - (+0.5) = 58$
$3\sigma = 58/2 = 29.0$

For uncoded data
$\bar{\bar{x}} = .229$
$\sigma = .059$

Percent out of:
Lower Spec: 0.8%
Upper Spec: 1.8%
Total 2.6%

% Below L.S. is 0.8%

U.S.=50σ $\bar{\bar{x}}$ = 29.5   L.S.=5   −0.5

Module 5, Series 1, Set 2. Probability plot.

Module 5, Series 1, Set 2.
Process capability study. Average and range chart method. Coded.

LIMITS FOR INDIVIDUALS
COMPARE WITH SPECIFICATION OR TOLERANCE LIMITS

$\bar{\bar{X}}$ = 31.18

$\dfrac{3}{d_2}\bar{R} = \dfrac{3}{2.326} \times 23.65$ = 30.50

$UL_x = \bar{\bar{X}} + \dfrac{3}{d_2}\bar{R}$ = 61.68

$LL_x = \bar{\bar{X}} - \dfrac{3}{d_2}\bar{R}$ = 0.68

US = 50

LS = 5

US − LS = 45

$6\sigma = \dfrac{6}{d_2}\bar{R} = \dfrac{6}{2.326} \times 23.65$ = 61.01

Module 5, Series 1, Set 2.
Process capability study. Average and range chart method. Uncoded.

LIMITS FOR INDIVIDUALS
COMPARE WITH SPECIFICATION OR TOLERANCE LIMITS

$\bar{\bar{X}}$ = 0.23118

$\dfrac{3}{d_2}\bar{R} = $ × = 0.23050

$UL_x = \bar{\bar{X}} + \dfrac{3}{d_2}\bar{R}$ = 0.26168

$LL_x = \bar{\bar{X}} - \dfrac{3}{d_2}\bar{R}$ = 0.20068

US = 0.250

LS = 0.205

US − LS = 0.245

$6\sigma = \dfrac{6}{d_2}\bar{R}$ = 0.26101

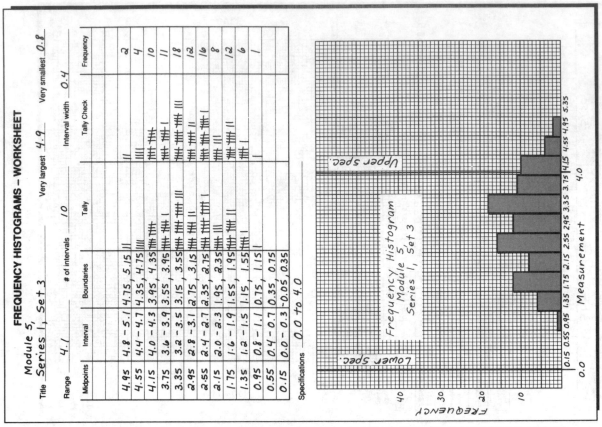

Module 5, Series 1, Set 3. Frequency histogram worksheet.

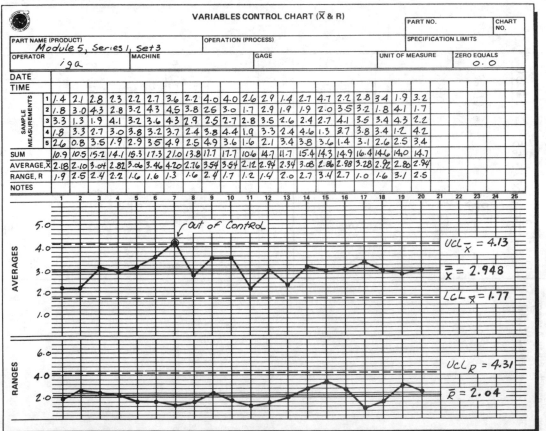

Module 5, Series 1, Set 3. Average and range chart.

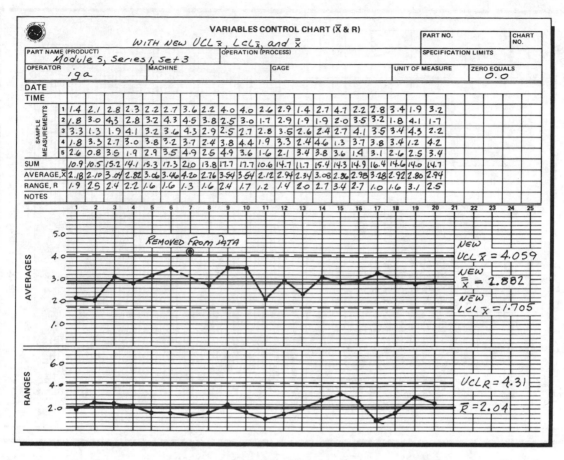

Module 5, Series 1, Set 3. Average and range chart with new UCL$_{\bar{x}}$, LCL$_{\bar{x}}$, and $\bar{X}$.

VARIABLES CONTROL CHART ($\bar{X}$ & R)

WITH NEW UCL$_{\bar{x}}$, LCL$_{\bar{x}}$, and $\bar{\bar{x}}$

PART NAME (PRODUCT): *Module 5, Series 1, Set 3*

OPERATOR: *iga*

ZERO EQUALS: 0.0

	1	2	3	4	5	6	7	8	9	10	11	12	13	14	15	16	17	18	19	20
1	1.4	2.1	2.8	2.3	2.2	2.7	3.6	2.2	4.0	4.0	2.6	2.9	1.4	2.7	4.7	2.2	2.8	3.4	1.9	3.2
2	1.8	3.0	4.3	2.8	3.2	4.3	4.5	3.8	2.5	3.0	1.7	2.9	1.9	1.9	2.0	3.5	3.2	1.8	4.1	1.7
3	3.3	1.3	1.9	4.1	3.2	3.6	4.3	2.9	2.5	2.7	2.8	3.5	2.6	2.4	2.7	4.1	3.5	3.4	4.3	2.2
4	1.8	3.3	2.7	3.0	3.8	3.2	3.7	2.4	3.8	4.4	1.9	3.3	2.4	4.6	1.3	3.7	3.8	3.4	1.2	4.2
5	2.6	0.8	3.5	1.9	2.9	3.5	4.9	2.5	4.9	3.6	1.6	2.1	3.4	3.8	3.6	1.4	3.1	2.6	2.5	3.4
SUM	10.9	10.5	15.2	14.1	15.3	17.3	21.0	13.8	17.7	17.7	10.6	14.7	11.7	15.4	14.3	14.9	16.4	14.6	14.0	14.7
AVERAGE, $\bar{X}$	2.18	2.10	3.04	2.82	3.06	3.46	4.20	2.76	3.54	3.54	2.12	2.94	2.34	3.08	2.86	2.98	3.28	2.92	2.80	2.94
RANGE, R	1.9	2.5	2.4	2.2	1.6	1.6	1.3	1.6	2.4	1.7	1.2	1.4	2.0	2.7	3.4	2.7	1.0	1.6	3.1	2.5
NOTES																				

AVERAGES

REMOVED FROM DATA

NEW UCL$_{\bar{x}}$ = 4.059

NEW $\bar{\bar{x}}$ = 2.882

NEW LCL$_{\bar{x}}$ = 1.705

RANGES

UCL$_R$ = 4.31

$\bar{R}$ = 2.04

Left panel:

Module 5, Series 1, Set 3. Process capability study. Average and range chart method. Original $\bar{X}$. See set 3, $\bar{X}$ and R chart with original calculations.

LIMITS FOR INDIVIDUALS
COMPARE WITH SPECIFICATION
OR TOLERANCE LIMITS

$\bar{\bar{X}} = 2.948$

$\dfrac{3}{d_2}\bar{R} = \dfrac{3}{2.326} \times 2.04 = 2.631$

$UL_x = \bar{\bar{X}} + \dfrac{3}{d_2}\bar{R} = 5.579$

$LL_x = \bar{\bar{X}} - \dfrac{3}{d_2}\bar{R} = 0.318$

$US = 4.0$

$LS = 0.0$

$US - LS = 4.0$

$6\sigma = \dfrac{6}{d_2}\bar{R} = \dfrac{6}{2.326}(2.04) = 5.262$

Right panel:

Module 5, Series 1, Set 3. Process capability study. Average and range chart method. Recalculated $\bar{X}$. See set 3, $\bar{X}$ and R chart with recalculations.

LIMITS FOR INDIVIDUALS
COMPARE WITH SPECIFICATION
OR TOLERANCE LIMITS

$\bar{\bar{X}} = 2.882$

$\dfrac{3}{d_2}\bar{R} = \dfrac{3}{2.326} \times 2.04 = 2.631$

$UL_x = \bar{\bar{X}} + \dfrac{3}{d_2}\bar{R} = 5.513$

$LL_x = \bar{\bar{X}} - \dfrac{3}{d_2}\bar{R} = 0.251$

$US = 4.0$

$LS = 0.0$

$US - LS = 4.0$

$6\sigma = \dfrac{6}{d_2}\bar{R} = \dfrac{6}{2.326}(2.04) = 5.262$

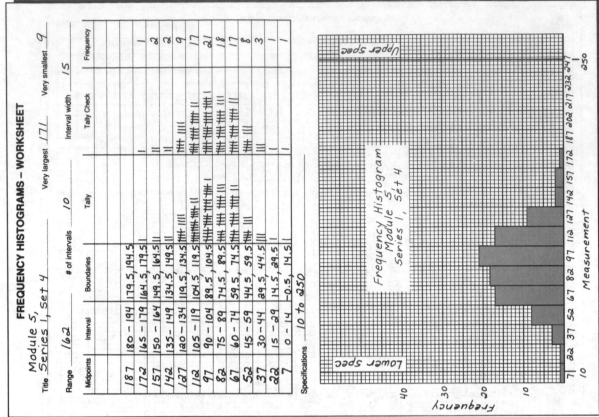

Module 5, Series 1, Set 4. Frequency histogram worksheet.

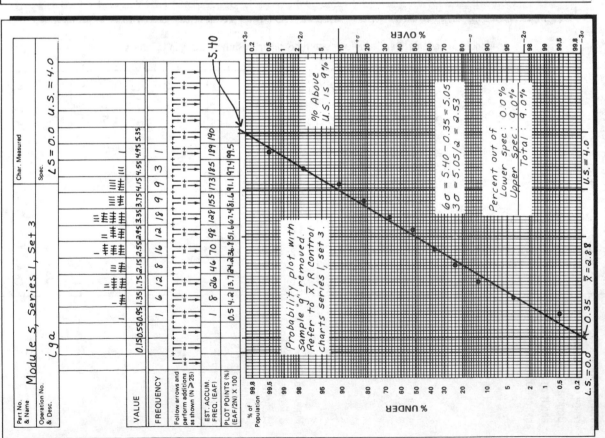

Module 5, Series 1, Set 3. Probability plot with sample "g" removed. Refer to X̄ and R control charts series 1, set 3.

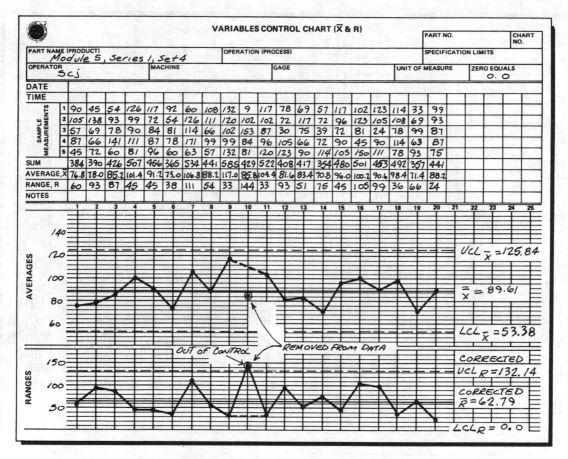

Module 5, Series 1, Set 4. Average and range chart.

LIMITS FOR INDIVIDUALS
COMPARE WITH SPECIFICATION
OR TOLERANCE LIMITS

$$\overline{\overline{X}} = 89.61$$

$$\frac{3}{d_2}\overline{R} = \frac{3}{2.326} \times 62.79 = \underline{80.985}$$

$$UL_x = \overline{\overline{X}} + \frac{3}{d_2}\overline{R} = 170.595$$

$$LL_x = \overline{\overline{X}} - \frac{3}{d_2}\overline{R} = 8.625$$

$$US = 250$$

$$LS = \underline{10}$$

$$US - LS = 240$$

$$6\sigma = \frac{6}{d_2}\overline{R} = \frac{6}{2.362}\left(62.79\right) = 161.969$$

**Module 5, Series 1, Set 4. Process capability
study. Average and range chart method.**

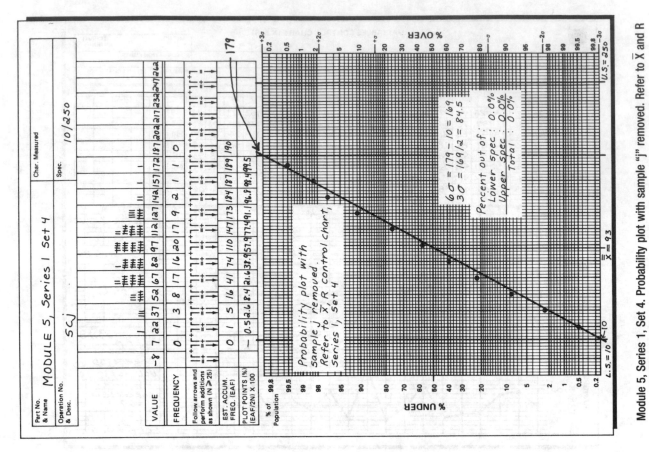

Module 5, Series 1, Set 4. Probability plot with sample "J" removed. Refer to $\bar{X}$ and R control chart, series 1, set 4.

Part No. & Name	12-1 (Series 2)											Char. Measured	
Operation No. & Desc.												Spec.	

VALUE																					
FREQUENCY			1	5	11	10	14	22	27	6	4										
Follow arrows and perform additions as shown (N ≥ 25)																					
EST. ACCUM. FREQ. (EAF)			1	7	23	44	68	104	153	186	196	200									
PLOT POINTS (%) (EAF/2N) X 100			0.5	3.5	11.5	22	34	52	76.5	93	98	X									

Module 5, Series 2. Practice chart for EAF's and plot points (12-1).

Part No. & Name	12-2 (Series 2)												Char. Measured			
Operation No. & Desc.													Spec.			

VALUE																				
FREQUENCY			3	0	5	12	16	25	19	13	7									
Follow arrows and perform additions as shown (N≥25)																				
EST. ACCUM. FREQ. (EAF)			3	6	11	28	56	97	141	173	193	200								
PLOT POINTS (%) (EAF/2N) X 100			1.5	3	5.5	14	28	48.5	70.5	86.5	96.5	X								

Module 5, Series 2. Practice chart for EAF's and plot points (12-2).

Part No. & Name	12-3 (Series 2)												Char. Measured			
Operation No. & Desc.													Spec.			

VALUE																				
FREQUENCY			1	2	5	8	15	21	30	12	3	2	1							
Follow arrows and perform additions as shown (N≥25)																				
EST. ACCUM. FREQ. (EAF)			1	4	11	24	47	83	134	176	191	196	199	200						
PLOT POINTS (%) (EAF/2N) X 100			0.5	2	5.5	12	23.5	41.5	67	88	95.5	98	99.5	X						

Module 5, Series 2. Practice chart for EAF's and plot points (12-3).

Part No. & Name	12-4 (Series 2)										Char. Measured									
Operation No. & Desc.											Spec.									

VALUE																				
FREQUENCY				5	12	23	37	15	5	1										
Follow arrows and perform additions as shown (N ≥ 25)																				
EST. ACCUM. FREQ. (EAF)				5	22	57	117	169	189	195	196									
PLOT POINTS (%) (EAF/2N) X 100				2.6	11.2	29.1	59.7	86.2	96.4	99.5	X									

Module 5, Series 2. Practice chart for EAF's and plot points (12-4).

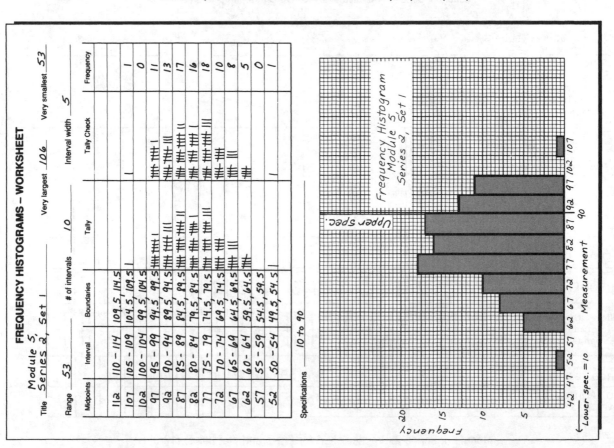

Module 5, Series 2, Set 1. Frequency histogram worksheet.

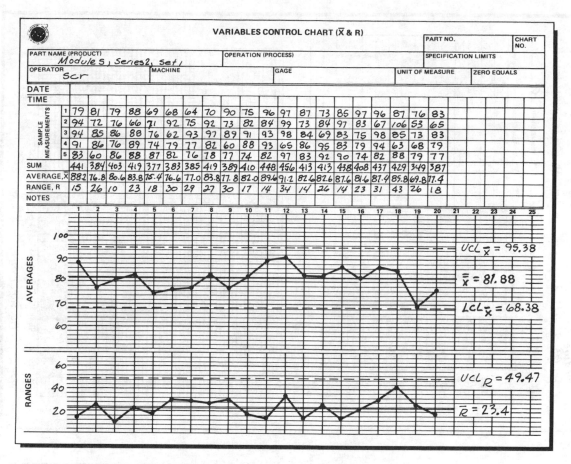

Module 5, Series 2, Set 1. Average and range chart.

LIMITS FOR INDIVIDUALS
COMPARE WITH SPECIFICATION
OR TOLERANCE LIMITS

$$\overline{\overline{X}} = 81.88$$

$$\frac{3}{d_2}\overline{R} = \frac{3}{2.326} \times 23.4 = 30.18$$

$$UL_x = \overline{\overline{X}} + \frac{3}{d_2}\overline{R} = 112.06$$

$$LL_x = \overline{\overline{X}} - \frac{3}{d_2}\overline{R} = 51.70$$

$$US = 90$$

$$LS = 10$$

$$US - LS = 80$$

$$6\sigma = \frac{6}{d_2}\overline{R} = \frac{6}{2.326} \times 23.4 = 60.36$$

Module 5, Series 2, Set 1. Process capability study. Average and range chart method.

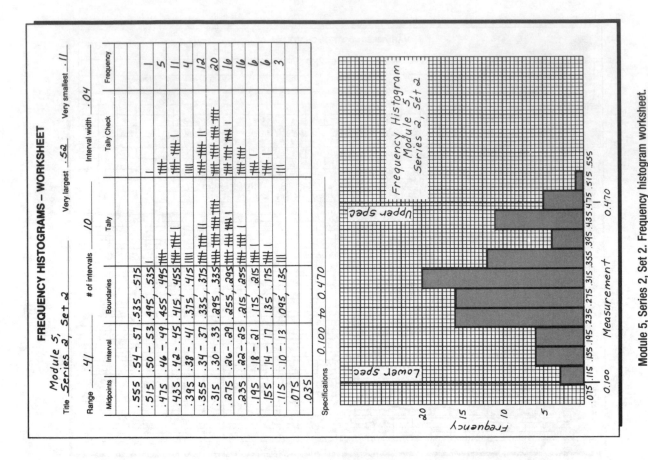

Module 5, Series 2, Set 2. Frequency histogram worksheet.

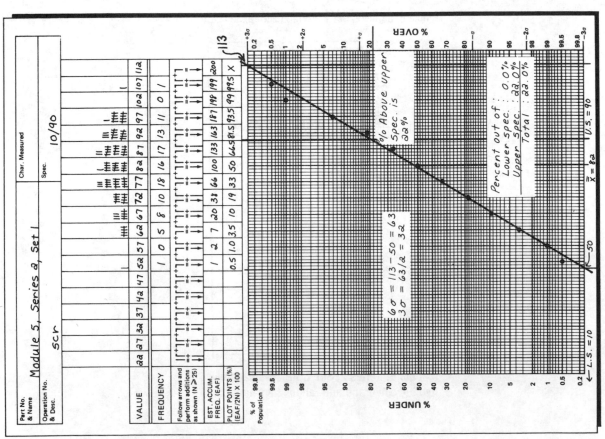

Module 5, Series 2, Set 1. Probability plot.

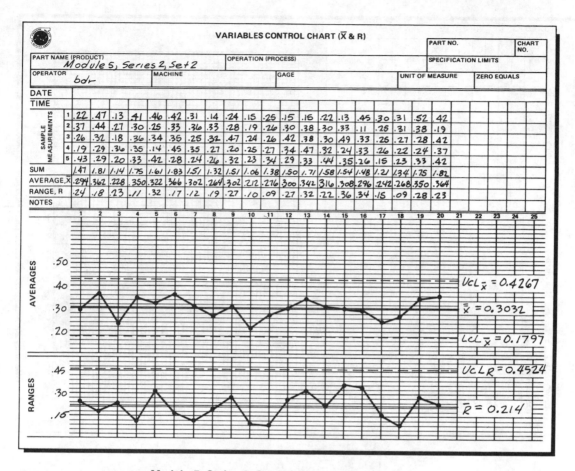

Module 5, Series 2, Set 2. Average and range chart.

LIMITS FOR INDIVIDUALS
COMPARE WITH SPECIFICATION
OR TOLERANCE LIMITS

$\overline{\overline{X}}$ = 0.3032

$\dfrac{3}{d_2}\,\overline{R} = \dfrac{3}{2.326} \times 0.214$ = 0.2760

$UL_x = \overline{\overline{X}} + \dfrac{3}{d_2}\overline{R}$ = 0.5792

$LL_x = \overline{\overline{X}} - \dfrac{3}{d_2}\,\overline{R}$ = 0.0272

US = 0.470

LS = 0.100

US − LS = 0.370

$6\sigma = \dfrac{6}{d_2}\,\overline{R}$ = 0.5520

Module 5, Series 2, Set 2. Process capability study. Average and range chart method.

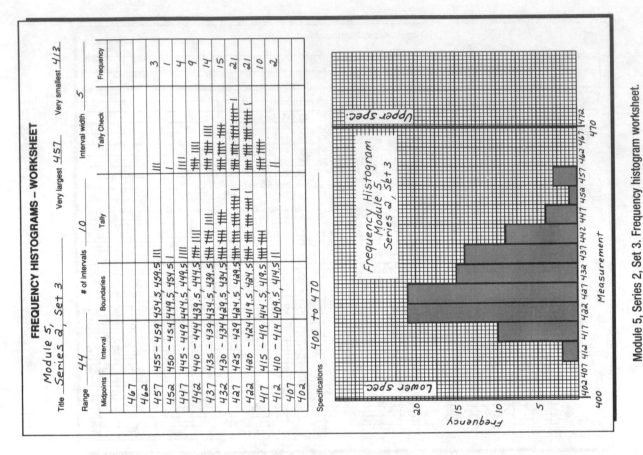

Module 5, Series 2, Set 3. Frequency histogram worksheet.

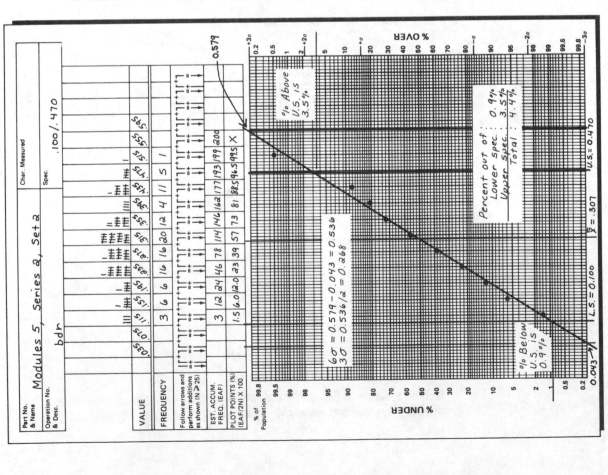

Module 5, Series 2, Set 2. Probability plot.

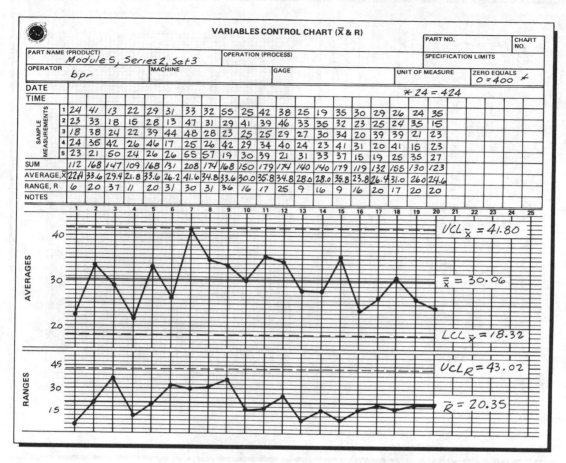

VARIABLES CONTROL CHART ($\bar{X}$ & R)

PART NAME (PRODUCT): Module 5, Series 2, Set 3
OPERATION (PROCESS):
PART NO.: CHART NO.:
SPECIFICATION LIMITS:
OPERATOR: bpr
MACHINE: GAGE:
UNIT OF MEASURE: ZERO EQUALS 0 = 400 *

DATE:
TIME: * 24 = 424

	1	2	3	4	5	6	7	8	9	10	11	12	13	14	15	16	17	18	19	20	21	22	23	24	25
1	24	41	13	22	29	31	33	32	55	25	42	38	25	19	35	30	29	26	24	35					
2	23	33	18	15	28	13	47	31	29	41	39	46	33	35	32	23	25	24	35	15					
3	18	38	24	22	39	44	48	28	23	25	25	29	27	30	34	20	39	39	21	23					
4	24	35	42	26	46	17	25	26	42	29	34	40	24	23	41	31	20	41	15	23					
5	23	21	50	24	26	26	65	57	19	30	39	21	31	33	37	15	19	25	35	27					
SUM	112	168	147	109	168	131	208	174	168	150	179	174	140	140	179	119	132	165	130	123					
AVERAGE, $\bar{X}$	22.4	33.6	29.4	21.8	33.6	26.2	41.6	34.8	33.6	30.0	35.8	34.8	28.0	28.0	35.8	23.8	26.4	31.0	26.0	24.6					
RANGE, R	6	20	37	11	20	31	30	31	36	16	17	25	9	16	9	16	20	17	20	20					
NOTES																									

AVERAGES:
$UCL_{\bar{X}} = 41.80$
$\bar{\bar{x}} = 30.06$
$LCL_{\bar{X}} = 18.32$

RANGES:
$UCL_R = 43.02$
$\bar{R} = 20.35$

Module 5, Series 2, Set 3. Average and range chart.

LIMITS FOR INDIVIDUALS
COMPARE WITH SPECIFICATION OR TOLERANCE LIMITS

$\bar{\bar{X}}$ = 30.06

$\frac{3}{d_2}\bar{R} = \frac{3}{2.326} \times 43.02$ = 55.49

$UL_x = \bar{\bar{X}} + \frac{3}{d_2}\bar{R}$ = 85.55

$LL_x = \bar{\bar{X}} - \frac{3}{d_2}\bar{R}$ = 25.43

US = 70

LS = 0

US – LS = 70

$6\sigma = \frac{6}{d_2}\bar{R}$ = 110.97

Module 5, Series 2, Set 3. Process capability study. Average and range chart method. Coded.

LIMITS FOR INDIVIDUALS
COMPARE WITH SPECIFICATION OR TOLERANCE LIMITS

$\bar{\bar{X}}$ = 430.06

$\frac{3}{d_2}\bar{R} =$ x = 55.49

$UL_x = \bar{\bar{X}} + \frac{3}{d_2}\bar{R}$ = 485.55

$LL_x = \bar{\bar{X}} - \frac{3}{d_2}\bar{R}$ = 425.43

US = 470

LS = 400

US – LS = 70

$6\sigma = \frac{6}{d_2}\bar{R}$ = 110.97

Module 5, Series 2, Set 3. Process capability study. Average and range chart method. Uncoded.

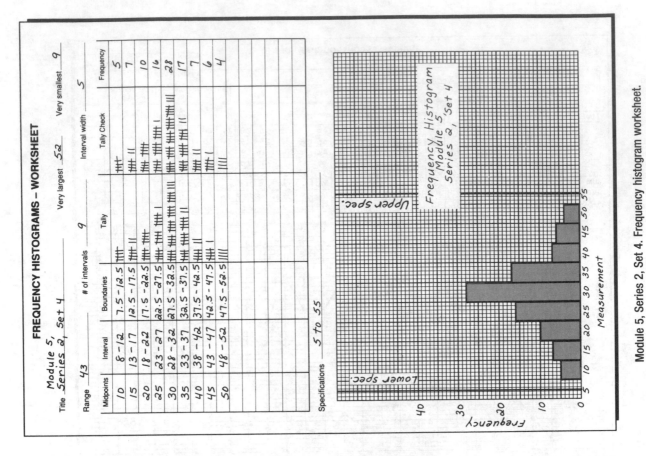

FREQUENCY HISTOGRAMS – WORKSHEET

Title Module 5,
Series 2, Set 4

Range 43   # of intervals 9   Very largest 52   Very smallest 5   Interval width 5

Midpoints	Interval	Boundaries	Tally	Tally Check	Frequency
10	8 – 12	7.5 – 12.5	₥₥	₥₥	5
15	13 – 17	12.5 – 17.5	₥₥ II	₥₥ II	7
20	18 – 22	17.5 – 22.5	₥₥ ₥₥	₥₥ ₥₥	10
25	23 – 27	22.5 – 27.5	₥₥ ₥₥ ₥₥ I	₥₥ ₥₥ ₥₥ I	16
30	28 – 32	27.5 – 32.5	₥₥ ₥₥ ₥₥ ₥₥ ₥₥ III	₥₥ ₥₥ ₥₥ ₥₥ ₥₥ III	28
35	33 – 37	32.5 – 37.5	₥₥ ₥₥ ₥₥ II	₥₥ ₥₥ ₥₥ II	17
40	38 – 42	37.5 – 42.5	₥₥ II	₥₥ II	7
45	43 – 47	42.5 – 47.5	₥₥ I	₥₥ I	6
50	48 – 52	47.5 – 52.5	IIII	IIII	4

Specifications 5 to 55

Frequency Histogram
Module 5, Series 2, Set 4

Module 5, Series 2, Set 4. Frequency histogram worksheet.

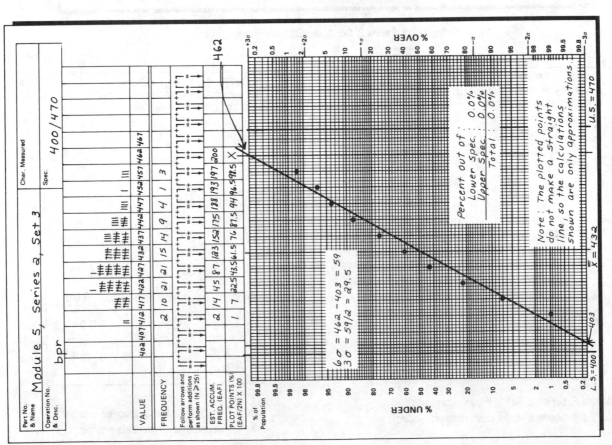

Part No. & Name: Module 5, Series 2, Set 3

Char. Measured: bpr

Spec.: 400/470

$6\sigma = 462 - 403 = 59$
$3\sigma = 59/2 = 29.5$

Percent out of:
Lower Spec.: 0.0%
Upper Spec.: 0.0%
Total: 0.0%

Note: The plotted points do not make a straight line, so the calculations shown are only approximations.

Module 5, Series 2, Set 3. Probability plot.

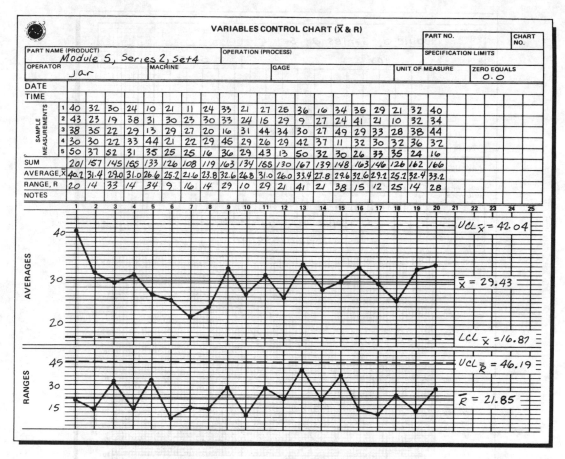

Module 5, Series 2, Set 4. Average and range chart.

LIMITS FOR INDIVIDUALS
COMPARE WITH SPECIFICATION
OR TOLERANCE LIMITS

$\overline{\overline{X}}$ = 29.43

$\dfrac{3}{d_2}\overline{R} = \dfrac{3}{2.326} \times 21.85$ = 28.18

$UL_x = \overline{\overline{X}} + \dfrac{3}{d_2}\overline{R}$ = 57.61

$LL_x = \overline{\overline{X}} - \dfrac{3}{d_2}\overline{R}$ = 1.25

US = 55

LS = 5

US − LS = 50

$6\sigma = \dfrac{6}{d_2}\overline{R}$ = 56.36

Module 5, Series 2, Set 4. Process capability
study. Average and range chart method.

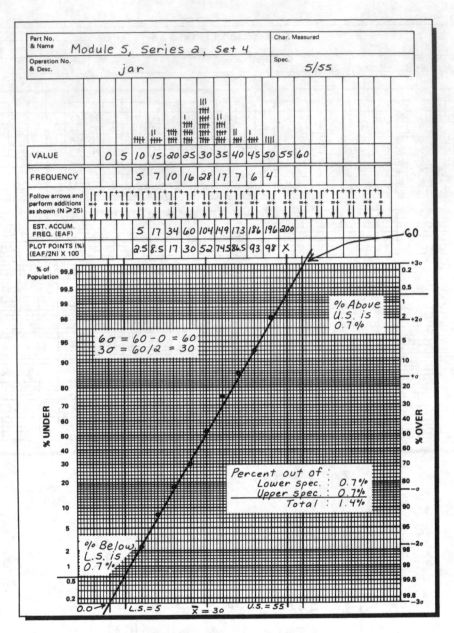

Part No. & Name	Module 5, Series 2, Set 4												Char. Measured							
Operation No. & Desc.	jar												Spec. 5/55							
VALUE	0	5	10	15	20	25	30	35	40	45	50	55	60							
FREQUENCY			5	7	10	16	28	17	7	6	4									
EST. ACCUM. FREQ. (EAF)			5	17	34	60	104	149	173	186	196	200								
PLOT POINTS (%) (EAF/2N) X 100			2.5	8.5	17	30	52	74.5	86.5	93	98	X								

$6\sigma = 60 - 0 = 60$
$3\sigma = 60/2 = 30$

% Above U.S. is 0.7%

Percent out of:
Lower spec.: 0.7%
Upper spec.: 0.7%
Total: 1.4%

% Below L.S. is 0.7%

L.S. = 5 $\bar{X} = 30$ U.S. = 55

Module 5, Series 2, Set 4. Probability plot.

MACHINE AND PROCESS CAPABILITY: ANALYSIS AND DISCUSSION OF CASE STUDIES

CASE 5-1

The measurements used in this problem were taken and recorded over a very short period of time. The 125 weights came from consecutively produced pieces. The variation seen in these weights is due mainly to the machine and tooling used. The time period was short enough that the variation in the weights due to materials, methods, people, and environment would not be significant under ordinary conditions. Most of the variation would have been contributed by the machine and tooling used. This, then, is a machine capability study.

Figure 5-A shows the calculation worksheet for this problem. You should complete the section headed "LIMITS FOR INDIVIDUALS" to determine the capability of this operation. When you developed the average and range chart in Case 3-1 (Figures 3-A and 3-B), you found that the averages for Samples 1 and 3 were below the lower control limit and were deleted from the calculations for the average control limits. No points were outside the recalculated limits, therefore the remaining averages were in control. We can proceed with the capability study. Using the overall average and the average range calculated in Case 3-1, you can determine the upper limit for individuals (UL_x) and the lower limit for individuals (LL_x).

The UL_x is determined by adding a value ($3/d_2$ times $\overline{R}$) to the overall average ($\overline{\overline{X}}$). The LL_x is determined by subtracting that same value from ($\overline{\overline{X}}$).

The value for $3/d_2$ is obtained from the table headed "FACTORS FOR CONTROL LIMITS." The sample size (n) is 5; the value is found in the column headed $3/d_2$. This value is 1.290. When it is multiplied by the range, 32.362 is the value to be added to $\overline{\overline{X}}$ to produce the upper limit for individuals. This same value is subtracted from $\overline{\overline{X}}$ to produce the lower limit for individuals. The upper limit for individuals is found to be 811.484; the lower limit for individuals is found to be 746.760.

The upper specification (US) is 790.0 grams; the lower specification (LS) is 730.0. The difference, or the tolerance, is 60.0. This value can be compared to the estimated spread of the weights of the pieces being produced by the operation. This estimate is known as three standard deviations around the overall average, or six standard deviations. This value is shown as 6σ, or $6/d_2$ times $\overline{R}$. The estimated value for this problem is 64.72. Because the six standard deviation (6σ) value is 64.72 and the specification spread is 60.0, it appears that the operation will be declared not capable. That is, the extruder will produce stock preparation pieces that vary 64.72 grams in weight when everything is

operating normally. Some of the pieces will be outside the specification limits on each production run.

The capability ratio has been calculated on the calculation work sheet shown in Figure 5-A. The CR is shown to be 107.8% of the tolerance.

The capability index (C_{pk}) has been calculated and is shown to be .336. This index value is calculated in two ways; the true capability index is the smaller of the two values obtained. In this case we obtain 1.52 and .336, so the capability index is .336.

All of these calculations are based on the assumption that the data or the weights coming from the extruder are normal; that is, the distribution of data approaches the shape of a bell, or a normal, curve. One way to verify this assumption is to construct a frequency histogram, as was done in Case 2-1. Another way is to make a probability plot of the data. This has been done in Figure 5-B. The probability plot for the stock prep operation was developed by using only the measurements in the samples that were inside the control limits of the average and range chart. The control chart signaled the presence of assignable causes when Samples 1 and 3 were taken. Something was distorting the bell-shaped curve, so we did not use the measurements taken from the pieces made during that time. We plotted the values using a class interval of five, as we did in constructing the frequency histogram in Figure 2-A.

If the distribution of data is truly normal, or bell-shaped, the plot points will fall on a straight line when placed on the graph portion of the probability plot. Because the number of measurements used is only a sample of the total number of measurements from the operation, it is possible that the plot points will not be in a straight line even if the output of the operation is exactly normal; 115, however, is a large enough number to ensure a close approximation of the true shape of the underlying distribution of the data. When all of the points are plotted, a line of best fit is placed on them. This is a straight line, and because we want the plotted points also to form a straight line, we can see how well they conform to the line of best fit.

When we place the line of best fit on the graph, the points near the middle of the line should receive more attention than those at the ends. We can see that the plot points fall fairly near the straight line, except for those on the ends. This shows that the weights of the pieces being extruded are close enough to forming a straight line to be considered normal.

Placing the specification limits on the probability plot shows that a significant portion of the pieces will be outside the specification on the high side of the tolerance. We should not expect to see any pieces out of specification on the low side. When a line is drawn from the point where the line of best fit crosses the upper specification line straight

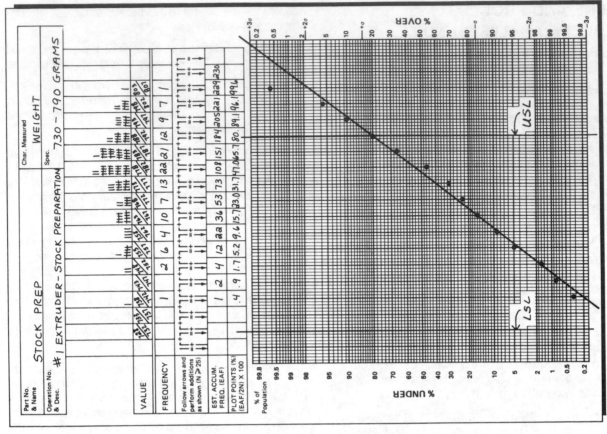

Figure 5-B. Probability plot, Case 5-1.

CALCULATION WORKSHEET

CONTROL LIMITS

SUBGROUPS INCLUDED = 23

$\bar{R} = \dfrac{\Sigma R}{k} = \dfrac{577}{23} = 25.087$

$\bar{\bar{X}} = \dfrac{\Sigma \bar{X}}{k} = \dfrac{1819.8}{23} = 79.122$

OR

$\bar{X}$ (MIDSPEC. OR STD.) =

$A_2\bar{R} = \quad \times \quad =$

$UCL_{\bar{x}} = \bar{\bar{X}} + A_2\bar{R} =$

$LCL_{\bar{x}} = \bar{\bar{X}} - A_2\bar{R} =$

$UCL_R = D_4\bar{R} = \quad \times \quad =$

LIMITS FOR INDIVIDUALS
COMPARE WITH SPECIFICATION OR TOLERANCE LIMITS

$\bar{\bar{X}} = 779.122$

$\dfrac{3}{d_2}\bar{R} = 1.290 \times 25.087 = 32.362$

$UL_x = \bar{\bar{X}} + \dfrac{3}{d_2}\bar{R} = 811.484$

$LL_x = \bar{\bar{X}} - \dfrac{3}{d_2}\bar{R} = 746.760$

$US = 790.0$

$LS = 730.0$

$US - LS = 60.0$

$6n = \dfrac{6}{d_2}\bar{R} = 64.7$

FACTORS FOR CONTROL LIMITS

n	A₂	D₄	d₂	3/d₂	Aₘ
2	1.880	3.268	1.128	2.659	0.779
3	1.023	2.574	1.693	1.772	0.749
4	0.729	2.282	2.059	1.457	0.728
5	0.577	2.114	2.326	1.290	0.713
6	0.483	2.004	2.534	1.184	0.701

MODIFIED CONTROL LIMITS FOR AVERAGES
BASED ON SPECIFICATION LIMITS AND PROCESS CAPABILITY. APPLICABLE ONLY IF: US − LS > 6n.

US = $\quad$ LS =

$A_m\bar{R} = \quad \times \quad = \quad A_m\bar{R} =$

$URL_{\bar{x}} = US - A_m\bar{R} = \quad LRL_{\bar{x}} = LS + A_m\bar{R} =$

NOTES

$CR = \dfrac{6\sigma}{USL-LSL} \times 100\% = \dfrac{64.7}{60.0} \times 100\% = 107.8\%$ (uses 107.8% of tolerance)

smaller of these two →

$C_{PK} = \dfrac{USL - \bar{\bar{X}}}{3\sigma} = \dfrac{790 - 779.122}{32.362} = .336$ ← less than 1.0 NOT CAPABLE

$C_{PK} = \dfrac{\bar{\bar{X}} - LSL}{3\sigma} = \dfrac{779.122 - 730}{32.362} = 1.52$

Figure 5-A. Calculation worksheet, Case 5-1.

across to the right-hand side of the graph, we see that approximately 20% of the pieces will be out of tolerance.

In applying the capability ratio we can say that even if the process were centered on the specification, some pieces would be out of specification tolerance.

The capability index shows that the operation as presently set up will not produce all pieces within specification.

The probability plot verifies that the previous information is true when no assignable cause is present. It enables us to estimate the percentage of pieces that will be out of specification.

When you have completed Cases 2-1, 3-1 and 5-1, you have used three different statistical tools to obtain the same estimates about the output of the same operation. In Case 2-1 you used a frequency histogram to estimate the shape and location of the distribution of the weights in relation to the specification. The frequency histogram gives an estimate of the average and the spread of the weights around the average. In Case 3-1 you used an average and range chart to estimate the overall average of the operation. You used the range of weights in a small sample to signal when something was distorting the output of the operation. The machine capability study in Case 5-1 gives an estimate of the shape of the output of the operation in relation to the specification limits.

Look again at each of these three charts and estimate the process average and spread from each.

	Process Average	Process Spread
Frequency Histogram	778/782	738/807
Average and Range Chart	779.122	unknown
Capability Study	779.122	746.7/811.5

Each of these estimates is made from one of the three statistical techniques you have studied. The frequency histogram enables you to make approximations of the average and spread of the process. The average and range chart and the capability study are more precise statistical tools and can make more precise estimates possible.

Do not be misled by the fact that the overall average and the process spread estimates obtained from the average and range chart and from the capability study are stated in decimal parts of a gram. These numbers are merely the result of the calculations; they do not indicate the accuracy or the precision of the estimate. Because the average and range chart detects the presence of distortions in the output of the operation and because the probability plot shows the degree of nor-

mality, they are better tools than the frequency histogram for estimating the process output.

CASE 5-2

Figure 5-C shows the calculation worksheet for the production setup using Hammer #2—Die #1. The control limits calculations show that all range values and all average values were within the control limits. The overall average ($\bar{\bar{X}}$) is shown to be 13.38. This value is stated in thousandths of an inch, so it must be written as .0134 when it is to be used to estimate machine capability. Stating the values to four decimal places is adequate for this study.

The "LIMITS FOR INDIVIDUALS" calculations are shown in the upper right-hand corner of the work sheet.

The value for $3/d_2$ is found in the "FACTORS FOR CONTROL LIMITS" chart. The sample size (n) used in this problem is five, so the $3/d_2$ value is 1.290. This value is multiplied by the average range ($\bar{R}$ = .0153) to produce .0197. When this product is added to the overall average ($\bar{\bar{X}}$ = .0134), the sum is .0331, the upper limit for individuals (UL_X). When we subtract the same value from the overall average ($\bar{\bar{X}}$), the result is a negative number. When measuring total indicator reading (TIR) we cannot have a measurement less than zero; therefore the value for the lower limit for individuals is zero.

The specified tolerance for this characteristic is .040 maximum. The upper specification limit is .040; the lower specification limit is zero. The total spread of the output of the operation is equal to 6σ, or $6/d_2$ times $\bar{R}$. This value is .0394. Using these two values, we calculate the capability ratio (CR) to be 98.5%. (See Figure 5-C.)

The capability index is calculated from the upper specification limit (US) and the overall average ($\bar{\bar{X}}$). This calculation gives a capability index of 1.35. A capability index of 1.0 or greater indicates that the machine is capable.

The closer to zero the measured value (TIR) is, the better the product. The capability index value obtained by using the lower specification limit of zero is less than one. This is not physically possible because it means that some of the measurements are distributed below zero; therefore the C_{pk} value obtained is to be ignored. This situation can occur in measuring concentricity and when the lower limit is not specified or is zero.

The factors for control limits and the calculations made with them are based on the assumption that the data are distributed around the average as in a bell-shaped curve—that is, normally. To make sure that the data you are working with are distributed approximately in the shape of a bell, you must make a probability plot using those data to see how well they fit a straight line.

Figure 5-D shows the probability plot developed with the measurements from Hammer #2—Die #1. This plot is constructed in the usual

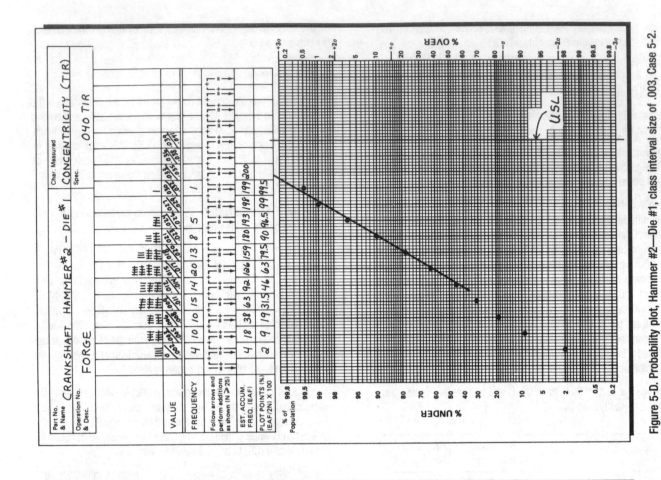

Figure 5-D. Probability plot, Hammer #2—Die #1, class interval size of .003, Case 5-2.

CALCULATION WORKSHEET

HAMMER #2 – DIE #1

CONTROL LIMITS	LIMITS FOR INDIVIDUALS
SUBGROUPS INCLUDED **2.0**	COMPARE WITH SPECIFICATION OR TOLERANCE LIMITS

$\bar{R} = \dfrac{\Sigma R}{k} = \dfrac{306}{20} = 15.30 \ (.0153)$ $\bar{X} = .0134$

$\bar{\bar{X}} = \dfrac{\Sigma \bar{X}}{k} = \dfrac{267.6}{20} = 13.38 \ (.0134)$ $\dfrac{3}{d_2}\bar{R} = 1.290 \times .0153 = .0197$

OR

$\bar{X}$ (MIDSPEC. OR STD.) = $UL_x = \bar{X} + \dfrac{3}{d_2}\bar{R} = .0331$

$A_2\bar{R} = .577 \times 15.30 = 8.83$ $LL_x = \bar{X} - \dfrac{3}{d_2}\bar{R} = 0$

$UCL_{\bar{x}} = \bar{\bar{X}} + A_2\bar{R} = 22.21$ US = .040

$LCL_{\bar{x}} = \bar{\bar{X}} - A_2\bar{R} = 4.55$ LS = 0

$UCL_R = D_4\bar{R} = 2.114 \times 15.30 = 32.344$ US – LS = .040

$6\sigma = \dfrac{6\bar{R}}{d_2} = .0394$

MODIFIED CONTROL LIMITS FOR AVERAGES

BASED ON SPECIFICATION LIMITS AND PROCESS CAPABILITY.
APPLICABLE ONLY IF: US – LS > 6σ.

$US = $ ____ $LS = $ ____

$A_M\bar{R} = $ ____ $\times$ ____ $A_M\bar{R} = $ ____

$URL_{\bar{x}} = US - A_M\bar{R} = $ ____ $LRL_{\bar{x}} = LS + A_M\bar{R} = $ ____

FACTORS FOR CONTROL LIMITS

n	A_2	D_4	d_2	$\dfrac{3}{d_2}$	A_M
2	1.880	3.268	1.128	2.659	0.779
3	1.023	2.574	1.693	1.772	0.749
4	0.729	2.282	2.059	1.457	0.728
5	0.577	2.114	2.326	1.290	0.713
6	0.483	2.004	2.534	1.184	0.701

$CR = \dfrac{6\sigma}{USL - LSL} \times 100\% = \dfrac{.0394}{.040} \times 100\% = 98.5\%$ (uses 98.5% of tolerance)

$C_{PK} = \dfrac{USL - \bar{\bar{X}}}{3\sigma} = \dfrac{.040 - .0134}{.0197} = \boxed{1.35}$ ← greater than 1.0 **CAPABLE**

Note: When no lower limit is specified or it is specified as zero, the calculation using the LSL is ignored.

NOTES

Figure 5-C. Calculation worksheet, Hammer #2—Die #1, Case 5-2.

manner, but because we are dealing with total indicator readings, it is often a good idea to remember that the upper half of the probability plot is the part of the data most important to our analysis. When drawing the line of best fit, give attention to the points plotted above the 50% value. The plot for this set of measurements shows a good fit to a straight line, indicating that the output of the operation is normal and has not been distorted by assignable causes.

A vertical line has been drawn on the probability plot at the point representing the upper specification limit of .040. The line of best fit crosses the top of the graph and does not cross the USL line. This is an indication that all pieces produced by this operation will be within specification. In other words, the operation is capable.

The calculations for the capability analysis of Hammer #3—Die #2 are shown in Figure 5-E. As can be seen in Figure 5-E, the calculations for the control limits of the average and range chart show assignable causes to be present. Subgroup 8 shows the range to be outside the control limit. When the measurements in this subgroup are deleted and when a new average range and a new overall average are calculated, Subgroup 15 is shown to be outside the control limit for averages. When these two subgroups are deleted, the remaining 18 subgroups are within the newly calculated control limits. When calculating the limits for individuals, we use the overall average and the average range that were determined when the two subgroups were deleted. The overall average ($\bar{X}$) used is 17.33 in thousandths of an inch, or .0173 in inches; the range is 21.22 in thousandths of an inch, or .0212 in inches.

The $3\bar{R}/d_2$ (3σ) is determined to be .0274. This value, when added to the overall average ($\bar{X}$), yields a UL_X of .0447. The LL_X is set at zero because the calculated value would be less than zero.

The capability ratio (CR) is calculated from the values shown, and is found to be 137%. This means that the operation has a normal spread that is 37% greater than the tolerance.

The capability index (C_{pk}) is calculated with the upper specification limit (USL) and the overall average ($\bar{X}$). This value, .828, is less than one, which indicates that the operation should be classified as not capable when it is used as presently set up. The C_{pk} using the lower specification limit (LSL) is not meaningful because we are dealing with a concentricity measurement and because the lower limit for individuals (LL_X) is calculated to be less than zero.

Figure 5-F shows the probability plot of the measurements from Hammer #3—Die #2. As can be seen, the half of the plot points above the 50% line on the graph fit a straight line fairly well. The plot points drop off steeply below this line, however, because there can be no measurement values below zero, but there are many near zero. The elimination of the two lowest subgroups leaves the data nearly normal.

The line of best fit crosses the upper specification limit (.040) at about 2 on the "% Over" line. This point of crossing is determined by starting at the point where the line of best fit crosses the upper specification limit line drawn on the graph, moving straight across the graph to the scale on the right-hand side, and reading the percent over on that scale. The fact that a percentage of the product is predicted to be outside the tolerance is an indication that the operation is not capable.

It is easier to make a direct comparison between the probability plots of the two production setups in this problem when the data from Hammer #2—Die #1, as shown in Figure 5-D, are plotted with the same class interval as was used in plotting the data from Hammer #3—Die #2 (Figure 5-F). This has been done in Figure 5-G. The two graphs (Figures 5-F and 5-G) may be used to make a direct comparison of the two tooling setups. The line of best fit on each of the graphs shows that there is less distortion in the distribution of the measurements for Hammer #2—Die #1 than in the distribution of the measurements for Hammer #3—Die #2. As stated previously, the distortion due to assignable causes is not a factor in deciding which tooling setup to recommend for use; when the probability plot presents a very good fit to a straight line, however, we have greater confidence in our decision.

Figure 5-G shows that the line of best fit does not pass through the upper specification limit line. This finding confirms the decision that the Hammer #2—Die #1 setup is capable.

Did you recommend that Hammer #2—Die #1 be used for current production schedules?

CASE 5-3

In this problem you are asked to determine the capability ratio of an operation assembling a left-hand stationary snap to an adjustable retainer. In the average and range chart for Case 3-3 (Figure 3-G) we found the process to be in statistical control, therefore we can proceed with the capability study.

The capability ratio will tell you whether the operation is potentially capable of producing all pieces within the specification limits, but it does not tell you whether that is actually the case. It may be necessary to make an adjustment in the average of the output of the operation before all pieces produced are within the specification limits. It may be easy to adjust the average of the output of some operations, but for other operations the adjustment may be very time-consuming and expensive. For instance, the diameter of a piece of metal can be adjusted by turning a knob or handle on a lathe. However, if the diameter of a molded product must be changed, a new mold must be constructed. If the thickness of the plating applied to a shaft must be changed, a new plating setup may have to be brought in at great cost.

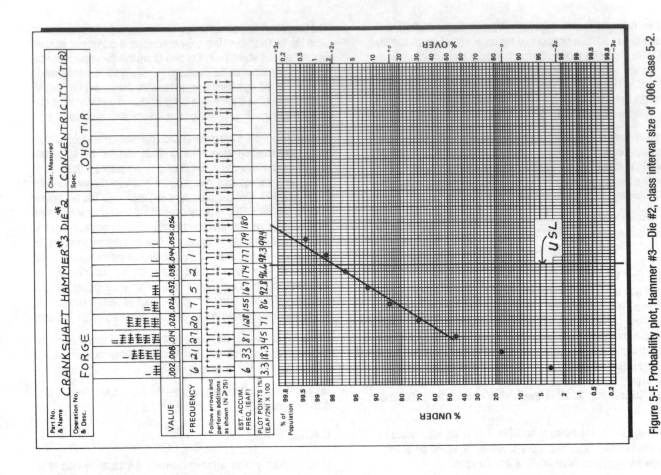

Figure 5-F. Probability plot, Hammer #3—Die #2, class interval size of .006, Case 5-2.

CALCULATION WORKSHEET

CONTROL LIMITS	HAMMER #3 – DIE #2		
SUBGROUPS INCLUDED	20	19	

$\bar{R} = \frac{\Sigma R}{k} = \frac{471}{20} = 23.55 \qquad \frac{417}{19} = 21.95$

$\bar{\bar{x}} = \frac{\Sigma \bar{x}}{k} = \qquad \frac{347.4}{19} = 18.28$

OR

$\bar{x}$ (MIDSPEC. OR STD.) =

$A_2 \bar{R} = \qquad \times \qquad = .577 \times 21.95 = 12.67$

$UCL_{\bar{x}} = \bar{\bar{x}} + A_2 \bar{R} = \qquad = 30.95$

$LCL_{\bar{x}} = \bar{\bar{x}} - A_2 \bar{R} = \qquad = 5.61$

$UCL_R = D_4 \bar{R} = 2.114 \times 23.55 = 49.78 \quad 2.114 \times 21.95 = 46.40$

LIMITS FOR INDIVIDUALS
COMPARE WITH SPECIFICATION OR TOLERANCE LIMITS

$\bar{\bar{x}} = .6173$

$\frac{3}{d_2}\bar{R} = 1.29 \times .02122 = .0274$

$UL_x = \bar{\bar{x}} + \frac{3}{d_2}\bar{R} = .0447$

$LL_x = \bar{\bar{x}} - \frac{3}{d_2}\bar{R} = 0$

$US = .040$

$LS = .000$

$US - LS = .040$

$6\sigma = \frac{6\bar{R}}{d_2} = .0548$

MODIFIED CONTROL LIMITS FOR AVERAGES
BASED ON SPECIFICATION LIMITS AND PROCESS CAPABILITY. APPLICABLE ONLY IF: US – LS > 6σ.

$US = \qquad LS =$

$A_M \bar{R} = \qquad \times \qquad = A_M \bar{R} =$

$URL_{\bar{x}} = US - A_M \bar{R} \qquad LRL_{\bar{x}} = LS + A_M \bar{R}$

FACTORS FOR CONTROL LIMITS

n	A_2	D_4	d_2	$\frac{3}{d_2}$	A_M
2	1.880	3.268	1.128	2.659	0.779
3	1.023	2.574	1.693	1.772	0.749
4	0.729	2.282	2.059	1.457	0.728
5	0.577	2.114	2.326	1.290	0.713
6	0.483	2.004	2.534	1.184	0.701

NOTES *Subgroups 8 ∮ 15 deleted*

$\bar{R} = 382/18 = 21.22$

$UCL_R = 2.114 \times 21.22 = 44.85$

$\bar{\bar{x}} = 312/18 = 17.33$

$A_2 \bar{R} = .577 \times 21.22 = 12.24$

$UCL_{\bar{x}} = 29.57$

$LCL_{\bar{x}} = 5.09$

$C_{PK} = \frac{USL - \bar{\bar{x}}}{3\sigma} = \frac{.040 - .0173}{.0274} = \boxed{.828} \quad \overset{less\ than\ 1.0}{\underline{NOT\ CAPABLE}}$

$CR = \frac{6\sigma}{USL - LSL} \times 100\%$

$= \frac{.0548}{.040 - 0} \times 100\%$

$= 137\% \; (uses\ 137\%\ of\ the\ tolerance)$

LSL is zero – do not calculate C_{PK} using LSL.

Figure 5-E. Calculation worksheet, Hammer #3—Die #2, Case 5-2.

In addition to determining the capability ratio, you were asked whether the operation should be classified as capable or not capable.

Figure 5-H shows the calculation worksheet for the average and range chart developed in Case 3-3. The section of the work sheet headed "LIMITS FOR INDIVIDUALS" was completed to arrive at the required answers. The overall average of the measurements was determined to be 3.19. Because the data are coded with 320 equal to zero, the overall average of 3.19 represents an actual overall average of 323.19 mm. This is the value recorded in the "LIMITS FOR INDIVIDUALS" section of the work sheet. The calculation of the value $3\overline{R}/d_2$ (3σ) gives 3.42. By adding this value to the overall average we obtain the upper limit for individuals, which is 326.61. The lower limit for individuals is obtained by subtracting 3.42 from the overall average; this value is 319.77.

The product specification is 323.0 ± 3.2 mm, so the upper specification (US) is 326.2 and the lower specification (LS) is 319.8. The difference between these two values is a total tolerance of 6.4 mm.

The estimated spread of the output of the operation is twice the $3\overline{R}/d_2$ value or (6σ), which is 6.84 mm.

The capability ratio (CR) is the ratio of the estimated spread of the operation (6σ) to the total tolerance, expressed as a percentage. The calculation of the CR is shown at the bottom of the calculation work sheet in Figure 5-H; this value is 106.9%.

The calculation of the capability index (C_{pk}) takes into account the location of the distribution of the measurements with respect to the tolerance limit of the dimension being studied. The C_{pk} is calculated twice, once with the upper specification limit and once with the lower specification limit. The smaller of the two values obtained is used as the C_{pk}. In order for a machine or a process to be classified as capable, the smaller of these values must be 1.0 or larger.

The C_{pk} calculation based on the upper specification limit (USL) is .88; the calculation based on the lower specification limit (LSL) is .99. We must use the smaller of the two values, so the capability index for this operation is .88, which is less than 1.0. Therefore the operation must be classified as not capable.

The factors used in calculating the C_{pk} are based on the assumption that the measurements used are distributed normally. That is, they take the shape of a bell-shaped curve. A graphic method of verifying this assumption is the probability plot. If the measurements as plotted on the graph fall in a straight line, we can be confident that our decision is correct.

A probability plot of the measurements is shown in Figure 5-1. The line of best fit has been placed on the plot points, and it shows only a fair fit of the points to a straight line. One end of the line of best fit crosses the upper specification limit line at approximately 1 on the "%

Over" line. The other end of the line of best fit crosses the lower specification limit line very near 0.2 on the "% Under" line. This is an indication that we could expect this operation to produce a small percentage of pieces below the specification limit and a small percentage over the specification limit. The C_{pk} values indicate the same thing.

This operation is very close to being capable of producing all pieces within the specification. In fact, none of the 100 pieces used in the development of the average and range chart, the probability plot, and the calculations of the C_{pk} was outside either the upper or lower specification limits.

CASE 5-4

In this problem you are asked to determine the capability ratio of an operation assembling a right-hand stationary snap to an adjustable retainer.

The calculation of a capability ratio will tell you whether the operation is potentially capable of producing all pieces within the specification limits, but it does not tell you whether that is actually the case. It may be necessary to make an adjustment in the average of the output of the operation before all pieces produced are within the specification limits. It may be easy to adjust the average of the output of some operations, but for other operations the adjustment may be very time-consuming and expensive.

In addition to determining the capability ratio, you were asked whether the operation should be classified as capable or not capable.

In Case 3-4 we determined that the process was in statistical control, therefore we can proceed with the capability study. Figure 5-J shows the calculation work sheet for the average and range chart developed in Case 3-4. The section of the work sheet headed "LIMITS FOR INDIVIDUALS" was completed to arrive at the required answers. The overall average of the measurements was determined to be 3.10. Because the data are coded with 320 equal to zero, the overall average of 3.10 represents an actual overall average of 323.10 mm. This is the value recorded in the "LIMITS FOR INDIVIDUALS" section of the work sheet. The calculation of the value $3\overline{R}/d_2$ (3σ) gives 4.64. By adding this value to the overall average we obtain the upper limit for individuals, which is 327.74. The lower limit for individuals is obtained by subtracting 4.64 from the overall average; this value is 318.46.

The product specification is 323.0 ± 3.2 mm, so the upper specification (US) is 326.2 and the lower specification (LS) is 319.8. The difference between these two values is a total tolerance of 6.4 mm.

The estimated spread of the output of the operation is twice the $3\overline{R}/d_2$ value or (6σ), which is 9.28 mm.

CALCULATION WORKSHEET

CONTROL LIMITS L.H. STATIONARY SNAP

SUBGROUPS INCLUDED: 20

$\bar{R} = \dfrac{\Sigma R}{k} = \dfrac{53}{20} = 2.65$

$\bar{\bar{X}} = \dfrac{\Sigma \bar{X}}{k} = \dfrac{63.8}{20} = 3.19 \; (323.19)$

OR

X' (MIDSPEC. OR STD.)

$A_2\bar{R} = .577 \times 2.65 = 1.53 \times$

$UCL_{\bar{x}} = \bar{\bar{X}} + A_2\bar{R} = 4.72$

$LCL_{\bar{x}} = \bar{\bar{X}} - A_2\bar{R} = 1.66$

$UCL_R = D_4\bar{R} = 2.114 \times 2.65 = 5.60 \times$

LIMITS FOR INDIVIDUALS
COMPARE WITH SPECIFICATION OR TOLERANCE LIMITS

$\bar{\bar{X}} = 323.19$

$\dfrac{3}{d_2}\bar{R} = 1.290 \times 2.65 = 3.42$

$UL_x = \bar{\bar{X}} + \dfrac{3}{d_2}\bar{R} = 326.61$

$LL_x = \bar{\bar{X}} - \dfrac{3}{d_2}\bar{R} = 319.77$

$US = 326.2$

$LS = 319.8$

$US - LS = 6.4$

$6\sigma = \dfrac{6}{d_2}\bar{R} = 6.84$

FACTORS FOR CONTROL LIMITS

n	A_2	D_4	d_2	$\dfrac{3}{d_2}$	A_M
2	1.880	3.268	1.128	2.659	0.779
3	1.023	2.574	1.693	1.772	0.749
4	0.729	2.282	2.059	1.457	0.728
5	0.577	2.114	2.326	1.290	0.713
6	0.483	2.004	2.534	1.184	0.701

MODIFIED CONTROL LIMITS FOR AVERAGES
BASED ON SPECIFICATION LIMITS AND PROCESS CAPABILITY.
APPLICABLE ONLY IF: US - LS > 6σ.

$US =$ $LS =$

$A_M\bar{R} = \quad \times \quad = \qquad A_M\bar{R} =$

$URL_{\bar{x}} = US - A_M\bar{R} = \qquad LRL_{\bar{x}} = LS + A_M\bar{R} =$

NOTES

$CR = \dfrac{6\sigma}{USL - LSL} \times 100\% = \dfrac{6.84}{6.4} \times 100\% = 106.9\%$

$C_{PK} = \dfrac{USL - \bar{\bar{X}}}{3\sigma} = \dfrac{326.2 - 323.19}{3.42} = .88 \;$ ← less than 1.0 **NOT CAPABLE**

smaller of these two

$C_{PK} = \dfrac{\bar{\bar{X}} - LSL}{3\sigma} = \dfrac{323.19 - 319.8}{3.42} = .99$

Figure 5-H. Calculation worksheet, Case 5-3.

Part No. & Name: CRANKSHAFT HAMMER #2 — DIE #1

Operation No. & Desc.: FORGE

Char. Measured: CONCENTRICITY (TIR)

Spec: .040 TIR

VALUE	.002	.008	.014	.020	.026	.032	.038	.044	.050	.056
FREQUENCY	14	25	34	21	5	1				
EST. ACCUM. FREQ. (EAF)	14	53	112	167	193	199	200			
PLOT POINTS (%) (EAF/2N) × 100	7	26.5	56	83.5	96.5	99.5				

Figure 5-G. Probability plot, Hammer #2—Die #1, class interval size of .006, Case 5-2.

CALCULATION WORKSHEET

CONTROL LIMITS

SUBGROUPS INCLUDED 20

$\bar{R} = \dfrac{\Sigma R}{k} = \dfrac{72}{20} = 3.6$

$\bar{\bar{X}} = \dfrac{\Sigma \bar{X}}{k} = \dfrac{61.92}{20} = 3.10 \ (323.1)$

OR

$\bar{X}'$ (MIDSPEC. OR STD.) =

$A_2\bar{R} = .577 \times 3.6 = 2.08$

$UCL_{\bar{x}} = \bar{\bar{X}} + A_2\bar{R} = 5.18$

$LCL_{\bar{x}} = \bar{\bar{X}} - A_2\bar{R} = 1.02$

$UCL_R = D_4\bar{R} = 2.114 \times 3.6 = 7.61$

MODIFIED CONTROL LIMITS FOR AVERAGES

BASED ON SPECIFICATION LIMITS AND PROCESS CAPABILITY. APPLICABLE ONLY IF: US – LS > 6σ.

US =   LS =

$A_M\bar{R} = \qquad \times \qquad = \qquad A_M\bar{R} =$

$URL_{\bar{x}} = US - A_M\bar{R} = \qquad LRL_{\bar{x}} = LS + A_M\bar{R} =$

LIMITS FOR INDIVIDUALS

COMPARE WITH SPECIFICATION OR TOLERANCE LIMITS

$\bar{\bar{X}} = 323.1$

$\dfrac{3}{d_2}\bar{R} = 1.29 \times 3.6 = 4.64$

$UL_x = \bar{\bar{X}} + \dfrac{3}{d_2}\bar{R} = 327.74$

$LL_x = \bar{\bar{X}} - \dfrac{3}{d_2}\bar{R} = 318.46$

US = 326.2

LS = 319.8

US – LS = 6.4

$6\sigma = \dfrac{6}{d_2}\bar{R} = 9.28$

FACTORS FOR CONTROL LIMITS

n	A_2	D_4	d_2	$\dfrac{3}{d_2}$	A_M
2	1.880	3.268	1.128	2.659	0.779
3	1.023	2.574	1.693	1.772	0.749
4	0.729	2.282	2.059	1.457	0.728
5	0.577	2.114	2.326	1.290	0.713
6	0.483	2.004	2.534	1.184	0.701

NOTES

$CR = \dfrac{6\sigma}{USL-LSL} \times 100\% = \dfrac{9.28}{6.4} \times 100\% = 145\%$

$C_{PK} = \dfrac{USL - \bar{\bar{X}}}{3\sigma} = \dfrac{326.2 - 323.1}{4.64} = .668$ ← less than 1.0 NOT CAPABLE

$C_{PK} = \dfrac{\bar{\bar{X}} - LSL}{3\sigma} = \dfrac{323.1 - 319.8}{4.64} = .711$

smaller of these two

Figure 5-J. Calculation worksheet, Case 5-4.

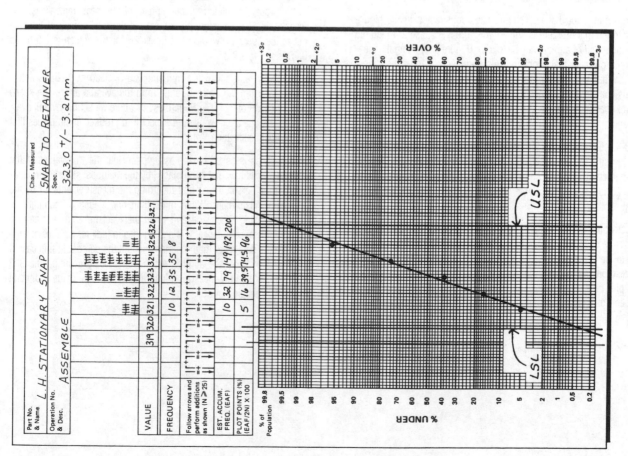

Figure 5-I. Probability plot, Case 5-3.

The capability ratio (CR) is the ratio of the estimated spread of the operation (6σ) to the total tolerance, expressed as a percentage. The calculation of the CR is shown at the bottom of the calculation worksheet in Figure 5-J; this value is 145.0%. On the basis of the 100 measurements used in this problem, we would estimate that the pieces produced from this operation will have a total spread that is 145% of the total tolerance. Further analysis is required before we can say more.

The calculation of the capability index (C_{pk}) makes use of the "LIMITS FOR INDIVIDUALS" calculations. This calculation takes into account the location of the distribution of the measurements with respect to the tolerance limit of the dimension being studied. The C_{pk} is calculated twice, once with the upper specification limit and once with the lower specification limit. The smaller of the two values obtained is used as the C_{pk}. In order for a machine or a process to be classified as capable, the smaller of these values must be 1.0 or larger.

The C_{pk} calculation for this problem is shown in Figure 5-J. The C_{pk} calculation based on the upper specification limit (USL) is .668; the calculation based on the lower specification limit (LSL) is .711. We must use the smaller of the two values, so the capability index for this operation is .668, which is less than 1.0. Therefore the operations must be classified as not capable.

The factors used in calculating the C_{pk} are based on the assumption that the measurements used are distributed normally. That is, they take the shape of a bell-shaped curve. We must first demonstrate stability with the average and range chart. Then a graphic method of verifying this assumption of normality is the probability plot. If the measurements as plotted on the graph fall in a straight line, we can be confident that our decision is correct.

The probability plot that you should have constructed in reaching a conclusion in this problem is shown in Figure 5-K. Case 2-4 required the development of a frequency histogram (Figure 2-1) using the measurements given in that problem. This frequency histogram shows a graph that has two class intervals near the middle of the graph. These intervals contain fewer values than do the intervals on either side. This indicates that something is not normal in the distribution of the measurements.

Case 3-4 required the development of an average and range chart (Figure 3-1) using the measurements given in that problem. The average and range chart does not show any points outside the control limits. This is an indication of a stable operation with no assignable causes present.

The plot points on the probability plot in Figure 5-K are such that a straight line of best fit cannot easily be placed on them. This difficulty is due to the class intervals 323.2 and 323.7, which contain seven and six measurements respectively and cause a sharp change of direction in the plot points near the middle of the graph. Two lines of best fit have been placed on the plot points, one on the lower portion of the

graph and one on the upper portion. These two lines are approximately parallel; they could indicate two distributions of measurements with approximately the same process spread but with different overall averages. The frequency histogram gave an indication of this condition, but the average and range chart gave no such signal. The probability plot, in fact, is a manipulation of the frequency histogram, which provides a graphic estimate showing how normal the data are.

In this problem, the probability plot signals that we should be wary of the machine capability estimates we make using the C_{pk} calculation method. When this is the case, often it is possible to estimate the machine capability by using a probability plot. This is done by selecting a section of the line of best fit that shows a portion of the plot to be normal. This portion is usually one-half of the total plot.

We can estimate the total spread of the output of this operation by using the probability plot as follows:

Follow the 50% line to the point where the line of best fit crosses that line. Follow a vertical line from that point up to the value of that class interval; estimate the value represented by that point on the line of best fit. In this case the value is 323.0

Next, find the -2σ line on the right-hand side of the chart and follow a horizontal line across to the point where it crosses the line of best fit. Follow a vertical line from that point up to the value of that class interval; estimate the value represented by that point on the line of best fit. In this case the value is 320.4.

Next, subtract the 320.4 value from the 323.0 value to obtain 2.6. This value is equal to 2σ of the total spread of the measurements when the operation is operating at the level depicted by that portion of the probability plot. The total spread of the measurements is represented by 6σ. Therefore an estimate of the total spread of the output of the operation would be 3 times 2σ, or 6σ, which is 2.6 times 3. This value is 7.8.

A capability ratio calculated by using 7.8 (instead of 9.28, as determined by using the average range from the average and range chart) will give a CR of 121.9%. Regardless of where we set the overall average of this operation, we would expect it to produce some pieces that are out of specification.

This analysis is based on the assumption that the true values of the measurements have not been biased by the methods, skills, or inclinations of the person taking and recording the measurements, or by the measuring instrument. When more than one statistical technique is used in making a decision and when that decision does not carry a high degree of confidence, it is a good idea to look for sources of variation in the data other than the machine and the person. In this case it may be found that the auditor was unconsciously avoiding the 323 numbers, or that the measuring instrument may have made it difficult to obtain a reading of 323.

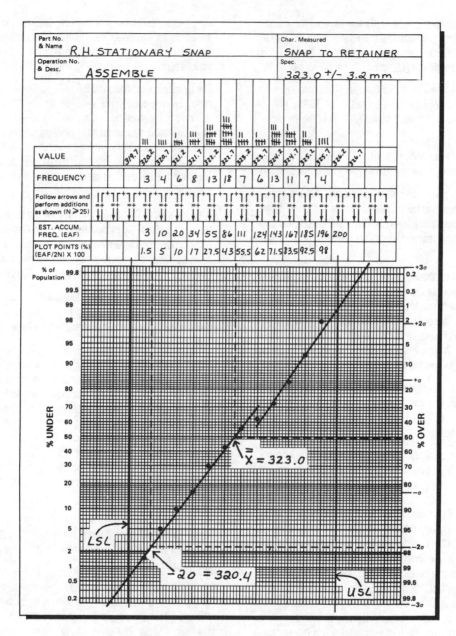

Part No. & Name	R.H. STATIONARY SNAP															Char. Measured SNAP TO RETAINER		
Operation No. & Desc.	ASSEMBLE															Spec. 323.0 +/- 3.2mm		
VALUE		319.7	320.2	320.7	321.2	321.7	322.2	322.7	323.2	323.7	324.2	324.7	325.2	325.7	326.2	326.7		
FREQUENCY			3	4	6	8	13	18	7	6	13	11	7	4				
EST. ACCUM. FREQ. (EAF)			3	10	20	34	55	86	111	124	143	167	185	196	200			
PLOT POINTS (%) (EAF/2N) X 100			1.5	5	10	17	27.5	43	55.5	62	71.5	83.5	92.5	98				

Figure 5-K. Probability plot, Case 5-4.

CASE 5-5

In this problem you are asked to determine the capability ratio (CR) and the capability of a process described as an automatic cutoff operation. Metal sleeves are cut rapidly to a length of 615.0 ± 3.2 mm. Since the average and range chart developed in Case 3-5 showed a stable process, the chart may be used as the basis for the capability analysis. Figure 5-L shows the calculation worksheet used to develop

the average and range chart. The overall average is shown to be 4.18. This average is developed with coded values for the length of the sleeves. Zero is equal to 610 mm, so the overall average of 4.18 represents 614.18.

The overall average is entered into the "LIMITS FOR INDIVIDUALS" section of the work sheet, and the value for $3\bar{R}/d_2$ (3σ) is calculated to be 4.19. Adding this value to the overall average gives the upper limit for individuals (UL$_X$); this value is 618.37. The lower limit for individuals (LL$_X$) is determined by subtracting the 3σ value from the overall average; this value is 609.99. The upper specification limit (US) is 618.2; the lower specification limit (LS) is 611.8; the 6σ value is 8.38.

The capability ratio (CR) now can be calculated. (This calculation is shown on the lower portion of Figure 5-L.) The CR is 130.9%; that is, the output of the operation is estimated to use 130.9% of the tolerance.

The capability index (C$_{pk}$) calculation yields the two values .959 and .568. The smaller of the two, .568, is the C$_{pk}$ of this operation. This value is less than 1.0; therefore the operation is declared not capable.

The CR and the C$_{pk}$ both give such strong indications that the operation is not capable that you may be inclined to stop at this point. However, it is a good idea to complete the capability study by constructing a probability plot to confirm your decision. This has been done in Figure 5-M.

The line of best fit has been placed on the plot points by giving more importance to the points near the 50% portion of the graph than to those at the outer ends of the distribution. The tolerance limit lines are drawn on the graph. The line of best fit crosses both the upper and the lower tolerance limit lines before crossing the top and the bottom lines of the chart; this shows that a percentage of the pieces will be out of tolerance on both the high and the low side.

In addition to the lack of capability, there is an indication of another problem at this operation. Did you notice that the operation was classified as not capable even though none of the measurements was recorded as out of specification?

The problem could be detected first when the frequency histogram was developed. The probability plot confirmed the frequency histogram, but the average and range chart did not detect the problem. Looking at the frequency histogram from Case 2-5 (Figure 2-J), we can see that 18 pieces were recorded as 612 mm, 12 were recorded as 613 mm, 21 as 614 mm, 37 as 615 mm, nine as 616 mm, one as 617 mm, and two as 618 mm. It is true that 612 mm is the smallest measurement that can be recorded and still be in specification on the low end; 618 mm is the largest measurement that can be recorded and still be in specification on the high end. Still, the fact that 18 measurements were recorded at the low limit and none was below the limit indicates a possible problem that may be solved by more complete training of the production associate. For whatever reason, there is a probability that pieces measuring below the low limit were produced but were not recorded at this operation.

CASE 5-6

This problem asks you to determine the capability ratio and the capability index of an operation that creates an .800 dimension. In addi-

tion, you are asked whether the associate was correct in deciding that the operation no longer needed to be checked after he had checked the output for about two months and had found no pieces out of specification.

The measurements collected by the associate were accumulated over a relatively long period. The variation seen in the measurements is not due only to the machine; during the time when the measurements were taken, variation also could have been caused by changes in the materials used, in operators, in the environment, or in the methods used. these are sources of variation for the process as a whole. These measurements, when used all together, should be employed for a process capability study.

A process capability study differs from a machine capability study in the way in which the measurements are collected. In a process capability study, the measurements are collected over a relatively long period of time in order to include the variation from different sources that would be expected when the process is running in production.

The average and range chart developed in Case 3-7 is used in this problem. Refer to Figure 3-Q or to your own chart. Figure 5-N shows the calculation worksheet. The control limits were calculated from the first 10 subgroups in Case 3-7.

Figure 5-0 is a probability plot of the measurements from these 10 subgroups. Because we are dealing with process capability, the overall average ($\overline{\overline{X}}$) and the limits for individuals are estimated from the probability plot, not from the calculations involving the average range. The line of best fit in Figure 5-0 enables us to estimate these values. At the point where the line of best fit crosses the 50% horizontal line, a vertical line is drawn up through the tallies at the top of the chart. This line passes through the "VALUE" row just below the middle of the .796 class interval, so the overall average ($\overline{\overline{X}}$) is estimated to be .7955.

At the point where the line of best fit crosses the top horizontal line of the graph, a vertical line is drawn up through the "VALUES" row of the chart. This line passes through the "VALUES" row at the lower end of the .808 class interval, so the upper limit for individuals (UL$_X$) is estimated to be .807.

At the point where the line of best fit crosses the bottom horizontal line of the graph, a vertical line is drawn up through the "VALUES" row of the chart. This line passes through the "VALUES" row at slightly above the middle of the .784 class interval, so the lower limit for individuals is estimated to be .7845. The difference between the upper limit for individuals and the lower limit for individuals is the estimated total spread of the process (6σ).

The calculation of the capability ratio (CR) for this process using only the first 10 subgroups is shown in Figure 5-N. T estimated to be 56.3%.

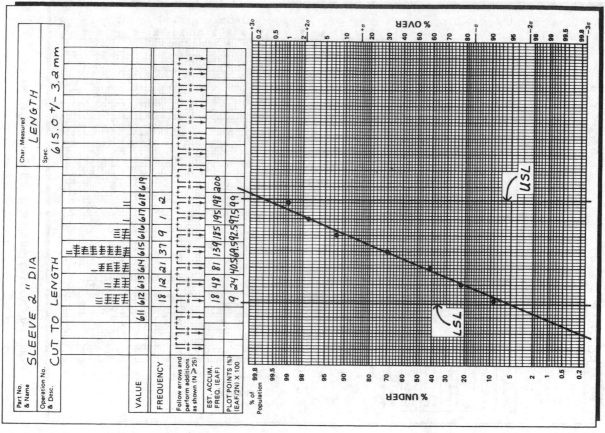

Figure 5-M. Probability plot, Case 5-5.

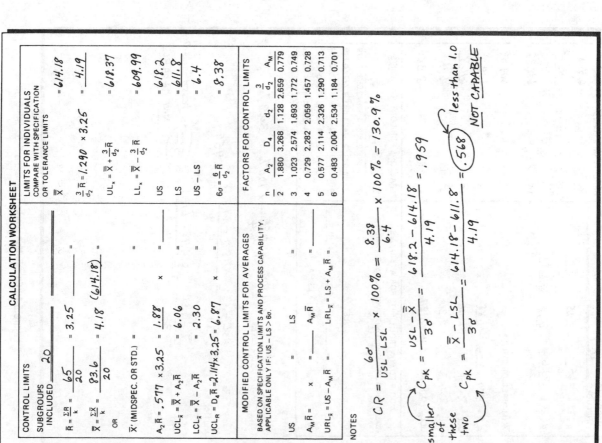

Figure 5-L. Calculation worksheet, Case 5-5.

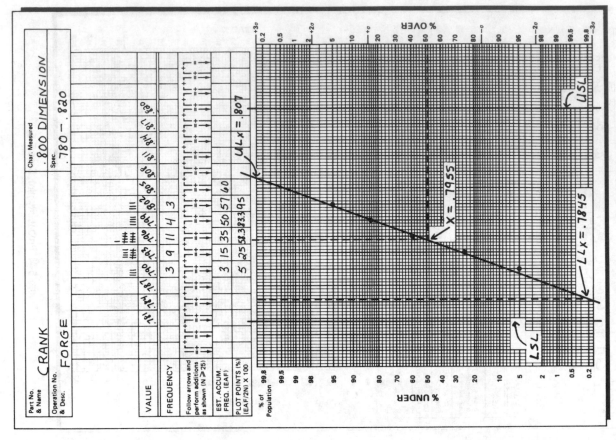

Figure 5-O. Probability plot based on first 10 subgroups, Case 5-6.

Figure 5-N. Calculation worksheet, Case 5-6.

The capability index (C_{pk}) for this process using only these 10 subgroups is shown in Figure 5-N. The CR is estimated to be 1.37. These estimates normally would be satisfactory if we had only the 10 subgroups from which to make our estimates, but the average and range chart developed in Case 3-7 and shown in Figure 3-Q gives additional information about the operation. Data taken over a longer period of time show that the process is subjected to additional variation. Figure

5-P is a probability plot developed from all the available measurements.

As before, the overall average ($\overline{\overline{X}}$) is estimated by locating the point where the line of best fit crosses the 50% line of the chart and by drawing a vertical line up through the "VALUES" row. This value is estimated to be .7985. The upper limit for individuals is estimated by starting at the point where the line of best fit crosses the top horizontal line

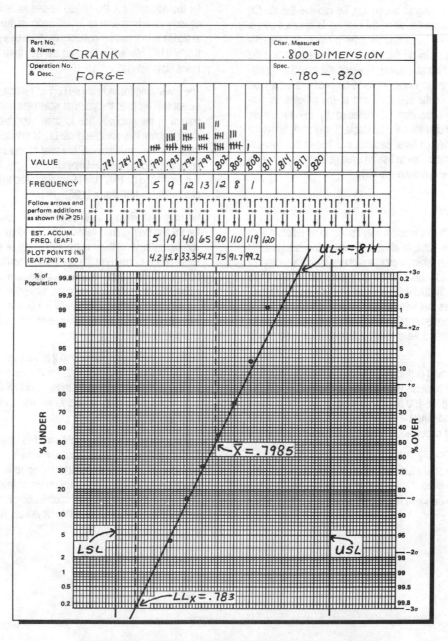

Figure 5-P. Probability plot based on all subgroups, Case 5-6.

of the graph and by drawing a line up through the "VALUES" row. This value is estimated to be .814. The lower limit for individuals is estimated by starting at the point where the line of best fit crosses the bottom horizontal line of the graph and by drawing a line up through the "VALUES" row. This value is estimated to be .783.

The total process spread (6σ) is the difference between the upper limit for individuals and the lower limit for individuals, which is shown to be .031. From this value the CR is calculated to be 77.5%.

The capability index is calculated from the estimated UL_x, the estimated LL_x, and the estimated $\bar{\bar{X}}$. The C_{pk} is estimated to be 1.19.

When we compare the estimates made using the first 10 subgroups with the estimates made using all subgroups, we can see that the CR is greater and the C_{pk} is smaller when the process is sampled over a longer period of time. The larger sample gives a more accurate estimate of the process capability. In this problem, the operation and the process would be classified as capable; however, the associate's decision that the operation no longer needed to be checked was not a good decision. The analysis of the operation and of the process as performed, based on the measurements collected by the supervisor, shows that although the operation will be stable, it may shift, from time to time, to a different average level. Because it is known that this can happen, it would be a good idea to use an average and range chart to monitor the output of the operation regularly.

CASE 5-7

The capability analysis in this problem may appear to be different from the analysis in most situations, in which the measurements to be used in the analysis have been taken in groups suitable for constructing an average and range chart. In this problem the measurements are single values obtained from individual batches of material produced by a mixing process. The batches that were measured were mixed over a long period of time. The measurements were not suitable for developing an average and range chart, but were used to develop an individual and range chart.

The analysis that you would perform with these data is rightly called a process capability study because 100 batches are involved. In addition, the time span for mixing the 100 batches is long enough that different lots of raw materials and different operators most likely were used in the operation. This kind of operation is not easily studied for machine capability.

The process capability study used to determine the capability ratio (CR) and the capability index (C_{pk}) is developed as follows. The individual and range chart developed in Case 3-9 is used to determine the

presence of any assignable causes in the process that would tend to distort the distribution of the tensile measurements. From the individual and range chart we learn that there was, in fact, a tensile value outside the lower control limit. This was Batch 39, plotted on Chart 2 at Sample Point 14. (See Figure 3-W.) Because we know that conditions in the process were not as they should have been when this batch was mixed, the tensile value for that batch will not be used in the analysis.

The 99 tensile measurements from batches mixed under stable conditions are used to develop a probability plot as shown in Figure 5-R. The line of best fit is placed on the plot points and the overall process spread is estimated. We do this by finding the value at the point where the line of best fit crosses the top of the graph. This is the upper limit for individuals (UL_x), the largest tensile value we would expect to see as long as the material is mixed under stable conditions. The value assigned to this point is obtained by drawing a straight line up through the "VALUE" row and estimating the UL_x from the position of the line in the class interval.

The lower limit for individual (LL_x) is estimated in a similar manner, except that we used the point at which the line of best fit crosses the bottom of the graph. A line is drawn up through the class interval directly above this point, and the LL_x is estimated from the position of the line in the class interval. The total process spread is the difference between the two values estimated in this way. In this problem the UL_x is estimated to be 1877; the LL_x is estimated to be 1841. The difference between these two values is 36.

We must estimate one more value from the chart in order to calculate the CR and the C_{pk}. This value is the overall process average. The most accurate estimate of the process average to be obtained from the probability plot is the value of the point where the line of best fit crosses the 50% line of the graph. The value for this point is estimated by drawing a straight line up through the class interval above it and then estimating the overall process average by the position of the line in the class interval. When this is done, the overall process average ($\bar{\bar{X}}$) is estimated to be 1859.

Using the values you obtained in this way, you should have calculated the CR as shown in Figure 5-Q. This value is 60.0%, which indicates a very capable process. You must calculate the C_{pk} before you can determine whether the process is set up to produce as the CR indicates.

The C_{pk} that you should have obtained has been calculated in Figure 5-Q. The smaller of the two calculated values is 1.06. This process can be classified as capable, but it is set up to operate so that the LL_x is very close to the lower specification limit. This condition can be seen graphically in Figure 5-R. The specification limits are indicated by the vertical lines at the specification limit values. The location of the line of

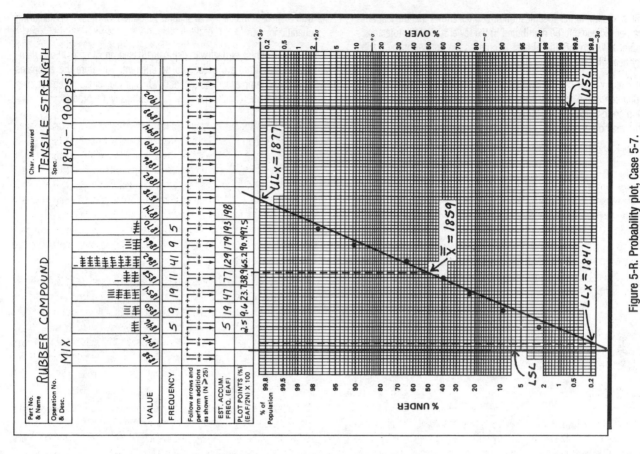

Figure 5-R. Probability plot, Case 5-7.

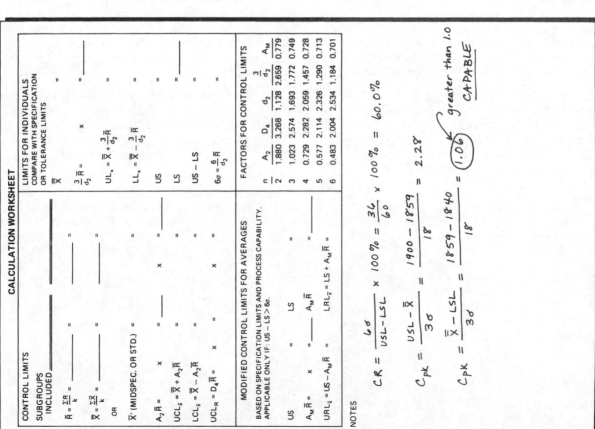

Figure 5-Q. Calculation worksheet, Case 5-7.

best fit in relation to the specification limit lines shows that the test values can be expected to be distributed in the lower half of the tolerance. The point at which the line of best fit crosses the bottom of the graph is very near the lower specification line.

All of these values can be obtained more precisely by mathematical manipulation of the tensile values; however, as long as care is taken in developing the probability plot and in drawing the line of best fit, this graphic method is easier to use and to understand. It is very adequate with respect to the degree of accuracy required for most manufacturing operations.

All SPC techniques deal with estimates based on samples. Each sample selected from a process will be different. Therefore the estimates from those samples will be different, whether the values in the samples are manipulated mathematically or graphically to produce the estimates.

BRAINSTORMING: REVIEW QUESTIONS

1. (a) A problem that happens over and over again.
   (b) A problem that only happens once in a while.
   (c) Chronic problems.
2. We make breakthroughs to new and better operating levels and in the way we improve quality and productivity.

BRAINSTORMING

1. (a) Helps identify problems.
   (b) Helps determine the causes of problems.
2. (a) A group problem-solving method.
   (b) (1) It encourages them to contribute to the group.
       (2) It helps develop trust.

WHAT IS NEEDED FOR BRAINSTORMING?

1. (a) People who are willing to work together.
   (b) Everyone concerned with the problem.
   (c) (1) Their ideas will be available to the whole group.
       (2) They help solve the problem.
   (d) They'll probably support the solution.
2. (a) Anybody.
   (b) (1) Guide the brainstorm to produce ideas.
       (2) Exercise enough control to keep it on track.
       (3) Encourage ideas and participation.
3. A place free from interruptions and distractions.
4. (a) Flipcharts.
   (b) Markers.
   (c) Masking tape.

HOW DOES A BRAINSTORM WORK?

1. Choose the topic to brainstorm.
2. What the brainstorm topic is.
3. (a) One idea per turn.
   (b) Say "pass."
   (c) Jot it down to use on your next turn.
4. (a) To write down the ideas.
   (b) Yes.
5. Yes.
6. They could trigger another idea.
7. (a) Criticism can block the free flow of ideas.
   (b) Quantity and creativity.

8. Laughter is OK, but don't overdo it. Laugh with, not at, people.
9. An incubation period allows the mind to come up with more ideas.
10. Review the rules, and then the leader starts.
11. About 12–15 minutes.
12. When the group is new to brainstorming.
13. As the group gains experience in brainstorming.

PRODDING TECHNIQUES

1. Group process is a fragile thing.
2. (a) Building on another's ideas.
   (b) When the brainstorm is slowing down.
   (c) (1) Suggesting opposites.
       (2) Quick associations.
3. (a) Work on a new area of possible causes.
   (b) Pursue one area in more depth.
4. (a) Be patient.
   (b) Remind the group to say "pass."
   (c) It gets the person off the hook, but it also breaks the sound barrier.
   (d) A direct question.
   (e) Know your group; know whether direct questions will help or hinder development.
5. (a) To capture additional ideas.
   (b) Do a second brainstorm with a time limit.
   (c) To gather all the ideas that have come to mind since the original brainstorm.
   (d) It allows people in the work area to contribute their ideas.
   (e) It helps them to feel like they are a part of the process.

COMPLETING THE BRAINSTORM

1. Make a list of all the general areas of possible causes and have the group look it over.
2. Production associate, machine, method, material, environment, money, etc.

DIFFICULTIES WITH BRAINSTORMING AND WHAT TO DO ABOUT THEM

1. (a) Training the group in brainstorming goals, and reminding the group that outsiders have different perspectives.

(b) They see things insiders do not.
2. At problems, not at people.
3. (a) Be firm but friendly.
   (b) Talk to the person privately and find out how they feel the group is doing. Give the person special jobs.
   (c) (1) Gently turn the conversation back to task.
       (2) Remind the group as a whole about criticizing. Review the rules.

BRAINSTORMING: EXERCISES, SERIES 1

(Keep in mind that the answers for these exercises are just suggestions; your answers may be different.)
2. (a) (1) Proportion of sugar and chocolate chips.
       (2) Too much baking powder.
   (b) (1) Draft in oven.
       (2) Poor circulation.
   (c) (1) Beams are too long.
       (2) Beams are not of right thickness.
   (d) (1) Capper not designed for the speed.
       (2) Capper out of sync with bottles at slow speed.
   (e) (1) Not cleaned often enough.
       (2) Wrong size mesh in strainer.
3. (a) Too large, too fine.
   (b) Not enough, too much.
   (c) Too fast, too slow.
   (d) Too tight, too loose.
   (e) Timely, late.
   (f) Too dark, too light.
   (g) Too loose, too tight.
   (h) Too shallow, too deep.
   (i) Overweight, underweight.
   (j) Too high, too low.
4. (a) Talk privately at first; find out why Sandy feels the problem is too technical. See if you can get him to teach some of the technical aspects. Point out that his behavior is making it hard for the others.
   (b) Look for what he does do in the group and thank him on the side. Encourage him privately. Perhaps, ask him a direct question.
   (c) Remind the group as a whole that it is to defer criticism until later. Say that all areas need to be looked at.
   (d) Have a breakout brainstorm for three minutes just on raw materials. Take some of the ideas that are in raw materials and ask for quick association, piggyback, and/or opposites.

BRAINSTORMING: EXERCISES, SERIES 2

2. (a) (1) Contaminants in fluid.
       (2) No maintenance.
   (b) (1) Sheets out of order.

(2) Routing incorrect.
   (c) (1) Poor storage of plates.
       (2) Labels on plates missing.
   (d) (1) Poor handling.
       (2) Design of scrubbers.
   (e) (1) Brownout.
       (2) Electrical short.
3. (a) Too large, too small.
   (b) Slow, fast.
   (c) Too high, too low.
   (d) Deep, shallow.
   (e) Too many, too few at peak hours.
   (f) Overweight of A, underweight of A.
   (g) Too short, too long.
   (h) Overcoated, undercoated.
   (i) Too high, too low.
   (j) Too many, too few.
4. (a) Remind the group as a whole to give one idea at a time and to jot down ideas between turns.
   (b) Choose one major area to concentrate on. Use producing techniques like piggybacking and opposites.
   (c) Remind the group to laugh with people, not at them. *All* ideas are important and could trigger the solution.

CAUSE AND EFFECT DIAGRAMS: REVIEW QUESTIONS

1. (a) So it can be used effectively.
   (b) In picture form, as a kind of graph.
2. (a) Production associate.
   (b) Machine.
   (c) Method.
   (d) Material.
   (e) Environment.

WHY USE THE CAUSE AND EFFECT DIAGRAM?

1. To organize the ideas from a brainstorm and to help sort them into basic categories.
2. It shows what area you forgot or didn't work on as much.
3. Helps keep track of where they are in the problem-solving process.

HOW TO CONSTRUCT A CAUSE AND EFFECT DIAGRAM

Step 1. (a) Flipchart.
        (b) Markers.
        (c) Masking tape.
        (d) Brainstorm idea list.

Step 2. (a) The leader and the brainstorm group.
   (b) Anyone who has something to do with solving the
      problem.
   (c) Draws the diagram.
Step 3. (a) On the right-hand side.
   (b) So everyone understands what is being discussed.
   (c) Draw a box around the problem statement.
Step 4. The spine of the fishbone.
Step 5. (a) (1) Production associate.
      (2) Machine
      (3) Method.
      (4) Material.
   (b) (1) Environment.
      (2) Money.
      (3) Management.
      (4) Gaging.
      (5) Causes outside the process.
      (6) Error in measuring/inspection.
      (7) Sampling errors.
      (8) Arithmetic errors.
Step 6. Group them logically under the appropriate headings.

THE PROCESS OF CONSTRUCTING
THE CAUSE AND EFFECT DIAGRAM

1. (a) (1) From the original brainstorm list.
      (2) Build as you go.
   (b) When you build as you go.
   (c) (1) Leader.
      (2) Recorder.
   (d) (1) Make contributions in turn.
      (2) Pass if you don't have an idea.
      (3) Hold criticism.
2. (a) Because there are lots of decisions to make about what
      goes where, and the group needs to stay focused on the
      problem, not on assigning blame.
   (b) On how to solve the problem.
3. (a) (1) Work through each cause in turn.
      (2) Freewheel brainstorm all main bones at once.
   (b) Work on it for a few minutes.
   (c) Put the idea under as many headings as it will fit.

TYPES OF CAUSE AND EFFECT DIAGRAMS

1. Fishbone diagram.
2. (a) The process C and E diagram.
   (b) It follows the product through each step in manufactur-
      ing or assembly.
   (c) Looks at each stage and determines which factors are
      involved.
   (d) Brainstorm each stage in turn.
3. (a) Find the causes of production problems.
   (b) (1) Finding possible causes.
      (2) Developing trial solutions.

CAUSE AND EFFECT DIAGRAMS:
EXERCISES, SERIES 1

(Keep in mind that the answers for these exercises are just
suggestions; your answers may be different. Representative
charts have been provided.)
1. *See the answer charts.*
   (a) (1) Machine.
      (2) Materials.
      (3) Method.
      (4) Production associate.
   (b) (1) Environment.
      (2) Money.
      (3) Management.
      (4) Gaging.
      (5) Bias/error in measuring/inspection.
      (6) Sampling errors.
      (7) Arithmetic errors.
      (8) Causes outside the process, such as government
         regulations.
   (c) Diagram 1: machine, method, associate, material.
      Diagram 2: machine, method, associate, material.
   (d) Diagram 1: Yes.
      Diagram 2: Yes.
   (e) Diagram 1: Environment.
      Diagram 2: Environment.
2. *See the answer chart.*
   (a) (1) Proportion of sugar and chocolate chips: materials,
         method.
      (2) Too much baking powder: associate, method, mate-
         rials.
   (b) (1) Draft in oven: machine.
      (2) Poor circulation: machine, environment.
   (c) (1) Beams too long: material, gaging.
      (2) Beams are not of right thickness: material.
   (d) (1) Capper not designed for speed: Machine, Method.
      (2) Capper out of sync with bottles at slow speed:
         machine, method.
   (e) (1) Not cleaned often enough: method, associate.
      (2) Wrong size mesh in strainer: machine, associate,
         method.
3. *See the answer chart.*

CAUSE AND EFFECT DIAGRAMS:
EXERCISES, SERIES 2

1. *See the answer charts.*
   (a) (1) Machine.
      (2) Materials.
      (3) Method.
      (4) Associate.
   (b) (1) Environment.
      (2) Management.
      (3) Sampling errors.
      (4) Bias/error in measuring/inspection.
      (5) Money.

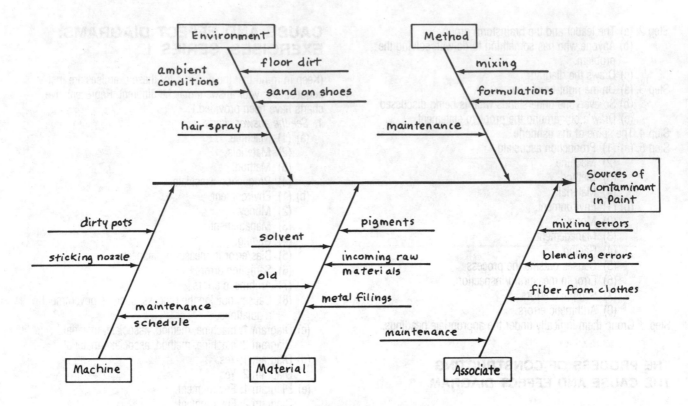

Module 6, Series 1, Question 1, Diagram 2. Cause and effect diagram.

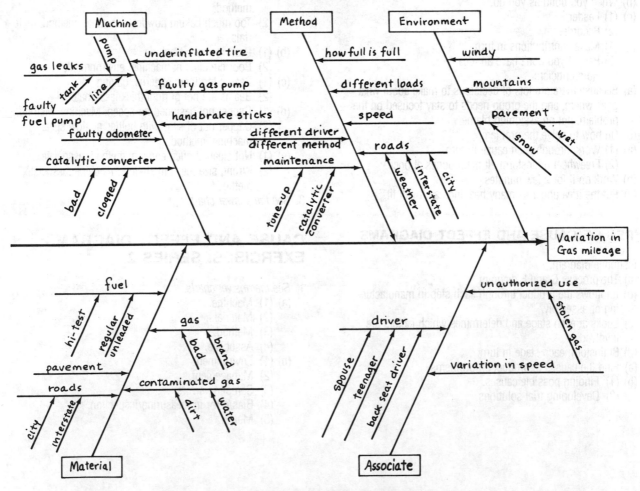

Module 6, Series 1, Question 1, Diagram 2. Cause and effect diagram.

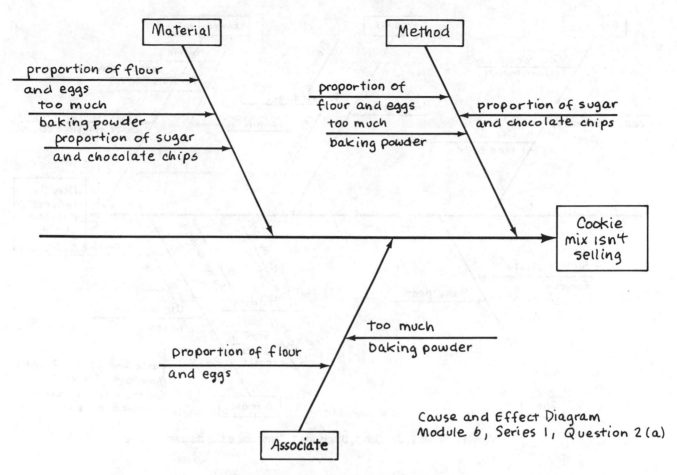

Cause and Effect Diagram
Module 6, Series 1, Question 2 (a)

Module 6, Series 1, Question 2 (a). Cause and effect diagram.

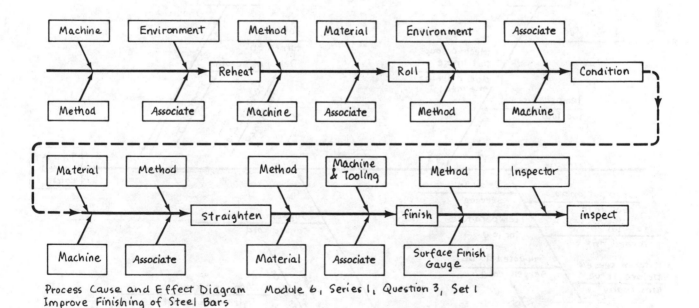

Process Cause and Effect Diagram   Module 6, Series 1, Question 3, Set 1
Improve Finishing of Steel Bars

Module 6, Series 1, Question 3, Set 1. Cause and effect diagram. Improve finishing of steel bars.

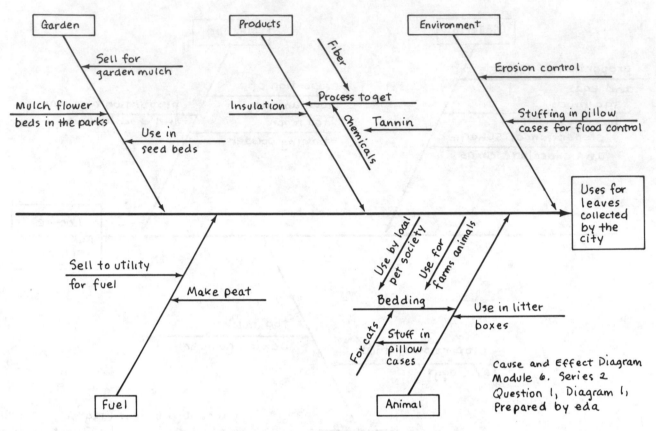

Module 6, Series 2, Question 1, Diagrs am 1. Cause and effect diagram.

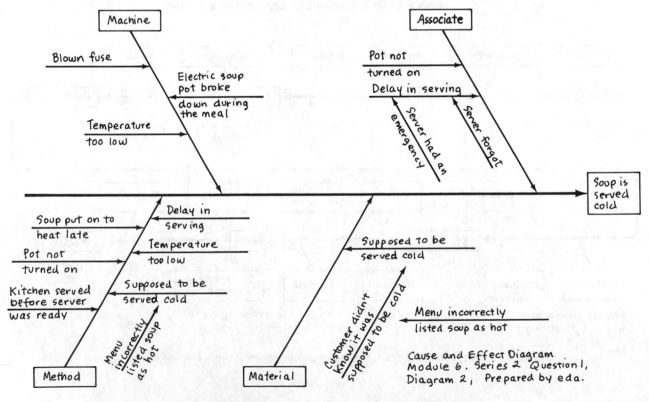

Module 6, Series 2, Question 1, Diagram 2. Cause and effect diagram.

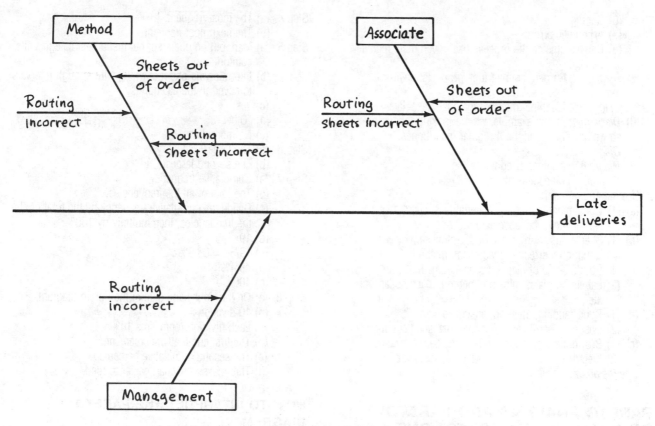

Module 6, Series 2, Question 2(b). Partial cause and effect diagram.

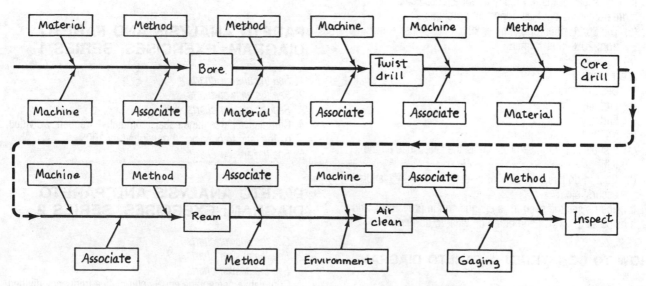

Module 6, Series 2, Question 3, Set 1. Cause and effect diagram.

    (6) Gaging.

    (7) Arithmetic errors.

    (8) Causes outside the process like government regulations.

  (c) *Diagram 1:* Garden, animal, fuel, products, environment.

    Diagram 2: Machine, method, material, associate.

  (d) *Diagram 1:* In this example, we are looking for "uses" so we have not used the 4 regular main bones.

    Diagram 2: Yes.

  (e) *Diagram 1:* Another category of use.

    Diagram 2: Management.

2. See the answer chart.

  (a) (1) Contaminants in fluid: material, associate

     (2) No maintenance: associate, method.

  (b) (1) Sheets out of order: method, associate.

     (2) Routing incorrect: management, method.

  (c) (1) Poor storage of plates: associate, method.

     (2) Labels on plates missing: method, machine, associate.

  (d) (1) Poor handling: method, associate.

     (2) Design of scrubbers: machine, management, money.

  (e) (1) Brownout: method, material, outside the process.

     (2) Electrical short: material, method, associate.

3. *See the answer chart.*

PARETO ANALYSIS AND PARETO DIAGRAM: REVIEW QUESTIONS

1. (a) It helps to decide which of several chronic problems to attack.

  (b) To see whether the solution has worked.

2. It helps separate the few really important problems from the more numerous but less important problems.

3. (a) The 80/20 rule: for example, 80% of business comes from 20% of customers.

  (b) Yes.

4. A bar graph.

5. (a) Dead motors.

  (b) Endplay.

  (c) Endplay.

  (d) It's the biggest problem.

6. (a) It shows the biggest problem as the tallest bar, on the left.

  (b) Cost in dollars, numbers of defects, how often a failure occurs, etc.

7. It helps us see the need for a change and improvement, and it helps set priorities and agree on what to do first.

HOW TO CONSTRUCT A PARETO DIAGRAM

Step 2. (a) Get the data yourself.

    (b) Audit inspection reports.

Step 4. (a) The most frequent.

    (b) The next most frequent.

Step 5. (a) Mark out numbers so that the largest category fits comfortably.

    (b) Into intervals of equal width, with enough intervals to cover all the categories.

    (c) Yes.

    (d) "Other."

    (e) No more than 10%.

Step 6. (a) The largest category.

    (b) The second largest.

Step 7. (a) Cumulative frequency.

    (b) The total of all the frequencies.

    (c) Divide the cumulative frequency by the total of all the frequencies, then multiply by 100%.

    (d) 19

    (e) 19/56 = 33.9%

    (f) 46.4%

    (g) 100%

Step 8. (a) On the right-hand side of the Pareto diagram.

    (b) 10 divisions.

    (c) Each division represents 10%.

    (d) The first cumulative percentage.

    (e) The second cumulative percentage.

    (f) This makes the chart easier to read.

HOW TO INTERPRET THE PARETO DIAGRAM

1. It can be duplicated, put on an overhead, or stored.

2. Politics and personal feelings.

3. You can see if the problem really has been reduced or eliminated.

PARETO ANALYSIS AND PARETO DIAGRAM: EXERCISES, SERIES 1

1. *See the answer charts.*

2. *See the answer charts.*

3. *See the answer charts.*

4. Cumulative percentage equals cumulative frequency divided by the total frequency, all multiplied by 100%.

5. *See the answer charts.*

PARETO ANALYSIS AND PARETO DIAGRAM: EXERCISES, SERIES 2

1. *See the answer charts.*

2. *See the answer charts.*

3. *See the answer charts.*

4. Cumulative percentage equals cumulative frequency divided by the total frequency, all multiplied by 100%.

5. *See the answer charts.*

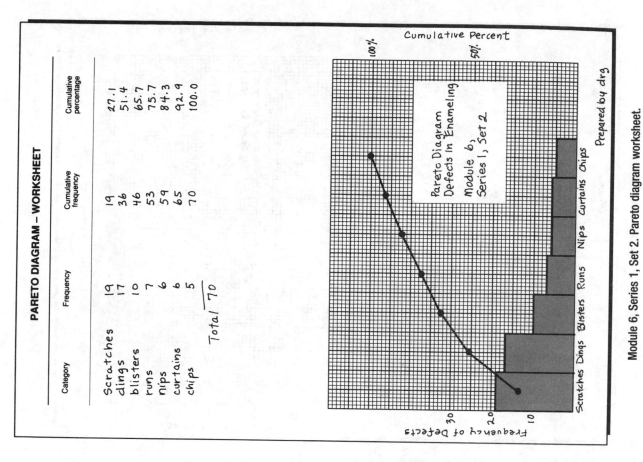

PARETO DIAGRAM – WORKSHEET

Category	Frequency	Cumulative frequency	Cumulative percentage
Scratches	19	19	27.1
dings	17	36	51.4
blisters	10	46	65.7
runs	7	53	75.7
nips	6	59	84.3
curtains	6	65	92.9
chips	5	70	100.0
	Total 70		

Module 6, Series 1, Set 2. Pareto diagram worksheet.

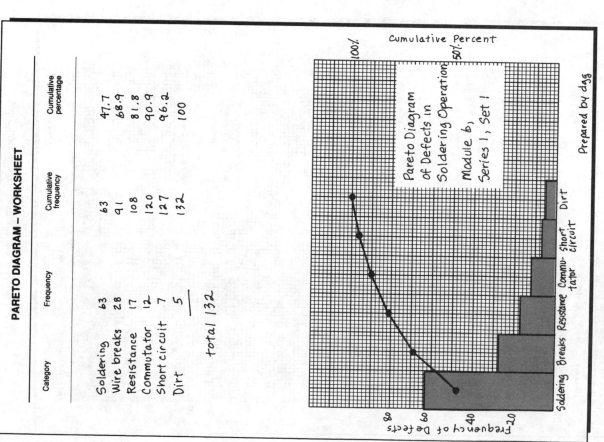

PARETO DIAGRAM – WORKSHEET

Category	Frequency	Cumulative frequency	Cumulative percentage
Soldering	63	63	47.7
Wire breaks	28	91	68.9
Resistance	17	108	81.8
Commutator	12	120	90.9
Short circuit	7	127	96.2
Dirt	5	132	100
	total 132		

Module 6, Series 1, Set 1. Pareto diagram worksheet.

PARETO DIAGRAM – WORKSHEET

Category	Frequency	Cumulative frequency	Cumulative percentage
zerks	19	19	26.0
verts	14	33	45.2
thrims	12	45	61.6
whiffles	10	55	75.3
warbles	7	62	84.9
tweets	6	68	93.2
other	5	73	100.0
Total	73		

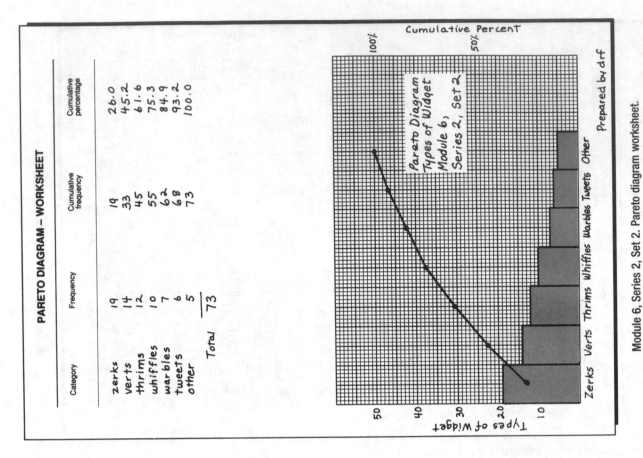

Module 6, Series 2, Set 2. Pareto diagram worksheet.

PARETO DIAGRAM – WORKSHEET

Category	Frequency	Cumulative frequency	Cumulative percentage
tow piece take-up	54 kg	54	36.0
intermediate cut	27 kg	81	54.0
wind on roller	23 kg	104	69.3
incorrect cut	19 kg	123	82.0
break	14 kg	137	91.3
first cut	13 kg	150	100.0
total	150 kg		

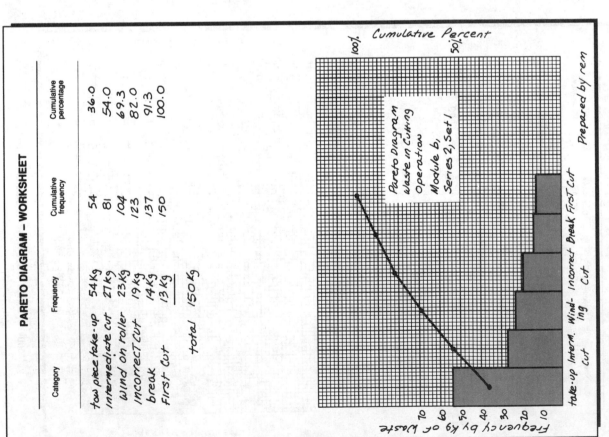

Module 6, Series 2, Set 1. Pareto diagram worksheet.

FLOW CHARTS: REVIEW QUESTIONS

1. A process flow chart is a special type of diagram that pictures in sequence the steps of a particular job.
2. The flow chart helps track the flow of subassemblies, parts, raw materials, and information through the system of manufacturing a product. This chart helps you find places in the process you can simplify, where trouble happens, or where control is needed.
3. The flow chart symbols are:
   (a) Operation (Circle)—This is work required to complete a task.
   (b) Move (Arrow)—Some thing, such as raw material, subassemblies, or the finished product, travels from one point to another.
   (c) Inspection (Square)—Someone tests or verifies that the raw material, subassemblies, or finished product is correct and meets requirements.
   (d) Delay (the Letter "D")—This is a wait. A delay can occur before or after an operation, inspection or move.
   (e) Decision (Diamond)—A point in the process at which alternative actions may be taken.
   (f) Storage (Triangle)—This is a point in the process at which something is stored.
   (g) Connector (Small circle)—Use this symbol whenever you need to continue the flow chart on another line.

CONSTRUCTING A PROCESS FLOW CHART

Step 1. Define the process.

(a) Determine what is the first thing to be done, and ask what the last step is.

Step 2. Identify the steps in the process.

(a) The easiest way to identify process steps is mentally to walk through the process as it usually happens.
(b) You could go to where the process actually happens; you can brainstorm process steps; or you can videotape them.
(c) A process step begins when a new activity is required.
(d) Trying to describe all aspects of a step in minute detail—this is usually not necessary.

Step 3. Draw the flow chart.

(a) Tell who is involved in the step, where the step is done, and what happens.
(b) Use the connector symbol whenever you need to continue the flow chart on another line.
(c) (1) When several operations need to occur at the same time.
    (2) When there is a conditional, or "if," situation.
    (3) When there is an inspection.

Step 4. Determine the time or distance for each step.

(a) Knowing the time for a step helps to find where to reduce or eliminate wasted time.
(b) To determine how long a step takes, measure the time between the beginning and ending of the step. Or track a part, for example, through the process.
(c) Delays and storage usually represent wasted time and are good places to target for improvements.
(d) Moves are also potential places where the process can be improved.

Step 5. Assign a cost for each step.

(a) Cost information may provide incentive to eliminate repetitive or unnecessary steps.

HOW TO USE THE PROCESS FLOW CHART

1. (a) The flow chart may reveal trouble spots that could be controlled using statistical methods, such as control charts, to monitor the process for unwanted change.
   (b) Two possible tools to help control a process are statistical control charts and process cause and effect diagrams.
2. (a) The flow chart helps find repeated steps and points out moves, delays, and/or storage that can be either shortened or removed.
   (b) Some tools to use to improve a process are cause and effect diagrams or brainstorming.
3. (a) Look for bottle necks, those points in the process that slow or restrict the flow of work or materials.
   (b) Think about the sequence of operations and try to make it more effective.
   (c) Can you improve workplace layout or the flow of components?
   (d) Think about how to reduce or eliminate having to correct, change, add, or rework things.
   (e) Ask yourself: Is there a better way?

FLOW CHARTS: EXERCISES, SERIES 1

SET 1. This flow chart shows what happens when branching is caused by "if" situations. In the start-up of the envelope machine, a branch occurs at step 3, when the operator inspects an envelope for proper fold and print line-up (registration). The results of this check could lead to three branches. *See answer flow chart.*

SET 2. In the flow chart we drew, we show arc weld as a parallel operation. Steering wheel rims wait at both arc welders for the hub/cup and spoke units. Then a cell associate loads the welders and runs the operation.

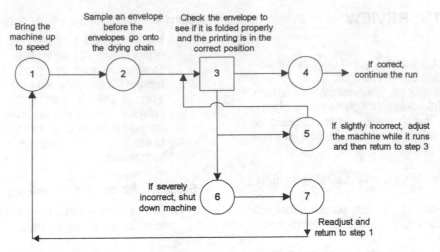

Module 6, Series 1, Set 1. Flow chart of the envelope machine-web process start-up.

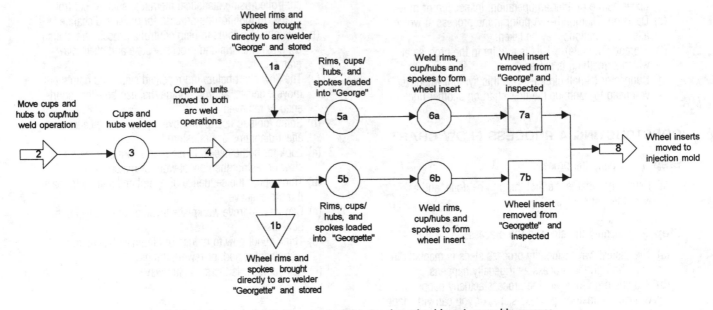

Module 6, Series 1, Set 2. Flow chart of the steering wheel insert assembly process.

When laying out the cell, the development team realized the arc weld operation was a potential bottleneck and so installed two welders. *See answer flow chart.* How does the flow chart you drew compare to this one?

FLOW CHARTS: EXERCISES, SERIES 2

SET 1. Preparing and assembling two metal parts. *See answer flow chart.*

1. There are two places in this process where branching occurs, namely at step 4 and at step 19. Both are inspection steps. Step 4 could be eliminated by a closer relationship with the supplier.
2. The supplier should use some type of control chart to monitor and control critical characteristics on the part in order to assure quality.
3. There are many steps in this process that waste time. Of the 25 process steps, 8 are moves. A possible solution is a different lay out, which would reduce distances parts travel. One large waste of both time and space are all the instances of storage.

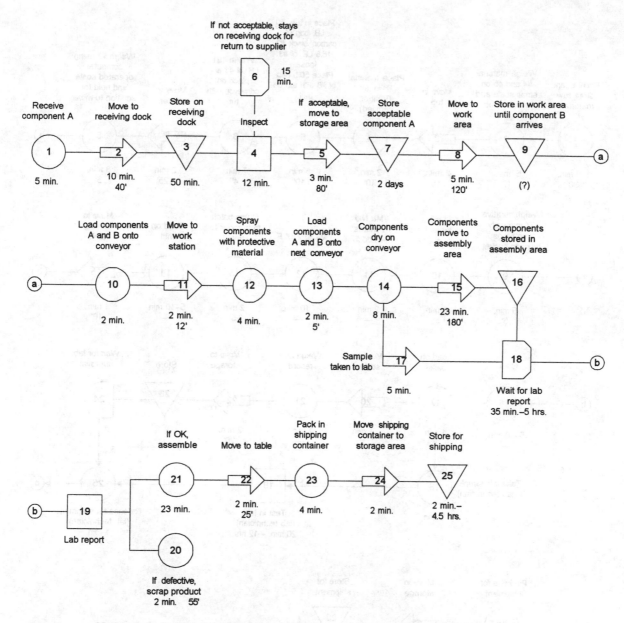

Module 6, Series 2, Set 1. Flow chart of the preparation and assembly of two metal parts.

4. The wait for the lab reports may be a bottleneck.

SET 2. Rubber mixing process. *See answer flow chart.*
1. Branching occurs after step 17 when the lab sample is taken.
2. Weighing operations and lab tests are possible places to use statistical process control.
3. The largest waste in time is the wait for the lab testing. Step 21, "weigh and record," may be unnecessary if the associates already know what has gone into the batch.

4. The big bottleneck here is the lab. An improvement team should definitely target this step for improvement.

SCATTER DIAGRAMS: REVIEW QUESTIONS

1. A scatter diagram is a type of graph that indicates how two variables may be related.
2. Use the scatter diagram whenever you want to see how two variables relate to each other. If there is a relationship, then

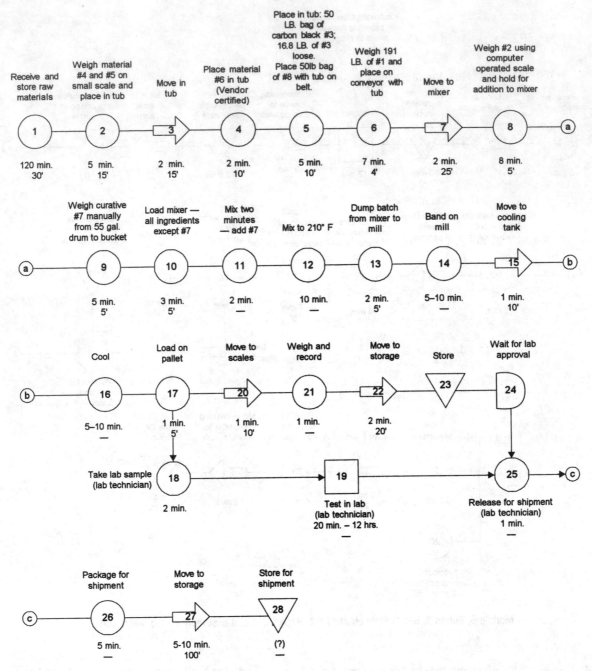

Module 6, Series 2, Set 2. Flow chart of rubber mixing process.

by controlling one variable you may be able to control the other.

HOW TO CONSTRUCT A SCATTER DIAGRAM

3. Each plotted point represents two variables.
4. (a) Variable data.
   (b) A few examples of variable data include temperature, length, weight, and time.

Step 1. Is the problem suitable for a scatter diagram?

(a) Does each point come from variable data; is it measurable?
(b) Are there two things, two variables, that you can measure, such as speed of a tool and length of a part?
(c) You are looking for a relationship between two variables.

Step 2. Collect your data.

Record anything interesting or peculiar. It may be of use later.

Step 3. Determine the scales for the graph and plot the data.

(a) When one variable results from or depends upon another variable.

(b) We usually plot the dependent variable on the vertical axis.

(c) Set the scale for the vertical axis so that the largest and smallest values will fit inside, not on, the edges of the chart. Use a scale that's easy to work with.

(d) Plot the other variable on the horizontal axis.

Step 4. Do the corner count test.

(a) (1) Whether it is obvious that there is a straight-line relationship between the two variables.

(2) Whether it is clear that such a relationship does not exist.

(3) When you must conduct the corner count test to determine the relationship, because it is not clear whether or not a straight-line relationship exists between the variables.

(b) A straight-line relationship is one where an increase in one variable always results in an increase or decrease in the other variable. When the points are plotted, they form a straight line.

(c) If such a relationship does exist, there may possibly be a cause and effect relationship between the variables.

(d) You may then be able to control one of the variables by controlling the other.

(e) The six steps for the corner count test are:
(1) Check whether you have enough data.
(2) Find the medians.
(3) Label each corner of the chart.
(4) Do the corner counts.
(5) Total the corner counts.
(6) Compare the total of the counts.

(f) The median is the point at which half the measurements are on one side of the median and half are on the other side. The medians are represented by a horizontal or vertical line, where half the points are above or below, or to the right or left.

(g) Because the dependent variable usually is drawn on the vertical axis, position the ruler at the bottom of the graph so that all the points are above the ruler. Move the ruler slowly toward the top of the diagram and count the points as they disappear underneath it; stop when you have reached half the count. Draw a horizontal line across the diagram.

(h) Draw the median for the independent variable on the scatter diagram in much the same manner, except start at the right side of the scatter diagram. When you start counting, all the plotted points will lie to the left of the ruler. Draw this median as a vertical line, where half of the points fall on the left side of the ruler and half are on the right side.

(i) (1) If the number of points is odd, divide the count in half and round off by adding 0.5. Then draw the median through that point so that there is an equal number of plotted points on either side of, or above and below, the median line.

(2) If the number of points is even, simply divide the count in half so that half the number of plotted points lie above and the other half are below the median line, or are on either side of it. Draw in the median.

(3) It's OK if more than one point is on a median.

(j) Label the upper right corner "+", or plus; the upper left corner "−", or minus; the lower left corner "+"; and the lower right corner "−".

(k) (1) Begin the count of plotted points from the right side of the chart. Slowly move toward the left side of the chart. Stop at the first point you come to and note the sign of the quarter. Continue moving in toward the left side and counting points until you meet a point that is in a different quarter or is on a median line. Stop and write down the total number of points counted so far (except the stopping point). Repeat starting from the top, left, and bottom of the chart.

(2) The sign of the quarter of the diagram where you find the first point will tell you.

(3) Stop counting when you meet a point that is in a different quarter or on a median.

(l) Add all the counts. If there are "+" and "−" values, simply subtract the minuses from the pluses.

(m) The important thing about the count is how big it is, not whether it is "+" or "−."

(n) (1) If the result is equal to or greater than 11, there probably is a straight-line relationship between the variables.

(2) If the result is less than 11, there may not be a straight-line relationship. The data do not tell.

SCATTER DIAGRAMS: EXERCISES, SERIES 1

1. The scatter diagram is based on variable data.
2. *See the answer diagrams.* The dependent variable is usually plotted on the vertical axis.
3. *See the answer diagrams.*
4. A straight-line relationship.
5. *See the answer diagrams.*

(a) The median on the scatter diagram is where half the points will be on one side of the median line and half will be on the other. In the case of the horizontal median, half the points are above it and half are below. For the vertical median, half the points will fall to the left of the line and half to the right.

(b) Set 1. odd   Set 3. even
Set 2 even   Set 4. odd

(c) If the number of points is odd, divide the count in half and round off by adding 0.5. Then draw the median through that point so that there is an equal number of plotted points on either side of, or above and below, the median line.

6. *See the answer diagrams.* Label the upper right corner "+", upper left corner "−", the lower left corner "+", and the lower right corner "−."

7. (a) *See the answer tables.*
(b) *See the answer tables.*

8. (a) Count total   Results greater/less than comparison
                       number 11
Set 1.   3   less than 11
Set 2. 23   greater than 11

Set 3. 18   greater than 11
Set 4. 22   greater than 11

(b) A straight-line relationship.

(c) Set 1. Since the count total is less than the comparison number 11, there is no evidence for a straight-line relationship between these two variables.

Set 2. The count total is greater than 11, the comparison number. There is evidence that a straight-line relationship exists between these two variables.

Set 3. The count total is greater than 11, the comparison number, so there is evidence for a straight-line relationship between these two variables.

Set 4. The count total is greater than 11, the comparison number, so there is evidence for a straight-line relationship between these two variables.

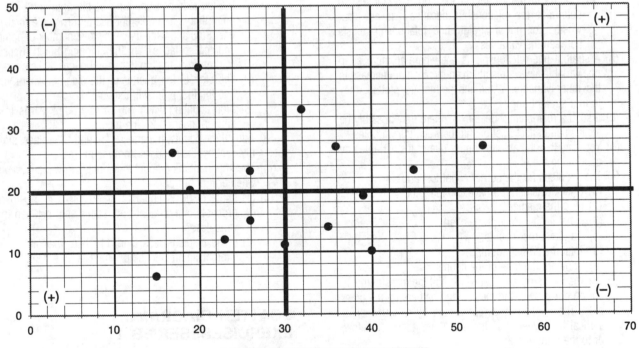

Corner Count Table Series 1, Set 1	
Move Ruler	Count
from right	+2
from top	−1
from left	+1
from bottom	+1
Total	+3
Without sign	3

Module 6, Series 1, Set 1. Scatter diagram.

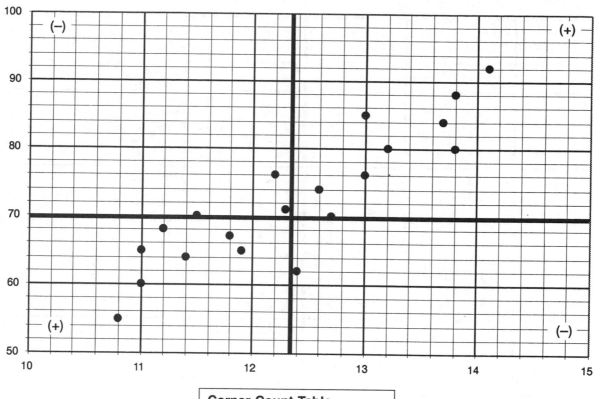

Corner Count Table Series 1, Set 2	
Move Ruler	Count
from right	+7
from top	+6
from left	+8
from bottom	+2
Total	+23
Without sign	23

Module 6, Series 1, Set 2. Scatter diagram.

SCATTER DIAGRAMS: EXERCISES, SERIES 2

1. The scatter diagram is based on variable data.
2. *See the answer diagrams.* The dependent variable is usually plotted on the vertical axis.
3. *See the answer diagrams.*
4. A straight-line relationship.
5. *See the answer diagrams.*
   (a) The median on the scatter diagram is where half the points will be on one side of the median line and half will be on the other. In the case of the horizontal median, half the points are above it and half are below.

   For the vertical median, half the points will fall to the left of the line and half to the right.
   (b) Set 1. odd
       Set 2 even
       Set 3. even
       Set 4. odd
   (c) If the number of points is odd, divide the count in half and round off by adding 0.5. Then draw the median through that point so that there is an equal number of plotted points on either side of, or above and below, the median line.

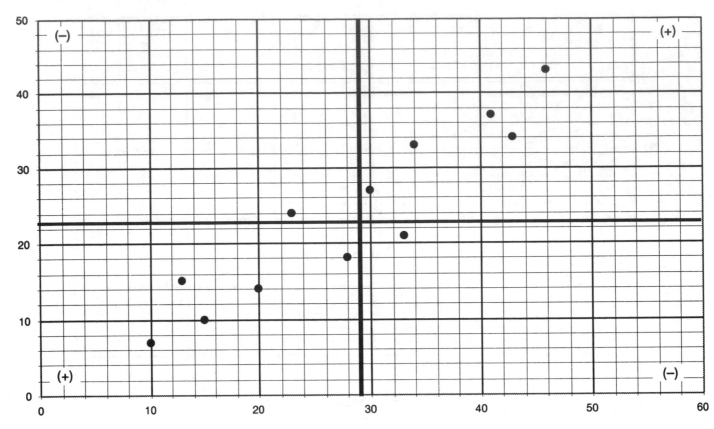

Corner Count Table
Series 1, Set 3

Move Ruler	Count
from right	+4
from top	+5
from left	+4
from bottom	+5
Total	+18
Without sign	18

Module 6, Series 1, Set 3. Scatter diagram.

6. *See the answer diagrams.* Label the upper right corner "+", upper left corner "−", the lower left corner "+", and the lower right corner "−:"

7. (a) *See the answer tables.*
    (b) *See the answer tables.*

8. (a)

	Count total	Results greater/less than comparison number 11
Set 1.	4	less than 11
Set 2.	12	greater than 11
Set 3.	12	greater than 11
Set 4.	15	greater than 11

   (b) A straight-line relationship.
   (c) Set 1. According to the results of the corner count, there is no indication of a straight-line relationship between these two variables. But be careful! The plotted points do form a pattern that looks as though some kind of relationship could be present. You should find someone in your organization with additional understanding of statistics to help you determine accurately just what is going on in this type of situation.

   Set 2. The count total is greater than 11, the comparison number. There is evidence that a straight-line relationship exists between these two variables.

   Set 3. The count total is greater than 11, the comparison number, so there is evidence for a straight-line relationship between these two variables.

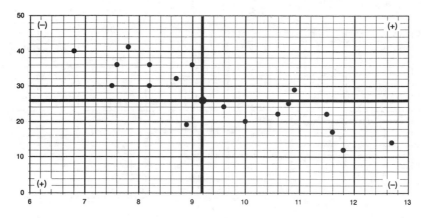

Corner Count Table
Series 1, Set 4

Move Ruler	Count
from right	−4
from top	−8
from left	−7
from bottom	−3
Total	−22
Without sign	22

Module 6, Series 1, Set 4. Scatter diagram.

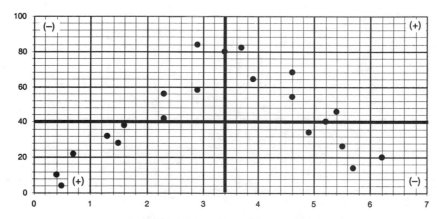

Corner Count Table
Series 2, Set 1

Move Ruler	Count
from right	−3
from top	−1
from left	+6
from bottom	+2
Total	+4
Without sign	4

Module 6, Series 2, Set 1. Scatter diagram.

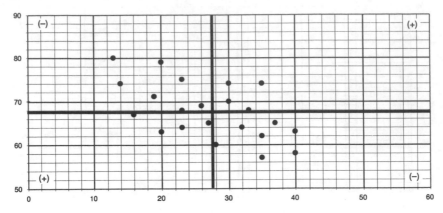

Corner Count Table
Series 2, Set 2

Move Ruler	Count
from right	−3
from top	−3
from left	−2
from bottom	−4
Total	−12
Without sign	12

Module 6, Series 2, Set 2. Scatter diagram.

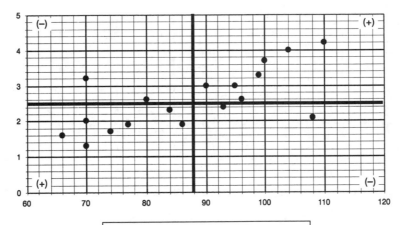

Corner Count Table
Series 2, Set 3

Move Ruler	Count
from right	+1
from top	+4
from left	+1
from bottom	+6
Total	+12
Without sign	12

Module 6, Series 2, Set 3. Scatter diagram.

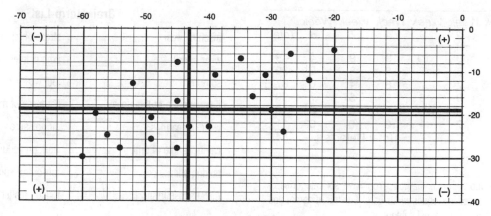

Corner Count Table Series 2, Set 4	
Move Ruler	**Count**
from right	+3
from top	+3
from left	+4
from bottom	+5
Total	+15
Without sign	15

Module 6, Series 2, Set 4. Scatter diagram.

Set 4. The count total is greater than 11, the comparison number, so there is evidence for a straight-line relationship between these two variables.

QUALITY PROBLEM-SOLVING TOOLS: ANALYSIS AND DISCUSSION OF CASE STUDIES

The problem analysis for the four case studies is based on the problem-solving process that real teams followed. The teams started with Pareto analysis to identify the best opportunity for improvements. Because Pareto analysis is a databased part of problem solving, the Pareto diagrams you construct ought to resemble closely the diagrams from the case studies.

It is quite likely that your brainstorm lists and your cause and effect diagrams will be different from those we have provided. Remember that brainstorming as well as cause and effect diagrams depend on the team members' individual experiences and perspectives. Different teams handle the same topic in different ways. How do your lists and diagrams compare with those in each case study? Do your cause and effect diagrams cover the four main bones? Are there other bones that might be appropriate? Did you follow the rules for brainstorming?

CASE 6-1

Problems with the crankshafts may well be the most obvious cause of rejected Z-7 engines, but this is only a guess until someone has data to prove that this is the case. The first place to look for data would be in the inspection reports that quality control keeps. You may be able to collect the inspection slips or cards.

After you have collected printouts on rejects for six weeks, you must first organize the data. Arrange the data in table form by types of rejected parts. Six different kinds of defects show up in the printouts: camshaft, #1 crankshaft, #2 crankshaft, manifold, block, and cylinder head. Count the number of defects for each part. Your data sheet might look like this:

Part	Week 1	Week 2	Week 3	Week 4	Week 5	Week 6	Total
Camshaft	5	7	7	8	4	6	37
#1 crank	6	0	6	5	5	7	29
#2 crank	0	6	5	0	0	8	19
Manifold	0	7	1	3	0	0	11
Block	8	9	10	9	9	4	49
Head	7	6	7	8	8	3	39

Now rank the categories of engine defects by frequency. Your data sheet will look like this:

Part	Week 1	Week 2	Week 3	Week 4	Week 5	Week 6	Total
Block	8	9	10	9	9	4	49
Head	7	6	7	8	8	3	39
Camshaft	5	7	7	8	4	6	37
#1 crank	6	0	6	5	5	7	29
#2 crank	0	6	5	0	0	8	19
Manifold	0	7	1	3	0	0	11
						Total Defects	184

Organize the data into a Pareto diagram. You have six categories of defects, so you will need six equal-width bars. For this diagram you don't need to combine the smallest categories.

The Pareto diagram with the bars drawn in should look like the diagram in Figure 6-A.

Determine the cumulative frequencies and percentages. The table below shows this.

Cumulative Frequencies and Percentages

Camshaft	Frequency	Cumulative Frequency	%
Block	49	49	27
Head	39	88	48
Camshaft	37	125	68
#1 crank	29	154	84
#2 crank	19	173	94
Manifold	11	184	100

Figure 6-B shows the completed Pareto diagram with the cumulative percentages drawn in.

Remember that several people have claimed that crankshafts are the largest source of trouble in the Z-7 engines. Has the Pareto diagram shown that this is actually the case? Your diagram will show that the single largest number of rejects in the Z-7 engines is coming from problems in the engine blocks. Crankshafts seem to cause the most problems only when you combine the rejects from Crankshafts 1 and 2; the combined number of rejects accounts for a total of 48 bad parts. You can see from the Pareto analysis that blocks (49 rejects) really are the greatest single problem. They provide the best opportunity for quality improvement.

There are several things you can do for the next step. Because you have shown that the block is the greatest source of difficulty, your team should conduct another Pareto analysis to see what kinds of defects there are in the block.

After a second Pareto analysis the team finds that the greatest source of rejects in the Z-7 block is defects in the bore holes. The team can brainstorm to determine the cause of these defects. The following is a list of possible brainstorm ideas.

Brainstorm List

machine wear	stress on spindle
wear of drill	bore diameter of first drill
spindle	tool wear
fluctuation in drill diameter	hardness of metal
wear of bearings	oil pressure
camber angle of drill	work procedure
cutting allowance	run-out of spindle
metal stress in block	foreign matter
drill setting	

When the team has finished the brainstorm session, the participants can use a cause and effect diagram to organize the brainstorm list. This diagram will help them to see relationships between the causes. It will also reveal causes that they have not discussed; in this case they overlooked "operator." The cause and effect diagram might look like the diagram in Figure 6-C.

Brainstorming and the cause and effect diagram are also useful in preparing possible solutions and safeguards. Once the team has implemented its solution, we recommend that it conduct a final Pareto analysis to see whether the rejection rate from the blocks actually has been reduced. This analysis will show where the next opportunity lies for further improvement in the Z-7 engine.

CASE 6-2

A preliminary look at the complaints suggests several possible sources of trouble. Some of the complaints appear to be office problems, others could have occurred at shipping, and there may be defects in the pipes themselves. Until you make a careful analysis, you will not know the source.

You can organize the information from quality control in table form, as follows:

Defect Type	Number
Wrong quantity	22
Order entry	8
Damage in transit	3
Billing errors	4
Mislabeling	33
Canceled orders	2
Quality	17
Total	89

Rank the categories of complaints, starting with the largest. Your data sheet will look something like this:

PARETO DIAGRAM – WORKSHEET

Category	Frequency	Cumulative frequency	Cumulative percentage

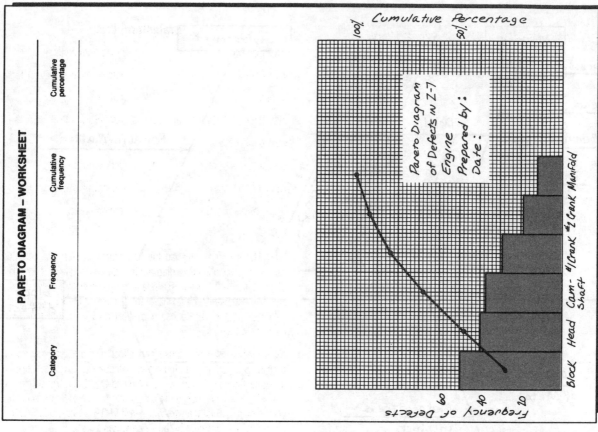

Figure 6-B. Pareto diagram with cumulative percentages drawn in, Case 6-1.

PARETO DIAGRAM – WORKSHEET

Category	Frequency	Cumulative frequency	Cumulative percentage

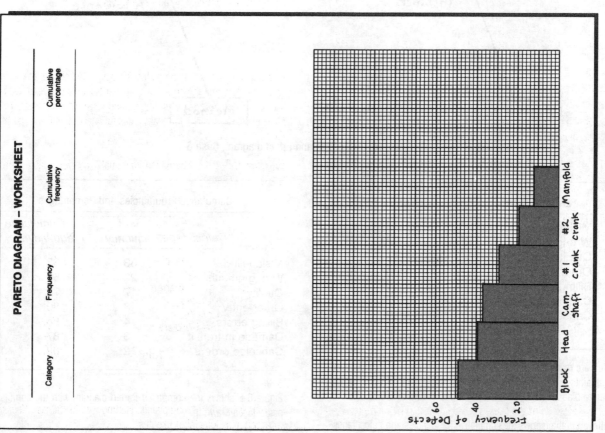

Figure 6-A. Pareto diagram with bars drawn in, Case 6-1.

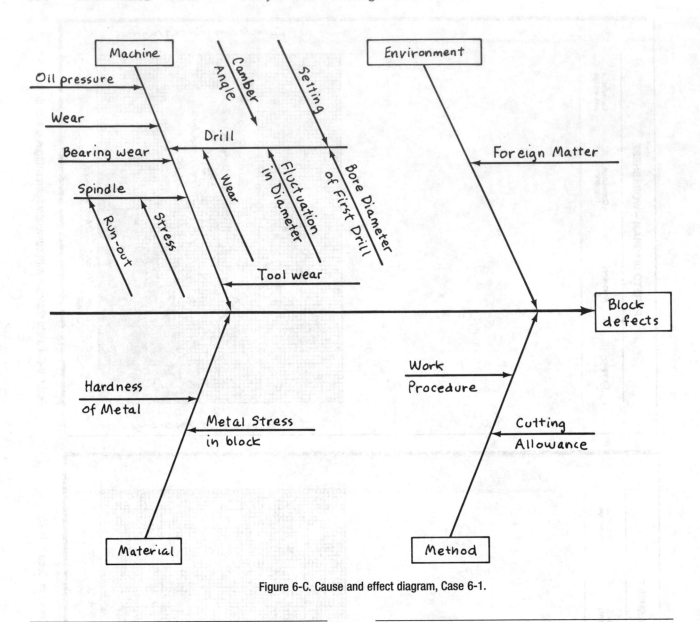

Figure 6-C. Cause and effect diagram, Case 6-1.

Defect Type	Number
Mislabeling	33
Wrong quantity	22
Quality	17
Order entry	8
Billing errors	4
Damage in transit	3
Canceled orders	2
Total	89

Now you are ready to develop a Pareto diagram. There are seven types of complaints, so your diagram will have seven bars of equal width. The Pareto diagram should look like the one in Figure 6-D.

The following table shows the cumulative frequencies and percentages.

Cumulative Frequencies and Percentages

	Frequency	Cumulative Frequency	%
Mislabeling	33	33	37
Wrong quantity	22	55	62
Quality	17	72	81
Order entry	8	80	90
Billing errors	4	84	94
Damage in transit	3	87	98
Canceled orders	2	89	100

Figure 6-E shows the completed Pareto diagram with the comulative percentages drawn in.

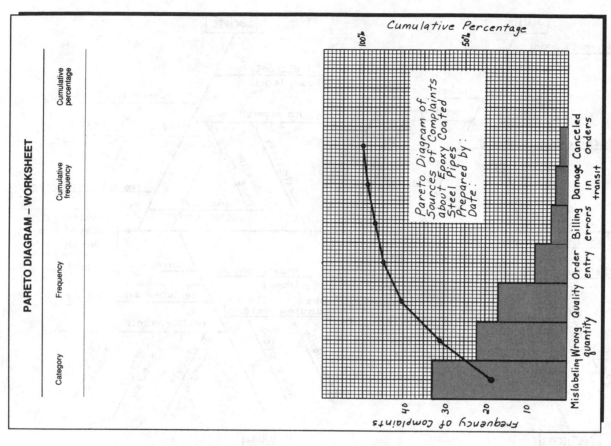

PARETO DIAGRAM – WORKSHEET

Category	Frequency	Cumulative frequency	Cumulative percentage

Figure 6-E. Pareto diagram with cumulative percentages drawn in, Case 6-2.

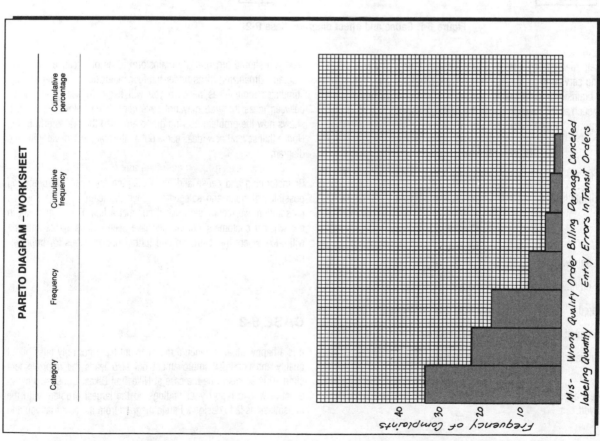

PARETO DIAGRAM – WORKSHEET

Category	Frequency	Cumulative frequency	Cumulative percentage

Figure 6-D. Pareto diagram with bars drawn in, Case 6-2.

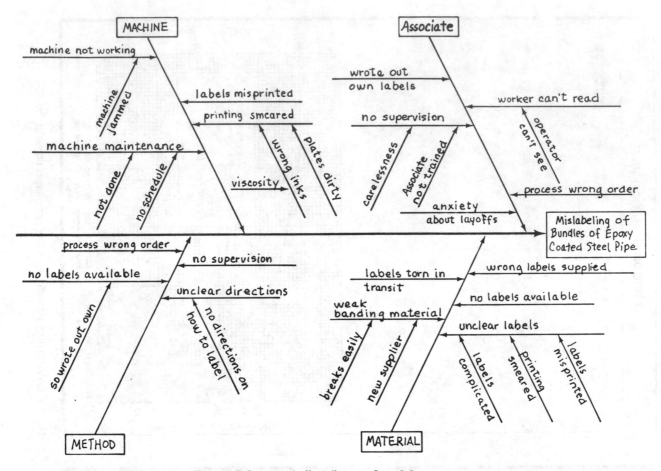

Figure 6-F. Cause and effect diagram, Case 6-2.

From the Pareto diagram in Figure 6-E, it is clear that the best way to start improving service is by solving the problem of mislabeling. The team should brainstorm for possible causes. A brainstorm list might include ideas such as the following ones that were generated in a problem-solving group. You will certainly think of others.

Brainstorm List

labels complicated	worker can't read
no labels available so wrote out own	wrong order processed
unclear labels	labels misprinted
associate not trained	no supervision
no directions on how to label	labeling machine not working properly
printing smeared	associate's carelessness
labels torn in transit	unclear directions
weak banding material so labels fall off	wrong labels supplied
workers' anxiety about impending layoff.	workers can't see

Next you should organize the brainstorm ideas on a cause and effect diagram. Organizing ideas under the four major bones or causes also stimulates more ideas because you will begin to see relationships between ideas that you may not have considered before. Figure 6-F shows how the problem-solving group arranged the brainstorm ideas. Notice that several new ideas came out as the team was developing the diagram.

Brainstorming and cause and effect diagram are useful in preparing possible solutions and safeguards. Once the team has implemented its solution, we recommend that it conduct a final Pareto analysis to see whether customers' complaints have been reduced. This analysis will show where the team can find further opportunities for improvement.

CASE 6-3

It is a happy situation when a management team not only talks about quality and continual improvement but also leads the improvement effort. This seems to be the case at Nike Trail Bikes. Consequently an effective way to report your findings on the largest problem with the transmissions is to design a Pareto diagram from the data that you and your workmate have collected. Your data sheet may look like the following table:

Source of Defects	Frequency
Suppliers	72
Assembly	113
Grinding	60
Gear cutting	19
Nicks	312
Scratches	3
Cracked	12
Dirt	2
Total	593

Rank the categories of source of defects, starting with the largest. Your data sheet will look something like this:

Source of Defects	Frequency
Nicks	312
Assembly	113
Suppliers	72
Grinding	60
Gear cutting	19
Cracked	12
Scratches	3
Dirt	2
Total	593

Once you have organized the data, you can easily construct a Pareto diagram. Although there are eight types of complaints, you will need only seven bars of equal width because you can combine the categories "scratches" and "dirt" in a bar labeled "other." The Pareto diagram with the bars drawn in should look like the one in Figure 6-G.

Determine the cumulative frequencies and percentages as in the following table.

Cumulative Frequencies and Percentages

	Frequency	Cumulative Frequency	%
Nicks	312	312	53
Assembly	113	425	72
Suppliers	72	497	84
Grinding	60	557	94
Gear cutting	19	576	97
Cracked	12	588	99
Other	5	593	100

Figure 6-H shows the completed Pareto diagram with the cumulative percentages drawn in.

From this Pareto diagram, it will be obvious to everyone that nicks are the largest source of problems with transmissions. This Pareto analysis with its diagram has helped to focus everyone's attention on the best place to start improving the quality of the transmissions. Management is confident that your team will dig deeper and find ways to reduce repair costs.

As your team begins to talk about possible causes of nicks, you all realize that different kinds of nicks are showing up. The team decides that they will need more data in order to be effective in finding the cause of the nicks. Over the next four weeks you collect further data on the types of nicks in the gears and list them on the following data sheet:

Nicks	Frequency
Drive gear	12
Clutch gear	72
Idle	12
Reverse gear	108
First gear	43
Second gear	27
Third gear	38
Total	312

Rank the categories of sources of defects, starting with the largest, "reverse gear." The data sheet will now look like the following table:

Nicks	Frequency
Reverse gear	108
Clutch gear	72
First gear	43
Third gear	38
Second gear	27
Drive gear	12
Idle	12
Total	312

You can use the arrangement of the data in this table to help construct a Pareto diagram showing the types of nicks. You have found seven types of nicks, so draw the Pareto diagram with seven bars of equal width. We don't recommend combining "drive gear" and "idle" into one bar because the combined figure would equal more than 10% of the defects. The diagram with the bars drawn in is shown in Figure 6-I.

PARETO DIAGRAM – WORKSHEET

Category	Frequency	Cumulative frequency	Cumulative percentage

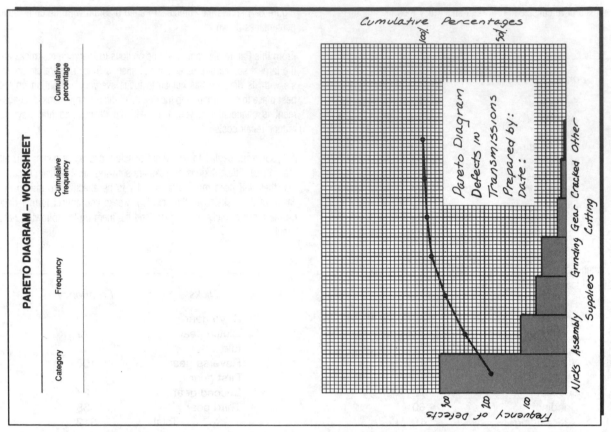

Figure 6-H. Pareto diagram with cumulative percentages drawn in, all sources of defects, Case 6-3.

PARETO DIAGRAM – WORKSHEET

Category	Frequency	Cumulative frequency	Cumulative percentage

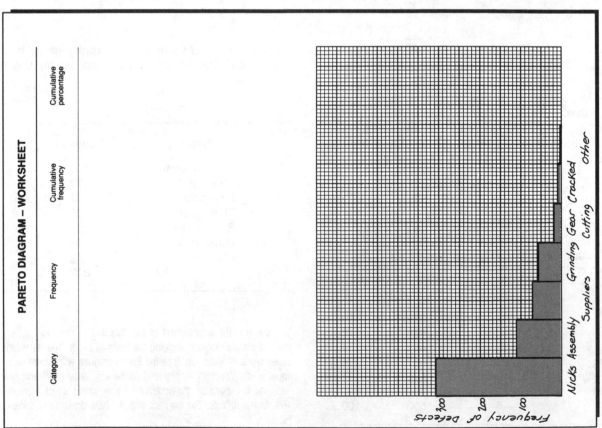

Figure 6-G. Pareto diagram with bars drawn in, all sources of defects, Case 6-3.

PARETO DIAGRAM – WORKSHEET

Category	Frequency	Cumulative frequency	Cumulative percentage

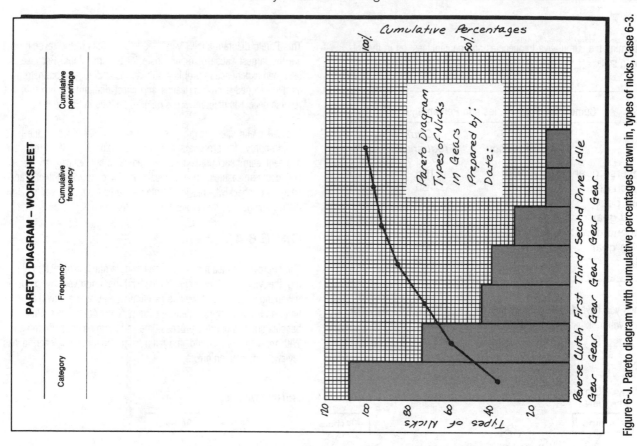

Figure 6-J. Pareto diagram with cumulative percentages drawn in, types of nicks, Case 6-3.

PARETO DIAGRAM – WORKSHEET

Category	Frequency	Cumulative frequency	Cumulative percentage

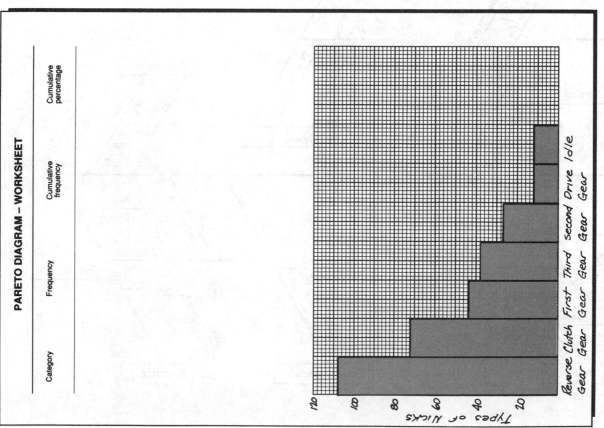

Figure 6-I. Pareto diagram with bars drawn in, types of nicks, Case 6-3.

Determine the cumulative frequencies and percentages, as in the following table:

Cumulative Frequencies and Percentages

	Frequency	Cumulative Frequency	%
Reverse gear	108	108	35
Clutch gear	72	180	58
First gear	43	223	71
Third gear	38	261	84
Second gear	27	288	92
Drive gear	12	300	96
Idle	12	312	100

When you have drawn in the cumulative percentages, the Pareto diagram will look like Figure 6-J.

This Pareto diagram shows very clearly that nicks in the reverse gear are the largest cause of repair costs for transmissions. Because the team had experience in problem-solving methodology, it brainstormed as it developed a process cause and effect diagram for nicks in the reverse gear. The diagram was similar to the one in Figure 6-K.

The cause and effect diagram revealed several places where the team could improve the process and so reduce repair costs. With the management team's encouragement, the team is enthusiastically trying several countermeasures. In four weeks it will conduct another Pareto analysis to check whether its countermeasures have removed nicks in the reverse gear as the largest source of repair costs.

CASE 6-4

The improvement team has been reviewing a number of factors affecting the yield of N-861006. Yields will be improved by reducing reworking of batches as well as by eliminating waste of raw materials, time, and labor. Improvements in the process could have additional benefits such as shorted process time and more batches out the door. With these goals in mind, the team from R&D and engineering has reviewed the data on errors.

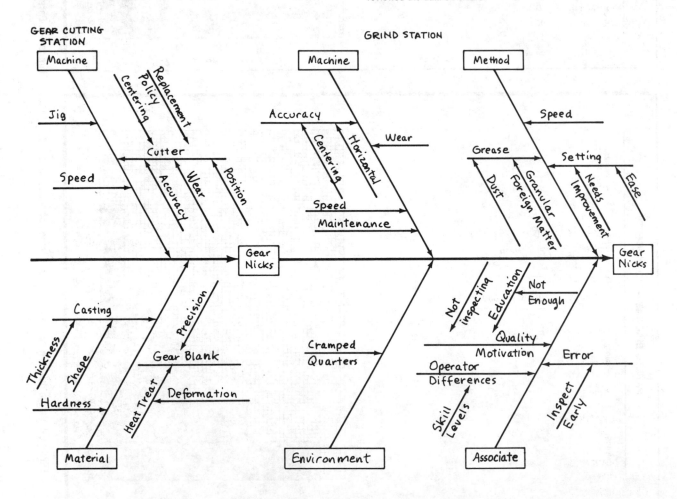

Figure 6-K. Cause and effect diagram, Case 6-3.

The team's first step was to make a Pareto analysis of the data. It organized the data as follows:

Source of Errors Affecting Yield	Frequency
Weighing raw materials	12
Poor maintenance	11
Damaged/illegible labels on raw materials	3
Unclear operation standards	43
Missing operational steps	37
Worker inexperience	29
Total	135

Next, the team ranked the errors, starting with the largest category, as follows:

Source of Errors Affecting Yield	Frequency
Unclear operation standards	43
Missing operational steps	37
Worker inexperience	29
Weighing raw materials	12
Poor maintenance	11
Damaged/illegible labels on raw materials	3
Total	135

From time to time, six sources of errors have had adverse effects on the yields of N-861006. On 43 occasions the cause was unclear operation standards. The next largest cause was missing operational steps. The Pareto diagram developed from this information appears in Figure 6-L.

The team developed a table similar to the following for cumulative frequencies and percentages.

Cumulative Frequencies and Percentages

	Frequency	Cumulative Frequency	%
Unclear operation standards	43	43	32
Missing operational steps	37	80	59
Worker inexperience	29	109	81
Weighing raw materials	12	121	90
Poor maintenance	11	132	98
Damaged/illegible labels on raw materials	3	135	100

The team drew the cumulative percentages on the Pareto diagram and completed it in time for the monthly management meeting. Figure 6-M shows the completed Pareto diagram.

Knowing that management would want some resolution to this problem, team members brainstormed possible causes for unclear operation standards, the largest source of errors. Several members pointed out that missing operational steps was also a serious issue. They thought it might be worthwhile to brainstorm for both topics because the causes of "unclear standards" and of "missing steps" might be similar. The team leader asked the others how they felt about combining the ideas; everyone agreed that it was OK. The brainstorm list included the following ideas:

Brainstorm List

misunderstanding of the process	poor training in how to follow standard operations
poor communication	change in raw materials
lack of planning	poor understanding of process in first place
inadequate planning	
lost gov't contract	poor supervision
R&D budget cuts	budget cuts
incompetent operators	change in formulations
gov't changed regulations	supervisors changing standards
poor machine design	operators changing standards
change in batching methods	engineering changed standards
change in formulations not passed on	lab changed standards
standards not updated	customers' needs not understood thoroughly
with change in raw materials, no change in operation standards	customers' needs not incorporated in operation standard

Notice how much piggybacking on ideas took place in this brainstorm. After time for further thinking, the team constructed a cause and effect diagram. The diagram showed relationships between causes that helped R&D and engineering to develop clearer operation standards and to set a timetable for regular review and updating of the standards. In addition, engineering found that clear and complete standards for batching N-861006 helped to reduce errors by workers when they switched over from another process. The preliminary cause and effect diagram is shown in Figure 6-N.

PARETO DIAGRAM – WORKSHEET

Category	Frequency	Cumulative frequency	Cumulative percentage

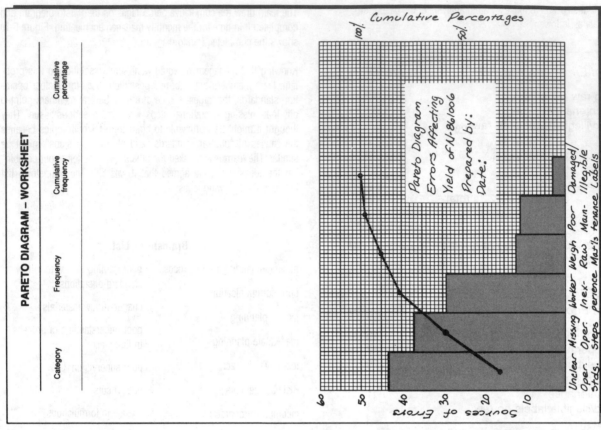

Figure 6-M. Pareto diagram with cumulative percentages drawn in, Case 6-4.

PARETO DIAGRAM – WORKSHEET

Category	Frequency	Cumulative frequency	Cumulative percentage

Figure 6-L. Pareto diagram with bars drawn in, Case 6-4.

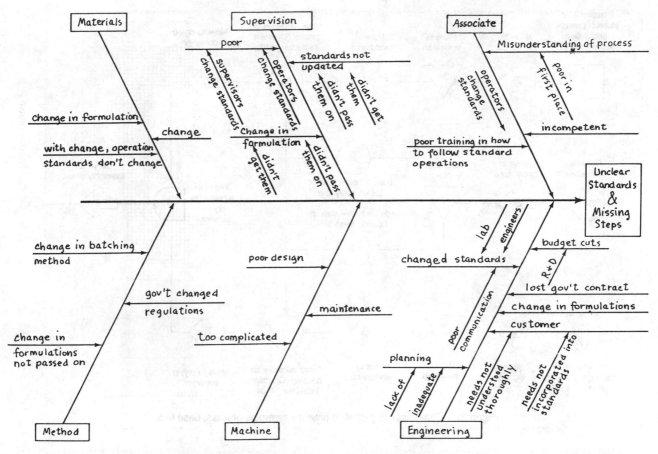

Figure 6-N. Cause and effect diagram, Case 6-4.

CASE 6-5

The gasket to housing assembly process, as depicted by the flow chart in Figure 6-O, begins with three parallel paths showing the flow of the three components—the gaskets, the adhesive, and the housings—starting with their reception into the plant.

The first flow path shows that the gaskets are received and inspected in accordance with Inspection Instruction #101, indicated by the inspect symbol and the numeral "1". The gaskets are moved to the work area and stored until needed, as indicated by the move and store symbols. The next symbol on the flow chart path is a move, showing that the gaskets are moved to the workbench where the adhesive is sprayed, in accordance with Operator Instruction #102. The next step on the flow chart is another move to the conveyor belt.

In the second flow path the adhesive is received and moved to be stored in the work area. The flow path is then split, showing that the adhesive is loaded into two supply tanks: Operation #1 fills a supply tank for spraying the adhesive on the gasket; and Operation #2 fills the supply tank for the housing spray workstation.

The third flow path shows that the housings are received and stored in the receiving area as described in Operator Instruction #103. They are then moved to the work area and stored until needed by the spray operator at the workbench. After the housings are sprayed with adhesive at Operation #4, in accordance with Operator Instruction #104, they are moved to the same conveyor as the gaskets following Operation #3. As the housings and gaskets move on the conveyor to the assembly press a delay is built into the process to allow them to dry. Obviously, delays are encountered at various points in the process from time to time, but this delay symbol indicates a planned delay that is significant to the product performance.

Operation #5, assembling the gasket to housing, is performed next, according to Operator Instruction #105. The assemblies are then moved to a table from which they are inspected and packed in accordance with Inspection Instruction #106. The next operation on the flow chart prepares the loaded shipping container for shipment. The closing and identification of the container are described in Operator Instruction #107. The flow chart next indicates that the products in the shipping container are moved to the shipping area and stored until shipped to the customer.

A review of the flow chart shows that the entire operation is made up of many more activities than first anticipated. Although the process used in this example is a simple one and was initially envisioned as a four-step process, the development of the process and the flow chart

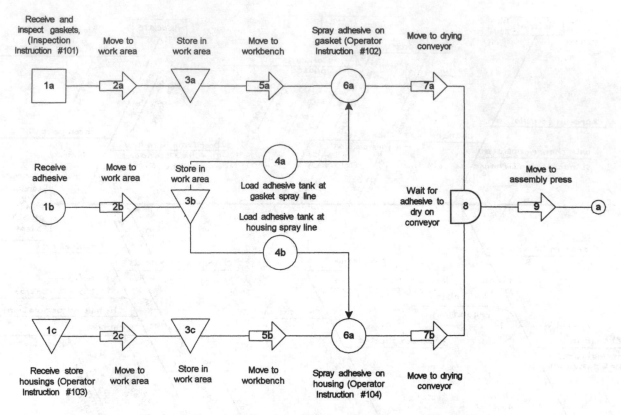

Figure 6-0. Flow chart of gasket to housing assembly process, Case 6-5.

shows that even simple products require many activities to produce them. We now can see the process consists of six production operations, two inspect operations, five store activities, and one built-in delay activity. All of these activities add cost to the product and affect productivity and profitability.

CASE 6-6

This problem involves a manufacturing process used by a company that buys the basic material from a source outside their own facilities. The material is received and inspected by taking a small sample representing a fairly large quantity of material. Various statistical process controls are used in the processing of the material. A process flow chart depicting a process such as this should include not only the operations performed by the production associate, but also the statistical process control activities of whomever is responsible for monitoring the performance of the process.

The process begins with the receipt of the basic material from the supplier. The inspection in Step 1 is performed to ensure the material was not damaged or contaminated in shipment from the supplier. A key characteristic is measured and the results plotted on an individual and range control chart. As long as the control chart shows the material is stable and within the control limits, the material is moved directly to the production area, where it is available for use by the production associate.

In this problem, the material is an elastomeric material, so it is first placed on a mill and rolled through the rolls to warm the material to make it pliable and more easily handled (Step 3) through the vulcanizing process. When it is sufficiently warm, the associate prepares the material (Step 4) by cutting it into pieces of the proper weight for loading into a mold. At this point, an X-bar-R chart is used to monitor performance of the stock preparation operation (Step 5). The stock is loaded onto a rack (Step 6) and moved to the vulcanizing press line where it is stored prior to the vulcanizing operation.

The prepared stock is loaded into the mold cavities and vulcanized to the shape of the cavities (Step 9). Next, an audit inspection of molded parts (Step 10) is performed by an audit inspector. The vulcanized parts are loaded into tubs by the production associate (Step 11) and moved to a lathe for the next operation. The tubs of parts are stored on a conveyor at the lathe until needed. Several parts are cut from one molded part on the lathe (Step 14). At this operation, the audit inspector also maintains an X-bar-R chart for the width of the pieces cut from the molded parts (Step 15) and a sample is taken on a specified time interval for a laboratory check of the compression set of the elastomeric material to ensure all the proper ingredients were in the original compound and the vulcanizing cycle was correct.

The pieces of material are then loaded onto a large rack (Step 16) to be moved to the inspect and pack area. In this area they are stored until they

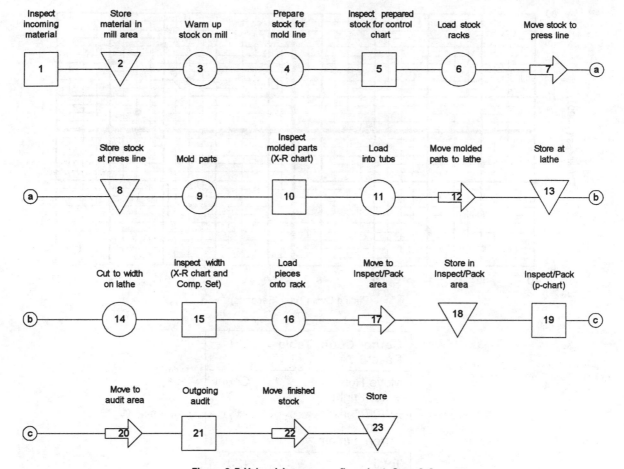

Figure 6-P. Vulcanizing process flow chart, Case 6-6.

are visually inspected and packed (Step 19). The packed parts are moved to an outgoing audit area where they are again inspected on an audit basis (Step 21) and then moved to the finished stock area and stored ready for shipment.

The CI team can make good use of the process flow chart developed for this part. A previous CI team was successful in greatly reducing the scrap on this job. The process flow chart shows there are seven production operations and six inspection operations. It is common for the number and frequency of inspections operations to grow and become embedded in a process that has a high rejection and scrap rate. Perhaps the CI team should use the process flow chart to examine the need or frequency of all of the inspection operations now that the scrap problems have been solved on this job.

CASE 6-7A

As a member of a CI team, you were asked to create a diagram in order to determine if the thickness of the chromium can be predicted based on the plating cycle time; in other words, is the chromium thickness dependent upon the plating cycle time. The variables in this problem are the plating cycle time and the chromium thickness.

The scatter diagram you created using the data provided should look like Figure 6–Q. To create this chart, first set up the horizontal and vertical scales; the vertical scale (thickness) values in the scatter diagram are set in inches and have been converted to whole numbers so that they are easier to use (multiply each number by .00001″ to obtain the true values). The horizontal scale values are in seconds. After plotting the thickness values on the scatter diagram, the next step is to determine and place the median lines on the diagram, which are necessary to properly analyze the plotted data.

To find the median lines, hold a straight edge vertically on the chart, moving across the scatter diagram from the right side of the chart and count each plotted point until you reach a count equal to half the number of the plotted points. In this case, there are 20 plotted values, so after you have passed 10 of the points draw a vertical line (the median line) between the tenth and eleventh points. The horizontal median line is obtained by moving across the chart from the bottom and following the same procedure as above. This time, however, because the tenth and eleventh points are on the same thickness value (66) we draw the horizontal median line through them, not between them. Now that values are plotted and the median lines are drawn, you are ready to perform the corner count test.

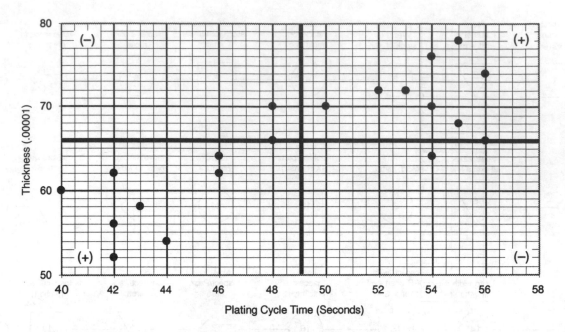

Figure 6-Q. Piston rod plating thickness, Case 6-7A.

Corner Count Table Case 6-7A	
Move Ruler	Count
from right	0
from top	+5
from left	+8
from bottom	+7
Total	+20
Without sign	20

Counting the plotted points from the right side of the scatter diagram to the left you encounter two points at the 56 value of the horizontal (cycle time) scale—one point is at the 74 thickness value and the other is at the 66 thickness value. Because the 74 thickness point is in the plus (+) quadrant and the .00066 thickness point is on the median line, you must not count these points; record a zero for the count from the right side.

Counting in from the top of the diagram down, you encounter five points in the plus (+) quadrant before you come to a point in the minus (−) quadrant. You should record a count of +5. Counting in from the left side of the scatter diagram, you count eight points in the plus (+) quadrant before stopping at a point on the horizontal median line and one point in the minus (−) quadrant. Adding eight to the five you already counted gives thirteen (13) so far. Finally, counting up from the bottom of the scatter diagram you come to seven points in the plus (+) quadrant before reaching a point in the minus (−) quadrant. When you add this seven to the 13 already counted, you get +20 (see Figure 6-Q). The plus sign means that you have positive correlation. In other words, when the plating cycle time is increased, the chromium thick-

ness will increase. If the sign came out to be negative (−) and you had a negative correlation, the chromium thickness would decrease as the plating cycle time increased.

The value of 20 you obtained in the counting is large enough to give you over a 99% confidence that the team is right to say that the amount of chromium thickness depends on the plating cycle time.

CASE 6-7B

The second part of this question asked you to create a scatter diagram using only the three plating cycle time settings, instead of the actual plating times recorded. Your scatter diagram should look like the one in Figure 6-R.

In creating a scatter diagram like the one in Figure 6-R, notice that the points for the dependent variable, the plating thickness, fall in three vertical lines. This is because you have used only three values for the plat-

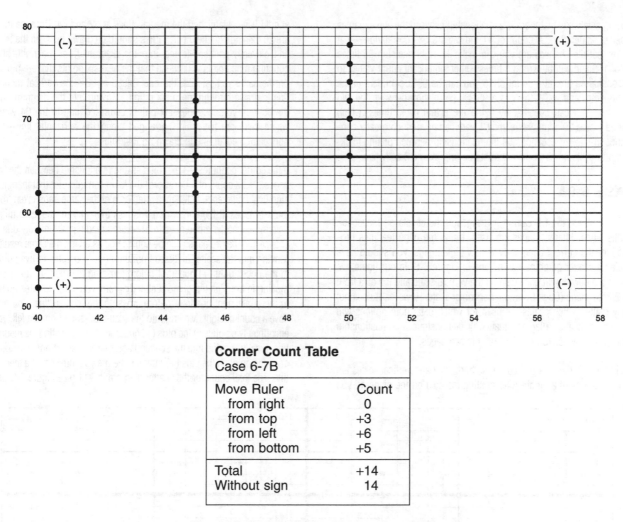

Corner Count Table	
Case 6-7B	
Move Ruler	**Count**
from right	0
from top	+3
from left	+6
from bottom	+5
Total	+14
Without sign	14

Figure 6-R. Piston rod plating thickness, Case 6-7B.

ing cycle time, the independent variable, creating a scatter diagram without much scatter on the horizontal scale. When you plot the median lines on the scatter diagram you find that all the plotted points for the 45-second plater cycle time setting fall on the median line. This is because the middle count of the total set of 20 data values falls between points 10 and 11, which are both in the group of 45-second cycle times. After you set the horizontal median line, the tenth and eleventh points fall on the horizontal median line. This creates a situation wherein all six of the plating thickness values for the 40-second cycle time are in the lower left plus (+) quadrant, all six of the 45-second cycle times are on the vertical median, and six of the 50-second cycle time values are in the upper right plus (+) quadrant with one point on the horizontal median line and one point in the lower right minus (–) quadrant.

Starting the corner count test from the right side of the scatter diagram, the first count is zero—because all the points from the 50-second cycle time are encountered at the same time and one point is on the median line and one point is in the minus (–) quadrant, you must not count any of the values. Moving in from the top of the scatter diagram,

you count three points in the plus (+) quadrant before coming to a point on the vertical median line. A count of +3 is recorded. Next, moving in from the left side of the scatter diagram you encounter all six of the 40-second cycle time points in the plus (+) quadrant before coming to the points on the vertical median line. This gives a count of +6 to add to the other count of +3, for a total of +9 so far. Finally, move in from the bottom of the scatter diagram and count five points in the plus (+) quadrant before stopping at a point on the vertical median line. This gives a total of +14 (see Figure 6-R), which is smaller than the 20 arrived at when the data was collected using the actual plater cycle times. Although this count of 14 also indicates that the thickness of the plating depends on the plating cycle time, the count of 20 obtained using the actual cycle times gives the team a higher degree of confidence in the relationship.

It should be noted here that although there are more complex ways to analyze data such as we have in this problem, a CI team can use a scatter diagram as a quick and easy way to make improvement decisions. The number to look for is 11. If your corner count is at least 11, you can safely say that there is a relationship between the two variables under consideration. A count of 11 indicates a 5% correlation—that means that the chances are you can make the right decision 95 times out of 100 and will be wrong 5 times. Other significant count values to be considered are: at a count of 15 you can be 99% confident in the relationship; and at 21 there is a 99.9% correlation between the two variables. You can see that by using the actual cycle times, which yielded a plus 20 count value, the CI team can have much greater confidence in making decisions on the relationship between plating thickness and cycle times in their continuous improvement activities.

CASE 6-8A

In this problem the CI team is investigating the effects on inspection results when different gages are used. Using the gage readings provided for the current gage and the new digital gage, you should have created a scatter diagram like the one in Figure 6-S. In our figure, we placed the new digital gage data on the vertical scale and the data from the current gage (Gage 6) on the horizontal scale. However, it does not really matter which scales are used for which data; both options will produce a scatter diagram that will demonstrate the relationship between the inspection results from the two gages.

In Figure 6-S, the data plotted on the horizontal and vertical scales are in thousandths of an inch. After plotting the data on the diagram, you should have established the median lines at 62 and 64. Because there are 20 data points, the median lines should be drawn between the tenth and eleventh points. Moving into the diagram from the right, after counting nine points you notice that the next six points that are plotted on the same vertical line, the one valued at 62—the vertical median line is drawn through these six points. Moving into the diagram from the bottom, you encounter six points before coming to the 64 value, where there are five points arranged along the horizontal line—the horizontal median line is drawn on that line.

If the corner count results exhibit a strong relationship between the two gages (i.e., a count of 11 or more) the team can interpret that there is a significant difference in the measurements of the same parts taken from the two gages. If the corner count is less than eleven, the team might determine that the differences in the paired readings are merely due to chance and the two gages can be considered as giving the same results. Moving into the scatter diagram from the right, you come to five points in the upper right (+) quadrant before crossing the median line. Next, moving in from the top of the scatter diagram, you count to three points in the upper right quadrant before crossing the median line. You now have a count of eight. Moving into the scatter diagram from the left, you encounter two points in the plus (+) quadrant before meeting the median line. Finally, moving into the scatter diagram from the bottom, you count only one point, in the plus (+) quadrant before you must cross a median line. The total count for the scatter diagram is +11 (see Figure 6-S), so

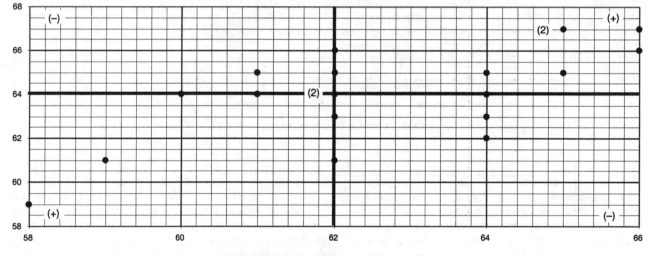

Corner Count Table Case 6-8A	
Move Ruler	**Count**
from right	+5
from top	+3
from left	+2
from bottom	+1
Total	+11
Without sign	11

Figure 6-S. Digital Gage Readings vs. Old Gage Readings, Case 6-8A.

the team can assume that there is a significant difference in the measurements of the same parts taken from the two gages.

CASE 6-8B

Figure 6-T is a scatter diagram depicting the differences between measurements taken by two different inspectors. Again, for simplicity the scales have been set to thousandths of an inch. Does your scatter diagram look similar to this one?

The median lines for this scatter diagram are set at 63 for the vertical median line and 64 for the horizontal median line (there are a total of 20 points). When counting the plotted points from the right side, we immediately come to two points at the 66 line, one point at the 65 line, and six points at the 64 line, for a total of nine. There are five points on the next vertical line of 63, so we draw the vertical median line at the 63 line. Moving in from the bottom of the scatter diagram, we come to one point at the 59 horizontal line, two points at the 61 horizontal line, one point at the 62 line, and three points at the 63 horizontal line for a total of seven points. There are five points on the next horizontal line, 64, making a total of 12 points, so we draw the horizontal median line through the 64 horizontal value.

Performing a corner count test, we enter the scatter diagram from the right, and the first vertical line with points is the 66 vertical line. One of the points is in the upper right quadrant, the positive quadrant, and the other one is in the lower right quadrant, the negative quadrant. We therefore must record a count of zero for the first value. Entering the scatter diagram from the top, we count five points on the 64 vertical line in the positive quadrant before coming to three points on the 65 horizontal line. One is in the positive quadrant, one is on the vertical median line, and one is in the negative quadrant, so we must stop our count from the top at +5. Next, counting in from the left side of the scatter diagram, we count one point in the lower left, or positive quadrant before encountering two points on the horizontal median line at the 60 vertical line, along with one point in the negative quadrant. Our count now totals six. Moving into the scatter diagram from the bottom, we get a count of +1 before finding a point on the vertical median line. Adding this +1 to the +6 we already have gets us a total corner count of +7 (see Figure 6-T). The rule is, if the count is greater than 11, we can say with some degree of confidence that there is a relationship between the two sets of numbers being studied. In this case, because our total is only 7 we cannot say with confidence that the inspection results are dependent upon the inspectors doing the gaging.

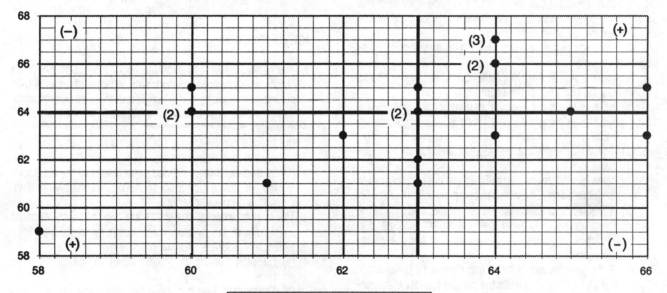

| Corner Count Table | |
Case 6-8B	
Move Ruler	Count
from right	0
from top	+5
from left	+1
from bottom	+1
Total	+7
Without sign	7

Figure 6-T. Inspection Results, Case 6-8B.

REVIEW QUESTIONS

WHAT IS TQM?

1. Traditional management assigned the responsibility for productivity to managers and the responsibility for quality to the quality control department. In a TQM system, companies empower the production associate at the lowest practical level in the organization with the responsibility to make decisions affecting both productivity and quality.
2. (a) TQM companies have realized that they must restructure their management and operations systems to respond to the wants, needs, and expectations of their customers.
   (b) Each member of a TQM company needs to understand that the quality of every action can be improved and that all improvements contribute to a better product and a more satisfied customer.
3. To meet the wants, needs, and expectations of its customers.
4. Customers are the next functional group in the process as well as the end user of the products.
5. (a) All employees are involved in quality improvement.
   (b) All strategic decisions are made with the customer in mind.
6. (a) The vision statement defines the direction of the company.
   (b) The vision statement establishes the basic processes to be followed in achieving the company vision.
7. (a) It requires that the employees know and understand the operating procedures for performing, maintaining, and improving the many processes used in the day-to-day operations.
   (b) TQM organizations publish and maintain a policy manual that clearly describes the current manner of operating and how the organization will operate in the future.
8. It is a part of the policy manual that lists specific projects to be undertaken to improve company operations and ensures the organization will constantly move toward its goals and objectives.
9. (a) Cross-functional activities are cooperative activities among the departments of the organization.
   (b) Cross-functional activities enable individuals in the organization to better understand the problems of co-workers and result in improved performance of the whole organization.
10. (a) To provide a written record of the responsibilities of each element of the organization.

(b) To provide a method for documenting the results of the important activities of each element.
11. (a) The importance of establishing a prevention mode of managing rather than a detection mode.
   (b) The need for training employees in the techniques of SPC and group problem solving.
   (c) The empowering of employees at all levels to improve their processes and the quality of the product.
   (d) The successful activities of cross-functional continuous improvement teams in meeting the wants, needs, and expectations of the customer.
12. (a) Level I—Mission statement.
   (b) Level II—Procedures.
   (c) Level III—Written instructions.
   (d) Level IV—Documentary evidence of performance (e.g., databases, documents, and forms).

KEYS TO TQM

1. The wants, needs, and expectations of the customers of an organization must be satisfied if the organization is to stay in business. Therefore, a TQM organization must be customer-driven, rather than driven by profits as in traditional management systems.
2. (a) Internal customers are the persons or group of persons next in line in the process.
   (b) Internal customers depend upon results of the actions of the individual or group of individuals supplying them with a product or service.
3. The final or external customers are the ones who must be satisfied with the product if the company expects to keep selling the products they are producing.
4. (a) Decision making is moved down to lowest possible level.
   (b) The person who has the information and the ability to make good decisions, often the one right on the production floor, is empowered to make decisions previously reserved for managers or supervisors.
   (c) The empowerment of employees at all levels working in cross-functional problem-solving teams is a key element in TQM success.
5. Improved quality and increased productivity.
6. Continuous improvement.

CONTINUOUS IMPROVEMENT

1. A clearly defined procedure for attacking and solving problems and developing improvements.

2. (a) Through the actions of teams of associates from various parts of the organization working together.
   (b) Continuous improvement is neither spontaneous nor self-directing. Many companies create steering committees to maintain their continuous improvement activities.
3. (a) A steering committee identifies and prioritizes the obstacles to attaining the goals and objectives of the business plan.
   (b) The steering committee recruits cross-functional teams to formally organize and attack individual problems and find solutions.
4. (a) PDCA represents PLAN, DO, CHECK, ACT.
   (b) PDCA makes use of the SPC and problem-solving techniques presented in *SPC Simplified* to analyze problems and find solutions.

PLAN

1. (a) Identify the problem.
   (b) Analyze the processes.
   (c) Propose potential solutions.
   (d) Determine the SPC and problem-solving tools to be used.
2. Team members learn what is to be done, how it will be done, when it will be done, and by whom it will be done.
3. The process flow chart.
4. (a) Formulate a strategy for arriving at a solution.
   (b) (1) A brief statement of how the team plans to go about obtaining information about the conditions surrounding a problem.
       (2) How they plan to identify possible causes.
       (3) How they plan to locate the causes in the processes.
       (4) How they plan to test possible corrective actions.
       (5) How they plan to recommend the best solution to the steering committee.
5. Conduct a brainstorming session.
6. Construct a cause and effect diagram.
7. Perform a Pareto analysis.

DO

1. Try out the solution in the process to demonstrate its effectiveness.

CHECK

1. (a) Control charts.
   (b) Histograms.
   (c) Scatter diagrams.

ACT

1. (a) Establish what needs to be done to keep the problem from recurring.
   (b) Report findings to the steering committee.
2. (a) Importance of customer satisfaction.
   (b) Company vision and mission statement drive activities.
   (c) Managerial leadership.
   (d) Prevention mode of managing.
   (e) Employee training.
   (f) Statistical process control.
   (g) Cross-functional teamwork.
   (h) Continuous improvement.
3. These concepts have been used in many state and national awards and standards.

THE MALCOLM BALDRIGE NATIONAL QUALITY AWARD

1. The U.S. National Institute of Standards and Technology.
2. U.S. companies who exemplify performance excellence.
3. (a) The Baldrige criteria provide companies with a common language and a common way to understand where to apply all of the theories, tools, and approaches that are part of running an effective organization.
   (b) They enable U.S. companies to share information on successful performance strategies and the benefits derived from using those strategies.
4. (a) Manufacturing companies.
   (b) Service companies.
   (c) Small businesses.
5. (a) Leadership.
   (b) Strategic planning.
   (c) Customer and market focus.
   (d) Information and analysis.
   (e) Human resource development and management.
   (f) Process management.
   (g) Business results.

QUALITY MANAGEMENT STANDARDS

1. While the Baldrige criteria focus on the quality improvement practices of the entire organization, the standards focus specifically on the capabilities of a company to control its internal processes.
2. It proves to the company's customers that the company is capable of doing what it says it does; that is, that the company is able to follow its own procedures.
3. Quality System Requirements QS-9000.
4. The QS-9000 standard expands on the ISO 9000 series to include the specific quality assurance requirements of each of the auto manufacturers.

FREQUENCY HISTOGRAMS – WORKSHEET

Title _____   Very largest _____   Very smallest_____

Range _____   # of intervals _____   Interval width _____

Midpoints	Interval	Boundaries	Tally	Tally Check	Frequency

Specifications _____

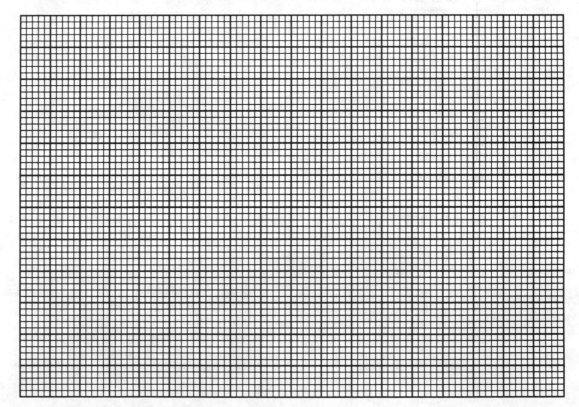

FREQUENCY HISTOGRAM CHECKSHEET

Title _____ Specifications _____

Anticipated largest _____ Anticipated smallest _____ Range _____

No. of observations _____ No. of intervals _____ Interval widths _____

First interval _____ Second interval _____

F
R
E
Q   **40**
U
E   **30**
N
C   **20**
Y
     10

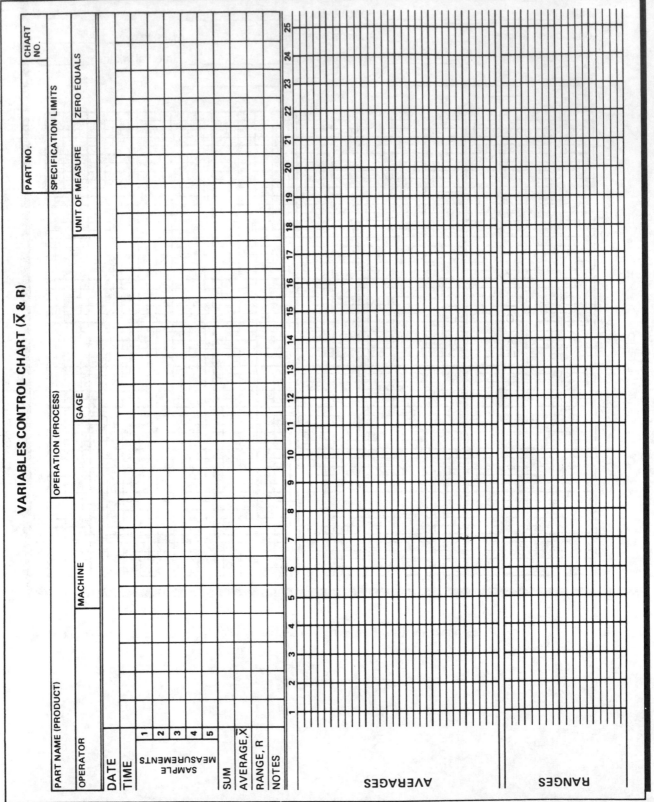

VARIABLES CONTROL CHART ($\overline{X}$ & R)

PART NAME (PRODUCT) | OPERATION (PROCESS) | PART NO. | CHART NO.

SPECIFICATION LIMITS

OPERATOR | MACHINE | GAGE | UNIT OF MEASURE | ZERO EQUALS

DATE
TIME
SAMPLE MEASUREMENTS: 1, 2, 3, 4, 5
SUM
AVERAGE, $\overline{X}$
RANGE, R
NOTES

AVERAGES

RANGES

CALCULATION WORKSHEET

CONTROL LIMITS

SUBGROUPS
INCLUDED _____   _____

$\bar{R} = \dfrac{\Sigma R}{k}$ = _____ = _____ =

$\bar{\bar{X}} = \dfrac{\Sigma \bar{X}}{k}$ = _____ = _____ =

OR

$\bar{X}'$ (MIDSPEC. OR STD.) =   =

$A_2 \bar{R}$ =   x   = _____ x = _____

$UCL_{\bar{x}} = \bar{\bar{X}} + A_2 \bar{R}$ =   =

$LCL_{\bar{x}} = \bar{\bar{X}} - A_2 \bar{R}$ =   =

$UCL_R = D_4 \bar{R}$ =   x   =   x   =

LIMITS FOR INDIVIDUALS
COMPARE WITH SPECIFICATION
OR TOLERANCE LIMITS

$\bar{\bar{X}}$ =

$\dfrac{3}{d_2} \bar{R}$ =   x   = _____

$UL_x = \bar{\bar{X}} + \dfrac{3}{d_2} \bar{R}$ =

$LL_x = \bar{\bar{X}} - \dfrac{3}{d_2} \bar{R}$ =

US   =

LS   = _____

US $-$ LS   =

$6\sigma = \dfrac{6}{d_2} \bar{R}$ =

MODIFIED CONTROL LIMITS FOR AVERAGES

BASED ON SPECIFICATION LIMITS AND PROCESS CAPABILITY.
APPLICABLE ONLY IF: US $-$ LS $> 6\sigma$.

US   =   LS   =

$A_M \bar{R}$ =   x   = _____ $A_M \bar{R}$ = _____

$URL_{\bar{x}} = US - A_M \bar{R}$ = $LRL_{\bar{x}} = LS + A_M \bar{R}$ =

FACTORS FOR CONTROL LIMITS

n	A_2	D_4	d_2	$\dfrac{3}{d_2}$	A_M
2	1.880	3.268	1.128	2.659	0.779
3	1.023	2.574	1.693	1.772	0.749
4	0.729	2.282	2.059	1.457	0.728
5	0.577	2.114	2.326	1.290	0.713
6	0.483	2.004	2.534	1.184	0.701

NOTES

PERCENT DEFECTIVE (p) CONTROL CHART

INSPECTED BY _____   PART NO. _____

MACHINE/OPERATION _____   PART NAME _____

PERCENT DEFECTIVE

2   4   6   8   10   12   14   16   18   20   22   24   26   28   30   32

% DEF

KINDS OF DEFECTS

NO. DEF.

NO. INSP.

DATE & TIME

REMARKS

NUMBER OF DEFECTS (c) CONTROL CHART

INSPECTED BY _____   PART NO. _____

MACHINE/OPERATION _____   PART NAME _____

INSPECTION UNIT _____

NUMBER OF DEFECTS

2   4   6   8   10   12   14   16   18   20   22   24   26   28   30   32

NO. DEF

KINDS OF DEFECTS

DATE & TIME

REMARKS

PROBABILITY CHART

Part No. & Name		Char. Measured
Operation No. & Desc.		Spec.

VALUE	
FREQUENCY	
Follow arrows and perform additions as shown (N ≥ 25)	
EST. ACCUM. FREQ. (EAF)	
PLOT POINTS (%) (EAF/2N) X 100	

% of Population

% UNDER

% OVER

99.8	0.2 +3σ
99.5	0.5
99	1
98	2 +2σ
95	5
90	10
80	20 +σ
70	30
60	40
50	50
40	60
30	70
20	80 −σ
10	90
5	95
2	98 −2σ
1	99
0.5	99.5
0.2	99.8 −3σ

PARETO DIAGRAM – WORKSHEET

Category	Frequency	Cumulative frequency	Cumulative percentage

Other Productivity Press publications that will help you achieve your quality improvement goals.

DOE Simplified
Mark J. Anderson and Patrick J. Whitcomb
ISBN 1-56327-225-3 / Forthcoming

SPC Simplified
Robert T. Amsden, Howard E. Butler, and Davida M. Amsden
ISBN 0-527-76340-3 / 304 pages / $24.95 / Item QRSPC

The Basics of FMEA
Robin E. McDermott, Raymond J. Mikulak, and Michael R. Beauregard
ISBN 0-527-76320-9 / 76 pages / $9.95 / Item QRFMEA

Mistake-Proofing for Operators: The ZQC System
Created by The Productivity Development Team
ISBN 1-56327-127-3 / 96 pages / $25.00 / Item ZQCOP

Target Costing and Value Engineering
Robin Cooper and Regine Slagmulder
ISBN 1-56327-172-9 / 400 pages / $50.00 / Item COSTB1

Quality Function Deployment: Integrating Customer Requirements into Product Design
Yoji Akao (ed.)
ISBN 0-915299-41-0 / 387 pages / $85.00 / Item QFD

Process Discipline
Norman M. Edelson and Carole L. Bennett
ISBN 0-527-76345-4 / 224 pages / $34.95 / Item PDISC

Fast Track to Waste-Free Manufacturing: Straight Talk from a Plant Manager
John W. Davis
ISBN 1-56327-212-1 / 425 pages / $45.00 / Item WFM

Productivity Press, Dept. BK, P.O. Box 13390, Portland, OR 97213-0390
Telephone: 1-800-394-6868   Fax: 1-800-394-6286